CW01597194

A Guide to the Housing Act 1988

Fourmat Publishing

A Guide to the Housing Act 1988
by James Driscoll, LL.M, Solicitor

London
Fourmat Publishing
1989

ISBN 1 85190 069 1

First published 1989

Published by Fourmat Publishing, 27 & 28 St Albans Place,
Islington Green, London N1 ONX
Typeset by Pentacor Ltd, High Wycombe
Printed in Great Britain by Billing & Sons Ltd, Worcester

Preface

In describing legal and political change, commentators often refer to the Government's break with the post-war consensus on matters of economic and social policy. However, there has rarely been agreement between the major political parties on the best way of providing rented housing. There was a short period in the early 1950's when the two main political parties were both committed to an expansion of public housing. Since that time, successive Labour and Conservative Governments have taken widely divergent approaches to the provision of public and private housing.

In the Housing Act 1988, the Government has pursued its two long-term goals of de-regulating the private sector and of reducing the role of local authorities as providers of housing. The Act introduces measures that substantially take away statutory controls over the rent which may be charged for private lettings; it expands the role of housing associations; it allows Central Government to intervene in local authority housing; and it enables private landlords to take over public housing. It will have a profound effect on the lives of tenants, whether they live in the private or the public sector.

Much of the Act came into force on 15 January 1989. The remainder will be in force by the middle of 1989. Copies of regulations and other material available on 15 January 1989 appear as appendices to this book, along with a copy of the Act. Readers will have to wait for the other regulations, which will be published during the next few months. These include regulations governing the new role of rent officers in assessing rents for housing benefit purposes; the setting up of housing action trusts; the balloting procedures and valuations for the change of landlord provisions; and the criteria for approval of landlords applying to buy housing from Housing Action Trusts. Additional standard tenancy agreements for housing associations are also awaited.

I have, in the text, commented on the available Statutory Instruments and other material.

This book is written with a wide readership in mind. It will assist lawyers, and others working in the areas of housing and landlord and tenant, who need an overview of this huge measure. It will also help housing advisors, local authorities, housing associations and others who need an account of the impact of the Act on public and private rented housing.

The Act is just over one hundred pages in length. I have tried to cover all the main features and the most relevant miscellaneous matters. However, no attempt was made to cover all of the details in the eighteen schedules, which run to nearly one hundred pages. Naturally such matters as tenancies that cannot be assured and grounds for possession are considered in full. However, many of the schedules deal with matters that are not directly connected with the main thrust of the Act. These, on the whole, are not considered. To have done so would have obscured the basic purpose of the Act which is to deregulate private rentals and to reduce further the role of local authorities as the primary providers of rented housing.

I have had the benefit of comments and advice from a number of friends and colleagues. Particular thanks are due to Sylvester Carrot and Juliet Bellis. Sylvester read and commented in detail on all of the chapters and assisted with the laborious task of reading the proofs. He and I have also had several long discussions of the Act as it progressed through Parliament. He has given me a good deal of his time, despite his own busy schedule. Juliet Bellis was good enough to read and let me have some very thorough and sensible advice on all of the chapters. Thanks also to Ole Hansen and Maurice Sunkin, both of whom read and discussed the book with me when it was in draft. Richard Gee discussed Chapter 7 with me. Rosalyn Malcom and Leslie Blake discussed a number of points on Housing Action Trusts and David Watkinson read Chapters 8 and 9 and let me have several helpful comments. Nick Raynsford read Chapters 10 and 11 and made several incisive comments. Any errors that remain are my responsibility alone.

During the four months that I have been writing this book, my family has shared the pressures of writing while working full time with their usual good humour, and I would not have finished this project without their warm support. Lelia has been encouraging and considerate throughout. My children, Jonathan and Sarah remained cheerful during this period, even though I was unable to accept their offer of help with the word-processing!

As usual in law books, I have, for the sake of clarity and simplicity, used "he", "his" and "him" to include "she" "hers" and "her"; no sexism is intended.

James Driscoll
January 1989, London

Contents

Table of Cases

page

page

Chapter 1

Introduction

The Housing Act 1988 is the most important measure affecting rented housing for more than forty years. It will, within a short space of time, affect the lives of many tenants, whether they rent from private or public landlords or from housing associations. Although the Act consists of 141 sections and 18 schedules, it does not tell the whole story. How different parts of the Act will work will depend on the drafting of several statutory instruments that will be published (for the most part) early in 1989. It will also depend on decisions taken by Central Government which has under the Act reserved to itself significant powers to intervene and control sections of public rented housing. Despite its length, the Housing Act 1988 is far from being a definitive statement of the rights and duties of residential landlords and tenants. Advisors will have to consider the Act in the general context of the wider legislative and common law framework of the landlord and tenant relationship. This chapter examines the background and the scope of the Housing Act 1988. It also describes other developments that will affect rented housing in the near future.

1. Background to the Housing Act 1988

(a) The scale of current housing problems

At the turn of this century most people rented their homes from private landlords. Few could afford to buy their homes and local authorities were only starting to build houses for rent. Today more than 60% of householders are owner-occupiers and the proportion of people renting from private landlords has shrunk to less than 8%. Local authorities have become the largest single landlord, housing some 30% of householders (see *Social Trends 1988*). The general condition of housing has been the subject of several recent inquiries (see for example, *The Private Rented Sector*, HMSO, first report, 3 vols., *English House Condition survey*, 1981, HMSO, 1982). A report that has attracted considerable interest is the *Inquiry into British Housing* published by the National Federation of Housing Associations in 1985. This was based on a survey undertaken by a committee chaired by the Duke of Edinburgh. It identified four main components of what it called the "housing problem". The first is a growing problem of the shortage of housing. This is a phenomenon of major proportions in London and other urban areas. Acute shortages also exist in rural areas, affecting specific groups such as the elderly and people with large families. With fewer new houses being built and local authorities experiencing reductions in their resources ". . . there are simply not enough homes available . . ." (page 4 of the Report). Linked to this problem is the increase in the numbers of the homeless. Local authorities have responsibilities for some categories of the homeless but many authorities can do little more at present than offer "bed and breakfast" accommodation.

The second dimension is the deterioration in housing conditions. Although fewer homes now lack basic amenities, an increasing number are falling into serious disrepair. Disrepair is most common in the owner-occupied sector and most concentrated in the private rented sector where it is estimated that some 30% of homes are substandard (*English and Welsh House Condition Surveys 1981*).

A third problem is that of unsatisfactory council estates. On the whole there are far fewer problems of unfitness in council housing than in the private sector. However, many council estates suffer major problems that appear to be the product of poor design and bad building. The problems include condensation, inadequate heating, structural defects and badly designed layouts in some estates (see also Hughes: *Housing Repairs: A Suitable Case for Reform*, 1984 Journal of Social Welfare Law 137).

The fourth issue identified in the Report is the lack of choice and the social divisions that are the product of the present range of tenures. For most households, the Report argued, there is little or no choice. The better off households have the option of owner-occupation but there is a lack of good quality private rented accommodation from which to choose. Those on low incomes, who cannot afford to buy, must become tenants, generally tenants of a local authority. With the reductions in local authority housing spending there is little opportunity for council tenants to move.

According to the report, a number of underlying factors have contributed to these difficulties. One is low investment in housing. At present Britain has the lowest investment in new house building of any comparable developed nation. In addition Central Government subsidies to local authorities have been drastically reduced. Local authorities are also inhibited from using capital receipts from the sale of council homes to finance their housing programme. On the other hand they face a major commitment in meeting the costs of providing "bed and breakfast" accommodation for the homeless. The Report identified two other factors. First, the continuing pressure to attract households into owner-occupation, which results in lower income households finding it difficult to meet the increased costs of ownership, maintenance and repair. Second, what the report called a "rigid administrative framework" in which housing is planned, provided and managed.

In its conclusion, the Report made four major recommendations. First, all existing personal subsidies would be replaced by one housing allowance payable to those on low or limited incomes. The subsidies replaced would include tax relief on mortgage payments, which would be gradually phased out. The Report argued that this tax relief—which costs some £4 billion each year—assists the better off household and is of no benefit to householders who no longer have a mortgage. The Report also suggested that a new basis for fixing rents should be set for all of the rented sectors. Broadly speaking, rents would be based on the capital value of the premises let. Under the report's third recommendation, local authorities would take on a different range of housing functions. In addition to being a provider of housing, local authorities would take on more of a stragetic role, being more involved in research and the co-ordination of different forms of renting. The final recommendations relate to the improvement of housing conditions. These include proposals for helping older and poorer owners and the development of area-based agencies. The report also argued that its other recommendations will generate the resources to target remedial action on the areas of worst housing.

(b) The Government's solutions

It was against this background of a rapidly diminishing private rented sector, falling investment in housing and deteriorating housing conditions that the Government published its White Paper on Housing in September 1987 (Cmnd 214). The paper made a number of observations that are similar to those in the *Inquiry into British Housing*. However the Government's analysis of the problems and its prescriptions are very different. In paragraph 1 of the White Paper, four principal aims are outlined as follows:

> "First, to reverse the decline of rented housing and to improve its quality; second, to give council tenants the right to transfer to other landlords if they choose to do so; third, to target money more accurately on the most acute problems; and fourth, to continue to encourage the growth of home ownership".

To promote this last objective, the Government will continue to offer tax relief on the interest element of mortgage repayments. It will also bring forward legislation to extend the "right to buy" and to change the administration of grants to enable repairs and maintenance to be carried out. None of these measures (apart from some changes to the right to buy) appear in the Housing Act 1988 and they will be the subject of future legislation.

It is the other three objectives that form the essence of the 1988 Act. First, there is the attempt to "put new life into the independent rented sector" (*op cit*, paragraph 1.15). Second, approved landlords will be able to take over local authority housing provided that a majority of the tenants affected do not vote *against* the proposal. Third, resources will be directed towards the worst areas of local authority housing through the creation of "housing action trusts".

Many of these measures presage a new role for local authorities—"Provision of housing by local authorities should be diminished, and alternative forms of tenure and tenant choice should increase" (*op cit*, paragraph 1.16). In addition to the provisions in the 1988 Act, there will be further legislation containing a new financial regime for local authorities. The extension of the right to buy and changes in the grants system will also affect the housing role of local authorities.

Apart from its general context and the future legislative plans, the 1988 Act should also be seen in the light of other fiscal and statutory changes affecting rented accommodation. There have already been significant changes to local authority housing finance. Central Government housing subsidies have been substantially reduced—from £2029 million in 1980 to £665 million in 1985 (figures cited in the *Inquiry into British Housing*, page 14). Since these figures have not been adjusted to take account of inflation, the actual rate of decline is even greater. As a result, only a small minority of authorities (50 of the 319 authorities in England and Wales) receive any subsidy at all. The Government has also inhibited capital spending by local authorities. Through the housing investment programme, the Government controls capital expenditure. Authorities currently can spend only 20% of the receipts from the sale of council homes (Hughes: *Public Sector Housing Law*, 2nd ed 1987, pages 11 to 15). This has led to the remark that "local authorities have been made subject to increased statutory duties while not being given resources commensurate to these new responsibilities" (Hughes, *op cit*, page 18). Local authorities have also been encouraged to sell off their housing stock by measures in the Housing Act 1985 and the Housing and Planning Act 1986.

(c) The Government's legislative plans

The White Paper, which appeared in September 1987, consisted of only nineteen pages; an extremely thin document considering the import of the Government's plans. More information was revealed the following month when a number of consultative documents were circulated. These consisted of a consultation paper on the private rented sector; a separate paper dealing with the implications for housing benefit; a paper containing financial proposals for housing associations; a paper on the housing action trust proposals and a paper detailing proposed rights for council tenants to transfer to a private landlord.

How much weight the Government gave to the representations it received is not clear, since the Housing Bill was published before the period allowed for consultation had elapsed. The Bill published in November 1987 was immediately withdrawn and then replaced with another version. This was because of a number of typographical errors in the original.

The Bill had its Second Reading in November 1987 and it went into its Committee stage the following month. After twenty-seven sittings, the Committee finished its deliberations in March 1988. Whilst the basic structure and principles of the Bill remained intact, the Government did make several concessions. One important change is that council tenants can only be transferred to an approved landlord under a new "tenants' charter". Several weeks passed before the Bill returned to the House of Commons for its Report Stage. At the Report Stage the Government introduced a number of amendments. It also introduced new clauses, such as that creating a separate Housing Corporation for Wales that had not been considered in Committee. There were also changes when the Bill was before the House of Lords. For example, the Opposition won a change requiring a ballot of council tenants before the Government can set up a housing action trust. The Bill completed its final Parliamentary stages in November and received Royal Assent on 15 November 1988.

The Housing Act 1988 differs on many points of detail from the original Bill. These changes are highlighted at appropriate places in the following chapters.

2. Existing statutory protections affecting rented accommodation

It is difficult to understand how the 1988 Act will influence rented accommodation without referring to the other regulatory statutes that already exist. Tenants protected before the Act came into force will continue to be protected by the Rent Act 1977. Local authorities will continue to let on secure tenancies under the Housing Act 1985. In addition to these transitional factors, the 1988 Act uses concepts that first appeared in earlier legislation. For these reasons it is necessary to review briefly the pre-1988 Act statutory regulatory schemes.

(a) Private rented accommodation

Tenants renting from private landlords first received statutory protection as to rent and security of tenure in 1915 (in the Increase of Rent and Mortgage Interest (War Restrictions) Act 1915). This was an emergency measure designed to halt rent and mortgage increases during the First World War. Although controls were relaxed during the 1920's and 1930's, they were re-introduced in 1939 (see Holman: *Housing Policy in Britain: A History* 1986, Chapters 2 and 3). Furnished lets had been left out of statutory protection. However, in 1946, these tenants were given a measure of protection by the Furnished Houses (Rent

Control) Act 1946. Newly created rent tribunals were given jurisdiction to set a "reasonable rent" for the premises and power to delay a landlord's notice to quit, thereby giving some security to furnished tenants. In 1957, a Conservative Government sought gradually to de-control tenancies protected under the Rent Acts. However, a Labour Government brought back most de-controlled lets into protection in the Rent Act 1965. The 1965 Act also introduced a new system for regulating rents, called "fair rents", under which landlords could obtain higher rents, with tenants being protected against inflation. A new system under which "rent officers" were to adjudicate on rent increases, with an appeal to a rent assessment committee was introduced. Before 1965, Rent Act protected tenancy rents were controlled by a statutory formula relating to the rateable value of the premises and any repairing obligations upon the landlords. As a result, there were two types of rent control for protected tenants: "controlled rents" for a tenant whose tenancy had not been de-controlled by the time of the 1965 Act and "fair rents" for a tenant who became protected by the 1965 Act.

The Housing Act 1969 made provision for controlled rents to be converted into fair rents if the landlord carried out defined improvements (and grants were available to landlords for this purpose). In the Housing Act 1980, all remaining controlled lets were converted into lets regulated by the fair rents scheme. Since that time all protected lets have been subject to fair rents. The statutory provisions governing protected and furnished lets were consolidated in the Rent Act 1968. Furnished lets were excluded from protection because it was assumed that a tenant taking such a let did not intend it as a permanent home. However, it became evident during the 1970's that many landlords were letting properties and using worthless or near-worthless furniture simply to exclude protection. Tenants were accepting furnished accommodation, not as a short-term arrangement, but because there was often little else available. This development was recognised by the Court of Appeal in *Woodward* v *Docherty* (1974). In this case, the annual rent was £520 and the amount attributable to the rent was found to be £40 per annum. It was held that since the value of the furniture compared with the rent was insubstantial, the let was not a furnished one for the purposes of the Rent Acts. The tenant was in consequence protected. This was a significant decision. Thereafter, landlords could not exclude protection simply by providing low cost furniture.

Shortly after *Woodward* v *Docherty* was decided, the Rent Act 1974 came into force. This Act had two related purposes. First, provision of furniture no longer took a tenant outside the protection of the Rent Acts. Second, it introduced the "resident landlord" exception to protection. If at the beginning of a let, the landlord lived in another part of the property, the tenant could not be protected so long as the landlord remained in residence. This was designed to encourage owner-occupiers to let part of their homes, without the tenant acquiring full protection under the Rent Acts.

Under the transitional provisions of the 1974 Act, all unfurnished lets existing at 14 August 1974 remained protected even if the landlord was resident. The rationale was that a protected tenant should not lose protection simply because his landlord had moved in. A furnished let also became protected *unless*, at the same date, the landlord was resident in the same premises. Here the rationale was that a tenant who was unprotected before the Act lost nothing by continuing to be unprotected (see Martin: *Security of Tenure Under the Rent Act*, 1986, page 42). In the light of *Woodward* v *Docherty*, this leaves an intermediate category. Consider the position of a tenant of furnished premises whose landlord was resident at 14 August 1974. If in reality it was an unfurnished let under the *Woodward* v *Docherty* test, it was protected at this date. Under the transitional provisions in the 1974 Act, it remains protected under the Rent Acts.

The Rent Acts of 1968 and 1974 were consolidated in the Rent Act 1977. Under the 1977 Act certain occupancies became known as "restricted contracts". The major example is a tenancy of a resident landlord. The tenant cannot be protected but he had the right to ask a rent tribunal to fix a reasonable rent, and the tribunal could also provide a modicum of security of tenure by deferring the operation of a notice to quit. This was based on the principles governing furnished lets before they became incorporated into full protection under the Rent Act 1974.

Further changes were made in the Housing Act 1980. As noted above, controlled lets were converted into tenancies governed by fair rents. In addition, this Act reduced the limited protection given to holders of restricted contracts. A restricted contract created before 28 November 1980 remains the subject of the limited security provisions of the Rent Act 1977. The holder of such a contract can refer a notice to quit to a rent tribunal, which can defer its operation (however, by definition this cannot apply to a fixed term which will come to an end by effluxion of time without the need for a notice to quit). But in the case of a restricted contract entered into after 28 November 1980, the security provisions are removed and replaced by giving the county court discretion to postpone a possession order for up to three months. A holder of a post-28 November 1980 contract can still refer the rent to the tribunal who can still fix a reasonable rent. However, it has no jurisdiction to deal with a notice to quit. To add to the complications, these functions have since the 1980 Act been exercised by the rent assessment committee which is called a "rent tribunal" when dealing with restricted contracts.

The Housing Act 1980 made other changes to the Rent Act 1977, including amendments to the resident landlord provisions and other parts of the Act. It also introduced two types of statutory regulation for new lets meeting certain conditions. These are "assured tenancies" and "protected shorthold tenancies" which are described more fully in Chapters 3 and 5. Under assured lets, approved landlords could let new or converted properties free of Rent Act controls and subject to the same degree of regulation as business tenancies. In the case of protected shortholds, the tenant has security of tenure during the period of his tenancy but the landlord is entitled to possession at the end of the term if he has complied with the statutory conditions. These new tenancies were introduced to try to stimulate new investment in private rentals. The Rent Act 1977 was also amended by the Rent (Amendment) Act 1985 in relation to one of the grounds for possession.

Thus the position of private tenants before the Housing Act 1988 was complex enough. If a tenant is protected, he can only be evicted if one or more of the grounds set out in Schedule 15 of the 1977 Act (as amended) is proved, and, in the case of a discretionary ground, providing the court is satisfied that it is reasonable to make an order. A protected tenant (or the landlord) can periodically ask a rent officer to fix a fair rent. An appeal lies to a rent assessment committee. The landlord cannot terminate a protected tenancy simply by serving a notice to quit in the case of a periodic let. Nor will a protected tenant be without protection at the end of a fixed term. In either case, a "statutory tenancy" comes into existence and this can only be brought to an end in the manner prescribed by the 1977 Act. If a protected tenant dies, his spouse or other member of his family will succeed to the tenancy. The tenancy can pass twice in this way. Some tenancies cannot be protected. A major example are tenants of resident landlords. Nor, by definition, can the holder of a licence to occupy be protected. These and other categories may hold a restricted contract. Others are completely outside the Rent Acts, although in most cases the owner must obtain a possession order before evicting them (under the Protection From Eviction Act 1977). In addition there are assured and protected shortholds to consider.

(b) Tenants of public landlords

Until the Housing Act 1980, tenants of a local authority (and other public landlords) had no statutory security of tenure. They were outside the protection of the Rent Acts. The 1980 Act introduced security of tenure for most local authority tenants. Under this Act a "secure tenant" has security of tenure similar to that enjoyed by protected tenants. The local authority can recover possession only if it establishes one or more grounds for possession (there are no mandatory grounds for possession). On the death of a secure tenant, the tenancy passes to his spouse or other member of his family. Unlike the position under the Rent Acts, there is only one succession. Secure tenants have other statutory rights not enjoyed by private tenants. They have qualified rights to sublet, take in a lodger, assign or exchange, and rights to be consulted over certain matters of housing management.

Perhaps the best known right is the right to buy. Before the Housing Act 1980, local authorities had the power to sell homes to their tenants. Since the 1980 Act they are under a *duty* to sell to secure tenants in most circumstances and the tenant is entitled to a discount in the sale price. These provisions are now to be found in the consolidating Housing Act 1985, which has in turn been amended by the Housing and Planning Act 1986. Additional changes appear in the Housing Act 1988.

(c) Tenants of housing associations

Most housing association tenants are not protected by the Rent Acts. However many of these tenants are "secure tenants" under the Housing Act 1985. Thus they have security of tenure under the 1985 Act and many of the other statutory rights enjoyed by secure tenants (there are limitations on their right to buy). These tenants can use the fair rents machinery of the Rent Act 1977.

3. Other recent and proposed legislation affecting rented housing

The Housing Act 1988 cannot be understood without reference to other recent measures that regulate rented housing. As already noted, the position of private tenants is largely regulated by the Rent Act 1977; the rights of secure tenants are regulated by the Housing Act 1985 (as amended); secure tenants of housing associations are also subject to the fair rent procedures of the Rent Act 1977.

The Housing Associations Act 1985 consolidated the law relating to housing associations. The Landlord and Tenant Act 1985 has consolidated several aspects of landlord and tenant relations including those relating to repairs and notices to quit. In 1987 another Landlord and Tenant Act introduced important changes to the rights of tenants and owners of long leases. These included consultation rights, a right of first refusal if the landlord sells and rights to challenge service charges. The Landlord and Tenant Act 1988 changes the law on covenants against assignment and subletting.

In addition to this there have been recommendations for changes to housing litigation in the Lord Chancellor's Department's *Civil Justice Review* which was published in July 1988. This review proposed a new rent arrears action whereby rent (and mortgage) arrears can be recovered without the threat of eviction. In addition, there is a proposal for a new "housing action" under which non-possession cases, such as repairs disputes, can be dealt with by arbitration.

Another matter to bear in mind is the Legal Aid Act 1988. Under this Act there is power to transfer certain classes of housing (and other) cases from solicitors to such advice agencies as Citizens Advice Bureaux.

Legislation will be brought forward in the 1988/1989 Parliamentary session to change local authority housing revenue accounts and housing capital programmes and receipts. These Government proposals are contained in two consultative documents published by the Department of the Environment in July 1988 (*Capital Expenditure and Finance*; *New Financial Regime for Local Authority Housing in England and Wales*). One effect will be to increase council tenants' rents.

Legislation is also likely in the near future to strengthen local authority powers to control "houses in multiple occupation" (*Houses In Multiple Occupation: Consultative Document*, Department of the Environment, July 1988).

Thus new legislation, dealing with these and possibly two other matters, will appear shortly. The first additional matter is changes to the homelessness provisions in the Housing Act 1985. The Government believes that local authorities should only have responsibility to provide temporary accommodation for the homeless. It has commissioned two surveys, only one of which has been published (*Responding to Homelessness: Local Authority Policies and Practice*, HMSO 1988). Although the results of the second survey have not been published, they were extensively leaked to the *Housing Journal*. The Government believes that many of the homeless use the legislation in order to jump the queue of applicants seeking council housing. However, the research provides little evidence to support this belief.

The second matter that is likely to be included in the forthcoming Bill concerns changes to the right of first refusal, which is available to certain tenants under the Landlord and Tenant Act 1987. There are changes to this Act in the Housing Act 1988. These are summarised on page 40 in the next chapter.

4. The scope of the Housing Act 1988

(a) Private rentals

The provisions affecting the private rented sector are contained in Part I of the Act. Since they were brought into force on 15 January 1989, it will (with limited exceptions) no longer be possible to create tenancies that are protected under the Rent Act 1977. Nor will it be possible to create new restricted contracts. Instead, new lettings will take one of two forms. The first is the "assured tenancy" where landlords will be able to charge market rents but the tenants will have security of tenure. The second is the "assured shorthold tenancy" where there will be some regulation of the rent but no security of tenure beyond the period of the agreement. However, contractual licences cannot be "assured" and Part I also prevents certain types of tenancy from attaining the assured status. These two new assured lets are different from those introduced by the Housing Act 1980.

How will these changes attract new investment into private rentals? The key, according to the Government, lies in allowing landlords to charge market rents and in confining security of tenure to the assured lettings. In addition the Government hopes that interest will be stimulated by the provision of tax incentives. Under the Finance Act 1988 investors in companies offering assured lettings will be eligible for income and capital gains relief. This is considered further in Chapter 3.

There will also be Government subsidies to private rentals through housing benefit. During the Parliamentary debates the Government affirmed its commitment to maintaining housing benefit for those in need. However in making this commitment the Government found itself in a dilemma. If it guarantees this subsidy and rents are allowed to rise, landlords will be tempted to charge exorbitant rents in the knowledge that they will be paid out of public funds. In an attempt to resolve this problem, the administration of housing benefit is being changed. In future, in the case of new lettings, a local authority will have to refer applications for benefit to a rent officer. The rent officer will have to assess whether the rent payable is excessive. If he concludes that it is, he must state what he believes is a genuine "market rent". This would not bind the landlord who can still demand the full rent. The new role of rent officers is explored in Chapter 2.

Although (with limited exceptions) there can be no further protected tenancies, existing tenants do not lose their rights under the Rent Act. Tenancies that are protected as the Act comes into force will continue to be regulated by the 1977 Act. However, there are significant changes to succession rights. These transitional matters are explained in Chapter 2. The Government accepted that there is a danger that protected tenants may be harassed by landlords eager to take advantage of the new assured tenancies (see White Paper, *op cit* paragraph 3.17). It is in order to discourage such practices that the Act seeks to strengthen the laws on harassment and illegal eviction.

(b) Housing associations

The Government believes that housing associations have a crucial role in its plans to revive the privately rented sector. However the Government also considers that housing associations should be less dependent on public resources to fund their operations. Under the Act housing associations will have to raise more money from the private sector and rely less on public grants. The powers of housing associations and their financial structure are changed by the Act. All new lets will be by assured or assured shorthold tenancies, thus increasing rental income. The position of existing tenants is unchanged. In future, many housing associations will have two types of tenants: secure tenants and assured tenants under the 1988 Act.

(c) Local authorities

The general content of local authority responsibilities for housing will remain largely as it was before the Housing Act 1988. Thus local authorities will continue to provide housing and will have the primary duty towards the homeless. Their other duties in relation to substandard housing and houses in multiple occupation will remain as before, although the 1988 Act makes changes to the repairs notices procedures under Part VI of the Housing Act 1985. However, local authorities will continue to operate under continuing financial constraints and in the shadow of forthcoming changes to the capital and revenue structures of their housing spending.

Their tenants' legal position is also largely unchanged although tenants will continue to face increases in their rents. There are some changes in the 1988 Act to the right to buy.

Under Part III of the Act, the Government has assumed powers to set up "housing action trusts" to take over council housing in particular areas. A trust, which will be given a number of local authority functions, will manage and renovate the housing and sell it to other forms of landlordship such as housing associations and private landlords. Tenants living in these properties will remain secure tenants so long as the properties are owned by the trust. However, unless the properties are resold to the local authority, the tenants will lose their secure status and will become assured or assured shorthold tenants. They will however, retain their right to buy.

Part IV of the Act will enable private landlords and others to purchase council housing, unless a majority of the tenants affected vote against the proposal. If the proposal comes into effect, a tenant will lose his secure status unless he elects to stay as a tenant of the council.

These two measures continue the process of selling local authority housing to the private sector. This complements the right to buy, and the existing provisions (in the Housing Act 1985 and the Housing and Planning Act 1986) that allow councils to sell their housing stock. These powers and procedures are also amended by the Housing Act 1988.

(d) The Housing Corporation

The Housing Corporation is given new responsibilities. In addition to its current role of promoting and regulating housing associations, it will have new functions in relation to administering grants to housing associations.

It will also have to approve prospective landlords who intend bidding for local authority housing under Part IV of the Act. It will have the power to give advice to council tenants who are interested in transferring to private landlords, and it will be able to offer legal advice and assistance to tenants who have transferred and who find themselves in dispute with the new landlord. A separate Housing Corporation is established for Wales.

(e) Miscellaneous

Part V of the Act makes a number of changes to the right to buy. It also makes minor changes to statutory repairing obligations and to premiums. In addition there are significant amendments to the repairs notices procedures under Part V of the Housing Act 1985.

5. Delegated legislation

As noted at the beginning of this chapter, much of the workings of the 1988 Act will depend on the drafting of several statutory instruments. In Part I of the Act, which deals with private rentals, several forms governing the service of notices and the procedures used by rent assessment committees, have been introduced by statutory instrument (see, for example, The Assured Tenancies and Agricultural Occupancies (Forms) Regulations 1988, 1988 No. 2203). Much of the workings of "housing action trusts" (under Part III of the Act) will depend on decisions taken by Central Government. For example, the Government will decide which local authority functions will be transferred to a housing action trust. Under Part IV of the Act private landlords will be able to compulsorily acquire council housing. However the details of how the council tenants will be affected by the compulsory acquisition are not set out in the Act and will appear in a statutory instrument to be published in 1989.

6. Glossary of terms

Because of the overlap between the 1988 Act and other legislation, it is important to appreciate the different terminology used, particularly in relation to rented accommodation. This is summarised as follows:

Protected tenant – this refers to a private tenant who is protected under the Rent Act 1977 as to security of tenure and rent. A "fair rent" can be fixed by a rent officer and reviewed by a rent assessment committee.

Statutory tenant – where a protected tenant's contractual agreement comes to an end, a statutory tenancy comes into existence. The tenant continues to enjoy the protection of the Rent Act 1977, so long as he occupies the premises as his residence. All protected or statutory tenancies existing on 15 January 1989 continue to be governed by the Rent Act 1977, although the Housing Act 1988 makes changes to the succession rights. With limited exceptions, no new Rent Act protected tenancies can be created after 15 January 1989.

Restricted contract – this refers to certain tenancies (and some contractual licences) that are excluded from the full protection of the Rent Act 1977. A restricted contract entered into before 28 November 1980 can be granted limited security by a rent assessment committee. Contracts created after this date do not enjoy this limited protection. Rent assessment committees can fix "reasonable rents" for all restricted contracts. No further restricted contracts can be created after 15 January 1989.

Protected shorthold tenant – this refers to certain private tenancies, where the tenant has security of tenure during the currency of the agreement, but where the landlord has a mandatory ground for possession at the end of the term. These tenancies are also subject to "fair rents".

Secure tenant – this refers to tenants (and some contractual licensees) of local authorities, other public bodies and many housing associations. Secure tenants have security of tenure and other statutory rights under the Housing Act 1985. Local authorities fix "reasonable" rents for their tenants.

Housing association tenancy – most housing association tenants have the right to have a "fair rent" fixed under the Rent Act 1977. After 15 January 1989, all new housing association tenancies (with limited exceptions), will not have this right. After this date most new lets by housing associations will be on "assured lets" under Part I of the Housing Act 1988.

Assured tenant – this refers to a tenant who has security of tenure under Part I of the Housing Act 1988 and who will be paying a market rent. A rent assessment committee has only limited jurisdiction over market rents for assured tenancies. Where it has jurisdiction, it is restricted to considering whether a rent is excessive, or more than a genuine market rent. Where an assured tenant applies for housing benefit, rent officers will have to consider whether the rent is excessive and/or whether the accommodation is too large given the needs of the tenant. However this determination only affects the payment of benefit and not the rent charged. Assured tenancies created under the Housing Act 1980 are converted into assured lets governed by the Housing Act 1988.

Statutory periodic tenancy – if an assured let is for a fixed term, a statutory periodic tenancy comes into existence at the end of that term under the Housing Act 1988, unless another assured let is granted.

Assured shorthold tenant – this refers to the other type of tenancy introduced by the Housing Act 1988. Such a tenant has very limited security of tenure. At the end of the agreement, the landlord has a mandatory ground for possession. A rent assessment committee has limited jurisdiction to regulate the rent. Rents are supposed to be lower than the market rents for assured tenancies, to reflect the lack of security.

Chapter 2

Commencement, transitional provisions, jurisdiction and miscellaneous matters

This chapter begins by explaining how the Act will be brought into force. The second section deals with the effect of the Act on tenants who enjoyed statutory protection at the date of its commencement. This is followed by a summary of the changes to the jurisdiction of the county courts, rent assessment committees and rent officers. The final section briefly examines a number of miscellaneous matters that appear in the Act.

1. Commencement and extent

The Housing Act extends to England and Wales (s 141(5), (6)). A separate Act (the Housing (Scotland) Act 1988) introduces similar measures to Scotland, although there are some changes to the Scottish legislation in the Housing Act 1988. These are not examined in this book.

Matters relating to the commencement of the Housing Act 1988 are dealt with in s 141. Part I of the Act, which deals with the private sector, came into force two months after Royal Assent which was on 15 November 1988. The private sector provisions came into force on 15 January 1989. The other private sector provisions that came into force on this date are those dealing with premiums and repairing obligations. However, the new role that rent officers will have in relation to housing benefit does not come into force until later, after regulations have been approved by Parliament (these are likely to be published in March 1989). With this exception, the transitional provisions, the new assured and assured shorthold lets and the harassment provisions came into force on 15 January 1989 (see also The Housing Act 1988

(Commencement No. 2) Order 1988, S.I. No. 2152.

The Housing Corporation and Housing for Wales started their new role of approving landlords and assisting generally with the change of landlord provisions on 15 January 1989. Their criteria for approving new landlords also came into effect on this date. However as will be seen in Chapter 10, the change of landlord provisions in Part IV of the 1988 Act will not be fully operative until regulations dealing with the consultation procedures and lease-back arrangements have been approved (these are likely to be published in May 1989).

The powers to set up housing action trusts will not be brought into force until mid-1989. As will be explained in Chapter 8, the Government has announced the areas it has selected, but no final decisions will be taken until it has received reports it has commissioned from consultants.

The general procedure for bringing the remainder of the Act into force is by the laying of a statutory instrument (s 141(2)).

It is likely that the whole of the Act will be operational by the middle of 1989.

2. Transitional provisions

As Part I came into force on 15 January 1989, there was a large group of tenants who enjoy the protection of various enactments such as the Rent Act 1977 and the Housing Act 1985. As explained in Chapter 1, these are tenants who are protected under the Rent Act 1977; holders of restricted contracts under the 1977 Act; tenants of public authorities who have rights under the Housing Act 1985; agricultural workers who are protected under the Rent (Agriculture) Act 1976; and housing association tenants who are enjoying the protection of either the Rent Act 1977 or the Housing Act 1985.

The basic principle is that tenants who are covered by these statutory provisions at the commencement of the 1988 Act, will continue to be regulated in the same way. However, there are some changes to the position of Rent Act protected tenants. Further, as Parts III and IV of the 1988 Act are brought into force, the legal position of tenants of public authorities will change if they are transferred to a private landlord. For a considerable time there is likely to be much anxiety if not confusion for many tenants. The transitional provisions are of major importance and their effects on the different categories of tenancy are now examined in turn.

(a) Tenants who are protected under the Rent Act 1977

Continuing protection: Under the Rent Act 1977, a tenant living in residential accommodation is protected unless he comes within one or other of the exceptional categories specified in Part I of that Act. A landlord may only recover possession under the discretionary or mandatory grounds set out in Sch 15 of the 1977 Act. A protected tenant's contractual agreement might come to an end after receipt of a notice to quit in the case of a periodic let, or at the end of a fixed term. When this happens, a statutory tenancy comes into being which is on the same terms as the old tenancy (s 2 of the 1977 Act). Both the tenant and his landlord may apply for a fair rent to be fixed and this rent may be less than the one that was contractually agreed. On the death of the tenant, the tenancy passes to his spouse or to another member of his family. There can be a further transmission of the tenancy on the death of the first successor (see generally, Martin: *Security of Tenure Under the Rent Act* 1986). All protected or statutory tenancies that existed when the 1988 Act came into force on 15 January 1989 continue to be regulated by the Rent Act 1977. Thus a landlord seeking possession must do so in the manner prescribed by the Rent Act 1977 (on this see Martin, op cit, Chapter 6). Moreover the fair rent procedures will continue to apply to these tenancies although local authorities will, under Sch 17 of the 1988 Act, lose the right to refer a rent to a rent officer (a procedure often used by local authorities on receipt of an application for housing benefit, see Martin, op cit page 138).

However, there are important changes to the succession rights of protected and statutory tenants. These are considered after looking at the other transitional effects of the 1988 Act on private rentals. With limited exceptions, no further Rent Act protected tenancies can be created after 15 January 1989 (s 34(1)). All new private tenancies will be either assured or assured shorthold tenancies if they meet the conditions in Part I of the 1988 Act. However contractual licences and tenancies that are excluded from the assured formula will, in most cases, be outside any form of statutory regulation.

In addition to the protected tenancies existing on 15 January 1988 there are four ways in which a *new* protected tenancy may be created:

(i) The first deals with the case where the parties entered into an agreement before 15 January 1989 that a tenancy would be granted (s 34(1)(a)). Assuming that the tenancy satisfies the basic requirements of the Rent Act 1977, it will be protected even though it takes effect after 15 January 1989. Although this exception will by its nature be of importance for a limited period, it is not without its difficulties. A tenant will have to show that he had a binding agreement that a tenancy was to be granted. Hence he must show that agreement was reached on the basic terms such as the extent of the premises to be let and the rent. Moreover, the agreement must usually be evidenced in writing and signed by the landlord or his agent (s 40 Law of Property Act 1925). If the agreement is not evidenced in writing, the tenant will have to show an "act of part performance" (Megarry & Wade: *The Law of Real Property* 5th ed 1984, pages 588 to 598). An example would be payment of a deposit that clearly relates to an agreement to take a tenancy. Indeed the landlord's or agent's receipt may satisfy the s 40 Law of Property Act 1925 requirement if it is signed and refers to an agreement to grant a tenancy.

(ii) The second exception applies to a protected or a statutory tenant who is offered a new tenancy by his landlord after 15 January 1989 (s 34(1)(b)). The new tenancy will also be protected or statutory, as the case may be, even though it takes effect after 15 January 1989. Thus a tenant who accepts a new tenancy does not lose his protection under the Rent Act 1977. This also applies to a letting to joint tenants or to a letting by joint landlords. For example, if one of the joint tenants leaves, an offer of a new tenancy by the landlord to the remaining tenant will be a protected tenancy. Similarly an offer by one of the joint landlords will be a protected tenancy. The way in which s 34(1)(b) is drafted means that an offer of a new tenancy of *other* accommodation will also be a protected tenancy, even though it takes effect after 15 January 1989.

(iii) The third exception deals with a protected or statutory tenant against whom a possession order has been made following a finding that suitable alternative accommodation is available. If the court is satisfied that the alternative accommodation let on an assured let would not give the tenant "the required security" it must direct that the new let should be of a protected tenancy. The expression "required security" is a reference to the Rent Act 1977 requirement that an offer of alternative accommodation is only suitable if it consists of a protected tenancy or a let with comparable security of tenure. As will be seen in Chapters 3 and 4, an assured let offers comparable security in several respects. It is likely that landlords will offer an assured let to a protected tenant hoping that a court will accept that it is suitable and provides the necessary security of tenure. However a tenant may argue that the succession rights are far more limited and that grounds for possession are more stringent with assured lets. Further, the market rent payable under an assured tenancy might be beyond the means of the tenant, rendering it unsuitable and also making it unreasonable for a court to make a possession order. This exception applies then if (a) a possession order is made on the ground that suitable alternative accommodation is available; and (b) the court is satisfied that a let of an assured tenancy would not give the tenant security comparable to a protected tenancy (on possession orders made on this basis, see Martin: *Security of Tenure Under the Rent Act*, 1986, pages 70 to 73).

(iv) The fourth exception deals with the position when a tenant of a New Town Corporation is transferred to a private landlord. The general situation is that a secure tenant loses his secure status if he is transferred from a public landlord to a private landlord after 15 January 1989 (s 38). He will usually become an assured tenant. However in the case of a tenant of a New Town Corporation, the cut-off date is extended for up to two years after Royal Assent, that is up to 15 November 1990. The effect of this is that a tenant might be transferred to a landlord on a protected tenancy during this extended period.

These transitional provisions apply to a protected or a statutory tenant only. They do not apply to a protected shorthold tenancy (s 34(2)(a)). If a new tenancy is offered to a protected shorthold tenant, it cannot be a protected tenancy. This deals with a tenant under a shorthold that was in existence on 15 January 1989. There is a second situation to consider and that is where a shorthold tenant's agreement came to an end before 15 January 1989. Although the landlord has a mandatory ground for possession under Case 19, Sch 15 of the Rent Act 1977, he does not have to take proceedings immediately at the end of a protected shorthold. During the interim, the tenant holds under a statutory tenancy. However this is a limited interest since the landlord has a mandatory ground for possession. Again, a grant of another tenancy to a tenant in this position cannot be a protected tenancy.

These transitional provisions are of great importance to protected and statutory tenants and they may be summarised in the following way:

1. All tenants who are protected under the Rent Act 1977 continue to enjoy their rights as to security and rent regulation. This includes a statutory tenant and a tenant whose tenancy started after 15 January 1989 in pursuance of an agreement reached before this date.
2. A protected or a statutory tenant who accepts a new tenancy from his landlord after 15 January 1989 will continue to be protected by the Rent Act 1977.
3. If a landlord obtains possession under the Rent Act 1977 on the basis that suitable alternative accommodation is available, the court *may* direct that the new tenancy should be a protected tenancy.
4. The 15 January 1989 cut-off date is extended in cases of transfers of tenants from New Town Corporations.
5. Subject to these exceptions, no new protected tenancies can be created after 15 January 1989.

In the long term points 2 and 3 will be of most significance to protected and statutory tenants.

Changes to succession rights: There are also the succession right changes to consider. The White Paper stated that ". . . minor changes will be made to the succession rules . . ." (*Housing: The Government's Proposals*, Cmnd 214 1987, paragraph 3.15). However, the later consultation paper on private rentals revealed that the changes may have a substantial effect on protected tenants and their families. Under the Rent Act 1977, a protected or statutory tenancy will pass to the deceased tenant's spouse. If there is no surviving spouse, it will pass to a member of the deceased's family who was living with the deceased for at least six months before his death. There could be a second succession on the death of the first successor—again to a surviving spouse or other member of the deceased's family. These succession rules for protected and statutory tenants are contained in s 2 and Sch 1 of the Rent Act 1977.

However, these rules are changed by s 39 and Sch 4 of the Housing Act 1988. As a result, after 15 January 1989 the 1977 Act rules must be read in the light of the 1988 Act amendments. These changes are summarised in the following paragraphs.

A distinction must be drawn between a tenant who was the original tenant and a tenant who himself is a tenant by succession. Where the "original tenant" dies his spouse will succeed to the tenancy. The expression "spouse" includes a person who was living with the original tenant at the time of his death as his spouse. If there is no surviving spouse, a member of the deceased tenant's family will succeed. However, there are three major changes to this:

(i) first, this family member must have lived with the deceased for at least *two years* before his death;

(ii) second, this family member will inherit an *assured tenancy* and not a tenancy protected under the Rent Act 1977. The main repercussion of this is that the successor will have to pay a market rent;

(iii) third, there can be no further transmission of the tenancy.

This covers the changes where the original tenant dies. There are also changes to the succession rules where the "first successor" dies. This applies to a tenant who succeeded before or after 15 January 1989. There can be a further transmission to a member of the first successor's family provided (a) he or she was also a member of the original tenant's family; and (b) he or she lived with the first successor for at least two years before that tenant's death. Again he or she will inherit an assured not a protected tenancy. However, there are transitional provisions governing the position where the tenant dies within eighteen months after 15 January 1989. If the successor lived with the deceased for six months before this date and was living with the deceased when he died, he is treated as having lived with him for the necessary two year period. This offers some additional protection to members of the deceased's family.

What is the position if there is more than one eligible person living with the deceased at the time of his death? As under the Rent Acts it is left to the family to decide who will take the tenancy. If they cannot agree, the dispute has to be referred to the county court. An example of how the courts deal with these disputes under the Rent Acts is *Williams* v *Williams* (1970). In this case the deceased tenant was survived by her husband and her son (the case was decided before the rules were altered to allow a husband as well as a wife to succeed). The court found that the son, unlike the father, had treated the deceased well. However the father, unlike the son, was in financial need. The father's claim was upheld. Although hardship is not the sole criterion, his circumstances outweighed the merits of the son's claim.

These remarks have been addressed to protected or statutory tenants. During the currency of a shorthold tenancy the tenant has security of tenure under the Rent Acts. If the tenant dies before the end of the shorthold it is possible for the statutory tenancy to pass on his death. However the successor only inherits an assured shorthold tenancy (s 39(7)).

The effect of these changes is to reduce, in most cases, the right of succession to one person. Where the person who inherits is a member of the deceased's family, he or she will succeed to an assured tenancy under the Housing Act 1988. These changes will work hardship in many cases, particularly in the case of a son or daughter who has stayed at home to care for an ageing parent. Such a person faces a significant increase in rent on the death of the parent. As the organisation *Age Concern* has put it ". . . the proposals on succession seem to contradict the Government's policy on care in the community" (quoted in *A Future for Rented Housing?*, National Housing Forum, 1988).

(b) Restricted contracts

A private tenant may be excluded from Rent Act protection for a variety of reasons as set out in the Act. For example, a tenant of a resident landlord cannot be a protected tenant. Nor by definition can a contractual licensee. In some of these cases a tenant who is excluded from protection will have a "restricted contract" (s 19 Rent Act 1977). This status may also be held by a contractual licensee who meets the conditions in s 19 (*Luganda* v *Service Hotels* (1969)).

Since the Rent Act 1974, the main example of a restricted contract is a letting by a resident landlord. Under s 12 of the Rent

Act 1977, a tenant cannot be protected if his landlord was living in another dwelling in the same premises at the beginning of the tenancy and has been resident during the tenancy. Such a tenant has a restricted contract. The other examples of restricted contracts are:

(i) where the tenant shares living accommodation with his landlord;
(ii) contractual licences where services or furniture are provided;
(iii) lettings where board is provided but the board is less than substantial; and
(iv) a tenancy where substantial "attendance" (that is services personal to the tenant) is provided.

As explained in Chapter 1, since 1980, the main right that the holder of a restricted contract has is the right to refer the rent to a rent assessment committee. The committee may confirm, reduce, or increase the rent. Before 1980 a tenant could also refer any notice to quit to what was then called a rent tribunal. The tribunal could defer the coming into effect of the notice, thereby giving a limited measure of security to the tenant. However, this power was abolished by s 69 of the Housing Act 1980 in relation to restricted contracts created after 28 November 1980. A holder of a restricted contract created before this date can still refer a notice to quit.

Once the security provisions were abolished, it became more difficult for holders of restricted contracts to complain about the rent in this way. Referring the rent to a rent assessment committee carries the risk of eviction. The diminished function of the restricted contract is taken a stage further by s 36 of the 1988 Act. After 15 January 1989 no new restricted contracts can be created other than one created following an agreement reached before this date.

Thus in the case of a new let by a resident landlord after 15 January 1989, the tenant will be unable to refer the rent to the rent assessment committee. As will be seen in Chapters 3, 4 and 5, a tenant of a resident landlord cannot be an assured tenant (para 10, Sch 1 of the 1988 Act). Nor will such a tenant be an assured shorthold tenant.

Holders of restricted contracts in existence as the Act comes into force can still refer the rent to a rent assessment committee. However, there are three changes to this. Before the 1988 Act a rent registered by the committee was the maximum that could be charged for a period of two years after the date of registration. This was the case where a tenant left (or was evicted) and was replaced by a new tenant. After 15 January 1989 this requirement will cease to have effect (s 36(4)). As a result a landlord will be able to argue at any time that the rent should be increased (on this matter, see, Martin, op cit, pages 117 to 118). The second change is that the power of a local authority to refer a contract to a rent assessment committee is abolished (para 5, Sch 14 of the 1988 Act). The third change deals with the situation where the parties agree on a variation of the rent. If this occurs a new contract is, under s 36(2), deemed to have come into existence. Since it will have come into being after 15 January 1989, it will not be a restricted contract. This only applies to a variation of the rent and it will not occur where some other term has been changed by consent (s 36(3)).

Taken together, these changes are likely to eliminate restricted contracts within a short period of time. These changes should also be kept in mind when considering changes to the laws requiring landlords to obtain a court order before evicting a tenant. As will be seen (in Chapter 6) many resident landlords will no longer have to obtain a court order before evicting a tenant in the case of certain lets created after 15 January 1989.

(c) Tenants of public bodies

Tenants of local authorities and other public bodies will continue to be secure tenants so long as the local authority remains their landlord. However, the Housing Act 1988 will alter the position of many secure tenants. Under Part IV of the Act, housing associations and private landlords may compulsorily acquire council homes (see Chapters 10 and 11). Tenants living in these properties will become tenants of the private landlord unless they elect to stay with the local authority. If they transfer to a private landlord or a housing association they will cease to be secure tenants although they will retain their statutory right to buy (s 38). They will become assured or assured shorthold tenants under the Housing Act 1988.

Where a housing action trust is set up under Part III of the 1988 Act local authority tenants in the area affected will be transferred to the trust. While their homes are managed by a trust, they remain secure tenants. However, housing action trusts are expected to manage and renovate the properties with a view to selling them to other forms of landlordship (see Chapters 8 and 9). If a trust transfers council tenants to a private landlord, they lose their secure status and will become assured tenants of the new landlord.

(d) Housing association tenants

After 15 January 1989, most *new* housing association tenancies will be either assured or assured shorthold tenancies. The expectation is that housing associations will generally use assured lets. A standard tenancy form has been produced by the National Federation of Housing Associations following consultations with the Housing Corporation. This and other matters affecting housing associations are examined in Chapter 7.

Before the 1988 Act, many housing association tenants enjoyed statutory protection as to rent and security of tenure. In practice most tenants (and certain holders of contractual licences) eligible for statutory protection are secure tenants (Alder and Handy: *Housing Association Law*, 1987, Chapter 4). In a much smaller number of cases, tenants are protected under the Rent Act 1977 since ss 15 and 16 of that Act prevent registered associations from granting protected tenancies. However, tenants of non-mutual associations may be protected under the 1977 Act. A housing association tenant who is protected under the 1977 Act is obviously subject to its fair rent provisions. The same system applies in a modified form to most other housing association tenants under what are known as "housing association tenancies" or "Part VI tenancies" under the 1977 Act.

The transitional provisions of the Housing Act 1988 will affect housing association tenants in two ways. First, no new Rent Act protected tenancies can be created with the exceptions outlined earlier in section (a) of this chapter (see page 21). Second, no further "secure" or "housing association tenancies" can be created (s 35 of the 1988 Act). This is also subject to similar exceptions deriving from the transitional provisions of the 1988 Act. There is an additional provision dealing with the case of a housing co-operative which has taken a lease from a local authority. Some co-operatives can continue to let under secure lets (s 35(3)(b) and see Alder & Handy op cit pages 33 to 34 on this subject). These are co-operatives governed by s 27B of the Housing Act 1985, a co-operative leasing from a local authority which has management powers delegated to it.

Thus as of the date of commencement, many housing association tenants are either secure or protected tenants. The former enjoy security of tenure and other statutory rights under Part IV of the Housing Act 1985 (for a general account of the position of secure tenants see Hughes: *Public Sector Housing Law*, 2nd ed 1987, Chapters 2, 3 and 4). In the case of protected tenants the position is regulated by the Rent Act 1977 (see Martin op cit). Whether the tenant is protected or secure, the fair rent machinery of the 1977 Act applies (see Alder & Handy op cit Chapter 5).

How were existing tenants affected on 15 January 1989? The basic position is that existing tenants did not lose their protection under the 1977 or 1985 Acts. However, there is one change to the administration of fair rents. Under s 89 of the Rent Act 1977, payment of a registered rent where there has been an increase is phased over a period of time (Farrand & Arden: *Rent Acts and Regulations*, 2nd ed 1981 page 123). These phasing procedures will cease to have effect after the date of commencement except in relation to phasing that occurred before this date (para 6, Sch 17 of the 1988 Act).

As a result of these changes, housing associations will have the following categories of tenant for a considerable period of time:

(i) secure tenants whose rents will continue to be determined by the fair rent procedures in the Rent Act 1977;

(ii) in limited cases, tenants protected under the Rent Act 1977;

(iii) assured tenants under the Housing Act 1988.

(e) Assured tenancies created under the Housing Act 1980

An analysis of the development of assured lets appears at the beginning of the next chapter. Under the transitional provisions of the 1988 Act, no further assured lets can be created under ss 56 and 58 of the Housing Act 1980 (s 37(1)). There are no exceptions to this. Thus a let following an agreement entered into before the date of commencement cannot be a 1980 Act assured let (s 37(4)). It will be an assured let that will be governed by the Housing Act 1988, the details of which are examined in Chapters 3 and 4. Moreover under s 1(3) existing assured lets created under the 1980 Act provisions are converted into assured lets regulated by the 1988 Act.

Under the 1980 Act provisions, which are shortly to become redundant, a tenant had to apply to a county court for a new tenancy once the original let came to an end (unless another tenancy was granted). It is possible that applications will have been pending in county courts as the 1988 Act came into force. In this event the tenant will continue to hold as an assured tenant under the Housing Act 1980 and when the court considers the application, the hearing will be governed by the principles set out in ss 56 to 58 of the Housing Act 1980. However if a new tenancy is granted, this will be an assured tenancy within the meaning of the Housing Act 1988 (s 37(2), (3)).

In summary, existing assured lets created under the 1980 Act are converted into assured tenancies regulated by the 1988 Act. Assured lets created following a pre-15 January 1989 agreement will also be governed by the 1988 Act. If a county court orders the grant of a new let following the resolution of proceedings started before 15 January it will also be regulated by the 1988 Act. Under the new provisions certain classes of tenancy are excluded from the assured let provisions (Sch 1 of the 1988 Act). With the exception of lettings by the Crown and public authorities, none of these exceptions can apply to the two transitional cases just referred to.

(f) Tenancies regulated by the Rent (Agriculture) Act 1976

The way in which some agricultural workers have security of tenure and rent regulation is dealt with in Chapter 5. After the date of commencement there will be a new arrangement for this category of tenant which is broadly similar to the new assured let. However these new arrangements apply only to tenancies created after the date of commencement. Moreover the principle that no new tenancies regulated under the Rent (Agriculture) Act 1976 may be created is subject to the same exceptions as those that apply to protected and statutory tenants, which were reviewed above (see page 20).

(g) Summary

The law relating to rented accommodation will thus be very complicated during the immediate future. Apart from the continuing problems with non-exclusive licences (discussed in the next chapter), tenants may come into the following categories:

- (i) tenants protected under the Rent Act 1977;
- (ii) holders of restricted contracts under the Rent Act 1977;
- (iii) tenants and licensees excluded from the provisions of the Rent Act 1977;

(iv) tenants and contractual licensees of public authorities who are secure tenants under the Housing Act 1985;

(v) assured tenants under the Housing Act 1988 (including tenants under the converted assured tenancies created under the Housing Act 1980);

(vi) assured shorthold tenants under the Housing Act 1988;

(vii) post 15 January 1989 tenants and licensees who are excluded from the new assured or assured shorthold regimes;

(viii) housing association tenants who may be—

- protected under the Rent Act 1977
- restricted contract holders under the Rent Act 1977
- secure tenants (and licensees) under the Housing Act 1985
- tenants and licensees who fall outside the 1977 and 1985 Acts
- assured and assured shorthold tenants under the Housing Act 1988
- post 15 January 1989 tenants and licensees excluded from the 1988 Act assured provisions;

(ix) tenants and licensees governed by the Rent (Agriculture) Act 1976;

(x) tenants and licensees who are agricultural workers and who qualify for protection under Part I of the Housing Act 1988;

(xi) agricultural workers who are not protected under any statutory provisions.

In addition to this complicated picture there are the long residential leases that are regulated by the Landlord and Tenant Act 1954 and the Leasehold Reform Acts 1967 and 1979. These leases, which are not affected by the Housing Act 1988, are not considered in this book (for an account, see Evans: *The Law of Landlord and Tenant*, 2nd ed by Smith 1985 chapter 18).

3. Jurisdiction

Under Part I of the Housing Act 1988, county courts will have the primary responsibility for dealing with any problems of interpretation. Rent officers and rent assessment committees will have additional powers to deal with rents and other terms of assured and assured shorthold lets. These factors are considered in turn.

(a) Changes to the jurisdiction of the county court

Apart from the new types of possession claim that county courts will be dealing with, they are given additional jurisdiction to settle disputes under different parts of the Act. For example, Part I of the Act, which deals with the private rented sector changes, will create problems of interpretation. County courts will have jurisdiction to deal with interpretational difficulties over the assured, assured shorthold and assured agricultural tenancies. The courts also have jurisdiction over the phasing out and the transitional provisions described earlier in this chapter. New provisions dealing with harassment and illegal eviction are examined in Chapter 6. They include a new civil action for damages. County courts will have jurisdiction to deal with these claims. This additional jurisdiction is conferred on county courts by s 40 of the Act. When hearing a claim brought under any of these matters, county courts can deal with the matter even if the damages award will exceed the prevailing limit for the purposes of the County Courts Act 1984 (s 40(2)). At present this means that a county court will be able to award damages in excess of £5,000. Further, it has power to deal with other proceedings that are joined to the main claim even though this would normally fall outside its jurisdiction (s 40(3)).

This additional jurisdiction is reinforced by s 40(4). Here it is provided that a person who takes proceedings in the High Court where the county court has jurisdiction will be penalised on costs. In other words he will only be allowed costs on the appropriate county court scale. This will not apply, however, if a person took High Court proceedings in order to be joined with proceedings that are already pending there (s 40(5)).

Part IV of the Act, which is examined in Chapters 10 and 11, deals with the Government's "change of landlord plans". Unless a majority of council tenants object, their local authority may be forced to hand over properties to a private landlord approved by the Housing Corporation. Disputes may arise between the new landlord and the local authority as well as the tenants affected. Section 113 gives the county court jurisdiction to deal with a number of matters under this part of the Act. (Disputes over which properties can be transferred or the price payable will not be dealt with by the county court—s 113(1)). It may grant a declaration even though no other relief is sought. The usual rule in the county court is that it may not grant a declaration unless other relief such as damages is sought.

(b) Rent officers

Changes to the role of rent officers: Since 1965, tenancies protected under the Rent Acts have been governed by a system of fair rents. Either a tenant or the landlord can ask a rent officer to fix a fair rent, which might be lower or higher than the rent that was contractually agreed (s 67 Rent Act 1977). Rent officers also fix fair rents for many housing association tenancies. A local authority may also refer the rent to a rent officer (s 68 Rent Act 1977). In practice they often do so when the tenant applies for a rent allowance (see Martin: *Security of Tenure Under the Rent Act*, 1986 Chapter 10). Under the transitional provisions discussed earlier in this chapter, a number of protected and housing association tenancies will continue to exist for a considerable period of time. Rent officers will therefore continue their role of reviewing rents under the 1977 Act.

However, local authorities lose their power to refer a rent to the rent officer except in relation to pending applications made before the 1988 Act. This is dealt with in para 22 of Sch 17 of the 1988 Act. They also lose their power to refer restricted contracts to a rent assessment committee (para 23 of Sch 14).

In addition to their role in fixing fair rents for protected and housing association tenants, rent officers are to be given a completely new function. This derives from the Government's plans to introduce "market rents" into the private rented sector and its concern that excessive rents may be charged where the tenant receives housing benefit. In its consultation paper on this subject, the Government stated that it was committed to retaining housing benefit so that those eligible would not suffer from increased rents in the new de-regulated rented sector (*Deregulation of the Private Rented Sector*, 1987). However, the Government also expressed fears that excessive rents might be charged where the tenant is eligible for housing benefit saying ". . . it will be particularly important to ensure . . . that the rent that attracts such support is not unreasonable" (ibid, paragraph 3).

In future whenever an application for housing benefit is received, the local authority will refer it to a rent officer who will have to consider whether the rent is excessive. In many cases the rent officer will have to carry out a valuation unless the rent appears reasonable by comparison with current market rents. The Department of the Environment will issue guidelines to assist in the valuation.

The rent officers' function here "will be substantially different from the rent fixing role performed in respect of regulated tenancies" (ibid, paragraph 7). Under this new role the officer will be assessing whether the rent charged is a genuine "market rent". If he concludes that the rent is genuine, benefit will be paid in full. If it is considered excessive, the rent officer notifies the local authority of his valuation which will be the maximum rent on which subsidy will be paid. However, this valuation is in no sense the maximum rent that can be charged. The local authority could subsidise the tenant to the rent that is being charged. If it does so, it will not be reimbursed by Central Government for the additional payments it has made. This may place some local authorities in an invidious position. If it pays only the amount assessed by the rent officer, the tenant will have to try to make up the difference, failing which he would fall into arrears and face eviction. If the full rent is subsidised the local authority will be penalised financially, which will affect its responsibilities to its own tenants. The Government expressed the rather optimistic view that ". . . it will be open to the landlord to reduce the rent to the maximum eligible level. . ." (ibid, paragraph 13). It is possible that some landlords will do this in the knowledge that a reduction will ensure a regular rental income. If this happens on a large scale it will produce a paradoxical result; a de-regulated market where in practice many of the rents are being set by rent officers.

This new role has another dimension. For housing benefit purposes the Government wants to be satisfied that the accommodation is neither too large for the tenant nor "unnecessarily expensive" for the tenant. Hence the rent officer may also be asked to consider whether the claimant is over-accommodated or living in "accommodation which the majority of people could not reasonably expect to afford" (ibid, paragraphs 17 to 26). A finding that the accommodation is either too large or too expensive (or both) will result in a reduction of the benefit payable.

To summarise, rent officers will continue to fix fair rents for Rent Act protected and housing association tenancies. In addition they have a new, and in many ways a contradictory, responsibility to assess whether rents in the de-regulated sector are excessive for housing benefit purposes. However there is little detail of this in the Act. Section 121 empowers the Secretary of State to direct rent officers to carry out specified functions. This power is exercisable by statutory instrument (s 121(2)). This section also makes the necessary changes to the Rent Acts and the Social Security Act 1986. The form these new functions will take will only become evident when the regulations are published. These regulations will not be published until several weeks after the private sector provisions came into force on 15 January 1988.

Changes to the appointment of rent officers: Under s 63 of the Rent Act 1977, rent officers are appointed by local authorities after approval of the general scheme for appointment for the area by the Secretary of State. By s 64 of the 1977 Act the Secretary of State may revoke a local authority scheme. There are some minor changes to s 63 made by Sch 14 of the 1988 Act. Rather more substantial changes appear in the second part of Sch 14. As a result of these changes the Secretary of State may direct the amalgamation of two or more registration areas. This may be done if there is insufficient work to justify the continuing existence of the separate areas or if it would "be beneficial for the efficient administration of the service" (part 2 of Sch 14). The local authority must be consulted and an amalgamation is made by statutory instrument. Schedule 14 inserts a new s 64A into the Rent Act 1977 to give effect to these changes.

The Secretary of State's power to revoke a scheme under s 64 of the Rent Act 1977 is extended. Schedule 14 inserts a new s 64B into the Rent Act 1977. Under s 64B, the Secretary of State is empowered to take away a local authority responsibility for rent officers. This power may be exercised generally and if it is, Central Government would assume responsibility for the administration of rent officers. As an alternative, the power may be exercised over a particular area. Again the power is exercisable by statutory instrument (s 64B(3)(b)).

(c) Rent assessment committees

Either a landlord or a tenant may appeal to a rent assessment committee against a rent officer's determination of a fair rent (Sch 11 Rent Act 1977). Rent assessment committees will continue to hear these appeals in cases involving protected and housing association tenants. When doing so, their deliberations are subject to the rules of natural justice and an appeal lies to the

High Court on a point of law. Their decisions are also subject to judicial review (see Farrand & Arden: *Rent Acts and Regulations*, 2nd ed 1981, pages 190 to 191).

They are given additional jurisdiction by the 1988 Act. Chapters 3, 4 and 5 examine the new assured and assured shorthold tenancies. As will be seen, a tenant or a landlord may, in limited circumstances, ask a rent assessment committee to consider a rent (or the terms of a statutory periodic tenancy). However this role is quite different from that of considering fair rents. Under the 1988 Act, the committee will have power to deal with:

(i) market rents for assured tenancies where a contractual periodic let has no rent review clause;

(ii) rents and other terms of a statutory periodic let; and

(iii) rent levels for assured shorthold lets.

Under s 41 of the Housing Act 1988, it can require a party to provide it with information. It must maintain a public register of rents that it has considered (s 42 of the 1988 Act). Detailed regulations relating to this register will be made by statutory instrument (s 42(4)).

Under the Rent Assessment Committees (England and Wales) (Amendment) Regulations 1988 (S1 1988 No. 2200; see page 411), the general procedures governing rent assessment are changed to take account of these new responsibilities. When dealing with a reference under Part I of the 1988 Act, the committee must give each of the parties at least seven days to make oral or written representations. If a party wishes to make oral representations he is entitled to be heard in person or by a representative, who need not be a lawyer.

4. Miscellaneous matters

An Act of Parliament will often contain matters that are not directly relevant to its legislative aims. The Housing Act 1988 is no exception. Part V, which deals with miscellaneous and general matters, contains the rent officer provisions described above. In addition, there are provisions dealing with repairing obligations, repairs notices procedures under the Housing Act 1985 and related matters.

There are also provisions that amend the right to buy.

(a) Repairs

Under s 116 of the 1988 Act, there are changes to the repairing obligations that are implied into many residential tenancies. These are the obligations implied by s 11 of the Landlord and Tenant Act 1985. The 1985 provisions apply to a residential tenancy which is of a term less than seven years. The obligation to repair therefore applies to most residential lettings which are weekly or monthly lets and to fixed terms of less than seven years. It applies to most private tenancies and to lettings by local authorities. This implied liability may not be excluded without leave of the county court. Except for fixed terms in excess of seven years, it will apply to most assured and assured shorthold lets.

Under this repairing obligation, a landlord must keep in reasonable repair the structure and the exterior of the premises and the installations for gas, water and electricity. However, the landlord must have notice of any disrepair before he is under any liability, and this is so even if the defect is latent (*O'Brien* v *Robinson* (1973)).

This repairing obligation does not extend to any common parts. Thus, in the case of a flat, the obligations extend to the structure and exterior of the flat and to its installations.

The changes introduced by s 116 of the 1988 Act extend this statutory repairing obligation to other parts of a building in which the landlord has "an estate or interest" (s 116(1)). However, this expanded liability only applies to tenancies created *after* the commencement of the 1988 Act (s 116(4)). Section 116 of the 1988 Act came into force on 15 January 1989 (s 141(3)). It does not therefore apply to tenancies created before this date or to tenancies entered into following a contract made before this date.

A new subs (1) is added to s 11 of the Landlord and Tenant Act 1985. As a result, where s 11 applies to tenancies entered into after 15 January 1989, it will extend to other parts (and to installations in that part such as a central heating boiler) of a building as well as the flat (s 11(1A) Landlord and Tenant Act 1985).

This statutory obligation implies a term into the tenancy agreement and it therefore creates a contractual liability. It will also expand liability in tort. Under s 4 of the Defective Premises Act 1972, a landlord is liable to anyone injured as a result of his failure to carry out repairs he is obliged to do. The significance of this is that under the 1972 Act, the landlord is liable if he had notice *or* where "he ought in all the circumstances to have known of the relevant defect" (s 4(2) Defective Premises Act 1972). In *Clarke* v *Taff Ely Borough Council* (1983), it was held that the local authority ought to have foreseen that the floorboards in a pre-war council house would rot. The tenant was awarded compensation for injuries suffered when a rotting floorboard gave way.

These changes to the landlord's liability in contract and in tort are not a major extension of liability, since at common law a landlord has obligations to take reasonable care of common parts (see *Liverpool City Council* v *Irwin* (1977)).

Where this expanded liability applies, the landlord has a defence if he does not have access to the part of the building affected and where "he used all reasonable endeavours to obtain" access (s 11(3A) Landlord and Tenant Act 1985).

(b) Repair notices under the Housing Act 1985

Under Part VI of the Housing Act 1985, local authorities have responsibilities to inspect properties in their area and to take action if a property is "unfit for human habitation". Action may also be taken where a property, though fit, requires substantial work or where its condition is interfering with the comfort of a tenant. Provided the property can be repaired at "reasonable expense", the local authority serves a repairs notice on the landlord who can appeal the notice to the county court. Unless the court quashes the notice, the landlord must carry out the works specified in the repairs notice. If he fails to do so, the local authority may carry out the works in default and recover the cost from the landlord (see Hughes: *Public Sector Housing Law*, 2nd ed 1987, pages 209 to 223). These important procedures are changed and strengthened by s 130 of the Housing Act 1988. First of all, the definition of "fitness for human habitation" in s 604 of the 1985 Act is amended in relation to flats. As a result of this change, not only must the condition of an individual flat be considered, but also any other part of the building of which it forms part. Second, s 130 and Sch 15 of the 1988 Act make other changes to the repairs notices provisions of the Housing Act 1985. The repairs notice procedure is extended where a building (or part of a building) in which a flat is contained is unfit or in need of substantial repairs. A local authority can serve a repairs notice in relation to this part of the building if it is rendering a flat unfit. Enforcement of repairs notices is also changed. A repairs notice may be registered as a local land charge. Further, where the owner (or person having control of the premises) intentionally fails to comply with a repairs notice, he commits a summary offence (new s 198A inserted into the Housing Act 1985).

(c) Premiums

Section 115 of the 1988 Act changes the law governing the payment of premiums on the grant or renewal of a long lease. Under the Rent Act 1977, a premium may not generally be charged on the grant (or the assignment) of a protected tenancy. To allow landlords to charge a premium would undermine the fair rent machinery of the Act. However, prohibiting a tenant from charging a premium on the assignment of his tenancy could cause hardship. This can arise where a tenant pays the landlord a premium on the grant of a long tenancy which is not a protected tenancy. However, the tenancy might subsequently become protected. For example the rent might have originally been less than two thirds of the rateable value of the property thereby taking it out of protection (s 4 Rent Act 1977). Later the rent might rise above this limit because of an increase in the service charge element, bringing the let within the Act. In these sorts of circumstance, the tenant is permitted to charge a premium on an assignment of the tenancy to enable him to recover his original payment (see Petitt: *Private Sector Tenancies*, 2nd ed 1981 Chapter 14).

Section 127 of the Rent Act is amended by the substitution of new subs (2) and (3). The effect of these changes is that the permissible charging of premiums applies to a lease where the landlord has no power (other than through forfeiture or re-entry for breach of the agreement) to bring the lease to an end during twenty years of its grant. A premium may be charged provided there is no term inhibiting the assignment or sublet of the whole of the premises. Even if there is such a term, a premium may be charged during the last seven years of the lease.

This applies to premiums payable after 15 January 1989 (s 115(1) and s 141(3) of the 1988 Act).

(d) Changes to sales of council homes

Part V of the Housing Act 1988 makes several changes to the right to buy. These are only briefly covered in this chapter. The principal right to buy provisions are contained in Part V of the

Housing Act 1985. Section 124 of the 1988 Act inserts new ss 153A and 153B into the 1985 Act. These give a secure tenant additional sanctions if he considers that his local authority is delaying consideration of his application to purchase. Section 129 of the Housing Act 1988 empowers local authorities to make grants to assist tenants to purchase or to renovate property. There are also amendments to the restrictions on the right to buy, concerning, for example, council properties in National Parks (ss 122, 123, 125, 126 and 127).

There are also important changes to disposals of local authority housing stock, which are considered in Chapter 10.

(e) Codes of practice for rented housing

The Race Relations Act 1976 is amended so as to extend many of its provisions to rented housing (s 137). The Commission for Racial Equality is empowered to publish codes of practice relating to the field of rented housing.

(f) Changes to the Landlord and Tenant Act 1987

The application of rights under the Landlord and Tenant Act 1987 to assured tenancies is considered on pages 70–71 in the next chapter. This Act is amended by s 119 and Sch 13 of the Housing Act 1988. Under Part I of the 1987 Act, certain qualifying tenants must be given notice if the landlord intends selling the freehold. This is to enable a qualifying tenant or tenants to purchase the freehold. An assured tenant is *not* a qualifying tenant for this purpose (para 1, Sch 13).

The definition of a "qualifying tenant" is changed so as to prevent tenants being excluded from this definition because they have the right to use common parts in the building (para 1(2) of Sch 13). Qualifying tenants will also have to be notified if there is to be a sale by a mortgagee (para 3, Sch 3).

As noted in Chapter 1, there is likely to be legislation to tighten up the 1987 Act. For example, a landlord may currently avoid some of the statutory protection by selling shares in a company that owns the freehold, rather than the freehold itself.

Chapter 3

Assured tenancies: background, definition and terms

1. Background

The notion of an "assured tenancy" first appeared in the Housing Act 1980. It was introduced as an experiment to see whether investors might be persuaded to build new homes to rent (see Farrand & Arden: *Rent Acts and Regulations*, 2nd ed 1981, page 322). Under s 56 of the 1980 Act, assured lettings fall outside Rent Act protection. To qualify for this exemption, the letting has to be made by an approved landlord of newly built premises which have not previously been let except under an assured tenancy. Landlords have to be approved by the Secretary of State of the Environment (see SI 1980 No. 1466). Section 12 of the Housing and Planning Act 1986 extended assured lettings to properties that have been converted to rent on assured tenancies.

Regulation of rent and security of tenure for these assured lets are achieved by the same procedures as apply to the renewal of business tenancies under Part II of the Landlord and Tenant Act 1954 (s 58 and Sch 5 of the 1980 Act). Under these provisions a landlord can bring a tenancy to an end by notice to quit, but the tenant can apply to a county court for the tenancy to be renewed. The court can fix a new rent which is to be a market rent. The landlord can oppose the application on stated grounds (see Martin: *Security of Tenure Under the Rent Act 1986*, Chapter 4).

Only three thousand assured tenancies were created in the eight years following their introduction. Most of them were set up by housing associations, building societies and other financial institutions (see *The Private Rented Sector: The Government's Legislative Proposals*, 1987, paragraph 20). As explained in Chapter 2, the 1980 Act scheme is brought to an end by the 1988

Act. All assured tenancies created under the 1980 Act provisions are converted into the new style assured lettings governed by the Housing Act 1988.

The Government claims that the new provisions are an extension of the 1980 scheme (*ibid*, paragraph 6). However, they differ in three fundamental ways:

- First, private individuals as well as companies and partnerships can create assured lettings;
- second, the requirement of prior approval is removed;
- third, there is no requirement that the premises let are either built or converted for renting.

The new provisions are likely to be far more successful than the 1980 scheme. The relaxation of the statutory requirements alone will make assured tenancies more attractive to landlords. Moreover, the Government expects most new housing association lets to be on assured lettings, and landlords seeking approval to purchase council lettings will be expected to offer assured lettings to the tenants affected. In addition, the Government is offering significant tax relief to individuals investing in companies offering assured lettings. Section 50 of the Finance Act 1988 extends the business expansion scheme to qualifying companies letting on assured lettings. An individual who invests in one of these companies receives income tax relief at his highest rate of tax. This may be claimed on an investment of up to £40,000 per annum invested in any one tax year. After five years the investor may sell the shares and any capital appreciation is exempt from capital gains liability.

2. Definition of an assured tenancy

Part 1 and Schs 1 and 2 of the 1988 Act deal with the definition and the regulation of assured tenancies. Many of the phrases are borrowed from the security provisions governing protected and secure lettings under the Rent Act 1977 and the Housing Act 1985. As a result, many of the problems of interpretation that have arisen in the past will affect assured lettings. In assessing whether a let is within the assured category, three questions have to be asked:

(a) has a tenancy been granted to an individual or individuals?

(b) if so, is it within the definition in s 1 of the 1988 Act?
(c) if it is, does it fall into any of the exceptional categories set out in the first schedule?

Assuming that an assured tenancy has been created, the tenant has security of tenure similar to that enjoyed by secure and protected tenants. His landlord can only bring the tenancy to an end by seeking a court order and after serving a notice in a prescribed form. Section 1 of the 1988 Act defines an assured let as "a tenancy under which a dwelling-house is let as a separate dwelling" and one that meets the following three conditions:

(a) the tenant must be an individual or, in the case of a joint tenancy, each of the joint tenants must be an individual (this is different from the position under the Rent Act 1977 where a company can hold a protected (but not a statutory) tenancy and can thereby apply for a fair rent to be fixed). However, a company cannot enjoy security of tenure under the Rent Act 1977 because of the residence condition for a statutory tenancy. Hence, company lets have been used by some landlords to avoid the Rent Acts. Under these arrangements, a landlord lets to a company, which in turn sublets or creates a licence to the actual occupier (see Martin, op cit, pages 55 to 57). In *Hilton* v *Plustitle Ltd and another* (1988), the Court of Appeal upheld the use of company lets and stated that they are effective and will not necessarily be treated as a sham. However, shortly after this decision, the House of Lords redefined the notion of a sham in the context of the lease/licence distinction. Under this reformulation, which is considered on pages 46–48 of this chapter, the courts are required to take a more realistic attitude towards shams. The validity of company lets is thus somewhat uncertain. Landlords wishing to charge higher rents and to avoid statutory security of tenure will probably let under assured shortholds;
(b) the tenant must reside in the dwelling as his only or principal home; this is the same as one of the requirements for a secure tenancy under s 81 of the Housing Act 1985. A recent example of how this residence test has been interpreted under the 1985 Act is *Crawley Borough Council* v *Sawyer* (1988). Here a secure tenant left the premises to live with his girlfriend. He continued to pay the

rent and the rates and visited the premises once a month. However, the gas and electricity supplies were disconnected. Following the break-up of his relationship with the girlfriend, the tenant returned to the premises, but the local authority, assuming he had given up the residence, served a notice to quit and brought possession proceedings. They appealed against the county court's refusal to order possession. The Court of Appeal dismissed the appeal. The court held that there is no material difference between occupying premises as a home and occupying them as a residence (the test under the Rent Act 1977). Further, two houses may be occupied at the same time as a home and physical occupation is not therefore necessary. The court held that there was sufficient evidence to support the finding that the tenant occupied his girlfriend's house on a temporary basis and that his principal home remained the premises let to him by the local authority. This decision indicates that the residence test for secure tenants is no more stringent than that for protected tenants;

(c) the tenancy must not be one that is specifically excluded from the assured category (s 1(1)(c)). There are two types of exception. The first and the major category are those tenancies set out in the first schedule of the 1988 Act. These are considered in detail at pages 50–57. The second are occupancies granted under a local authority's duties towards the homeless under Part III of the Housing Act 1985. When considering an application for accommodation a local authority must, while it carries out its statutory enquiries, arrange temporary accommodation for applicants with a priority need. A let by a local authority cannot be an assured tenancy (para 12, Sch 1 Housing Act 1988). Nor will it be a secure tenancy (para 4, Sch 1 Housing Act 1985). However, a local authority may enter into an arrangement with another landlord such as a housing association, whereby that landlord provides the temporary accommodation. Where this occurs, this let cannot be an assured tenancy before the end of a period of twelve months after the applicant is notified of the outcome of the local authority's statutory enquiries (s 1(6), (7)).

Returning to the basic elements of the definition in s 1(1), it is evident that only a *tenancy* and not a *licence* can be an assured let. During the Parliamentary debates, the Government was urged to extend the definition to include contractual licences, as it had done when it introduced security of tenure for council tenants in the Housing Act 1980. The Government declined to do this, claiming that the distinction between a tenancy and a licence had been simplified by the decision of the House of Lords in *Street* v *Mountford* (1985) (see Hansard, Standing Committee G, Second Sitting, 15 December 1987, columns 42 and 43).

However, the Government under-estimated the uncertainties that have been caused by a number of post-*Street* v *Mountford* decisions. This question of an assured tenancy having to be a "let" is considered next. This is followed by considering the other basic difficulties that may arise under Part I of the 1988 Act, before moving on to examine tenancies that are specifically excluded from the assured status.

(a) The distinction between a tenancy and a licence

In *Street* v *Mountford* it was held that an agreement that gives an occupier exclusive possession for a term (that is a fixed term or a periodic letting) where rent is paid, creates a tenancy unless the landlord provides the occupier with services or attendance. Lord Templeman emphasised the importance of "exclusive possession". Where a landlord needs continuing access to the premises to provide the services or attendance, the occupant will be a lodger rather than a tenant. In *Street*, the occupier signed a "licence agreement", but the landlord (a solicitor) conceded that the tenant had exclusive occupation. Since she had exclusive occupation, for a term, and paid rent, the agreement created a tenancy even though it was described as a licence.

Lord Templeman added that where these three "hallmarks" (exclusive occupation, a term and payment of rent) exist, a tenancy is created. The only exceptions to this are (a) where on the facts there was no intention to create legal relations or (b) if there was an intention to create legal relations, there was no intention to create a tenancy. Examples of the first exception are family arrangements or where occupation was allowed as an act of friendship or generosity. Examples of the second exception are a service occupancy (such as accommodation occupied by a caretaker as part of his duties) or where a purchaser of property is allowed into occupation following exchange of contracts and before completion of the sale.

In addition to formulating this test, the House of Lords

disapproved a number of Court of Appeal decisions on the so-called "non-exclusive" licence agreements. These agreements had become popular with many landlords as a way of denying their tenants protection under the Rent Act 1977. Under these arrangements landlords would let to two or more occupants who would have to sign separate licence agreements, stating amongst other matters that each would share with the other and with the landlord if he chose to move in. The agreement would also allow the landlord to introduce another occupant should one of the current occupiers leave. If the agreements are binding, none of the occupants can claim to have the exclusive occupation necessary to found a tenancy. Despite the obvious intent to escape Rent Act regulation, the validity of these devices was upheld in several cases before the *Street* decision. These decisions (such as *Somma* v *Hazelhurst* (1978)) were disapproved by the House of Lords. Lord Templeman described non-exclusive licence agreements as "shams" and "artificial transactions".

Following *Street* v *Mountford* many lawyers assumed that non-exclusive licence agreements could no longer be used by landlords to avoid the Rent Acts. However, many landlords continued to do so and the continuing vitality of these evasionary devices is attested by two conflicting and confusing lines of Court of Appeal decisions. In the first line of decisions the Court of Appeal has striven to apply the *Street* v *Mountford* test to licence agreements. However a second line of decisions has exposed a problem with the House of Lords description of non-exclusive arrangements as "shams" or "artificial transactions". These phrases were defined in *Snook* v *London and West Riding Investments* (1967) as a transaction designed to confuse a third party and by which the parties never intended to be bound. On this definition, non-exclusive licence agreements cannot be shams. The other strand to the reasoning in this second line of cases is that in *Street* v *Mountford* it was *conceded* that the occupant had exclusive occupation. The courts are therefore free to consider whether exclusive occupation exists where the premises are occupied by two or more persons under separate agreements. It was inevitable that the House of Lords would have to consider this question again and it did so recently in considering appeals in *AG Securities* v *Vaughan* (1988) and *Antoniades* v *Villiers* (1988). The first case concerned a let of a large flat to a number of individuals, each of whom signed a non-exclusive licence agreement. The flat consisted of four bedrooms, a lounge and a living room in addition to a kitchen and bathroom. The flat was kept full by four occupants, each of whom had a bedroom, and they shared the remainder of the premises. Whenever an occupant left, the landlord's agents, with the concurrence of the remaining occupants, would introduce another person into the flat. That person would also sign a non-exclusive licence agreement. When a new occupant moved in, the practice was that the others would change the bedroom they each used, leaving the remaining and least desired bedroom to the newcomer. Each occupier was individually responsible for payment of rent under the separate agreements. Were the occupants licensees or tenants? A majority of the Court of Appeal decided that they were joint tenants since between them they had exclusive occupation. For a joint tenancy to be created, what are known as the "four unities" must be present. These are the unities of possession, interest, title and time (see Megarry & Wade: *The Law of Real Property* 5th ed 1984 pages 419 to 422). The Court of Appeal concluded that this requirement was satisfied even though the occupants entered into their individual agreements at different times.

The House of Lords held that this case was wrongly decided. None of the occupants had exclusive occupation of any part of the flat. Nor could they be joint tenants since the four unities did not exist. The arrangement was described by the House of Lords as "a sensible and realistic one to provide accommodation for a shifting population of individuals who were genuinely prepared to share the flat with others".

However the position would be different if each occupant had exclusive occupation of a bedroom and shared the remainder of the accommodation. Under that type of arrangement each occupant would have a tenancy and the share of the remaining accommodation would not take them outside the protection of the Rent Acts. However, this analysis could not be applied to this case, since the occupants changed bedrooms as one left to be replaced by another.

In the *Antioniades* v *Villiers* case, a couple signed separate non-exclusive licence agreements under which they agreed (amongst other matters) to share with the landlord. The Court of Appeal upheld the validity of the licence agreements. The court concluded that the agreements expressed the intention of the contracting parties. As a result, neither of the occupants had the necessary exclusive occupation to found a tenancy. They were therefore licensees and not joint tenants.

The House of Lords also decided that this case had been wrongly decided by the Court of Appeal. It held that the two agreements were interdependent since the couple would have signed either both or neither. Taken together, the agreements gave the couple exclusive occupation. Following *Street* v *Mountford*, the couple had exclusive occupation of the flat, for a term and in consideration of a rent. They were in consequence joint tenants and protected under the Rent Acts. The owner could not exercise his right under the agreements to occupy the premises, since this would violate the tenants' rights under the Rent Acts. Moreover, on the facts, there was no serious intention by the owner to use the premises. He had devised the licence agreements simply to avoid the Rent Acts.

The House of Lords also reaffirmed its disapproval of the non-exclusive licence cases referred to in *Street* v *Mountford*. Lord Templeman, noting that his description of these cases as "shams" and "artificial transactions" may have caused misunderstanding, described them instead as "pretences". The House also disapproved of the post *Street* v *Mountford* decisions that had reverted to a test based on the intention of the parties.

As a result of these appeals, the use of non-exclusive licence agreements as a method of avoiding statutory protection is limited. In a situation where a shifting group of individuals agree to share with persons who are initially strangers and there is a shifting use of individual parts of the premises (such as the bedrooms), there may genuinely be a licence arrangement. However, where two or more people apply jointly to rent premises and they are given exclusive occupation together and pay rent, a joint tenancy is created. Any power reserved to the landlord to share the accommodation is inconsistent with the tenants' exclusive occupation. Moreover the introduction of such a power is a pretence which is only intended to defeat the tenants' statutory rights.

(b) "a dwelling-house is let as a separate dwelling" (s 1(1))

There can only be an assured let if "a dwelling-house is let as a separate dwelling" (s 1(1)). As noted in the previous paragraphs, only a tenancy and not a licence can have assured status. Moreover, it must be a let for residential purposes. The only explanation of the expression "dwelling-house" appears in s 43.

This states that a dwelling may be a house or part of a house. There will obviously be assured lettings of flats as well as of houses. However, a house must be let as a separate dwelling. The same requirement appears in the definition of a protected tenancy under s 1 of the Rent Act 1977. In *Horford Investments* v *Lambert* (1976), there was a letting of a house that was previously converted into several living units. This was held not to be a single letting and therefore not a protected tenancy.

(c) Sharing accommodation with others

There will be many assured lettings of flats and in some of these cases a tenant may have to share accommodation with others. Does this have any effect on his position? Part of the answer to this question depends who the tenant shares with. Clearly the tenant must have exclusive use of some premises, otherwise he will not have a tenancy. If he shares with another tenant this does not affect his status as an assured tenant if he meets the basic requirements outlined above (s 3(1) of the 1988 Act). The same holds true if he shares with someone else, unless that person is his landlord. If the tenant shares with the landlord and the landlord also lives in the premises no assured tenancy can usually arise. This is because of the resident landlord exception which is considered later in this chapter. There is another possibility. A landlord might not live on the premises but might reserve the right to share the use of rooms with the tenants in the premises he lets. This may not commonly arise. An agreement under which a landlord reserves the right to use living accommodation simply to avoid the assured lettings principles, will almost certainly be regarded as a "pretence" (*Antoniades* v *Villiers* (1988)).

In any event, only a share of "living accommodation" prevents a tenant having a separate letting. Unfortunately, the expression "living accommodation" is not clearly defined in the 1988 Act. Section 3(5) describes it as accommodation that would prevent the tenancy being an assured letting. This oblique reference is, in effect, leaving it to the courts to decide whether the shared accommodation is a share of "living accommodation".

The courts have had to consider this issue under the Rent Acts. The basic test is whether the shared use is of "living rooms". Thus a kitchen or sitting room has been held to be living accommodation (*Neale* v *Del Soto* (1945)). Generally a bathroom or hall is not living accommodation (*Goodrich* v *Paisner* (1957)). There is also the question of the extent of the shared use. If the landlord's use is intermittent it may be disregarded. In *Marsh Limited* v *Cooper* (1969)) the kitchen was used by the landlord's employees as well as by the tenant. However, the employees used the kitchen for occasional washing up and the drawing of water. It was held that this shared use was negligible and should be ignored.

Section 3 addresses another issue that may arise where a tenant is sharing accommodation. Any term in a tenancy agreement that allows the landlord to terminate or modify the right to share living accommodation is void and will have no effect (s 3(3)). However, it is open to a landlord to reserve the right to vary the number of persons with whom the tenant shares (s 3(4)).

An assured tenant might be given the right to sublet part of the premises. If, under the terms of the sublet, he shares living accommodation with the subtenant, this factor by itself does not affect his assured status (s 4).

(d) Lettings with other land

As under the Rent Acts special provision is made where a dwelling is let with other land. The let of the dwelling may be assured. Do the tenants' statutory rights extend to the other land? This is dealt with in s 2. Provided the main purpose of the letting is to provide a home for the tenant, then this other land is treated as part of the dwelling and will form a part of the assured let (s 2(1)(a)). Where there are joint tenants, the main purpose must be to provide a home for one of them. If the main purpose is not the provision of a home, then the tenancy is treated as one where there is no let of a dwelling as a separate let, in which case it cannot be assured.

These rules do not affect any of the excluded categories in Sch 1 (s 2(2)). Under the first schedule, lettings of agricultural land cannot be assured lettings.

3. Tenancies that cannot be assured lettings

Even if the tenancy meets the requirements of s 1, it may still fall outside the ambit of assured lets for one or more of the reasons set out in part 1 of Sch 1. This schedule is similar to Part I of the Rent Act 1977 which excludes certain lettings from the protection of the Act. The 1988 Act exceptions fall into one of three categories:

(a) those based on the nature of the let (such as a business tenancy);
(b) those deriving from the terms of the let (such as a let at a low rent); and
(c) those based on the nature of one of the parties (such as a let by a local authority or a student letting).

(a) Tenancies created before 15 January 1989

A tenancy which was entered into or made pursuant to a contract made before the date of commencement cannot be assured (para 1, of Sch 1). This exception is self-explanatory although as noted in Chapter 2 (see page 21), there may be cases where there is some doubt as to whether a binding contract was actually concluded before 15 January 1989.

(b) Tenancies of premises with a high rateable value

As with the Rent Acts, premises with high rateable values cannot be let on assured lets. The reason for this appears to be that tenants who rent "up market" properties can negotiate their own terms and do not need statutory protection. The upper rateable value limits are set out in para 2 of Sch 1 of the 1988 Act. In Greater London, a let of a property with a rateable value of more than £1,500 cannot be assured. The upper limit for properties outside Greater London is £750.

Part 2 of the first schedule deals with the method of calculating the rateable value for the purposes of para 2. The basic rule is that the value shown in the valuation list is the one to be taken (para 14(1)). What is the position where there is a let of premises which form part of a larger building, for example a let of a flat? Another issue will arise if there is a let of a dwelling which forms part of more than one building. In these cases there must be an apportionment or aggregation as the case may be (paragraph 14(1)(b)). If the parties cannot agree on the appropriate calculation, the dispute must be referred to a county court, whose decision is final (para 14(2)). In the case of a let of a dwelling with other land, which is treated under s 2 as an assured let, the rules of calculation apply to that other land.

This exception, which, because the values are relatively high, may not be of much practical importance, will have to be changed once the community charge is brought into force under the Local

Government Finance Act 1988. The Government will publish a consultation paper on this subject in 1989.

(c) Tenancies at a low rent

A let where the rent is less than two thirds of the rateable value cannot be assured. The same applies to a let where no rent is payable (para 3(1), Sch 1). Since assured lets will be at market rents this exception is unlikely to be of much practical importance. However, a landlord might let at a low rent and require payment of a large premium in order to take advantage of this exception. Unlike the position under the Rent Act 1977, there is no prohibition of the taking of a premium (see also page 68).

The use of premium as an evasionary device was considered in the context of the Rent Acts in *Samrose Properties* v *Gibbard* (1958). Here there was a let for a year at a rent of £1 payable quarterly with payment of a lump sum of £35. The object of the arrangement was to avoid the Rent Act by creating a let at a low rent. It was held that this was a sham and the arrangement was treated as a let at an annual rent of £39 with the result that the Rent Acts applied.

Even though premiums are allowable under the 1988 Act clearly they should not be used to avoid the machinery of the assured let.

(d) Lettings of business, licensed and agricultural properties

Again these exceptions will be of little practical significance. They all relate to tenancies that are either regulated by other statutory provisions or excluded because of commercial use. Thus a business let that is regulated by Part II of the Landlord and Tenant Act 1954 cannot be assured (para 4, Sch 1). The same applies to a tenancy of an agricultural holding under the Agricultural Holdings Act 1986 (para 7, Sch 1).

Where the premises are used for the sale or consumption of intoxicating liquor (licensed premises), there cannot be an assured let (para 5, Sch 1).

Under s 2 a let with other land can be assured. However, if the let includes agricultural land exceeding two acres, it cannot be an assured tenancy (para 6, Sch 1).

(e) Lettings to students

Under the Rent Act 1977, a let by certain educational institutions to its students cannot be protected. The same exception applies to assured tenancies. Thus, where an educational institution lets residential property to students, the student cannot be an assured tenant (para 8, Sch 1). The intention here (as under the Rent Act 1977) is to prevent students acquiring an assured status on a letting of college accommodation such as a hall of residence. The institutions that can take advantage of this are to be specified by statutory instrument (para 8(2), Sch 1).

This exception applies to lets to students during term time only. A landlord can let during the vacation *direct* to students with a mandatory possession ground provided he complies with the conditions in Ground 4 of Sch 2. This is covered in more detail in Chapter 3, which examines grounds for possession.

Lettings *to* educational institutions will be significant for another reason. A private landlord can let to an institution with a covenant prohibiting subletting except to its students. This lease cannot be an assured let since the institution cannot qualify under s 1 of the 1988 Act. It cannot satisfy the residence qualification. Moreover a letting of a house converted into separate living units would not be a let of a dwelling. In *St Catherines College* v *Dorling* (1980) a house was let to the college for subletting to its students. The college applied for a fair rent to be fixed, contending that it had a protected tenancy. It was held that the house had been let as several dwellings and not as *a* dwelling. As a result, the college did not have a protected tenancy.

Not only will an educational institution be precluded from taking an assured tenancy, but the students to which it sublets cannot qualify because of paragraph 8. Thus private landlords can let to educational institutions who in turn sublet to students. In neither case will an assured let be created.

Schemes of this nature became popular under the Rent Acts. They may also be popular under the 1988 Act. However, institutions (and ultimately their students) face the prospect of paying higher rents. It is unlikely that these arrangements will be as widespread as they used to be unless landlords can obtain increased rents. On the other hand an advantage to a landlord is that the rent payable under the lease is the responsibility of the institution which has the task of collecting the rents under the sublets from its students.

Another point to consider is whether a lease of this type could become regulated by the business tenancies rules in Part II of the Landlord and Tenant Act 1954. This was reviewed in the Rent Act context in *Groveside Properties Ltd* v *Westminster Medical*

School (1983). Here the landlord let a furnished flat to the school to be occupied by its students. The school paid the outgoings, kept the keys and its secretary frequently visited the premises. It was held that the school thereby had the necessary degree of occupation and was running a business for the purpose of the 1954 Act. Thus it could take advantage of the provisions allowing it to apply to the county court for a new tenancy. This result was reached on the unusual features of this lease. It does not apply generally to the grant of leases to educational institutions. As a practical point an institution seeking to take advantage of the 1954 Act would find it difficult to persuade landlords to assist it in providing accommodation for its students.

(f) Holiday lets

Again this is similar to one of the exceptional categories in the Rent Act 1977. Where the purpose of the let is to allow the tenant to occupy the premises for a holiday, it cannot be an assured let (para 9, Sch 1 of the 1988 Act).

Under the Rent Acts, some landlords used this exception to avoid the tenant's protection, rather than for the genuine provision of holiday accommodation. The courts have considered the scope of such evasionary devices. In *Buckmann* v *May* (1978), it was held that the onus of proving that a holiday let is a sham lies with the tenant. A case where tenants succeeded in proving that the arrangement was a sham is *R* v *Rent Officer for the London Borough of Camden ex parte Ibiri* (1981). This case concerned a six month let to student nurses. The landlord knew that they took the let to carry out their work as student nurses and he could not in consequence claim that there was a genuine holiday let.

Where there has been a holiday let, the landlord can let the property out of season with a mandatory ground for possession. This is dealt with in Ground 3 of the second schedule; see Chapter 4, pages 83 to 84.

(g) Lettings by resident landlords

The resident landlord exception was introduced by the Rent Act 1974. It is designed to encourage owner-occupiers to let spare rooms in their homes. In order to guard against abuse, the statutory scope of this exception is complex (see now s 12, Sch 2 Rent Act 1977 as amended by s 65 Housing Act 1980).

Under paragraph 10 of the first schedule to the 1988 Act, there is a similarly drafted exception whereby a tenant of a resident landlord cannot hold under an assured let. This may prove to be the most important exception to the assured status. Because of the transitional provisions explained in the previous chapter, there can be no more restricted contracts. After 15 January 1989, all *new* lets by resident landlords will be deregulated, provided the conditions set out in paragraphs 10 and 17 to 22 of the first schedule are met. This means that a tenant of a resident landlord will have no security of tenure and no way of challenging the rent. Moreover, as will be shown in Chapter 6, in many cases, resident landlords will no longer have to obtain a court order before evicting the tenant at the end of the tenancy. In future tenants of resident landlords will not be in a strong bargaining position when it comes to reviewing the rent or dealing with disrepair. The resident landlord exception can only apply if the conditions set out in paragraph 10 are satisfied. These conditions are of two types:

(i) those relating to the structure of the premises let; and

(ii) those relating to the residence of the landlord.

In considering these conditions it should be remembered that the purpose of this exception is to encourage owner-occupiers to let spare accommodation, not to enable investment landlords to avoid the assured let provisions.

The first set of conditions then, relate to the structure of the premises. There must be a let of a dwelling that forms part of a building which is not a purpose-built block of flats. Thus an owner of a block of flats cannot take advantage of this exception by living in one of the flats and letting the others and claiming that he is a resident landlord. However, there is one exception to this. An owner of a flat in a purpose-built block can let part of the *flat* and rely on the resident landlord exception if he lives in the other part of the flat (para 10(1)(a), Sch 1).

The expressions "purpose-built" and "building" have led to some problems under the Rent Acts. Although many of the cases on these points depend very much on their facts they are useful illustrations of the difficulties that can arise. In *Barnes* v *Gorsuch* (1982), it was held that a house that was converted into flats did not become a purpose-built block. Another case involving a house converted into flats is *Bardrick* v *Haycock* (1976). The difference here was that the owner demolished an adjoining garage and built an extension with its own entrance. He lived in the extension, but this was held not to be part of the other building so that the resident landlord exception did not apply.

Under the second set of conditions, relating to the landlord's residence, the landlord must have occupied another dwelling in the same building at the beginning of the let and during it. To satisfy this condition, the landlord must occupy this dwelling as his "only or principal home" (para 10(1)(b), (c), Sch 1). This is the same test as the residence condition in s 1 which defines assured lets and which was considered earlier in this chapter (see page 43). In the case of a letting by joint owners, residence by one of them satisfies the residence condition (para 10(2), Sch 1).

It is possible for a landlord to claim the benefit of this exception even though he owns more than one property. In this event he will have to establish that he occupies the tenanted property as his principal home. It would be contrary to the policy underlying this exception to allow a landlord to claim the exception for more than one property.

As under the Rent Acts, there are certain periods of non-residence by a landlord that are to be disregarded. These exist to deal with a sale of the property or the winding up of the landlord's estate on his death. Details of these periods of "disregard" are contained in part 3 of the first schedule.

As a practical matter, a landlord selling the property would undertake to give vacant possession on completion of the sale. However, the purchaser can purchase a property occupied by a tenant who is excluded from having an assured let because of his landlord's residence and take advantage of the exception. He has twenty-eight days after completion of the purchase to move in. This period will be extended for up to six months if he gives the tenant written notice of his intention to move in (para 17(1)(a), (b), Sch 1). Whatever the period, the purchaser's non-residence is ignored. However, if he fails to take up residence during one or other of these periods the tenant will become an assured tenant.

On the landlord's death, his personal representatives have two years to sell or otherwise dispose of the property. During this period they may take steps to evict the tenant and the late landlord's non-residence will be disregarded (para 17(1)(c), (2) and para 18 to 20, Sch 1). Until possession is sought the tenant is treated as an assured tenant and possession may only be sought on the grounds mentioned in the second schedule (para 21), Sch 1).

Can a landlord purchase a property subject to an assured tenancy, move in, persuade the *assured tenant* to take another tenancy in the same building and then claim the benefit of this exception? The answer to this obvious ploy is no. Where a landlord (or in the case of joint landlords, one of them) grants a new tenancy to an assured tenant this will continue to be assured if it relates to the same dwelling or to another dwelling in the same building (para 10(3), Sch 1).

(h) Lettings by the Crown, local authorities and others

Where the property is owned by the Crown or by a Government department a residential letting cannot be an assured let (para 11(1), Sch 1). However, this does not apply to lettings by the Crown Estate Commissioners who may therefore let under assured tenancies. As noted in Chapter 2, local authorities (and other public bodies) can continue to let on secure tenancies under the Housing Act 1985. They cannot let on assured tenancies. This exception applies to local authorities, new towns, urban development corporations, housing action trusts and other public authorities listed in paragraph 12 of the first schedule.

(i) Transitional cases

The previous chapter outlined the way in which the position of tenants who benefit from other statutory protection will be affected after the 1988 Act is in force. Protected tenants, housing association tenants, secure tenants and protected occupiers (under the Rent (Agriculture) Act 1976) retain their statutory rights (with some modifications). This is underlined by the last exceptional case defined in paragraph 13 of the first schedule. Under paragraph 13 none of these categories can be assured tenancies.

4. Terms of an assured tenancy

The philosophy underlying assured lettings is that the rent and other terms are to be set by the market forces of supply and demand. Hence the parties are very much left to themselves to negotiate the terms of the agreement. As the Government stated in its consultative document on the private rented sector, "they would be free to agree the duration and terms of the tenancy, including the rent and any mechanism for reviewing it" (paragraph 7).

Nevertheless there will be substantial legal and other regulation of assured lettings in the following four ways:

- First, there is the matter of security of tenure. Although the parties are free to agree the duration of the tenancy, the Act guarantees security of tenure for most assured lets. A landlord cannot end a *periodic* assured let by simply serving a notice to quit. He has to serve a notice of intended possession proceedings before bringing possession proceedings. If a tenant has a *fixed term* assured let, the landlord's right to seek forfeiture is limited by the 1988 Act. At the end of a fixed term a statutory periodic assured let comes into being (unless another assured tenancy is granted).
- Second, there are (limited) ways in which the tenant can challenge the rent. Most assured lets will have a provision permitting the rent to be increased from time to time (a rent review clause). However in the case of a *contractual periodic let* that does not have a rent review clause, the Act makes provision for a rent to be assessed by a rent assessment committee if the parties cannot agree a figure. The committee can also fix the rent and other terms of an asssured statutory periodic tenancy.
- Third, the 1988 Act contains provisions dealing with assignment, subletting and succession rights.
- Fourth, there are rights and procedures implied by other statutes as well as the general body of the common law as it affects the landlord and tenant relationship.

These matters are now considered in turn.

(a) Security of tenure

As noted earlier, most assured tenancies are guaranteed security of tenure. The only exceptions are those where a landlord has certain mandatory grounds for possession, such as the case of an out of season holiday let or a vacation let to a student. It is the *availability* of security of tenure that marks the major difference between an assured and an assured shorthold tenancy. The way in which security of tenure is guaranteed differs according to whether the tenancy is periodic or for a fixed term.

Assured tenancies that are periodic: Many, if not most, assured tenancies will be of periodic nature, for example, weekly or monthly tenancies. Under s 5(1) of the 1988 Act, a landlord cannot end an assured tenancy that is a periodic tenancy by serving a notice to quit. As explained in the next chapter, the landlord has to follow the general procedure set out in Part I of the 1988 Act. In summary he must:

(i) serve a notice of intended possession proceedings which tells the tenant which ground or grounds for possession will be relied on and giving particulars of that or those grounds; and

(ii) bring a claim for possession.

This is quite different from the position of Rent Act protected tenants. Under the Rent Acts, a landlord must serve a valid notice to quit, bringing the contractual periodic tenancy to an end, as a pre-condition to launching possession proceedings. When the contractual periodic interest is terminated in this way, a statutory tenancy comes into being.

The position is therefore simpler with assured tenancies which are periodic. They remain contractual in nature unless terminated by a court order.

Fixed term assured tenancies: Most fixed term lets will have a clause enabling the landlord to seek forfeiture of the remainder of the term if the tenant breaks the agreement. However, a landlord's use of forfeiture is limited by the 1988 Act. During the currency of a fixed term, possession may only be sought if:

(i) the agreement contains a forfeiture (or a similar) clause; and

(ii) then only on a limited number of the grounds for possession that are set out in Sch 2 of the Act (s 7(6)).

Schedule 2 contains the mandatory grounds for possession – a claim brought by a mortgagee; serious rent arrears; and all of the discretionary grounds, save those dealing with alternative accommodation and a claim against a service tenant. In other words, a landlord can only recover possession during the period of a fixed term if the tenant has broken a term of the agreement or in the limited case where a mortgagee is claiming possession. In either case there *must* be a forfeiture clause in the agreement.

By the end of a fixed term the parties *may* have negotiated a new fixed term or a contractual periodic let. If they fail to reach agreement for a new assured let, a "statutory periodic tenancy" will come into existence (s 5(2)). This statutory periodic tenancy has the following five characteristics:

(i) it comes into effect automatically at the end of the fixed term (unless of course a new agreement has been reached);

(ii) it is deemed to have been granted by the person who was the landlord under the expired agreement (and of course to the person who was the tenant under that agreement);

(iii) the premises let will be the same as those let under the expired agreement;

(iv) if the fixed term provides for how often the rent will be reviewed, the same period applies to the statutory periodic tenancy;

(v) the other terms will be the same as those in the expired fixed term (s 5(3)).

As a result, a landlord cannot evict an assured tenant by simply refusing to offer him a new fixed term letting. The statutory periodic tenancy can only be brought to an end by the landlord obtaining a possession order in the manner prescribed by the Act.

Summary: To summarise, a contractual periodic assured let cannot be terminated by a landlord serving a notice to quit. A fixed term cannot be terminated before its expiry, unless there is a forfeiture clause in the agreement and then only on certain grounds set out in Sch 2 of the 1988 Act. At the end of a fixed term, a statutory periodic tenancy comes into being unless a new assured let has been granted to the tenant. To underline these security provisions, any surrender, notice to quit or other device that a tenant was required to sign before or at the time the agreement started is of no effect (s 5(5)). Thus a tenant cannot lose his rights under the 1988 Act by being required to sign a surrender or other such document as a condition of the assured let being granted.

The basic terms of the statutory periodic tenancy were set out above. In addition, provision is made for the resolution of any disputes over precise terms of the statutory periodic let. There is also provision for disputes over the rent for a statutory periodic let and a contractual periodic let which does not contain a rent review clause. The way in which the terms of the statutory periodic let may be fixed is dealt with in the next paragraph. For disputes over rents, see pages 62 to 67.

Fixing the terms of a statutory periodic tenancy: Section 6 sets out the procedure for fixing the terms of a statutory periodic tenancy. In the first instance it will be on the same terms as those contained in the expired fixed term. However, either the landlord or the tenant may serve a notice on the other proposing terms different from those implied into the statutory tenancy. Where appropriate a change to the rent may be suggested to take account of the changes proposed. The notice must be in a prescribed form and it must be served no later than the first anniversary of the date when the previous tenancy came to an end (s 6(2)). As a result, the parties have a period of twelve months to reach agreement on the terms of the new statutory periodic tenancy. There may be, for example, proposals for a change to service charges or a suggestion that the accommodation offered is altered, and that the rent be adjusted to take account of such changes. In other words the landlord cannot simply propose an increase in the rent. An increase would have to be justified in light of any other changes to the tenancy he is proposing. If the landlord wants simply to raise the rent he must use the procedure under s 13 which is described at page 65. Assume for illustrative purposes that the landlord serves a notice on the tenant. It proposes that he provides different services and that the accommodation remains the same as that provided under the statutory periodic tenancy. He also proposes that the rent is increased to take account of the change in the level of services provided. If the tenant agrees with these proposals, they will take effect from whatever date is specified in the landlord's notice (s 6(3)(b)). If the tenant disgrees, he has three months from the date of service to apply to a rent assessment committee for their adjudication (s 6(3)(a)). The application must be made in a prescribed form. These and other forms under Part I of the 1988 Act have been prescribed in The Assured Tenancies and Agricultural Occupancies (Forms) Regulations 1988 (SI 1988 No. 2203). A copy appears in Appendix B to this book.

Here the rent assessment committee will be exercising one of its new responsibilities under the 1988 Act, described in Chapter 2. The committee must consider whether the terms proposed are those that "might reasonably be expected to be found in an assured periodic tenancy of the dwelling-house concerned" (s 6(4)). It must work on the assumption that there is to be a let by a "willing landlord" on the terms of the statutory periodic tenancy as they would be changed by the landlord's proposals (s 6(4)(a), (b)). They must also consider whether there should be an adjustment to the rent in the light of their view of the appropriate terms and they may make an adjustment even though one was not suggested in the landlord's notice (s 6(5)). However, they may not fix a different rent simply because the new let is being granted to a "sitting tenant" (s 6(6)). In dealing with s 6 notices, the committee will be applying an open market test and the parties will no doubt introduce evidence from valuers and others as to what they believe are the current market conditions in the area.

The preceding paragraph has described what might happen if a landlord serves a notice. The same procedure applies if the tenant takes the initiative and serves a s 6 notice on the landlord.

There is then the question of the date that the committee's decision will come into effect. Section 6(7) gives the committee a discretion. The terms of its decision will come into effect "from such date as the committee may direct" unless the parties agree on a date. This gives the committee power to backdate the new terms. However, any adjustment to the rent cannot be backdated beyond the date specified in the s 6 notice.

Where under the Rent Acts, a rent assessment committee is considering what should be a fair rent for a protected tenancy, the parties may not usually withdraw the application before the committee has reached its decision. The reason for this is that it is in the public interest that fair rents are registered, since registration can affect a future determination for neighbouring properties. This is not the case where the committee is dealing with s 6 notices (or notices asking it to consider a rent for an assured let). The committee does not have to proceed if notified by both parties that they no longer require a determination. Whilst this is consistent with the market philosophy of the 1988 Act, it may reduce the numbers of decisions that parties can study when considering whether to make an application.

(b) Rents

The basic position is that it is for the parties to agree the rent and any provision for reviewing it. Rent assessment committees will only be involved in two limited situations. First to consider changes in the rent of a statutory periodic tenancy when the parties cannot agree (this is separate from their role in dealing with s 6 notices). Second, where, in the case of a periodic assured letting, there is no contractually agreed method of periodically reviewing the rent. In the case of a fixed term assured let, it is for the parties to agree a method of reviewing the rent. Here the committee can only become involved at the end of the fixed term when a statutory periodic tenancy comes into being and one of the parties asks the committee to consider a s 6 notice.

Many (in all probability most) assured tenancies, whether they are for a fixed term or are periodic, will contain a clause providing for the rent to be reviewed periodically. Rent review clauses must state a clear formula for assessing the rent and a mechanism, such as arbitration, for deciding what the new rent will be if the parties cannot agree (see Evans: *The Law of Landlord & Tenant*, 2nd ed by P. F. Smith 1985 pages 114 to 120). This will be a relatively new development with private rentals, and advisors will have to consider the overall body of law concerning rent review clauses which has hitherto been largely concerned with business leases (see Clarke & Adams: *Rent Reviews and Variable Rents*, 2nd ed 1983). There has been a large body of litigation on rent review clauses, caused, it has been said, by poor drafting (see Yates & Hawkins: *Landlord and Tenant Law*, 2nd ed 1986, page 179). The general form of such clauses is to allow the landlord to serve a notice proposing a rent and for the tenant to serve a counter-notice suggesting a different rent. In the event of disagreement, the rent is to be fixed by a nominated valuer. It is likely that rent review clauses in assured tenancy agreements will permit annual reviews, linking any increase to, for example, changes in the Retail Prices Index.

With many assured tenancies then, rents will be fixed in accordance with the procedures in a rent review clause with independent valuers fixing a rent increase where the parties fail to agree. However, as will be explained in Chapter 7, housing associations are expected to charge rents below market levels, to take account of their responsibilities for housing the lower paid and other disadvantaged groups. The standard form tenancy agreement for use by most housing associations allows reference of a proposed rent to a rent assessment committee where the tenant does not accept a proposed increase (see Appendix C). However, if housing associations keep their rents below market level, few tenants will invoke this contractual right, since rent assessment committees are required to fix a market rent for the letting.

When a rent assessment committee is involved, the 1988 Act and regulations published under it, prescribe the procedures and the principles to be used in fixing a rent. There are three matters to consider: notices of increase; determination of the rent by the committee; and the procedures involved.

Notice of increase: If the landlord wants to increase the rent he must first serve a notice on the tenant in a prescribed form (s 13(2)). This notice must propose a new rent to take effect from the beginning of the new period specified in the notice. There are statutory restrictions on the date the new rent will become payable. These are set out in s 13(3). Where the periodic let runs from year to year, the new rent cannot come into effect until after a minimum period of six months. In what is likely to be the more usual case of a periodic let of less than one month (such as a weekly tenancy), the new rent cannot come into effect until after a minimum period of one month. In any other case the minimum period is the same as the period of the tenancy.

How often can a landlord increase the rent in this way? He cannot try to increase the rent until after a year from the beginning of a contractual periodic tenancy (s 13(2)(b)). However where a statutory periodic tenancy comes into being at the end of a fixed term, a s 13 notice can be served right away. There may therefore be cases where both a s 13 and a s 6 notice are served simultaneously and application may be made to a rent assessment committee in both cases. Where this occurs the committee can hear both applications together. In many cases the only area of disagreement will be over the rent payable under the statutory periodic tenancy, in which case a s 13 notice will have to be served.

Whether it is a contractual or a statutory periodic tenancy a landlord cannot serve another notice of increase until one year after an earlier increase (s 13(2)(c)). The effect of this is that landlords can seek to increase the rents of periodic assured lets every year but not more frequently than this.

Unless the tenant disagrees with the landlord's proposals, the new rent comes into effect on the date specified in the notice (s 13(4)). If he decides to challenge the increase, he must apply (in a prescribed form) to the rent assessment committee before the new period mentioned in the notice (s 13(4)(a)). For example, a weekly tenant will have only one month to do this.

It is of course open to the parties to agree a different rent from the one in the landlord's notice (s 131(4)(b)). Section 13 provides a means of increasing the rent. It does not affect the right of the parties to agree any term of the tenancy (s 13(5)). They could for example agree to include a rent review clause in the agreement if the original agreement does not contain one.

Determination of rents by a rent assessment committee: this is the second new role given to rent assessment committees. It is quite different from their role of assessing fair rents for protected tenants under the Rent Act 1977 (a role they will of course continue to have for protected tenants). Their decisions determining rents under the 1988 Act do not bind the parties, who are free to agree a different rent. The rent the committee deems to be appropriate for the letting is not a maximum rent in the way that it is when they fix a fair rent.

If an assured tenant asks a committee to consider a s 13 notice, the committee's basic task is to consider whether what is proposed is the sort of rent at which the dwelling "might reasonably be expected to be let in the open market by a willing landlord under an assured tenancy" (s 14(1)). In doing this the committee looks at the terms and the period of the let at the time at which the new rent period is to start (s 14(1)(a),(b), (c)). It will also have to examine another factor where the landlord will have a mandatory ground for possession at the end of the tenancy because he has served a notice under Grounds 1 to 5 of Sch 2. These, which are examined in the next chapter, include a ground whereby an owner-occupier can let under an assured let with the certainty of recovering possession at the end of the term. As a result, rents for these sorts of assured let ought to be lower than those for standard assured lets to take account of the limited degree of security of tenure.

The committee must disregard certain factors. Some will favour the tenant. Thus the fact that the new period is, in effect, being granted to a sitting tenant should be ignored (s 14(2)(a)). If the tenant has carried out certain improvements, these are to be ignored. Without this provision the landlord would obtain a double advantage; first by the improvement to his property and secondly by obtaining a greater rental income as a result. The improvements to be ignored for this purpose are effectively those voluntarily carried out by the tenant (s 14(2)(b)). A factor that will benefit the landlord is contained in s 14(2)(c). Where the value of the premises has deteriorated because the tenant has not discharged his contractual obligations, this is to be disregarded in assessing the rent. This may arise where a landlord contends, for example, that the tenant has not used the premises in a tenant-like manner. The reason for this is self-explanatory.

Other factors to be disregarded are any service charges and rates where the landlord is responsible for their payment (s 14(4), (5)). However in the case of a furnished assured let, the committee can consider the amounts attributable to the tenant's use of the furniture (s 14(4)).

Once the committee has reached its decision it has only a limited discretion in fixing the starting date for the new rent. The basic rule is that the new rent starts from the date specified in the notice that proposed a new rent. However, the committee can postpone this date to a later date if the tenant would otherwise suffer undue hardship (s 14(7)). The expression "undue hardship" is not further defined. An example of a case where the committee could exercise this discretion is where it reaches a decision several weeks after the tenant applied for a determination and the tenant is a weekly tenant. If an increased rent is back-dated the tenant could be faced with considerable arrears and would face eviction if he is unable to clear these arrears quickly. The latest the new rent can be postponed is to the date of the committee's decision (s 14(7)).

The position where both s 6 and s 13 notices are referred was mentioned above. A landlord might serve both notices on the tenant at the start of a statutory periodic tenancy and the tenant might apply for both to be considered by the committee. If the date the new terms are to start from is not later than the date when the proposed new rent becomes payable, the committee must consider the s 6 notice first (s 15(6)). Obviously the committee must consider the terms of the statutory periodic tenancy first, since one of the factors it must look at in assessing the rent proposed in a s 13 notice is the terms of the tenancy.

Under the 1980 Act version of assured lets, the market rents were assessed by county court judges who also have jurisdiction is assessing market rents for business tenancies. However in its consultative document, the Government stated that it is better if this task is given to rent assessment committees, although it did not explain why it had reached this conclusion (para 9).

Rent officers will also have to assess market rents for housing benefit purposes, as outlined in the previous chapter. In principle there should be consistency in the way in which rent assessment committees and officers determine what are market rents for comparable properties. Committees and rent officers are not without experience of dealing with the concept. After all under the fair rents procedures one of the factors they must ignore is the "scarcity value" of lets in a local area, precisely the type of factor that is supposed to influence the market.

(c) Other terms that are implied into an assured tenancy by the Housing Act 1988

In addition to the provision of security of tenure and the limited regulation of rents, Part I of the Housing Act 1988 implies a number of other terms into assured lets. Consistent with the philosophy that the terms of assured lets should be matters for negotiation between the parties, these rights are on the whole of a limited nature. They deal with:

(i) assignments of assured lets;
(ii) access to view the state of repair;
(iii) succession rights;
(iv) the position of subtenants where the intermediate tenancy comes to an end; and
(v) regulation of any right reserved to levy distress for rent arrears.

Assignment of assured lettings: The standard tenancy agreement to be used by housing associations contains a covenant against assignment, although there are qualified rights to transfer and to exchange tenancies. This will give contractual rights to some assured tenants similar to the statutory rights enjoyed by secure tenants. These agreements, which are reviewed in Chapter 7, will apply to most new lets by registered housing associations. In most other cases of assured lets it is likely that a landlord will insist on an absolute covenant against assignment. However there may be a qualified right to assign, that is the right to assign with the landlord's consent. These and related matters are the subject of s 15.

Part I of the 1988 Act deals with assignment in a limited way. Under s 15, it is an implied term of every *assured periodic tenancy* that the tenant may only assign, sublet or part with possession with his landlord's consent.

In the case of a periodic assured tenancy it will be an implied term that the tenant will not assign the whole (or part) of the dwelling without his landlord's consent (s 15(1)(a)). Nor can a periodic tenant sublet or part with possession of the whole or part of the premises without consent (s 15(1)(b)). In the case of most leases (including commercial lets) this consent must not be unreasonably withheld. This is the result of s 19 of the Landlord and Tenant Act 1927. However this 1927 Act provision does not apply to the implied right under s 15(1) of the 1988 Act. Thus a landlord can refuse consent and this cannot be reviewed by the courts, however unreasonable it is. As a result this qualified right is unenforceable and in this sense illusory.

A periodic let may be created by the original agreement or arise as a statutory periodic tenancy at the end of a fixed term. In the case of the former, the s 15(1) rule does not apply if there is a provision dealing with assignments (s 15(3)). Such a provision may be an absolute or qualified covenant against assignment or subletting. If it is qualified, then the 1927 Act will apply. The reason for this is that it is only excluded where there are rights to assign *implied* by s 15(1).

Section 15(1) does not apply if a premium was paid as a condition of granting the tenancy or of renewing it (s 15(3)(b)). For these reasons it is unlikely that landlords will agree to either a qualified covenant against assignment or subletting or that they will take a premium. The expression "premium" includes any fine or like sum, any other pecuniary payment in addition to rent and a deposit other than one that does not exceed one-sixth of the annual rent (s 15(4)).

Access for repairs: Under s 16 a landlord has an implied right of "reasonable facilities" to carry out any repairs he is under an obligation to carry out. Liability for repairs is considered later in this chapter.

Succession to an assured tenancy: The original Bill made no provision for members of an assured tenant's family to succeed to the tenancy on the tenant's death. However the Government was persuaded that these important rights should be extended to assured lets. Succession rights are governed by s 17.

When the tenancy is in the sole name of the tenant it passes on death to the surviving spouse who was occupying the dwelling as the only or principal home. This will occur whatever is stated in the deceased's will or under the intestacy rules. Not only is the right limited to sole tenants, but the tenant must not be a successor in the way described in this section. A tenant is treated as a successor if:

(i) the tenancy was inherited under s 17; or
(ii) under the will or intestacy of a previous tenant; or
(iii) where he was originally a joint tenant and he became a sole tenant by survivorship (that is on the death of the other tenant); or
(iv) where a member of the deceased protected tenant's family succeeded to an assured tenancy (s 17(2)).

A tenant will also be treated as a successor if he had an earlier tenancy of the same or substantially the same dwelling (s 17(3)).

Only a surviving spouse can succeed, although someone living with the deceased as "his or her wife or husband" is entitled to inherit the tenancy (s 17(4)). There appears to be no requirement that the survivor must have been living with the deceased at the time of death. Perhaps this explains the otherwise peculiar language of s 17(5) which deals with the situation where there is more than one person eligible to succeed. If this happens the eligible persons must decide who will inherit the tenancy. In default of an agreement an application must be made to the county court. Thus where a tenant dies leaving a spouse with whom he once lived and another person with whom he was living as a spouse, both are eligible to succeed. This will also apply where he was not married to the first "spouse" but lived with her as a spouse.

Reversion of assured tenancies and the effect on subtenancies: A landlord of an assured tenant may himself be a tenant of a superior landlord. What is the position of the assured tenant if his immediate landlord's tenancy comes to an end? This issue is addressed in s 18. It achieves much the same result as s 136 of the Rent Act 1977, which deals with this issue in relation to protected tenants. The basic answer is that the assured tenant becomes the tenant of the superior landlord. However, this will not apply if the nature of the relationship between the tenant and the superior landlord is such that one of the exceptions in Sch 1 applies. An example of this is a lease by a local authority to a landlord who in turn lets to a tenant on an assured let. If the lease between the authority and the landlord comes to an end, s 18 does not assist the tenant since he cannot become an assured tenant of a local authority (because of para 12 Sch 1). Another example is a let by a resident landlord to a subtenant. The subtenant cannot be an assured tenant because of the resident landlord exception in para 10 of Sch 1. If this subtenant himself sublets (with the landlord's consent), the second subtenant has no rights against the head landlord once the intermediate tenancy comes to an end. If however the lease in this example was granted by a company, the tenant would become an assured tenant of that company if the lease comes to an end, assuming that one of the other exceptional categories applies.

Section 18 cannot apply to an unlawful sublet by an assured tenant. If the assured tenant gives up possession completely he will lose his assured status because of the residence requirement in s 1. If he continues to live in the premises, subletting part, he will be a resident landlord of the subtenant who will thus fall outside the assured regime (para 10 Sch. 1).

Levying distress for rent arrears: The agreement may empower a landlord to seize a tenant's goods if he is behind with the rent. In addition landlords have common law and statutory rights to levy distress (Yates and Hawkins: *Landlord and Tenant Law*, 2nd ed 1986, pages 200 to 202). This remedy has been described as archaic and both the Law Commission (Law Com. No. 5) and the *Committee on the Enforcement of Judgment Debts* (Cmnd. 3909) have argued that it should be abolished.

As with protected tenancies, leave of the county court must be obtained before exercising this remedy (s 19).

(e) Rights under the Landlord and Tenant Acts 1985 and 1987

The Landlord and Tenant Act 1985 contains measures regulating service charges and setting out consultation procedures for tenants. These rights are amended by the Landlord and Tenant Act 1987 which also introduces other statutory rights for certain tenants. These measures are generally aimed at improving the rights of flat owners. However, they are relevant to many ordinary tenants, including assured tenants, who pay variable service charges; and other rights in the Acts, such as applying for a manager, may be important.

Service charges: where a landlord makes charges for the provision of services a tenant has rights under ss 18 to 30 of the 1985 Act. A "service charge" is any charge for "services, repairs, maintenance or insurance or the landlord's costs of management" (s 18(1)(a) of the 1985 Act). The 1985 Act enables a tenant to challenge a service charge on the basis that it is unreasonable. In many cases, a landlord must consult his tenants and obtain estimates before incurring service charges. He must also provide information, at the request of a tenant, on the costs incurred. Where there is a "recognised tenants' association", the landlord must consult the association.

The 1987 Act changes these provisions in several ways. The rights are extended to houses as well as flats and there are provisions requiring service charge contributions to be held on trust for the tenants; additional regulation of payments for insurance; and consultation rights over the appointment of managing agents.

There are several requirements governing the reasonableness of a service charge. First, where a landlord intends incurring charges in excess of £1,000 (or £50 times the number of flats, whichever is the greater) he must obtain at least two estimates for the works. One of the estimates must be from a person wholly unconnected with the landlord. Notices must be served on the tenants, describing the proposed works and inviting observations on the proposals and the estimates. Where there is a recognised tenants' association, notice must be given to the association's secretary, specifying the proposed works and inviting the association to nominate others from whom estimates can be obtained. (A recognised tenants' association is one recognised either by the landlord in writing, or by a certificate of a member of a local rent assessment committee, s 29 of the 1985 Act).

There are also limitations on recovery. A charge cannot be recovered more than eighteen months after it was incurred (new s 20B added to the 1985 Act by Sch 2 of the 1987 Act). Tenants also have the right to apply to a county court for an order that part or all the charges should not be recoverable (new s 20C added by Sch 2 of the 1987 Act).

Tenants or any recognised association may request a summary of costs incurred (s 21 of the 1985 Act) and inspect the landlord's accounts and other documentation relating to the charges (s 22 of the 1985 Act).

Tenants may have to contribute payments to service charges in advance of expenditure. Under s 42 of the 1987 Act, these advance payments (and any investment on these payments) must be held on trust for the tenants. As a result the tenants are entitled to share any residue in this fund (s 42(4)).

Section 43 of the 1987 Act adds a new Sch 3 to the 1985 Act dealing specifically with payments towards insurance. Where a landlord is under an obligation to insure the premises, the tenant has rights to a written summary of the insurance cover and to inspect the insurance policy. There is also a right to challenge the choice of insurer if the tenants believe that the cover is unsatisfactory or the premium is excessive.

Appointment of a manager: Under ss 21 to 24 of the 1987 Act, tenants may apply to a court for a manager to be appointed if the landlord has broken his obligations and it is likely that this will continue. As a preliminary step, the tenant must serve a notice on the landlord setting out the complaints and requiring the landlord to put matters right (if the breach is capable of remedy). Assuming that the breach continues, application can be made to the court under s 24. The court has power to appoint a manager to carry out such management functions as it thinks fit. If an order is made it may be registered against the title to the property to discourage the landlord from disposing of the property before the breaches are remedied. These new remedies will assist tenants who cannot, for example, persuade the landlord to carry out repairs or other obligations under the tenancy agreement.

Other rights under the Landlord and Tenant Act 1987: An assured tenant cannot exercise the right to buy under Part I of the 1977 Act. Under Part I certain tenants have the right of first refusal if the landlord decides to sell. This is denied to assured tenants by Sch 13 of the Housing Act 1988. However, a council tenant who becomes an assured tenant following a transfer to a private landlord retains his right to buy.

(f) Repairs

The question of repairs is addressed only indirectly by the 1988 Act. As noted in this and in the previous chapter, there are minor amendments to the repairing obligations implied by s 11 of the Landlord and Tenant Act 1985 and a landlord is given a statutory right of facilities to carry out repairs. Although the spirit of the assured tenancy regime is that the parties are free to negotiate the terms of the tenancy, s 11 of the 1985 Act imposes limitations on this. It will be recalled that in the case of a lease for less than seven years, a landlord cannot contract out of the implied repairing obligations without the consent of the county court.

Obviously if a lease for more than seven years is granted, repairing obligations may be the tenant's responsibility under the agreement. Most assured fixed term lets are likely to for a term of less than seven years. The standard agreements for housing associations and approved landlords include the s 11 obligations. In other cases, the impact of the business expansion scheme may result in fixed terms of less than seven years being granted. It will be recalled that after five years an investor may dispose of his shares without capital gains tax liability. As a result, companies specialising in assured lets may let on fixed terms of five years followed by a periodic term.

The scope of the s 11 liability was considered in the last chapter.

(g) Other terms

Other terms will either be implied or will be the subject of express agreement. These include the covenants for quiet enjoyment and non-derogation from grant (Megarry & Wade: *The Law of Real Property*, 5th ed 1984, pages 692 to 722). These are important in relation to harassment and illegal eviction and they are considered in Chapter 6.

Chapter 4

Possession proceedings and assured tenants

1. Introduction

The manner in which possession may be sought is closely regulated by the Act. A landlord can usually bring an assured tenancy to an end only by serving on the tenant notice of his intention to seek possession. This notice must state the grounds on which possession will be sought. The period of the notice depends on the ground upon which the landlord brings his claim. If the tenant does not leave, the landlord must apply in the county court for an order for possession. As under the Rent Acts, there are discretionary grounds upon which possession may be granted, subject to the court's discretion; and mandatory grounds where possession must be granted if the relevant ground is proved. If possession is ordered on a discretionary ground, the court has power to stay or suspend enforcement of the order. These procedures are an amalgam of those in the Rent Act 1977 and the Housing Act 1985. Since the wording of many of the 1988 Act provisions is similar to that in the 1977 and 1985 Acts, it is useful to look at how the earlier provisions have been interpreted when examining this part of the Act.

There were some important changes made to the possession provisions whilst the Act was in Parliament. For example, an offer of alternative accommodation and certain categories of rent arrears were originally mandatory grounds for possession. This was changed at the Report Stage and they are now discretionary (although there remains one mandatory ground based upon three months rent arrears).

A possession claim therefore has two stages:

(i) service of a notice of intended possession proceedings; and
(ii) starting possession proceedings in the county court.

However, before examining these two stages, the different ways in which fixed term and periodic asssured tenancies enjoy security of tenure must be summarised. As noted in Chapter 3, a landlord cannot terminate a periodic assured tenancy by serving a notice to quit. A periodic assured let remains contractual in character and it can only be brought to an end by a court order. In the case of a fixed term, a statutory periodic tenancy comes into existence at the end of the term, unless another assured tenancy is granted. The statutory periodic tenancy cannot be terminated by notice to quit, but only by a court order. If, during the currency of a fixed term, a landlord wishes to bring possession proceedings, he can only rely on certain of the grounds for possession and there must also be a forfeiture clause in the agreement.

2. The notice of intended possession proceedings

This stage of the possession procedure is modelled on the procedures that apply to claims against secure tenants under the Housing Act 1985. Under s 8 of the Housing Act 1988, a court may not consider a possession claim against a secure tenant unless:

(a) a notice under s 8 has been served; or
(b) it is "just and equitable to dispense with the requirement of such a notice" (s 8(1)).

Where there are joint landlords, at least one of them must serve the notice (ibid).
There are three matters to consider:

(a) the contents of the s 8 notice;
(b) the timing of the notice; and
(c) the circumstances in which the notice requirement may be dispensed with.

These matters are now considered in turn.

(a) Contents of a s 8 notice

A s 8 notice must be in writing and in a prescribed form (see Appendix 2, page 417). It must state the ground (or grounds) on which the landlord will base his possession claim. However, the landlord may seek leave of the court to amend the ground originally stated or to add other grounds. This enables a landlord to correct any errors in the original notice or to add matters he wishes to complain of after service of the notice. Leave to amend may be sought at the hearing of the possession claim, although the tenant would be entitled to ask the court to exercise its discretion to adjourn the claim to enable the tenant to, if need be, amend his defence.

Not only must the s 8 notice state the ground or grounds on which the possession claim will be based, it must also set out particulars of the ground(s). Thus it is not enough for a landlord to claim (for example) that the tenant has been guilty of annoying his neighbours (under Ground 14 of Sch 2 of the Act); he must also particularise this allegation in the notice. A s 8 notice gives the tenant advance warning of the landlord's complaints, enabling him to deal with the complaints or to try to put matters right if he accepts their substance. Hence the importance of the grounds and particulars being set out in the s 8 notice.

A similar provision applies to notices of intended possession proceedings against secure tenants (s 83(2)(c) Housing Act 1985). In a case alleging rent arrears against a secure tenant, it was held that a notice that merely alleged "non-payment of rent" was defective. The notice should have given details of the arrears. This failure to particularise the allegation invalidated the notice and the court could not consider the merits of the possession claim (*Torridge District Council* v *Jones* (1985)). Another example of this problem is a county court decision in *South Buckinghamshire County Council* v *Francis* (1985). Here, the local authority served a notice containing complaints that the tenant had damaged the premises, had been guilty of nuisance and that he had failed to cultivate the garden and keep it free of rubbish. It was held that a notice of intended possession proceedings is analagous to a notice under s 146 of the Law of Property Act 1925 (the latter must be served by a landlord who wishes to take forfeiture proceedings alleging breach of a lease). As with a s 146 notice, it must particularise the landlord's allegations. In this case the local authority had failed to do so, although the allegation in relation to the garden was valid, since it must have been clear to the tenant what was being alleged in this case.

(b) Timing of a s 8 notice

The notice must also inform the tenant that:

(i) possession proceedings will be started on or after the date specified in the notice; and

(ii) that proceedings will be started no later than twelve months after the date of service of the s 8 notice (s 8(3)).

The date after which proceedings may be started is also regulated by s 8 and can be summarised in the following way:

(i) the basic period is *two weeks* of the date of service (s 8(3)(c));

(ii) however, a longer period is required when one or more of the following grounds is specified in the s 8 notice –

- an owner's mandatory possession claim (ground 1);
- the mandatory possession claim by a mortgagee (ground 2);
- the mandatory ground available for dwellings let to ministers of religion (ground 5);
- the mandatory ground when the landlord intends reconstruction or demolition of the premises (ground 6);
- a mandatory claim against an occupier following the death of the tenant (ground 7);
- a discretionary claim that suitable alternative accommodation is available (ground 9);
- a discretionary claim against a service tenant.

When any of these grounds are specified in a s 8 notice, the date after which proceedings may be started is *two months* and this date must be stated in the s 8 notice (s 8(4)). This period may extend to over three months with certain assured periodic tenancies. The date must not be earlier than the date on which the landlord could have terminated the let by service of a notice to quit (but for s 5(1)). Thus, in what may be the unusual case of a quarterly periodic tenancy, the minimum notice is one quarter (in the absence of an express notice provision). However, for most practical purposes, the minimum period when one of the grounds stated above is relied on, is two months. Proceedings must be started within twelve months of the date of service. If they are not started within this period, a fresh notice must be served.

(c) Dispensing with the notice requirement

With one exception, a court may dispense with the s 8 notice requirement if it is "just and equitable to do so" (s 8(1)(b)). There are no criteria in s 8 as to how a court should exercise its discretion. The exception to the court's power to dispense with notice is where a landlord is relying on ground 8 under which possession must be granted if there are three months rent arrears at the date of the s 8 notice and at the date of the hearing.

There are comparable powers of dispensation in the Rent Acts. For example a landlord who grants a protected shorthold tenancy must, at the beginning of the tenancy, serve a notice on the tenant stating that the tenancy is shorthold. Another example is case 11 of Sch 15 of the Rent Act 1977. This enables an owner-occupier to let with a mandatory ground for possession, if he gives the tenant notice that possession might be recovered on this ground. In both cases the court can dispense with the notice requirement.

In *Fernandes* v *Parvardin* (1982), the landlord gave the tenant an oral notice under case 11. The Court of Appeal held that the written notice requirements should be dispensed with. The majority of the judges felt that there was no injustice or inequity to the tenant since he was under no misunderstanding as to the type of tenancy that had been granted. However, Stephenson L J felt that a court's discretion is wider and that it should consider all of the circumstances of the case, including the balance of hardship to the parties if the discretion is exercised.

This issue was also considered in *Bradshaw* v *Baldwin-Wiseman* (1985). Here the landlord gave no notice at all at the start of the tenancy and the tenant thought that he had an ordinary protected tenancy. It was held that the notice requirement should not be dispensed with. The tenant must be apprised of his position at the beginning of the let. The court also stated that it preferred the minority view expressed in the *Fernandes* decision. As a result, where an oral notice is given, the court can still refuse to dispense with the full requirement by weighing the balance of hardship.

In *Minay* v *Sentongo* (1983) the power of dispensation was exercised where the landlord sent a correct notice but it was not received.

If the courts adopt a similar analysis in interpreting s 8, the failure to serve a notice should not be excused if no effort is made to notify the tenant of intended possession proceedings. It might be excused if the landlord notified the tenant orally; or if he wrote but failed to serve a notice in the prescribed form; or if the dates were incorrectly stated. It is arguable that the failure to serve a s 8 notice should only be excused in exceptional cases. The consequence of a failure to serve the notices under the Rent Acts is that the tenant obtains protection. Following the "balance of hardship" test, it is not unreasonable to excuse a landlord where an effort was made to explain to the tenant that he has limited protection. However, in the assured let cases, the only consequence of failure to serve the s 8 notice is that the landlord's possession claim will be dismissed. Fresh proceedings can be launched provided a proper notice is served. There will be even less justification to excuse a failure to comply with s 8 where the landlord employs an agent to manage the premises.

(d) Summary of the s 8 requirements

A court cannot consider a claim for possession unless a s 8 notice is served or it is just and equitable to dispense with this requirement. A notice must be served in a prescribed form, stating:

(i) the landlord's intention to start proceedings;
(ii) the ground(s) the landlord will rely on;
(iii) particulars of this ground;
(iv) the date after which possession proceedings will be started; and
(v) that proceedings will be started no later than twelve months of service of the notice.

3. Orders for possession

The basic proposition is that the court can only make an order on one or more of the grounds set out in Sch 2 to the Act (s 7(1)). Where the court if satisfied that one or more of the grounds set out in Part I of that schedule is made out, it *must* order possession (s 7(3)). However, where the grounds established are one or more of those in Part II of the schedule an order can only be made if the court "considers it reasonable to do so" (s 7(4)).

4. The mandatory grounds for possession

There are eight grounds upon which the court *must* order possession if the relevant condition is established. Four of them are modelled on grounds for possession against protected tenants; the others are new.

(a) Ground 1 (claim by owner-occupiers)

Under the Rent Act 1977 there are three ways in which an owner-occupier can let his home with the assurance of recovering possession at the end of the tenancy. These are cases 11, 12 and 20 of Sch 15 of the 1977 Act. (There is also a discretionary ground available to owner-occupiers in certain situations under case 9 of Sch 15). An owner-occupier can let his home for a limited period while he is not living there, or let a property that he will eventually occupy as a retirement home. A member of the armed forces may let with the assurance of recovering possession when he needs it.

Ground 1 in the 1988 Act is intended to be "an amalgam of Cases 11, 12 and 20 in the Rent Act 1977" (Consultative Document, paragraph 16). An owner can now let on an assured let and recover possession at the end of the term if *either*:

(i) he has lived in the property; *or*

(ii) he needs it as a home for himself or his spouse.

In either case the tenant must be told, at the beginning of the let, that possession may be recovered under ground 1. During the currency of the let, the tenant is an assured tenant and he can only be evicted on one or more of the grounds in Sch 2. At the end of the tenancy however, he has no defence to a possession claim, provided his landlord complied with two conditions.

The first is that a written notice must be given to the tenant no later than the beginning of the tenancy. It must tell him that possession might be recovered on this ground. Unlike the position under the Rent Acts, there is no prescribed form that has to be used. This notice condition may be dispensed with if the court considers it just and equitable to do so. A similar power of dispensation appears in s 8 and was considered earlier in this chapter. The same considerations on excusing failure to serve notice apply here.

The second condition deals with the landlord's reason for seeking possession. There are two possibilities. The first is that the landlord occupied the dwelling as his only or principal home "at some time before the beginning of the tenancy". The expression "only or principal home" also appears in the definition of an assured let and was considered in the last chapter (see page 43). It will be noted that there is no requirement that the landlord lived in the property *immediately* before it was let. As a result, there can be successive lets under ground 1, provided the landlord lived in the property at some stage. Indeed if the landlord grants a second or subsequent let to the same tenant, there is no need to serve a fresh notice (para 8, part 4, Sch 2). This means that a landlord can take advantage of ground 1 by letting on a succession of fixed term lets with the guarantee of vacant possession if he chooses to recover possession. This may help achieve the Government's goal of encouraging new investment in private rentals, but it undermines the conceptual basis of assured lets. Under ground 1, the tenant has limited security even though he pays a market rent.

The second possibility is that the landlord needs the property for himself or his spouse to use as his or her only or principal home. There is no requirement that he must have lived in the property before the letting or at any time before his possession claim. Thus an individual can purchase a property and let it on an assured let with the certainty of recovery of possession at the end of the term provided he complies with the ground 1 conditions. There is one case where a landlord cannot use ground 1. If the landlord buys a property which is already subject to an assured let to which ground 1 applies, he cannot claim possession under this ground. In practice, this qualification may not be of much significance since a purchaser will usually want vacant possession on completion of the purchase. However, this provision should prevent a claim that the landlord wishes to live in the property if his real intention is to sell it.

For the sake of simplicity the explanation above has been in the context of a let by an individual. In the more usual case of joint owner-occupiers, the relevant conditions are satisfied if only one of them has lived in the property or wants to live in the property, as the case may be. The ground 1 notice may be served by either of them (para 7, part 4, Sch 2).

There are two other points to consider: first the s 8 notice must give two months' notice of the impending possession claim and secondly, this ground may not be used during the currency of a fixed term.

(b) Ground 2 (claim by a mortgagee)

This ground was not mentioned in the Government's consultative document. It enables a mortgagee to recover possession where the owner lets under a ground 1 assured let. There are four conditions:

(i) the mortgage must have been created before the assured tenancy;

(ii) the mortgagee must be entitled to exercise a power of sale under s 101 of the Law of Property Act 1925. This power arises if the mortgage was created by deed; the mortgage is in arrears (or there has been some other breach of the mortgage); and there is nothing in the deed precluding this power of sale. In practice this power is always reserved by building societies and other lenders and it is the most common remedy used by mortgagees when owner-occupiers fall into arrears (see Gray: *Elements of Land Law*, 1987, pages 614 to 626);

(iii) the mortgagee must need possession to exercise the sale power with vacant possession. It is possible that the property could be sold subject to the assured let and that there would still be sufficient equity to recover the loan. For this reason it has been argued, in relation to the Rent Acts, that a tenant might defend the possession claim contending that the mortgagee does not need vacant possession to exercise the power of sale (Farrand & Arden: *Rent Acts and Regulations*, 2nd ed, 1981, page 208). However mortgagees might resist this. They are under a duty to obtain the best price they can on a sale and they hold any balance after recovery of the mortgage debt on trust for the former owner and mortgagor. They would be liable to the mortgagor in damages if they failed to obtain the best price (see Gray, *op cit*, pages 620 to 622); and

(iv) the owner must have given a notice under ground 1 or if he failed to do so, it must be just and equitable to dispense with the notice.

Ground 2 therefore relates to owner-occupation and it may encourage building societies to agree to property being let under ground 1. Most mortgage deeds prohibit the creation of a tenancy without the mortgagee's consent. A tenancy granted *after* the creation of the mortgage without their consent is not binding on them (*Dudley and District Benefit Building Society* v *Emerson* (1949)). In such a case the mortgagee can exercise its power of sale (or exercise other remedies for a breach of the mortgage) and recover possession without having to use ground 2. A Rent Act case that is relevant to this ground is *Quennell* v *Maltby* (1979). Here a husband owned a house subject to a mortgage. Without the consent of the mortgagee and in breach of the mortgage, he let the property to tenants who later claimed the protection of the Rent Acts. The husband wished to sell with vacant possession. He tried unsuccessfully to persuade the mortgagee to exercise its power of sale and recover possession against the tenants, as they could have done. The husband then persuaded his wife to pay off the mortgagee and she took a transfer of the mortgage. She then brought possession proceedings on the footing that the tenancies were unlawful. The Court of Appeal found that the wife's motive in the transaction was to obtain, with her husband, vacant possession in order to sell the house at a profit. The court decided that her claim as mortgagee should not be enforced. This should serve as a cautionary tale for a landlord seeking to evade the assured tenancy regime in this fashion.

In a claim under ground 2, two months' notice of proceedings is required. Ground 2 can be used during the currency of a fixed term if the letting agreement contains provision for the letting to be terminated.

(c) Ground 3 (out of season holiday accommodation)

This and the next two grounds are easier to follow. Ground 3 is concerned with out of season lets of holiday accommodation. A genuine letting for a holiday cannot be an assured let (para 9, Sch 1, discussed in Chapter 3; see page 54). Under this ground a landlord can let for a period of up to eight months with a mandatory ground for possession provided two other conditions are satisfied:

(i) that he gave written notice that possession might be recovered on this ground (there is no power to dispense with this notice requirement);

(ii) that during the twelve months before this tenancy began, the dwelling was occupied as a holiday let. As before, the tenant has an assured status during the term of the tenancy but he has no defence to a possession claim at the end of the term.

This ground is not available during the currency of a fixed term. At least two weeks' notice of proceedings must be given.

(d) Ground 4 (out of term student accommodation)

This enables landlords to let during the academic vacations. A let to an educational institution cannot be an assured let (para 8, Sch 1, discussed in Chapter 3). Under ground 4, the landlord can let the dwelling for a period of up to twelve months on an assured let and have a mandatory ground for possession at the end of the tenancy. Written notice that possession might be recovered on this ground must be given to the tenant at the start of the tenancy. This notice requirement cannot be dispensed with. During the twelve months preceding the start of the tenancy the dwelling must have been let to an educational institution under para 8 of Sch 1. The letting does not have to be to a student. This is based on the same policy as ground 3.

This ground may not be used during the currency of a fixed term and at least two weeks' notice of proceedings must be given.

(e) Ground 5 (minister of religion's house)

This applies to a let to a minister of religion where the purpose of the let is to enable the tenant to perform his duties as a minister. Under this ground the landlord can recover possession if the property is needed for occupation by another minister. The ground is only available if notice was given to the tenant at the beginning of the let that possession might be recovered under this ground. As with grounds 3 and 4, there is no power to dispense with this condition. This ground is similar to a mandatory ground in the Rent Act 1977 (case 15, Sch 15).

This ground cannot be used during the currency of a fixed term. Two months' notice of proceedings is required.

(f) Ground 6 (demolition or reconstruction of the premises)

This is the most complicated of the mandatory grounds. It enables a landlord to recover possession to enable him to carry out major reconstruction or demolition of the premises. There is no analagous ground in relation to protected or secure lets; ground 6 is adapted from the law relating to business tenancies in the Landlord and Tenant Act 1954. It was available as a ground for possession against assured tenancies created under the Housing Act 1980.

There are essentially two matters to consider: the landlord's intentions to demolish or reconstruct the premises; and whether he needs vacant possession to carry out his plans.

The first matter that has to be established is that the landlord intends to:

(i) demolish the premises (or part of the premises); or
(ii) reconstruct the whole or a substantial part of it; or
(iii) carry out substantial works to it.

Under the 1954 Act it has been held that an objective test must be used in assessing the landlord's intentions (*Poppett's (Caterers) Ltd* v *Maidenhead Borough Council* (1971)). That is to say, there must be some objective evidence that the works will be carried out once the landlord obtains possession. If, for example, planning permission is necessary, the landlord must have taken steps to obtain it (*Gregson* v *Cyril Lord Ltd* (1963)). Other evidence could include plans; that tenders for the work have been put out; that the necessary finance will be available; and, where the landlord is a corporation, extracts from the company's board minutes (Yates and Hawkins: *Landlord and Tenant Law* 2nd ed 1986 page 705). The requisite intention is to be established at the date of the hearing (*Betty's Cafés* v *Phillips Furnishing Stores* (1959)). Under the 1954 Act, it has been held that "reconstruction" means a substantial interference with the existing structure (Yates & Hawkins, op. cit, page 698). A similar approach should be adopted in the interpretation of ground 6.

The second factor is whether vacant possession is necessary before the works can be carried out. The landlord can show this in one of four ways:

(i) that the tenant will not give him the necessary access and other facilities to have the works done. (Since many assured tenancies will have a clause giving the landlord a right of access on notice, this may not be of much practical significance); or
(ii) the nature of the intended work is such that it could not be carried out even if the landlord had access and other facilities; or
(iii) that the tenant has refused an offer of an assured tenancy

of part of the dwelling, as would enable the works to be carried out; or

(iv) that the nature of the works is such that such a tenancy is impracticable.

As a result of these conditions, the court has considerable discretion in applying ground 6 and the tenant may have several lines of defence. For example, he can put the landlord to strict proof of his intentions, or argue that the works can be carried out without evicting him.

There is another condition which relates to the identity of the landlord. The landlord must have acquired his interest in the property before the grant of the assured let. This precludes a landlord buying a property subject to an assured tenancy and then seeking possession under ground 6. A tenant may have been granted a new assured let following the end of a previous let. For the purposes of excluding a landlord by purchase using ground 6, the relevant tenancy is the first tenancy. For example, if a landlord grants a one year tenancy and sells the property before the end of that term, the new landlord cannot take advantage of ground 6 before the end of that yearly term or during another term that he might grant on its expiration. The same would apply if he did not offer another term and the tenant continues in occupation under an assured statutory periodic tenancy.

All the references have been to a landlord. This can include a superior landlord where the immediate landlord is either a registered housing association or a charitable housing trust. Where such an association or trust has a lease from the owner and sublets to its tenants, the owner will be able (subject to the terms of the lease) to use ground 6 in order to obtain vacant possession.

Although ground 6 will give a court considerable discretion in its application, the court will be bound to make an order if it is satisfied that the conditions are met. Thus a landlord will have a mandatory claim without having to offer alternative accommodation or compensation, if he plans to demolish or reconstruct. (In the case of business tenancies compensation may be payable to the displaced tenant where possession is ordered under the analagous ground in the 1954 Act). He will however have to pay the tenant's removal expenses (s 11 of the Housing Act 1988).

Two months' notice of proceedings must be given. This ground is not available during the currency of a fixed term.

(g) Ground 7 (death of the tenant)

This applies where the tenant has died and the tenancy passes under his will (or under intestacy) to another person. If that person was the deceased's spouse, she/he will succeed to an assured tenancy provided the conditions in s 17 are met (see Chapter 3). Ground 7 deals with the situation where the tenancy passes to someone else.

Where this happens, the landlord has twelve months to bring possession proceedings. This period may be extended to the date on which the landlord discovered that the original tenant has died. If a landlord accepts rent from the new tenant, ground 7 states that this does not of itself create a new periodic tenancy unless the landlord agreed in writing to a change in the terms of the tenancy.

The purpose of this ground is to enable a landlord to bring proceedings where he was unaware of the original tenant's death, or accepted rent while he investigated the situation, without being bound by a new tenancy.

It only applies to periodic tenancies (including a statutory periodic tenancy). Two months' notice of proceedings is required.

(h) Ground 8 (rent arrears)

This final mandatory ground deals with rent arrears. There are also two discretionary grounds dealing with rent arrears which are considered later (see page 92).

Under ground 8 it must be proved that rent was in arrears both at the date of the service of a s 8 notice *and* at the date of hearing the possession claim. It will be recalled that this is a case where a court cannot dispense with service of a s 8 notice.

The size of the arrears requisite to establish ground 8 is specifically defined and depends on the manner in which rent is payable under the agreement. The details are as follows:

(i) where the rent is payable weekly or fortnightly, at least thirteen weeks' rent must be owing;

(ii) where the rent is payable monthly, at least three months' rent must be unpaid;

(iii) where the rent is payable quarterly, at least one quarter's rent must be more than three months in arrears;

(iv) where the rent is payable yearly, at least three months' rent must be more than three months in arrears.

In all cases, the rent must be lawfully due. Under ss 47 and 48 of the Landlord and Tenant Act 1987, landlords must notify their tenants of their address at which notices may be served and any written demand for rent or service charges must state the landlord's name and address. Failure to notify the tenant of the landlord's address renders the rent irrecoverable until the landlord complies with this requirement. Failure to comply with the written demand requirements only renders service charges irrecoverable.

A tenant might have other legitimate reasons for withholding rent. This is examined, along with other defences to possession proceedings, later in this chapter.

Although a tenant may have a defence, if the rent is lawfully due, the court must order possession *if* the requisite arrears are established. Under ground 8 the court is precluded from considering any explanation the tenant might offer for the arrears. Such matters as illness, unemployment or delays in receiving housing benefit are now irrelevant if a landlord proves the requisite arrears. Ground 8 may cause hardship in many cases and it is a striking departure from a centuries-old tradition of granting relief from eviction in rent arrears cases.

At least two weeks' notice must be given of proceedings under this ground. It can be used to end a fixed term provided there is a forfeiture clause in the agreement.

It is likely that a claim under this ground will often be accompanied by alternative claims under the discretionary rent arrears grounds.

5. Notices relating to recovery of possession

Grounds 1 to 5 require the landlord to serve notices on the tenant. Part 4 of the second schedule contains some additional matters and was briefly referred to in the previous section.

Paragraph 7 of Sch 2 states that where there are joint landlords, at least one of them must give the notice.

Where the landlord gives a notice under grounds 1 to 5 and he grants another tenancy to the tenant, he does not have to serve a fresh notice. This point was noted in relation to ground 1. A fresh notice does not have to be served if the new tenancy is granted to the same tenant and is of "substantially the same dwelling-house" (paragraph 8(2)(b)). However, this does not apply if the landlord notifies the tenant that the relevant ground for possession will not apply to the new tenancy (para 8(3)).

In a case where a notice was served under ground 1, only the landlord who served the notice can take advantage of this ground (para 9). Paragraph 10 of the second schedule deals with notices given under grounds 3 and 4 – out of season and academic vacation lets. In either case a landlord can let for a further term to the same tenant without having to serve a fresh notice (paragraph 8(1)). Where this happens, the subsequent let is treated as if it was the original let for the purposes of a possession claim. The effect of this is that a landlord can let to an educational institution and after let on successive ground 4 lets. One condition is that there must have been an institutional let during the previous twelve months. Without paragraph 10, this could not be established if, for example, there were successive twelve month lets to the same tenant.

Again, this may encourage more lettings, but the potential for abuse is obvious.

6. The court's discretion

When bringing a claim based on one or more of the discretionary grounds the landlord must also satisfy the court that it is reasonable to make an order (s 7(3)). A similar expression appears in the Rent Act 1977 and the Housing Act 1985. As a result there are decisions on the 1977 and 1985 Acts that are relevant here. It has been said that these cases are of little assistance as precedents (Farrand & Arden: *Rent Acts and Regulations*, 2nd ed 1981 page 128). The cases are best understood in the context of the particular ground relied upon, since the courts are often influenced by the conduct of the parties. Another point to be emphasised is that issues of reasonableness are for county court judges to decide. As a result the Court of Appeal will not interfere unless there has been an error of law (see Martin: *Security of Tenure Under the Rent Act*, 1986 page 74).

7. The discretionary grounds for possession

There are eight discretionary grounds and they are set out in part 2 of the second schedule.

(a) Ground 9 (suitable alternative accommodation)

This is a claim that suitable alternative accommodation for the tenant is available or will be available when the possession order is made. As noted earlier in this chapter, the Government was persuaded that this should be a discretionary and not a mandatory ground. Part 3 of the second schedule sets out the criteria that a court must apply when considering whether or not the alternative accommodation on offer is suitable.

If the tenant's local authority certifies that it will offer suitable accommodation by a certain date, this is conclusive evidence that this ground is satisfied (para 1, part 3, Sch 2). However, the landlord must still satisfy the court that it is reasonable to make an order. Because of the current length of most local authority's waiting lists it is unlikely that many of these certificates will be forthcoming.

The other criteria in part 3 relate to the security that the alternative accommodation will give the tenant and its environmental features. As to security, the offer must consist of either another assured tenancy or one that is equivalent in terms of security. If an assured let is on offer, it must be a letting of separate accommodation and not one that gives the landlord a mandatory ground for possession under grounds 1 to 5 which were considered above. Nor will an offer of an assured shorthold let be suitable (para 2, part 3, Sch 2). What alternative can be equivalent to an assured tenancy in terms of security? It cannot be a protected tenancy since no new protected tenancies can be created (s 34 of the Act). Nor will it be an offer of a secure let by a local authority in most cases. However, an offer of a long fixed term might be found to be equivalent. This was considered, in the context of the Rent Acts, in *Scrace* v *Windust* (1955). Here it was held that an offer of accommodation that would not be protected under the Rent Acts was not suitable. However, the Court of Appeal intimated that an offer of the same accommodation for a fixed term, rather than on a weekly tenancy, might be considered suitable.

Turning to the environmental considerations, the accommodation must be "reasonably suitable to the needs of the tenant and his family as regards proximity to place of work" (para 3(1), part 3, Sch 2). It must also be comparable with that enjoyed by local authority tenants as to rent and size of the accommodation.

Alternatively, it must be within the means of the tenant and be comparable in its extent and character (para 3(1)(a) and (b)). Because of the market rents chargeable on assured lets, there may not be many local authority lets with which to make a valid comparison. However, a certificate from a local authority dealing with this comparison is conclusive evidence on these factors.

There are two other matters to consider. First, if furniture was provided, the offer must include furniture which is similar to that which the tenant currently has or "reasonably suitable to the needs of the tenant and his family" (ibid). Second, the accommodation offered must not be of a size as would make the tenant and his family statutorily over-crowded under Part X of the Housing Act 1985 (para 4, part 3, Sch 2).

Some of the decisions on alternative accommodation in protected or secure tenancy cases are instructive, even though there are some differences in the wording of the respective statutory formulae.

In *Redspring* v *Francis* (1973), a Rent Act case, it was held that general environmental factors can be taken into account. Here the tenant had lived in a quiet location for some thirty years. An offer of larger accommodation was held to be unsuitable since it was in a noisy road adjacent to a cinema, public house, a fish and chip shop and a hospital.

Thus the general environment can be considered as well as the physical condition of the premises offered to the tenant (see also the discussion in Martin: *Security of Tenure under the Rent Acts*, 1986, pages 70 to 73).

Even if the offer is considered suitable, there is also the question of whether it is reasonable to make an order. Here the court can consider the general circumstances of the tenant. Thus in *Battlespring* v *Gates* (1983) it was held to be unreasonable to make an order where the tenant, who was a widow, had lived in the property for more than thirty-five years and was emotionally attached to it. An order was refused even though the offer was of a more comfortable flat.

If an order is made on this ground, the court has a power that is not available in claims against protected or secure tenants. That is the power to order the landlord to pay the tenant's reasonable expenses in moving to the new premises (s 11(1)). It is left to the parties to agree on the sum of money. If they cannot agree, application will have to be made to the county court. However, unless the sum of money is large it may be difficult for a tenant to obtain legal aid (assuming the tenant is financially eligible). If the sum involved is less than £500, a tenant could use the small claims procedure (under the recommendations of the Lord Chanceller's *Civil Justice Review* referred to in Chapter 1, the small claims procedure will be expanded). Any sum payable to the tenant may be recovered as a civil debt (s 11(3)). The power to award payment of removal expenses also applies to mandatory ground 6 which was considered earlier.

A tenant must be given two months' notice of proceedings under this ground. This ground is not available during the currency of a fixed term.

(b) Ground 10 (rent arrears)

This is one of three grounds (one of them mandatory; see page 87) dealing with rent arrears. Under ground 10 it must be proved that some rent was owing when the proceedings were started and was owing when the s 8 notice was served, unless this requirement is dispensed with. Under ground 10, therefore, a court could allow a landlord to proceed with a possession claim based on rent arrears even though no s 8 notice was served. It was argued earlier (see page 78) that the power to dispense with the s 8 requirement should be exercised sparingly. It would be hard on a tenant to dispense with the requirement in a ground 10 case, since he might only be a small sum in arrears and would suddenly face eviction without prior warning that his landlord was considering possession proceedings. The issue of reasonableness is very important in rent arrears claims and it will be considered further (see page 93) after dealing with the next rent arrears ground.

At least two weeks' notice of possession proceedings must be given.

(c) Ground 11 (persistent rent arrears)

Under this ground, a landlord can seek possession even if no rent is owing at the start of the proceedings. He has to show that the tenant "has persistently delayed paying rent which has become lawfully due". This is an entirely new ground for possession and one that does not appear in either the Rent Act 1977 or in the

Housing Act 1985. In the Government's original Bill it was to have been a mandatory possession ground. However, the Government agreed that a mandatory ground of this sort would be too harsh, particularly on tenants on low incomes who experience delays in payment of their housing benefit. There is a similar ground under the 1954 Act in relation to business lets. There, it has been held that persistent delay refers to a course of conduct over a period of time. The courts have looked at the frequency of non-payment, the reasons for non-payment, and the steps the landlord has had to take in the past to recover arrears (see *Evans: The Law of Landlord and Tenant*, 2nd ed P. F. Smith, 1985, page 397).

Ground 11 deals with a tenant with a poor record for paying rent, such as a tenant who pays only after the threat of proceedings. Thus a court will have to consider the conduct of the tenant in the context of his relationship with his landlord. There is no definition of "persistently delayed". However, given the reasons for introducing this ground, an order should not be made unless there is a history of poor payments. For the same reasons, a court will have to consider any explanation offered by the tenant. The delays might be due to illness, unemployment, break-up of a relationship or a genuine dispute over the tenant's liability for the rent. The tenant might, for example, have withheld rent because the landlord failed to carry out repairs. Under grounds 10 and 11 the reasonableness issue is particularly important. A landlord has, after all, other methods of recovering arrears such as a claim for debt (under the *Civil Justice Review* proposals, there will be a streamlined arrears action). In analagous claims against protected and secure tenants, courts have rarely ordered possession if the arrears were cleared by the date of the hearing. Possession might be ordered where there is a long history of arrears or where the landlord had repeatedly to start proceedings to recover the rent (*see Dellenty* v *Pellow* (1951)).

In a secure tenancy case it was held that a possession order should not be made where the tenants had a good record of rent payment and where the explanation for the arrears was illness and unemployment (*Woodspring District Council* v *Taylor* (1983)). Here the Court of Appeal dismissed an appeal against the refusal of the county court to grant possession.

Another relevant case is *Lal* v *Nakum* (1982). This concerned a claim against a protected tenant who had withheld rent because of his landlord's failure to carry out repairs. A possession order was refused since the complaints were genuine (although the tenant was ordered to pay the arrears as a condition for not making a possession order). Tenants may have a defence (and counterclaim) because of disrepair. This and other defences are considered in more detail later in this chapter (see page 98). In all claims based on a discretionary ground the court may suspend enforcement of the order and allow the tenant to stay in the property, subject to conditions as to payment of the arrears. Orders based on rent arrears in claims against protected and secure tenants are often suspended. This area of discretion is examined further below (see page 100).

Two weeks' notice must be given of proceedings under this ground.

(d) Ground 12 (breach of another obligation)

Grounds 10 and 11 deal with breach of the specific obligation to pay rent. Ground 12 deals with a claim that the tenant has broken some other term in the agreement. It refers to *any* obligation that has been broken or not performed. As a result, it can apply to any breach whether it is continuing or not. However, if the breach has been remedied, there will be a compelling argument for saying that it is not reasonable to order possession. This view has been taken in Rent Act decisions on this point (*Brown* v *Davies* (1958)). A landlord may not be able to rely on this ground where he has waived or lost his right to complain of the breach. This is also dealt with at page 98 when defences to possession claims are considered.

Again at least two weeks' notice of possession proceedings must be given.

(e) Ground 13 (deterioration of the premises)

Under this ground a landlord can seek possession if he proves that the condition of the dwelling or any of the common parts has deteriorated and that this was caused by the tenant. To establish that it was the tenant's fault, he must show that the deterioration was caused by an act of waste, neglect or default on the tenant's part. Alternatively, the landlord must prove that it was the fault of someone living with the tenant as a lodger or a tenant. In this case, however, the landlord must also show that the tenant failed to take reasonable steps to remove the person responsible. The expression "waste" means any unauthorised alteration to the premises (Megarry & Wade: *Law of Real Property*, 5th ed, pages

95 to 96). Under the similarly drafted Rent Act provision, it has been held that there may be grounds for possession even though there is no actual breach of the agreement (*Lowe* v *Lendrum* (1950)). Proceedings may also be brought where the tenant is in breach of the implied obligation to use the premises in a "tenant-like manner". As a breach of obligation this would also constitute a claim under ground 12.

The scope of this obligation is not entirely clear. A case on the point is *Wycombe Area Health Authority* v *Barnett* (1982) which concerned a secure tenant. It was stated that in very cold weather, a tenant may have to lag water pipes or to take other steps to prevent the sort of damage that can arise during periods of extremes of temperature.

However, there was held to be no liability in this case, where the tenant left the property for a short period, during which there was a cold weather spell resulting in burst water pipes. In an earlier case it had been said that the tenant should take proper care of the premises, cleaning chimneys and windows, replacing light bulbs, mending fuses and clearing a blocked sink (*Warren* v *Keen* (1954)).

Liability under this ground is wider than that under the Rent Act 1977, since it extends to the common parts. This expression is defined in ground 13 as parts which the tenant is entitled to use in common with other tenants of the same landlord. Where a landlord is bound by the repairing covenant implied by s 11 of the Landlord and Tenant Act 1985, his liability is extended to the common parts by s 115 of the 1988 Act (see Chapter 2). Further, a landlord is under a duty at common law in relation to the common parts (*Liverpool City Council* v *Irwin* (1977)). Thus the primary responsibility for the common parts will usually rest with the landlord. Ground 13 only applies to deterioration caused by the tenant or someone residing with him.

Two weeks' notice of proceedings is required.

(f) Ground 14 (nuisance, annoyance, illegal or immoral use)

This involves an allegation of misconduct. It is similar to grounds for possession against secure and protected tenants. Ground 14 deals with two types of misconduct. First, that the tenant has been guilty of conduct that has caused a nuisance or annoyance to adjoining occupiers. Second, that the tenant has been convicted or either *using* the dwelling for an immoral or illegal use; or of *allowing* the premises to be used in such a way. Where an assured let has been created in writing, these matters may be the subject of express covenants on the part of the tenant. Where this is so, there could also be a claim under ground 12 (see page 94). As with ground 13, liability under ground 14 arises where the misconduct was committed by someone else living in the dwelling. This is not limited to someone living with the tenant as a lodger or subtenant. However, here the tenant is not expected to have taken steps to evict the person responsible (indeed it will often be impossible for a tenant to do this).

Rent and Housing Act cases on this point are useful illustrations of the limits of this ground. For example, it has been held that possession may be ordered even if the nuisance or annoyance has stopped if it is likely that it will happen again (*Florent* v *Horez* (1984)). The question of who is an "adjoining occupier" was considered in *Cobstone Investments* v *Maxim* (1984)), where it was said that occupiers are adjoining if they are near enough to be affected. They need not live in premises that are physically adjacent (the liability is expressed more clearly under the Housing Act 1985 where the expression "neighbours" is used instead of adjoining occupiers).

Under the Rent Acts it has been held that immoral or illegal use creates a ground for possession only if the tenant (or another resident in the premises) has been convicted of an offence in a criminal court (*Schneiders & Sons* v *Abrahams* (1925)). Moreover, it has to be shown that there was a connection between the offence and the use of the premises. For example, a conviction for handling stolen goods would create grounds for possession where the tenant had stored the goods in the dwelling. On the other hand where drugs were found in the tenant's clothing and there was no evidence that the tenant was using the dwelling for drugs dealing this would not amount to a ground for possession (*Abrahams* v *Wilson* (1971)). Even where illegal or immoral use is proved, the court can at its discretion find that it is unreasonable to evict the tenant. In a Rent Act case the tenant had been convicted of possession of a small amount of cannabis which was found in her flat. The Court of Appeal held that to evict her would not be reasonable. The conviction had not brought the premises into disrepute and eviction would in her case amount to punishing her twice. She was unemployed, a single parent and eviction would have caused her hardship (*Abrahams* v *Wilson* (1971)).

The tenant must be given two weeks' notice of proceedings.

(g) Ground 15 (damage to furniture)

Damage to furniture first became a ground for possession in the Rent Act 1974. This Act extended protection to tenants of furnished lets and it also introduced the "resident landlord" exception to protection. The Government at that time was told that some furnished tenants would damage the furniture provided and that their landlords would have no redress. As a result damage to furniture became a ground for possession. A similar ground for possession exists against secure tenants although few local authorities provide furniture to their tenants.

With assured lets it is a ground for possession that, in the opinion of the court, the condition of any furniture provided under the agreement has deteriorated and that this was the tenant's fault. As with ground 13 a tenant may also be evicted if the damage was caused by a lodger or subtenant and the tenant failed to take reasonable steps to remove that person.

Unless landlords decide to provide furniture when letting on assured lets this ground will be of little practical significance.

Again two weeks' notice of proceedings must be given.

(h) Ground 16 (service tenancies)

This final discretionary ground applies to a service tenancy. This is a tenancy provided by an employer to an employee, as part of the terms and conditions of employment. It must be distinguished from a service *occupancy* where accommodation is provided to enable an employee to carry out his duties effectively. An occupier of this sort, such as a caretaker, has a licence not a tenancy and cannot by definition be an assured tenant (see also the discussion of tenancies and licences in Chapter 3, page 45). If the tenant's job comes to an end, the landlord may seek possession. This ground is wider than the corresponding Rent Act ground in this respect: the landlord does not have to show, as he would in a Rent Act claim, that he requires the dwelling for occupation by another employee. However, the reason the landlord seeks possession and the possible hardship to the tenant would be relevant when considering whether it is reasonable to evict the tenant. As under the Rent Act the landlord seeking possession need not be the tenant's employer. If the previous landlord was the employer his successor in title can seek possession on this ground.

Two months' notice of proceedings is required and this ground is not available during the currency of a fixed term.

8. Defences to a possession claim

In many cases the tenant's defence may consist of a simple denial that there are grounds on which the court can make an order for possession. In the case of a claim made under one of the discretionary grounds there may be an additional argument based on the question of reasonableness. These matters were reviewed in the previous section of this chapter; see pages 89 to 97. In addition there may be a defence where the landlord has waived or lost his right to complain about the tenant's default. At common law, a landlord loses his right to forfeit where, with knowledge of a breach, he does something that in effect recognises the continuing existence of the lease (Yates and Hawkins: *Landlord and Tenant Law*, 2nd ed, page 195). A common example of a waiver is a demand for or acceptance of rent after discovering that the agreement has been broken. This can amount to a waiver even if the rent was accepted "without prejudice" (*Segal Securities Ltd* v *Thoseby* (1963)). There may be a waiver if the landlord's agent became aware of the breach but failed to report it to the landlord. In *Metropolitan Properties* v *Cordery* (1979), the landlord's agents became aware that a flat had been unlawfully sublet. They failed to pass this information on to the landlord who continued to accept rent. It was held that the landlord had waived his right to complain of this breach of the tenancy agreement.

This assumes that there has been a single breach. Where the breach is continuing (continuing nuisance, for example) acceptance of rent may operate as a waiver of past breaches. However it cannot affect any breaches that continue into the future.

An assured tenant may in this way have a defence to a possession claim if his landlord has waived the breach. This should, in principle, apply to a fixed term and a contractual periodic let. What is the position, however, when the tenant occupies under a statutory periodic tenancy? In Rent Act cases on this point, it has been held that the waiver rules should not be applied strictly to a statutory tenancy (that is a tenancy that comes into being when a contractual tenancy comes to an end). The reasoning is that the waiver rules derive from forfeiture of leases and should not be strictly applied to a tenancy that comes into existence because of a statute. Hence acceptance of rent does not necessarily amount to a waiver even if the acceptance was unqualified (*Trustees of Henry Smith's Charity* v *Willson* (1983)). However, it is arguable that a statutory periodic tenancy is different in several respects from a statutory tenancy arising under the Rent Acts, so that the waiver rules *should* apply.

Another line of defence may exist where the tenant has a money claim against the landlord. For example, at common law a tenant may, after notice to his landlord, carry out repairs that are the landlord's responsibility and then recoup the expenditure out of future rent. He will then have a defence against an action to recover the rent (*Lee Parker* v *Izzet* (1971)). This principle was extended in *British Anzani (Felixstowe) Ltd* v *International Marine Management (U.K.) Ltd* (1980). Here it was held that a tenant also has an equitable right to set off against rent an unquantified claim for damages. It has also been held that the right of set off applies to rent that has been withheld in the past (*Asco Developments Ltd.* v *Lowes* (1978)).

As a result, a tenant may have a considerable amount to set off against a claim based on arrears of rent, whether a mandatory or discretionary ground is relied on. Since the Court of Appeal's decision in *Calabar Properties Ltd.* v *Stitcher* (1984), the courts have become more generous in awarding damages in cases of disrepair. Damages can be awarded not only for any actual losses suffered by the tenant, such as damage to his belongings, but also to compensate him for any loss of enjoyment of the premises. A recent example of a case where damages for disrepair was considered is *Personal Representatives of Chiodi* v *De Marney* (1988). Here the tenant complained of disrepair in October 1980 and, following advice, she stopped paying rent the next month. Her complaints included a defective bedroom window and the absence of hot water. She was temporarily housed by her local authority in September 1983, whilst repairs were carried out. She returned to the premises in March 1985 once the repairs were completed. After the landlord's death his personal representatives started possession proceedings. The tenant defended and counterclaimed for damages because of the disrepair. The possession claim was withdrawn and the plaintiffs conceded responsibility so the only question was that of damages. The county court judge awarded damages for distress at £30 per week for the period up to September 1983, making a total of £5,460; special damages of £4,657.63 (for her actual losses); and £1,500 for injury to the tenant's health. The appeal attacked the first damages item only. Although the Court of Appeal felt that the award was high (and towards the top of the range of damages in these cases) it upheld the trial judge's decision.

This right of set off applies only in relation to a breach of the lease (*British Anzani*, above) and not for some collateral matter. However, there may also be claims based on other types of breach such as the covenant for quiet enjoyment.

Given the current preponderance of unfit and poorly maintained property in the private sector (see Chapter 1) a defence based on a set-off could be of considerable significance. However, tenants and their advisors will have to consider withholding of rent very carefully, given the three grounds for possession for rent arrears, particularly the mandatory ground. It may be advisable in most cases to use other methods of getting the repairs done and to consider a claim for damages.

9. Suspension of the possession order

When dealing with a discretionary claim, a court has powers, similar to those it has in connection with claims against secure and protected tenants, of adjournment and suspension of a possession order. It may adjourn for "such period or periods as it thinks fit" (s 9(1)). If a possession order is made, there is power to stay or suspend execution or to postpone the date of the order. This power may be exercised at the date of the possession order or at any time after, provided the order has not been enforced (s 9(2)). If the court makes such an order, it must usually impose conditions. A common condition is that the tenant pays off any rent arrears by instalments. The court may also impose "such other conditions as it thinks fit" (s 9(3)).

There is an important qualification to the power to impose conditions. A condition should not be imposed if it would cause hardship to the tenant or "would otherwise be unreasonable" (ibid). The court should consider the size of the arrears payments when a tenant has a low income or is receiving benefit. There is evidence that some county courts are failing to consider the hardship criterion in Rent and Housing Act possession claims—see Ffloukes *Legal Action*, March 1983.

The power to suspend on a subsequent application may be exercised even though the original order was absolute (*Vandermolen* v *Toma* (1983)). This point was also underlined in *R* v *Ilkeston County Court ex parte Kruza* (1985). Here a tenant was subject to a possession order suspended on condition that the rent arrears were paid by instalments. He fell into further arrears and his landlord applied for a warrant for possession. The tenant applied for a further suspension of the possession order. The county court registrar rejected the application stating that he had no jurisdiction to make a further order. On appeal it was held that the registrar was wrong since a court has power to suspend not only at the time possession was ordered, but also on a subsequent application.

However, an application for a suspension does not of itself stay any warrant of execution issued on behalf on the landlord (*Moore* v *Registrar of Lambeth County Court* (1969)). A tenant must also *apply* for a stay of execution. Once the conditions of any suspension have been complied with, the court may rescind or discharge the possession order (s 9(4)). What is the position of a tenant who resides subject to a suspended possession order? This issue have been considered in relation to protected and secure tenants. In a Rent Act case it was held that a suspended possession order can pass on the tenant's death under the succession rules. The successor takes subject to the terms of the suspended order (*Sherrin* v *Brand* (1956)).

Some confusion has been caused by the Court of Appeal's decision in *Thompson* v *Elmbridge Borough Council* (1987). It was held that a single breach of the terms of a suspended possession order against a secure tenant brings the secure let to an end. As a result the court no longer has jurisdiction to suspend. As the author has argued elsewhere, the court overlooked a number of previous decisions which emphasise its broad powers in these cases. It also under-estimated the power to suspend on a subsequent application by a tenant (Driscoll: *Rent arrears, suspended possession orders and the rights of secure tenants*, 51 Modern Law Review 371 (1988)).

Quite apart from the powers in s 9, the County Court Rules enable a tenant to apply to have the original possession order set aside. In hearing such an application the court may also set aside a warrant of execution. This is so even if it has been enforced and the landlord has recovered possession (*Governors of Peabody Trust* v *Hay* (1987)). An order might be set aside, for example, if the original possession summons was not properly served.

There is also the position of the tenant's spouse to consider. She may have rights under the Matrimonial Homes Act 1983. These include the right to tender the rent, even though she is not the tenant. She also has the right to apply to be joined in any possession proceedings (s 1(9) of the 1983 Act) and she could seek the transfer of the tenancy to herself on divorce or judicial separation (under s 7 of the 1983 Act or s 24 of the Matrimonial Causes Act 1983). If a possession order is made, she has the same rights to apply for orders under s 9 provided she remains in occupation (s 9(5)).

There is room for improvement of these procedures. A non-tenant spouse remains vulnerable where the tenant spouse does not reveal that possession proceedings have been started or concluded. It would be fairer, and would cause little inconvenience to landlords, if they were required to serve notice of the proceedings on a non-tenant spouse, assuming they are aware of her existence, as they usually are. The s 9 procedures could also be strengthened, with minimal inconvenience, to require a landlord to apply for leave before obtaining a warrant of execution.

10. Special provisions applicable to shared accommodation

The problems of shared accommodation were addressed in the previous chapter. A tenant can hold an assured let even though he shares living accommodation with others (except the landlord). Under s 3 the landlord cannot alter this arrangement apart from controlling the persons who can use the shared living accommodation (s 9(3), (4)). Section 10 deals with some questions that may arise when making possession orders against a tenant who shares living accommodation. The effect of this section may be illustrated by the following example. Assume a landlord lets a house which contains three living units, but the occupants share a kitchen, dining room and a living room. The house is occupied by three assured tenants. The fact that they share the kitchen and living rooms does not take them out of protection because of s 3. If the landlord has grounds for possession against one of the three tenants, s 10 enables him to recover possession not only of the unit let to that tenant, but also of that tenant's use of the shared accommodation (s 10(3)). A landlord cannot claim possession of the other tenants' right to use the shared accommodation (s 10(2)). Thus the landlord can recover possession of one tenant's separate unit and of his use of the shared accommodation without affecting the use of the shared accommodation by the remaining tenants (s 10(4)).

11. Compensation for misrepresentation or concealment

A landlord may obtain possession to carry out demolition or reconstruction under ground 8 of Sch 2. What is the position if, after recovering possession, he does something else such as selling the property? Similar issues may arise in connection with proceedings under other grounds where a landlord may have misrepresented his intentions or concealed material facts. Under s 12 a court may award the displaced tenant compensation for the damage and loss sustained as a result of a possession order having been made if it is subsequently discovered that it was obtained by misrepresentation or a concealment of material facts. There is a similar remedy under s 102 of the Rent Act 1977, although this is limited to claims made under cases 8 and 9 of Sch 15 (where the landlord obtains possession for an employee or himself or a member of his family). In one case damages were awarded where a landlord sold the property immediately after a consent order (*Thorne* v *Smith* (1947)). In addition to this statutory remedy, there may be other remedies such as a claim alleging deceit (Farrand & Arden: *Rent Acts and Regulations*, 2nd ed, 1981, page 132). Whatever the basis of the claim, it must be proved that the misrepresentation or concealment was made in the possession proceedings and that the order was obtained as a result of this deceit. However, many displaced tenants may never discover that a deceit was practised on the court.

Section 12 did not appear in the original version of the Bill, but the Government was persuaded that such a remedy is necessary and the Bill was amended in this respect at the Report Stage.

Chapter 5

Assured shorthold tenancies and assured agricultural occupancies

1. Assured shorthold tenancies

(a) Background

As noted in the previous chapters, the Housing Act 1980 introduced two new types of tenancy, the assured and the protected shorthold lets. Both were introduced in an attempt to revive investment in the private sector. A protected shorthold let consists of a fixed term of between one and five years. The landlord must serve a notice on the tenant before the start of the let informing him that he has a shorthold let. During the period of the fixed term, the tenant has security of tenure and he is covered by the fair rent procedures of the Rent Act 1977. However, at the end of the fixed term the landlord has a mandatory ground for possession.

Originally, there was a requirement that a fair rent be registered or a fair rent certificate obtained before the grant of a protected shorthold. However, the Government reserved the right to withdraw this requirement from different areas. It was gradually withdrawn from all areas outside Greater London (see Martin: *Security of Tenure Under the Rent Act*, 1986, pages 47 to 52). In 1987, it was also withdrawn from Greater London. Protected shorthold tenants can still apply for a fair rent to be registered. However, many tenants may be reluctant to do so if they are hoping to obtain a renewal of their tenancy.

Unlike the position with the 1980 style assured lets, protected shortholds will not be governed by Part I of the Housing Act 1988.

For a time there will be two types of shorthold: those created under the 1980 Act and the new version introduced by the Housing Act 1988. However, given the limited security of tenure available to protected shortholds, they are likely to disappear within a short period as landlords switch to the new version.

(b) The Government's proposals

In its consultative paper on the private rented sector the Government stated "There will be many landlords who wish to let their property for a fixed term and to be sure of regaining possession at the expiry of the lease" (paragraph 21). Assured shortholds are designed to meet their needs. They differ from protected shortholds in the following ways:

(i) they can be for a minimum period of six months (there is no maximum period);

(ii) a fixed term can be followed by a periodic let which will also be an assured shorthold;

(iii) in the first instance, the rent payable is a matter for negotiation between the parties. A tenant can apply once and once only for reduction of the rent. However in considering the rent, the rent assessment committee must look at market rents, making allowance for the tenant's limited security of tenure. As the Government put it "it is expected that rents for shortholds will generally be slightly lower than rents for assured tenancies" (ibid, paragraph 23).

Landlords wishing to take advantage of the business expansion scheme tax concessions, described at the beginning of Chapter 3, cannot let on assured shorthold lets. Nor will most housing associations or landlords approved under Part IV of the Act let on assured shorthold lets. However these new lets are likely to become popular with other private landlords, given the limited term, limited security of tenure and higher rents.

(c) Definition of an assured shorthold tenancy

The definition is contained in s 20 and it has the following three elements:

(i) it must satisfy the basic definition of an assured let;

(ii) it must be for a minimum period of six months;

(iii) the landlord must serve a notice before the start of the let.

These three elements are considered in turn.

Assured: An assured shorthold must itself satisfy the basic conditions for the creation of an assured let (see page 42 *et seq*). Thus there must be *let* of a separate dwelling to an individual who occupies it as his only or principal home. By definition a licence cannot be an assured shorthold. It must not be a let that cannot be assured because of the exceptions set out in Sch 1 of the Act.

The most relevant exception in likely to be the resident landlord exception. This underlines a point made in Chapter 2 (see page 25). Lets (with very limited exceptions) by resident landlords after 15 January 1989 will not be restricted contracts under the Rent Act 1977. Nor can they be assured or assured shorthold lets. As a result the tenant has no method of challenging the rent and he has no security beyond that given to him under his contract. If, as is likely to be the case, new resident landlord lets are periodic, the landlord will be able to evict the tenant with relative ease. As explained in Chapter 6, in many cases a landlord will be able to evict without obtaining a court order.

In addition, a holiday let and a let by an educational institution to its students cannot be assured shortholds (or assured lets).

Term: There must be a term of not less than six months (s 20(1)(a)). The agreement must not contain a provision empowering the landlord to bring the let to an end earlier than six months from the start of the tenancy (s 20(1)(b)). There is no maximum term. At the end of the fixed term, a new assured shorthold can be granted to the same tenant which can be for a shorter term. For example, a landlord can create an assured shorthold for a period of six months and then grant a periodic let to the same tenant. The subsequent periodic let will also be an assured shorthold (s 20(4)).

Notice: *Before* the start of the assured shorthold a notice has to be served by the person who is to be the landlord on the person who is to be the tenant (s 20(1)(c)). Where there are joint landlords, at least one of them must serve the notice (s 20(6)). This notice must be in a prescribed form (see prescribed form number 7 in Appendix 2, page 425), The notice must inform the person who is to be the tenant that the tenancy will be an assured shorthold tenancy (s 20(2)(d)). The prescribed form also advises the prospective tenant of his right to apply to a rent assessment committee and that his fixed term cannot be terminated before six months. If an incorrect notice or no notice is served, the tenant will become an assured tenant, provided he meets the basic conditions outlined above (and which were examined in Chapter 3). A court has no power to dispense with this notice requirement. However, if the landlord grants another assured shorthold let to the same tenant, he does not have to serve a fresh notice (s 20(4)).

Summary: An assured shorthold is (1) an assured let; (2) for a minimum term of six months (with no power for the landlord to terminate before six months); and (3) where a notice was served before the beginning of the term. However, a subsequent let by the landlord to the same tenant can be for a term of less than six months and there is no need to serve a fresh notice.

Assured tenants and assured shortholds: if before the grant, a tenant was an assured tenant (and not an assured shorthold tenant), he cannot be granted a shorthold by his landlord. This is to prevent tenants from being induced into signing an agreement that would result in their losing their security of tenure. A similar rule prevents protected shortholds being granted to protected or statutory tenants.

(d) Security of tenure

During the period of the fixed term, the landlord cannot bring it to an end for six months following the start of the tenancy (s 20(1)(b)). If the fixed term is longer than six months, it can only be terminated in the same way as can an assured tenancy (see Chapters 3 and 4). Thus the landlord must have a ground for possession under Sch 2 of the Act (see page 75 *et seq*). He would also have to serve a notice of intended possession proceedings and there would have to be provision in the agreement for termination. Moreover, it will be recalled that only limited (fault) grounds may be used during the currency of a fixed term. For these reasons, it will be surprising if many landlords will be persuaded to grant terms longer than six months. At the end of the fixed term, the tenant will become a statutory periodic tenant, unless he is offered another assured shorthold.

However, it is relatively easy for the landlord to obtain possession. He has to give the tenant not less than *two months*' notice stating that he requires possession (s 21(1)(b)). Where there are joint landlords, at least one of them must give notice (ibid). This notice may be given before, on, or after the day on which the fixed term comes to an end, and this has effect even though a statutory periodic tenancy has come into effect (s 21(2)). In other words, a separate notice does not have to be served to terminate the statutory periodic tenancy. In practice a landlord may grant a fixed term of six months, and notify the tenant that he requires possession two months before the end of the term. He then becomes entitled to possession at the end of the term and has a mandatory ground for possession. There is no stipulation that the landlord requires possession for any particular reason.

This deals with the case where the landlord decides to recover possession at the end of a fixed term. However he may have granted another subsequent shorthold to the same tenant. Here it is also relatively easy for the landlord to recover possession. Again, he can use the general grounds for possession available against assured tenants. However, he also has a mandatory ground for possession on notifying the tenant that he requires possession. The period of the notice depends on whether the second or subsequent shorthold is for a fixed term or is periodic.

If it is a fixed term, then the same procedure as mentioned above has to be used. Thus not less than two months' notice that he requires possession must be given either before, on or after the day on which the term comes to an end (s 21(2)).

In the case of a shorthold that is periodic, the notice requirement is slightly different. It has two features (s 21(4)):

(i) the landlord must give the tenant notice that possession will be required after a particular date. This must be the last day of the period of the tenancy and no earlier than *two months* of the date the notice was given. For example, a weekly or monthly periodic tenancy can only be terminated by four weeks' notice. However, the landlord would still have to give two months' notice that he requires possession and the notice is to expire on the day on which the particular period ends;

(ii) the date specified must also not be earlier than the earliest day on which the tenancy could be terminated. This deals with a tenancy with a period longer than two months. As a practical matter, assured shorthold periodic tenancies are likely to run from week to week or month to month. This second condition is unlikely to be of practical importance.

To summarise:

(i) During the currency of an assured shorthold, a landlord can recover possession only on the grounds in Sch 2. In the case of a new let, he cannot recover possession during the first six months.

(ii) In the case of a fixed term, a landlord can recover possession by giving two months' notice before, on or after the end of the term. This applies to a fixed term or a fixed term plus a *statutory* periodic tenancy.

(iii) In the case of a periodic shorthold, the two months must expire on the last day of the period. In the case of periodic lets with a period longer than two months, the date must be no earlier than the date it could have been terminated by notice to quit.

(iv) In cases (ii) and (iii), the landlord has a mandatory claim for possession.

Curiously, neither a s 21(1)(b) or 21(4) states that notice must be given in writing. However the expression "has given the tenant notice" implies that it should be in writing. In any event, there would be problems of proof that a valid notice had been given if it was not in writing. There will be no prescribed form published under the Act. In the case of joint landlords, at least one of them must give notice. Unlike a notice of intended possession proceedings against an assured tenant, there is no stipulated period within which proceedings must be begun.

The combined effect of these provisions is that it is relatively easy for a landlord to recover possession and this obviously places him in a strong bargaining position if he negotiates a new shorthold with his tenant. A shorthold tenant's relative lack of security may also inhibit him from exercising his right to refer the rent to a rent assessment committee.

(e) Referring the rent to a rent assessment committee

It will be recalled that rent assessment committees have two functions in relation to assured lets. They can deal with disputes over the terms of the statutory periodic tenancy which arises at the end of a fixed term (assuming that a new assured let was not granted). They also have jurisdiction in connection with contractual periodic assured lets which do not have a rent review clause.

They also have a limited jursidiction in relation to assured shortholds. However, there are two pre-conditions to their considering a rent under an assured shorthold:

(i) first, that there "is a sufficient number of similar dwelling-houses in the locality let on assured tenancies (whether shorthold or not)" (s 22(3)(a)). There is no definition of "locality". This pre-condition will obviously make it difficult for committees to consider shorthold rents during the period immediately following commencement of the Act;

(ii) second, they must be satisfied that the rent referred to them, "is significantly higher" than the level of rents in the locality (s 22(2)(b)). There is no definition of "significantly higher".

Assuming that these two pre-conditions are satisfied, they can consider an application by a tenant who considers that the rent is too high. However, only a tenant under an initial fixed term (where a notice under s 20(2) had to be served by the landlord) can apply (s 22(1)). Moreover, only one application can be made during this fixed term (s 22(2)(a)). As a result a tenant who has been granted another assured shorthold after the initial fixed term has expired cannot refer the rent to the committee (s 22(2)(b)).

If the committee makes a determination, the rent assessed takes effect "from such date as the committee may direct" (s 22(4)(a)). However, this must be no earlier than the date of the application. If the rent determined is less than the one contractually agreed, the difference is irrecoverable from the tenant (s 22(4)(b)). In other words if a committee decides that the contractual rent is too high, the rent they assess becomes the maximum payable. The combined effect of these provisions is that the landlord could owe monies to the tenant. For example, if the rent is (effectively) reduced to take effect from the date of the original application, the landlord will owe the difference to the tenant.

If, following a fixed term, the tenant holds under a statutory periodic tenancy, the landlord can use the general procedure of serving a notice of increase under s 13(2) (see Chapter 3). This will also apply if the tenant is granted a contractual periodic let. However, a notice of increase may not be served until twelve months after the date of any determination under s 22 (4)(c)).

As with rents determined by the committee for assured lets, the rent must be assessed exclusive of rates. Who pays the rates depends on the terms of the agreement.

To summarise:

(i) a tenant holding under the initial fixed term may refer the rent to the committee once during the currency of the fixed term;

(ii) the committee may reduce the rent if it is significantly higher than rents for other assured lets in the locality (assuming that there is a sufficient number of lets to make a comparison);

(iii) a rent reduced is the maximum payable under the agreement;

(iv) if at the end of the agreement the tenant holds under a statutory periodic tenancy or is granted a contractual periodic tenancy the landlord can serve a notice of increase. However he cannot do this until twelve months after the date on which the committee made its decision.

Thus committees have a limited function in relation to assured shortholds. Many tenants will feel inhibited from exercising this right because of their limited security. For example, a tenant holding under an initial fixed term of six months can refer the rent to a committee, but he runs the risk that the landlord will serve notice that he requires possession, with the consequence that the tenant faces eviction at the end of the fixed term. Hence tenants hoping to obtain a further term will be reluctant to exercise this right. The Government is empowered to terminate this function of the rent assessment committee, by laying a statutory instrument, which must be approved by resolution of each House of Parliament (s 23). It will be recalled that the requirement to obtain a fair rent certificate as a condition of granting a protected shorthold under the Housing Act 1980, was gradually withdrawn (see page 104).

It is difficult to understand why these new shortholds have been named "assured". The only assurance is that the landlord can recover possession and can charge rents close to market rents.

2. Assured agricultural occupancies

(a) Background

The way in which agricultural workers may have security of tenure and rent regulation under the Rent (Agriculture) Act 1976 was explained in Chapter 2. Tenants enjoying this protection on 15 January 1989 will continue to be regulated by the 1976 Act. With limited exceptions, no new tenancies can be created that will be protected under the 1976 Act.

In its consultative document on the private sector, the Government explained that new "agricultural occupancies" will be offered in the case of new tenancies granted to agricultural workers. The grounds for possession will be "broadly the same as those of the main assured tenancy regime" (paragraph 31).

(b) Definition of an assured agricultural occupancy

The definition of an assured agricultural occupancy is contained in s 24 of the 1988 Act. Both tenancies and contractual licences are covered. There are two elements to the s 24 definition:

(i) the arrangement must fall within the description in s 24(2); and
(ii) the agricultural worker condition must be satisfied (s 24(1)).

The types of arrangement that come within the s 24 definition are:

(i) an assured, but not an assured shorthold, let;
(ii) a tenancy that would be assured if it were not excluded because it is a let at a low rent; thus a tenancy at a low rent can be an assured occupancy;
(iii) where the tenant also has an agricultural let under the Agricultural Holdings Act 1986;
(iv) a tenancy where the factors just mentioned both apply;
(v) a licence under which the worker has exclusive occupation of premises which are a separate dwelling and would otherwise be a tenancy under any of the arrangements just described.

Thus contractual licences as well as tenancies can be agricultural occupancies (similarly some licensees can be secure tenants under the Housing Act 1985). However, in light of the decisions in *Antoniades* v *Villiers* (1988) and *AG Securities* v *Vaughan* (1988), which were considered in Chapter 3 (see pages 45 to 48), this last category may not be of much practical importance. If exclusive occupation is granted, at a term and for a rent, this will usually create a tenancy and not a licence.

Under the second element in the definition, the worker must

satisfy the "agricultural worker condition" under the provisions set out in Sch 3 of the 1988 Act. This schedule borrows much of the phraseology from the 1976 Act and as a result, it has to be read in conjunction with the 1976 provisions. Space does not permit a full description of these complicated rules (on the 1976 provisions, see Evans: *The Law of Landlord and Tenant*, 2nd ed, 1985, pages 308 to 314). The main feature of this condition is that the worker has to undertake defined agricultural work for minimum hours over a minimum number of weeks each year. However, the strict hours condition is relaxed where the tenant is unable to work because of an accident or disease contracted at work (para 2, Sch 3 of the 1988 Act). This condition may also be fulfilled if the premises are occupied by a deceased tenant's widow (or widower as the case may be) or another member of his family providing the deceased was fulfilling the agricultural worker condition at the time of his death (para 3, Sch 3 of the 1988 Act).

Where an agricultural worker lives in premises and fulfils the two basic conditions, a modified form of an assured tenancy applies (s 24(3)). The rent may be referred to a rent assessment committee in the same limited circumstances as apply to assured tenants (s 24(4)). He will have security of tenure under Part I of the 1988 Act. If he was granted a fixed term, a statutory periodic tenancy comes into existence at the end of the term if there is no further grant of an assured let to him. He will hold under this statutory periodic tenancy so long as he fulfils the agricultural worker condition (s 25(1)(a)).

The grounds for possession contained in Sch 2 of the Act apply, with the exception of ground 16. Thus the fact that the tenancy was granted in consequence of his employment does not give the landlord grounds for possession. Moreover, if a tenant terminates his employment, his notice does not of itself constitute a notice to quit the occupancy (s 24(4)).

Chapter 6

Harassment and illegal eviction

1. Background

The Government acknowledged that de-regulating private rentals might tempt some landlords to harass or evict protected and other existing tenants in order to "obtain vacant possession and to re-let at higher rents" (*Housing: The Government's Proposals* Cmnd 214, 1987, paragraph 3.17). This happened after the Rent Act 1957, when many tenants were driven from their homes (Holman: *Housing Policy in Britain* 1987, pages 419 to 420).

In order to deter harassment and illegal evictions, the criminal sanctions in the Protection From Eviction Act 1977 are tightened up. However the requirement that a landlord obtains a court order before evicting a tenant is removed in the case of many new lets by resident landlords as well as holiday lets and hostel lets.

The civil law is also strengthened by the creation of a new civil remedy coupled with a new statutory measure of damages where a tenant has been unlawfully evicted.

The Act also creates a new criminal offence and it makes changes to the 1977 Act provisions governing rent books.

2. Possession orders

In 1964, provisions (The Protection From Eviction Act 1964) were introduced to deter harassment and illegal eviction following a Labour Government's announcement that it planned to introduce a new Rent Act. In Part III of the Rent Act 1965 offences relating to harassment and illegal eviction were created. These, and a provision governing rent books in the Rent Act

1957, were consolidated in the Protection From Eviction Act 1977. The 1977 Act was amended by the Housing Act 1980.

(a) Requirement for court orders

Section 2 of the 1977 Act provides that a forfeiture clause cannot be enforced except by court order so long as the premises are occupied. This protects a tenant who is outside the Rent Acts or, now, a tenant outside Part I of the Housing Act 1988. In the case of a protected tenant forfeiture does not of itself end the tenant's rights. The landlord must seek possession on one or other of the grounds in Sch 15 of the Rent Act 1977. A forfeiture clause in an assured tenancy can only be enforced by court order (see Chapters 3 and 4). Forfeiture proceedings against a secure tenant do not of themselves give the landlord possession, which must be sought under one or more of the grounds in Sch 2 of the Housing Act 1985.

Under s 3 of the Protection From Eviction Act 1977, a court order must be obtained before evicting certain occupiers who are not statutorily protected. For example a court order must be sought before evicting a holder of a restricted contract. In addition, s 3 applies to service licensees who have exclusive possession of premises and a licensee who has a restricted contract. Finally, a court order must be obtained following the death of a statutory tenant when there is no statutory tenant by succession.

To summarise, tenants who are statutorily protected by the Rent Act 1977, the Housing Act 1985 or the Housing Act 1988 cannot be evicted otherwise than by court order. This is because their tenancies can only be ended in the manner prescribed by the legislation and by court proceedings. Many occupants who fall outside these various codes of statutory protection cannot be evicted without court order (ss 2 and 3 of the Protection From Eviction Act 1977).

The Housing Act 1988 makes two changes to this:

(a) it takes away the requirement of obtaining a court order from several classes of occupation (called "excluded tenancies" and "excluded licences"); and

(b) it extends the protection of the 1977 Act to additional categories of licensee.

(b) Excluded tenancies and excluded licences

Section 31 of the Housing Act amends the Protection From Eviction Act 1977. Under s 3 of the 1977 Act, the prohibition on eviction without court order does not apply to a "statutorily protected tenancy". As explained above, the reason for this is that a court order must be obtained before the statutory protection can be terminated. This reference is replaced by a reference to a statutorily protected tenancy *or an excluded tenancy or licence* (s 3(1)). In addition a new s 3A is inserted into the 1977 Act which sets out the various categories of excluded tenancy and licence. Thus in any of these cases the s 3 requirement that a court order be obtained is removed.

The various types of excluded tenancy and licence are now considered in turn.

Sharing with a landlord or licensor: under what is now s 3A(2) of the 1977 Act, a tenancy or a licence is excluded if:

(i) under its terms the occupier shares any accommodation with the landlord or licensor (as the case may be); *and*

(ii) immediately before the start and at the end of the tenancy (or licence) the landlord (or licensor) lived in another part of the building as his only or principal home.

"Accommodation" does not include a staircase, passage, corridor or other means of access or an area used for storage (s 3A(5)(a) of the 1977 Act). However, subject to these limited exceptions the sharing of any accommodation will make these tenancies or licences excluded. In other words, it is not limited to living accommodation. Thus, sharing a bathroom or toilet brings the occupier into this excluded category. Sharing of accommodation means that the occupier has "the use of it" in common with others and where there are joint landlords (or licensors), sharing with one of them makes an occupier "excluded" (s 3A(4)).

Sharing with a member of a resident landlord's or licensor's family: Under s 3A(3) a tenant or licensee is also excluded in the following circumstances:

(i) where, under the terms of the agreement, he shares with a member of the landlord's (or licensor's) family; *and*

(ii) this family member occupied another part of the building as his only or principal home both at the beginning and at the end of the occupant's agreement; *and*

(iii) the landlord (or licensor) also occupied another part of the building as his only or principal home, both at the beginning and at the end of the agreement.

The expression "member of the family" is given the same meaning as in s 113 of the Housing Act 1985 (s 3A(5)). This is a wide definition, covering a spouse (or someone living with another as a spouse), parent, grandparent, child, grandchild, brother, sister, uncle, aunt, nephew or niece and a stepchild.

The expression "accommodation" was explained above.

Trespassers: Where a person entered the premises as a trespasser, any tenancy or licence granted to him subsequently is excluded if it was granted as a temporary expedient. This applies not only to an agreement in relation to the premises he originally entered as a trespasser, but to any other premises (s 3A(6)).

Holiday lets: A holiday let (or licence) cannot be an assured (or an assured shorthold) let (para 9, Sch 1 of the Housing Act 1988). It is also excluded. As remarked in Chapter 3, holiday lets were often abused under the Rent Acts. Removing the requirement that a possession order be obtained removes one opportunity for a tenant to try to demonstrate that a holiday let agreement is bogus.

The reference here is to a "holiday let" (s 3A(7) of the Protection From Eviction Act 1977), *not* an out of season let. In the latter case, a landlord must obtain a court order to recover possession (he has a mandatory claim for possession under ground 3 of Sch 2 of the Housing Act 1988).

This excluded category also includes a let or a licence which was granted "otherwise than for money or money's worth" (s 3A(7)(b)). Thus a gratuitous let or licence is also excluded.

Local authority and other hostel accommodation: Where the occupier has a licence and is living in a hostel, he is also excluded (s 3A(8)). This applies to hostel accommodation provided by local authorities, a development corporation, a New Town, an urban development corporation, a housing action trust, the Development Board for Wales, the Housing Corporation or Housing for Wales and a housing trust. In addition, the Secretary of State is empowered to introduce further categories. This must be done by a statutory instrument subject to annulment by a resolution of either House of Parliament (s 3A(9)).

(c) Extension of the possession order requirement

The previous paragraph dealt with cases where the possession order requirement is *removed*. However, this requirement is also extended in some cases.

As explained above, s 2 of the 1977 Act provides that a right of re-entry or forfeiture cannot be enforced otherwise than by court order. The Housing Act 1980 extended this requirement to a licence that is a restricted contract. It did this by inserting a new subs (2A) into s 3 of The Protection From Eviction Act 1977.

This is taken a stage further by s 30 of the Housing Act 1988. It inserts new subss (2B) and (2C) into The Protection From Eviction Act 1977. Under subss (2B) and (2C) the possession order requirement is extended to *any* licence other than one that is an excluded licence, provided the licence was created after the date of commencement, that is 15 January 1989. However, given the relatively narrow scope of genuine contractual licences and the width of the excluded categories, this extension, although important, may be of limited practical significance.

(d) Summary of the possession order requirements

(i) If the tenant is a protected tenant, a secure tenant, an assured or assured shorthold tenant, the landlord must obtain a court order before recovering possession.

(ii) If an agreement contains a re-entry or a forfeiture clause, this cannot be enforced without a court order.

(iii) A holder of a restricted contract cannot be evicted without a court order. This is so whether he has a tenancy or a contractual licence.

(ii) A court order must also be obtained in the case of other licences, other than excluded licences.

(v) In the case of excluded tenancies and licences, the court order requirement does not apply if the tenancy or licence was entered into *after* 15 January 1989. These excluded categories are –

- sharing with the landlord or licensor,
- sharing with a member of the landlord or licensor's family,
- a let or licence granted to a former trespasser,
- a holiday let or licence or an agreement where the occupier has not given consideration,

- local authority and other hostel accommodation.

The Government justifies the removal of the possession order requirement, arguing that it will encourage more lettings and that it will make the use of hostel accommodation more workable. It was stated during the Report Stage that "we want to encourage resident landlords properly to use their property and to let spare accommodation. We know that they will not do that if it means sharing with someone they cannot easily remove if relations deteriorate" (Hansard, 9 June 1988, column 1091).

Nevertheless, a prudent landlord will seek a possession order. Eviction without process of law can quite easily involve the landlord in unpleasant civil and criminal disputes. For example, it is an offence to use or threaten violence for the purposes of securing entry to premises (s 6 Criminal Law Act 1977). Theatening behaviour and other public order offences might be involved. Some of these offences under the Public Order Act 1986 can be committed in private as well as in public (see Driscoll: *Protest and Public Order*, (1987) Journal of Social Welfare Law).

3. Offences of harassment

Under s 1 of the Protection From Eviction Act 1977 it is an offence to unlawfully evict or to harass a "residential occupier". Section 29 of the Housing Act 1988 strengthens these offences and introduces a new harassment offence.

It is an offence to deprive a residential occupier of his occupation or to attempt to do so (s 1(2) of the 1977 Act). There is a defence available if the landlord, or others acting on his behalf, believed, on reasonable grounds, that the occupier had ceased to reside in the premises.

It is also an offence if any person, intending the occupier to leave or to refrain from exercising his rights, does acts calculated to interfere with the occupier's peace or comfort, or that of his family, or persistently withdraws or withholds services reasonably required for occupation of the premises (s 1(3) of the 1977 Act). This offence is often difficult to prosecute because of the very specific intent that has to be proved. The courts have emphasised that a positive intent to cause the occupier to leave etc. must be proved by the prosecutor (Ormrod J. in *McCall* v *Abelesz* (1976)).

The definition of the s 1(3) offence is strengthened by replacing the word "calculated" with the word "likely" (s 29(1) Housing Act 1988). Thus in relation to any prosecution under s 1(3) after 15 January 1989, it must be proved that (say) the landlord, intending the occupier to leave etc., did acts that were *likely* to result in the occupier's leaving or refraining from exercising his rights. It must still be proved that the landlord had the specific *intent*. If there is any doubt about this issue, the new offence created by s 29 of the 1988 Act may be used.

Section 29 inserts a new subs (3A) into s 1 of the 1977 Act. Under what is now s 1(3A) of the 1977 Act, the landlord or his agent commits an offence if he does any act of the type described in s 1(3). As already noted, these are acts interfering with the occupier's peace and comfort or the withholding of services. The difference with the s 1 (3A) offence is in the type of "intent" that has to be proved. Here the prosecutor must prove that the landlord (or his agent) either:

(i) knew; or

(ii) had reasonable cause to believe,

that his conduct was likely to cause the occupier to leave or refrain from exercising his rights.

The s 1 offences serve to protect a "residential occupier" who is defined in s 1(1) as a person occupying premises as a residence whether under a contract, any enactment or rule of law that gives him the right to occupy, or any restriction on the landlord's right to recover possession. It covers the following categories:

(i) an ordinary contractual tenancy or licence;

(ii) a restricted contract;

(iii) a statutory or statutory periodic tenant;

(iv) a tenant or licensee who is protected by s 3 of the 1977 Act (as amended).

The primary responsibility for prosecuting offences under the 1977 Act rests with officers employed by local authorities (tenancy/harassment officers). There are considerable variations in the prosecuting policies of different local authorities and their officers. Some see their role as conciliators rather than as prosecutors (Arden: *Manual of Housing Law*, 3rd ed 1986, page 136). In practice it is the availability of civil remedies that is of most importance to occupiers.

4. Notices to quit

Under s 5 of the Protection From Eviction Act 1977, a notice to quit served by a landlord or by the tenant must be in writing and given not less than four weeks before the date on which it is to take effect. The notice must contain prescribed information, such as a statement of the tenant's rights (Notice to Quit (Prescribed Information) Regulations 1980; see page 412). This requirement is extended to licences, apart from excluded licences (see page 116), whether created before or after the commencement of the Act. Failure to comply with this statutory requirement invalidates the notice to quit. However the notice to quit requirement is removed from excluded tenancies created after 15 January 1989, unless entered into following a contract made before this date. These changes are made by s 32 of the 1988 Act which inserts new subs (1A) and (1B) into s 5 of the 1977 Act.

5. Civil remedies

An occupier who has been harassed or illegally evicted has a number of civil remedies that are independent of the 1988 Act. Indeed the new civil remedy in s 27 expressly states that it does not affect an occupier's right to enforce other remedies he may have, although he cannot be compensated twice for matters arising out of the same event (s 27(5)).

Where the occupier is a tenant, there is an implied covenant that the landlord will not disturb his quiet enjoyment of the premises (see, for example, Yates and Hawkins: *Landlord and Tenant Law* 2nd ed 1986, pages 128 to 130). A written agreement may contain express provision to this effect. This implied or express covenant applies to leases generally and it is not confined to harassment or illegal eviction in its residential setting. It provides an important course of action for harassed or dispossessed tenants. It is also a covenant that may be implied into contractual licences. In *Smith* v *Nottinghamshire County Council* (1981), it was held that it applied to students occupying a college hall of residence. It was a term of their contractual licence.

Examples of behaviour that is a breach of this covenant are banging on the tenant's door and shouting threats of physical eviction (*Kenny* v *Preen* (1963)); cutting off the gas and electricity supplies (*Perera* v *Vandiyar* (1953)); failure to pay the bills with the result that these supplies are disconnected (*McCall* v *Abelesez*

(1976)); and changing the locks and throwing out the tenant's belongings (*Drane* v *Evangelou* (1978)).

In addition to this liability, there is also an implied covenant that the landlord will not derogate from his grant (Yates and Hawkins, *ibid*). Again this may be the subject of an express term in the agreement. If for example, a landlord uses adjoining premises in such a way that it frustrates the tenant's residential use of his premises, the landlord is derogating from his grant to the tenant.

Breach of either of these covenants is a breach of contract. There may also be liability in tort. A landlord may commit a trespass if he enters premises occupied by a tenant without the tenant's consent. There may also be torts of assault and nuisance. However, if a landlord commits one of the offences under the Protection From Eviction Act 1977, this has been held not to create a civil remedy based on breach of statutory duty (*McCall* v *Abelesz* (1976)). An exception to this derives from *Warder* v *Cooper* (1970) when breach of what is now s 3 of the 1977 Act was held to amount to a civil breach of statutory duty. Thus harassment and illegal eviction lead to a number of possible causes of action in the case of both a tenancy and a licence.

The occupier can seek damages both for his actual losses and for his inconvenience and suffering. In a case of particularly egregious conduct on the part of the landlord, exemplary or aggravated damages may also be awarded. An example is where a landlord evicts in order to sell with vacant possession. With this kind of misconduct, it has been said that exemplary damages may be awarded "to teach a wrongdoer that tort does not pay" (*Rookes* v *Barnard* (1964)). These types of damages may only be awarded if a tort is proved.

An occupier may also need an injunction to restrain further harassment and/or to reinstate him in the premises. In an urgent case, an injunction may be granted on an *ex parte* application by the occupier (Arden, *op cit*, pages 137 to 139). If the landlord fails to comply with such an injunction, he would be in contempt of court and could face imprisonment and/or payment of a fine (see Driscoll: *Committal to Prison for Contempt of Court*, (1986) Legal Action).

6. New cause of action under s 27 Housing Act 1988

This new cause of action is retrospective and applies to any unlawful eviction after 9 June 1988 (the date of the first debate on the Report Stage of the Bill in the House of Commons). A landlord is liable to pay damages in two situations:

(a) where he unlawfully evicts a residential occupier; and
(b) where as a result of his harassment or attempted eviction, the occupier gives up possession.

The measure of damages is the difference in the value of the *whole* premises subject to the right to the occupancy and its value without the occupancy. Thus the measure of damages could be very considerable if (say) a protected tenant is evicted. However, damages cannot be awarded if the occupier is reinstated. Liability under s 27 is in the nature of a tort (s 27(4)(a)).

There are four matters to examine in considering s 27:

(a) the two types of eviction;
(b) defences to a s 27 claim;
(c) factors that may reduce the compensation; and
(d) which occupiers can bring a s 27 claim.

(a) Eviction

The first and most straightforward case is where the landlord "or any person acting on behalf of the landlord" unlawfully deprives an occupier of his occupation of part or all of the premises (s 27(1)). The second situation is where the occupier is driven into leaving or giving up part of the premises. Here evictions are actionable in two situations. First, where the landlord (or others acting on his behalf) attempts to evict unlawfully as a result of which the occupier leaves (s 27(2)(a)). The second situation is defined in a similar way to the new s 1(3A) offence inserted into the 1977 Act by s 29 of the 1988 Act. This, which was reviewed above (page 120), covers conduct that is likely to cause the occupier to leave or to refrain from exercising his rights. If this is done by interfering with the occupier's peace or comfort (or that of his family) or the persistent withholding or withdrawal of services, it is actionable if the landlord knew or had reasonable cause to believe that the occupier would leave or refrain from exercising his rights. Again it must be shown that as a consequence the occupier left the premises. This connotes an element of causation. However where the offending behaviour and state of mind of the landlord is proved, it should not be difficult to establish a link between this and the occupier's leaving.

(b) Defences

There are three defences to a s 27 claim.

The first is that the occupier was reinstated in the premises before the date on which the s 27 proceedings were finally disposed of (s 27(6)(a)). For these purposes, proceedings are finally disposed of when they come to an end, or, where there has been an appeal, when the appeal is determined and the time for any further appeal has passed (s 27(6)). If an appeal is abandoned, the relevant time is the date of abandonment (ibid).

The second is where the tenant has been reinstated following a successful application for an order that he be allowed back into the premises (s 27(6)(b)). The difficulty with this is that many dispossessed occupiers may be reluctant to return. They may also be reluctant to apply for an order if advised that this will prevent them from bringing a s 27 claim. Hence a landlord has a defence if he reinstates the occupier. What is the position if he offers to reinstate and the occupier declines the offer? This is one of the mitigating factors that are covered in the next section (see below).

The third is where the landlord proves that he believed *and* had reasonable cause to believe either:

(i) that the occupier had left the premises *or*

(ii) in a case where he did acts or withdrew services, that he had reasonable grounds for doing so (s 27(8)).

The onus of proof lies with the landlord who must establish not only his belief but also that there was a reasonable basis for it. Thus it must be a belief based on objectively reasonable grounds.

(c) Factors that may reduce compensation

A court may reduce damages under s 27 for two reasons.

First, where *before* proceedings were begun, the landlord offered to reinstate the occupier *and* it was either unreasonable of the occupier to refuse the offer; *or* if he obtained other accommodation before the offer was made, it would have been unreasonable to refuse the offer had he not obtained the other accommodation. It is left to the courts to decide whether the refusal is unreasonable, since there is no definition of this expression. Much will depend on the nature of the landlord's misconduct and the general relationship between the parties. The more egregious the misconduct, the less likely it is that the occupier is being unreasonable in refusing an offer of reinstatement in the premises.

The second factor that might reduce damages is where the conduct of the occupier "or any person living with him" is such that it is reasonable to mitigate the damages (s 27(7)(a)). This covers conduct that occurred before the events that led the occupier to leave. It is an open-ended definition and again it is left to the courts to assess the occupier's conduct and its relationship with the eviction. In a sense the courts are required to assess whether the landlord was provoked into acting in the way that he did. This mitigating factor is not on the face of it limited to a breach of the agreement, although it would be harsh to penalise an occupier for behaviour that is not a breach of the agreement. This provision will cause uncertainty and it is doubtful if it is needed. If a landlord has a legitimate grievance, he could bring a counterclaim in the occupier's proceedings.

(d) The measure of damages

Measure of damages is dealt with in s 28 and is based on the profit the landlord has made in unlawfully evicting the tenant, in terms of difference in the value of the landlord's interest in the premises subject to the right to occupy, and its value free of this right. The valuation is to be made at the time immediately before the occupier left (s 28(1)). The valuation is of the landlord's interest in the *whole* of the building. Thus in the case of flat, the measure of damages is based on the value of the building subject to the tenancy (or licence) of the flat compared with the value of the building without this tenanted flat.

The valuation is to be made on the following assumptions:

(i) that the landlord is selling to a willing buyer on the open market;

(ii) that neither the occupier nor any member of his family is willing to buy;

(iii) that is unlawful to carry out substantial development or a demolition of the building (s 28(2)).

Thus it is the market value of the building that is to be assessed, ignoring the possibility that the occupier or any family member might have been willing to buy ("family member" has the same meaning as for the purposes of the "excluded" categories; see page 116). Thus its value is not to be deflated because of any element of a possible sale to a sitting tenant. The effect of assumption (iii) above is that any development value of the building is to be ignored—the tenant will not recover its development value. A development for this purpose is one that requires planning permission. A development under a general development order or a change of use is excluded (s 28(6)). It is possible that a landlord might be tempted to evict where a building has substantial development value, in the knowledge that he, not the tenant, will realise its development value. This, however, would be the type of case where a court could award exemplary damages. If a protected tenant is evicted and the landlord stands to make a large profit, damages could be very high.

(e) Summary

If a landlord evicts or causes an occupier to leave, the displaced occupier has a statutory cause of action. Subject to certain defences, he can claim damages equal to the profit the landlord has made in evicting him. Damages may be reduced because of the occupier's own conduct (or that of someone living with him) or where the occupier unreasonably refused an offer of reinstatement made before proceedings were started. A claim may be brought under s 27 as well as under other causes of action that the occupier may have in contract and in tort. The statutory s 27 claim will be most relevant where a statutorily protected tenant has been evicted. Where an unprotected tenant or licensee is unlawfully evicted, it is unlikely that a large award can be made under ss 27 and 28. Their occupation may not significantly affect the value of the premises.

Chapter 7

Housing associations

Although housing associations have a major role in the Government's plans for the private rented sector, there is relatively little in the 1988 Act that addresses them directly. They will continue to be regulated by the general body of law that deals with housing associations. However Part II of the Act gives effect to Government's desire to see housing associations raising more money from the private sector. Part II of the Act also increases some of the powers of housing associations, and a separate Housing Corporation is established for Wales. These matters are best understood by first examining the general background of housing associations.

1. Background

(a) The growth of housing associations

The origins of these associations lie in the voluntary housing movement which gathered strength in the nineteenth century (Burnett: *A Social History of Housing*, 1986). A combination of charitable bodies, philanthropic associations and co-operative associations led to the movement's being poised to become a major force at the opening of the twentieth century. Although the voluntary housing movement became very important in other European countries, it was overshadowed in Britain by the vast extension of municipal housing (Birchall: *Building Communities The Co-operative Way*, 1988, Chapter 4).

Since the 1960's, successive governments have encouraged the expansion of housing associations by financial and other means.

The Housing Corporation was set up in 1964 to register associations, administer grants and generally to supervise and control them. Housing associations will continue to expand as council housing declines.

However, at present housing associations house approximately 3% of households only (*Inquiry Into British Housing* 1985, page 23). There are more than 4,500 associations (Hughes: *Public Sector Housing Law*, 2nd ed 1987, page 39). In 1988 there were 2,665 housing associations registered with the Housing Corporation (Annual Report 1987/88 page 24). A housing association must register with the Corporation if it is to receive public funds.

Housing associations vary considerably in their size and legal arrangements; 80% have fewer than 250 units of accommodation. They exist on the whole to provide housing for people on low incomes and those with special needs. Approximately 30% of lettings are to the elderly; 16% to young single people; and 10% to single parent families. Housing association tenants are predominately people on low incomes or in receipt of benefits (Hughes, ibid).

(b) Legal regulation of housing associations

Housing associations are subject to the general framework of relevant areas of law. They operate within the areas of public law, landlord and tenant law and property law, as well as the law governing charities, taxation and companies.

The only legislation that deals specifically with housing associations is the Housing Associations Act 1985. This has already been amended by the Housing and Planning Act 1986. It is amended further by the Housing Act 1988 and these changes are addressed in the second part of this chapter. The 1985 Act (as amended) is primarily concerned with financial matters and Government controls.

It has been remarked that "in two senses . . . there is a body of special 'housing association law'" (Alder & Handy: *Housing Association Law*, 1987, page 7). First, an association will fall into a particular category such as a charitable or a fully mutual association. It is then entitled to benefits, privileges and immunities flowing from its status. Second, an association may be eligible for registration with the Housing Corporation. If it is registered it is eligible for grants. It will also be regulated by the Corporation.

The definition of a housing association appears in s 1(1) of the Housing Associations Act 1985. It has three elements:

(i) First, it may consist of a "society, body of trustees or company" (ibid). The term "society" is not defined. It could be an unincorporated association. In practice however, most associations seek incorporation as a society under the Industrial and Provident Societies Act 1965 (Alder & Handy *op cit*, page 12). Some of the older established associations take the form of a trust, having been established by sums of money donated for charitable purposes. In rare cases an association may be registered as a company.

(ii) Second, associations are prohibited from trading for a profit, or if they do, they must not pay interest or dividends above a rate prescribed by the Government. Payment of excessive dividends will endanger an association's status under the 1965 Act. It may also prejudice its eligibility to receive grants from the Housing Coporation (Alder & Handy, *op cit*, page 14). The word "profit" must be distinguished from surplus funds at the end of any particular accounting period. A surplus will only be treated as a profit if it is used for something other than its housing objectives, such as payment of the surplus to its members.

(iii) Third, its "purposes" must be providing, constructing, improving or managing, or facilitating or encouraging the construction or improvement of, housing accommodation (s 1(1)). An association may have other objects as well, but it must have at least one of these objects if it is to qualify as a housing association (Alder & Handy, *op cit*, page 14).

The relationship between an association and its tenants may also be statutorily regulated. As noted in Chapter 2, many tenants enjoy the secure status under Part IV of the Housing Act 1985. A smaller number are protected under the Rent Act 1977. However with limited exceptions, all tenancies granted after 15 January 1989 will be assured lets. Although they are publicly funded and centrally regulated, housing associations are still regarded as part of the private rented sector. For example, in *Peabody Housing Association* v *Green* (1978) it was held that the public law concepts of "fairness" and "reasonableness" do not apply to an association's decision to evict tenants. The Government also considers housing associations to be part of the private sector (*Housing: the Government's Proposals*, 1987 Cm 214, chapter 4). However, when viewed from their social, economic and administrative perspectives, housing associations "are closely connected with the public sector" (Alder & Handy, *op cit*, page 10).

(c) Other forms of regulation

Since Central Government provides most of the public funds payable to housing associations, it obviously exerts considerable influence over their operations and development. It also has powers to lay down accounting standards and certain matters requiring Government approval (Alder & Handy, *op cit*, pages 150 to 151). In addition, the Government issues circulars to guide the Housing Corporation in the manner in which it should carry out its functions.

Most of the work in regulating housing associations is carried out by the Housing Corporation. Its powers and duties are laid down by the Housing Associations Act 1985 (as amended). Apart from its general duty to promote the voluntary housing movement, it has the important responsibilities of registration of, administering grants and loans to, and the supervision of, registered associations. It has a wide discretion in the way it exercises its powers and its decisions are not usually subject to any right of appeal. It has been remarked that "it acts in relation to housing associations as promoter, banker, policeman, judge and executioner rolled into one" (*ibid*, page 151). However many of its decisions are subject to judicial review and there is some scrutiny by Parliament (*ibid*, pages 152 to 153).

The Corporation is given additional functions under Part IV of the Housing Act 1988. These are considered in Chapters 10 and 11. Apart from the Housing Corporation, there is supervision by the Registrar of Friendly Societies where an association has been incorporated under the 1965 Act or by the Charity Commissioners in the case of a charitable association. Local authorities also have responsibilities to promote and fund housing associations under the Housing Act 1985. In practice there is a good deal of liaison between local authorities and housing associations (*ibid*, pages 175 to 180).

(d) The funding of housing associations

Apart from its power to make loans, the Housing Corporation may pay grants to housing associations ("housing association grant"). The grant is calculated on the difference between the amount of a mortgage loan that can be repaid out of rental income and the approved costs of an association's project (Part II Housing Associations Act 1985). For example, an association wishing to purchase and renovate a property in order to rent it, will usually receive a loan from the Corporation. Once the project is completed, grants are payable and used to repay part of the loan (Alder & Handy, *op cit*, page 211).

Central Government can also make grants direct to housing associations. For example, it can pay a "revenue deficit grant". As the name implies, this grant assists an association that faces a deficit in its revenue account. A similar grant is available to an association that provides hostel accommodation (a "hostel deficit grant").

If a housing association has received a grant it must set up a "grant redemption fund". An association may receive greater rental income as a result of renovating or purchasing properties to rent. The purpose of the grant redemption fund is to account for the increased rental income from the properties that were the subject of a grant. Associations may be required to pay surplus rental income to the Department of the Environment, who may use it as part of its fund allocation to the Housing Corporation (Alder & Handy, *op cit*, page 219).

2. The Government's proposals

In its consultative document *Finance for Housing Associations*, which was published in September 1987, the Government stated that it wants housing associations to "increase the volume of rented housing . . . for any given level of public expenditure" and to "deliver their services in the most cost-effective manner" (paragraph 2). As previously noted, all new lets will be assured lets. Although rents will rise, the Government does not expect housing associations to charge "profit rents" (*ibid*, paragraph 4). Hence rents for housing association lets should be below market rents, enabling associations to cater for tenants on low incomes and for tenants with special needs. Existing tenants (that is secure and protected tenants as at 15 January 1989) will continue to have their rents regulated by the fair rent provisions of the Rent Act 1977. However, the system of phasing in a rent increase under the Rent Act 1977 has been abolished by the 1988 Act (see Chapter 2). This was also announced in the consultative document paragraph 5).

The Government also expects housing associations to increase the amount of funding they receive from the private sector. This obviously carries implications for the grant system and for rents. At a national level the Government will negotiate an "appropriate annual fund of mixed funding" with the Housing Corporation (paragraph 9). An assumption will be made that private finance "would be raised on a low start or indexed basis".

Under the existing system, housing association grants are influenced by fair rent regulation, since their rental income influences the amount of expenditure they can undertake. This too will change as housing associations acquire discretion in fixing rents with the introduction of assured lets. Tenants will continue to be eligible for housing benefit and the new rents are to be "significantly below the free market level" (*ibid*, paragraph 14). Another result is that revenue deficit will be gradually phased out (*ibid*, paragraphs 22 to 24).

The Government also wants the Housing Corporation to take on new functions. Its new responsibility for administering the change of landlord provisions is considered in Chapters 10 and 11. In the context of housing associations, the Government plans to transfer its own grant-making responsibilities, including the revenue deficit grants and the powers to recover grants. This is part of the Government's policy of transferring executive functions from its departments under its "financial management initiative" (*ibid*, paragraph 29).

This summarises the proposals for changes in funding and administration. In addition the Government wants to broaden the powers of housing associations. These are currently specified in s 4 of the Housing Associations Act 1985 which contains the rules of eligibility for registration with the Housing Corporation. The Government believes that these rules are too restrictive. It gives as an example housing associations' inability to deal commercially with shops below flats (*ibid*, paragraph 33). Moreover, associations should be empowered to convert derelict commercial units into small shops or workshops. However these powers will be ancillary or incidental to the main function of providing rented housing. Thus these additional functions will not be publicly funded: "the units must be disposed of or let on commercial terms and must pay their own way (*ibid*, paragraph 35).

3. Changes introduced by the Housing Act 1988

(a) Separate Housing Corporation for Wales

Under s 46 of the Act, a separate body is established for Wales. It is to be known as "Housing for Wales" (s 46(1)). Details of its constitution and related matters are set out in Sch 5 to the Act (s 46(2)). These are modelled on and resemble those governing the Housing Corporation under Sch 6 of the Housing Associations Act 1985.

Appointment of the members, chair and deputy chair of Housing for Wales will be a matter for the Secretary of State (paras 2, 3 and 4, Sch 5 of the 1988 Act). Their remuneration and pension entitlement will also be matters for the Secretary of State subject to Treasury consent (paras 5 and 6, Sch 5). Subject to Government approval, a chief executive will be appointed and provision is also made for the appointment of staff, including transfer from the Housing Corporation of staff who are responsible for the Corporation's functions in Wales (paras 7 to 11, Sch 5).

Once established, all property held by the Housing Corporation in Wales will be transferred to Housing for Wales. Housing associations which are registered with the Housing Corporation and whose registered office is in Wales, and charitable associations which have a Welsh address for the purposes of registration by the Charity Commissioners in Wales (s 47(1)), are transferred to Housing for Wales.

There was nothing on this in the White Paper, the consultative papers or in the original Bill. These provisions were introduced at the Commons Report Stage of the Bill. Although they are not controversial, they were not scrutinsed during the committee stage in the Commons.

Housing for Wales became a corporate body on 1 December 1988 (The Housing Act 1988 (Commencement No 1) Order 1988).

(b) Changes to the functions and powers of the Housing Corporation and Housing for Wales

A number of grant functions are to be given to the two Corporations. Under s 50 of the 1988 Act, they are given responsibility for the making of grants. The procedures involved, including methods of calculation, will be left to the Corporations (s 50(2), (3)). These functions may (with Government approval) be delegated to a local housing authority which would be acting as agent for the relevant Corporation (s 50(4), (5)). Under s 51 the responsibility for administering revenue deficit grants is transferred to the two Corporations. Again it is left to the Corporations to develop the principles on which these grants are calculated (s 51(2)).

Central government had powers to reduce, suspend, cancel or recover grants from housing associations under s 52 of the Housing Associations Act 1985. For example if a condition imposed on the making of a grant has not been complied with, the Secretary of State may reduce, suspend, cancel or recover the grant as the case may be (s 52(2) of the 1985 Act). These powers are also transferred to the Corporations by s 52. When negotiating grants with housing associations, the Corporations may make general determinations as to such matters as conditions and levels of grants (s 53). These decisions must be preceded by consultation with "bodies appearing to it to be representative of housing associations" and the decisions must be published (s 53(3)). Approval and consent must be sought from the Secretary of State and the Treasury (s 53(2)).

Other Central Government functions may also be transferred to the Corporations under s 57 of the 1988 Act. These are the Secretary of State's powers under ss 54 and 55 of the 1988 Act, relating to tax relief grants and surplus rental income (see below). The Secretary of State may also transfer a number of powers under ss 53, 54, to 57, 62 and parts 1 and 2 of Sch 5 of the 1985 Act. In summary these relate to recovery of surplus rental income, deficit grants, grants for obtaining tax reliefs and residual subsidies.

In addition to these financial matters, the general functions of the Corporations are expanded. Section 75 of the 1985 Act, which sets out the general functions of the Corporations, is amended by s 56 of the Housing Act 1988. As a result the Corporations will be under a statutory duty to promote and improve race relations. This duty, which applies to local authorities under s 85 of the Race Relations Act 1976, is extended to the Corporations.

Section 36 of the Housing Associations Act 1985 specifies Government functions with respect to legal proceedings applying to property held by housing trusts. This section is amended by s 49 of the Housing Act 1988. It inserts a new s 36(A) into the 1985 Act. This new section empowers the Corporations to promulgate guidance to housing associations concerning the management of their housing accommodation. The guidelines must be approved by the Secretary of State, as must any subsequent revisions (new s 36(A) of the 1985 Act). As with the general determination of grants, the Corporations must consult representatives of housing associations (new s 36(A) of the 1985 Act). These guidelines are of major importance, since they deal with the nature of the housing demands for which associations will make provision and their policies for allocation of tenancies. They will also cover the terms of new tenancies, rent levels, standards of repair and maintenance and consultation and communication with tenants (new s 36(A) of the 1985 Act). The guidelines on tenancy agreements are considered below; see pages 137–141.

(c) Changes to the powers of housing associations

Section 48 of the 1988 Act gives effect to the Government's plan to expand the powers of individual housing associations. It does this by amending s 4 of the Housing Associations Act 1985. Under s 4(3) and (4) of the 1985 Act the scope of permissible housing association activities is particularised for the purposes of eligibility for registration with the Corporations. These subsections are replaced and s 48 inserts new subss (3) and (4) into s 4 of the 1985 Act. Examples of these new powers are the power to acquire commercial premises as an incidental part of a housing association's projects (new s 4(4)(a)). Housing associations will also be empowered to repair, improve or convert commercial premises and to carry on for a limited period any business it acquires (new s 4(4)(b)). The Secretary of State may add to these new purposes, objects and powers (s 48(2) of the 1988 Act). This may be done by the laying of a statutory instrument subject to annulment by resolution of either of the Houses of Parliament (s 48(4) of the 1988 Act).

There is one change to certain housing associations that was not canvassed in the consultative paper. It affects the right to buy. Schedule 5 of the Housing Act 1985 sets out various exceptional cases where a secure tenant cannot exercise this right. Under the first exception, a tenant cannot exercise the right to buy if his landlord is either a housing trust or a charitable housing association. Section 58 of the Housing Act 1988 concerns a tenant who lives in a "publicly-funded" house and who does not have a right to buy because his landlord falls into one of the categories listed in the first exception mentioned above. A house is "publicly funded" under s 58 if certain grants were paid for a project which included its purchase; purchase of a building which was converted into this house; or of land and the construction of the house (s 58(2)). The relevant grants are those under s 50 of the 1988 Act, namely those administered by the Corporations, and under s 41 of the Housing Associations Act 1985 (or under the corresponding section in earlier legislation). This is a reference to the pre-1988 Act system before transfer of Central Government grant functions to the Corporations. Although the tenant does not have the right to buy, his landlord might decide to offer the property to him. If it does, a number of provisions in the Housing Associations Act 1985 apply to such a sale. They include the need to secure consent of the Corporations, the Corporation's power to lend money for this purchase and matters affecting the discount available to a secure tenant. What s 58 of the 1988 Act does is to extend these procedures to a case where a housing association of the sort described above enters into a contract to buy a property and sells if at a discount to the tenant (s 58(3), (4)). Without this section a housing trust or a charitable housing association could dispose of a house in this way and avoid regulation by the 1985 Act.

(d) Changes to the grant functions of the Secretary of State

The transfer of many of the Secretary of State's grant functions were explained in (*b*) above. There are two other matters to consider. The first is a reformation of the Secretary of State's power to give "tax relief grants". Many housing associations other than charities are treated for most tax purposes in the same way as private landlords. However, since 1965, their tax disabilities have been recognised by a power to pay to them the amount of income or corporation tax for which they are liable. This is in recognition of their role as non-profit making organisations (Alder & Handy, *op cit*, pages 189 to 190).

This power is now contained in s 54 of the 1988 Act. Broadly speaking, a tax relief grant may be paid to a registered non-profit making housing association which has been providing housing for rent and incidental matters (s 54(1), (21).

The second matter relates to surplus rental income. Section 55 reformulates the statutory requirements relating to this. Grant aided associations must keep separate accounts relating to any increase in their rental income flowing from a grant-aided activity which leaves them with a surplus (s 55(1)). These surpluses are to be kept in a "rent surplus fund" (s 55(2)). However, it is for the Secretary of State to determine the method of calculation of the surplus. The factors and assumptions that can lie behind this calculation were explained earlier in this chapter (see page 129). Amongst other matters, the Secretary of State is to consult representatives of housing associations as to the manner in which he reaches decisions on the calculation of surplus rental income (s 55(5)). He can require an association to pay (with interest) any sums standing in the rent surplus fund at the end of the relevant accounting period (s 55(6), (7)). To carry out this task the Secretary of State may require an association to furnish him with information (s 55(9)).

Both of these functions (in ss 54 and 55) may be transferred to the Corporations under the procedure in s 57 (see page 134).

(e) Other changes to the Housing Act 1985

Other changes to the 1985 Act are listed in Sch 6 to the 1988 Act. Many of these changes are in consequence of the creation of Housing for Wales. Thus various amendments are made to the 1985 Act to ensure that references to the Housing Corporation include a reference to Housing for Wales. Other changes are made in consequence of other relevant changes made by the 1988 Act. For example the 1985 Act is variously amended to include references to assured lettings and to the new provisions relating to grants.

4. Changes affecting housing association tenants

Changes to the position of tenants of housing associations were covered in Chapter 2 and are only briefly reviewed here. After 15 January 1989, all new housing association tenancies will have to be made on assured or assured shorthold lets. The expectation is that most new lets will be on an assured basis. The only exceptions are agreements made before this date which may be on a secure or protected status. Tenants who are secure or protected before this date retain their statutory security of tenure and rent regulation.

Under the new assured lets, tenants will have security of tenure and other statutory rights under Part I of the 1988 Act. These matters were considered in Chapters 3 and 4. If housing associations keep rents below market level (as the Government expects them to), it is unlikely that any of their assured tenants will refer rents to a rent assessment committee in the limited cases available under the 1988 Act. Moreover, many assured lets will contain a provision for the rent to be reviewed, thus ousting the rent assessment committee's jurisdiction until the end of the contractual term. In any event the committee only has jurisdiction if the rent is excessive.

Hence the major implications for new tenants of housing associations are the statutory provisions governing security of tenure and the limited succession rights. In addition the Corporations are to issue guidance on the management of accommodation by registered housing associations (new s 36A of the Housing Associations Act 1985). In advance of the Act, the Housing Corporation produced three documents: guidance for the management of lets under assured tenancies; separate notes of guidance for co-operative housing associations; and a standard tenancy agreement. Separate drafts are to be produced for tenancy agreements to be used by almshouse charities and co-ownership societies. These documents have been produced following consultations with the Department of the Environment, the National Federation of Housing Associations and others. As of 15 January 1989 there are three documents that will take effect. These are:

- *The Tenants' Guarantee* (guidance on the management of registered housing associations);
- a standard tenancy agreement for assured lettings by registered housing associations;
- Housing Corporation Circular No. HC/43/88 (December 1988).

See Appendices 4 and 5. They are on the whole self-explanatory and only the more salient points are covered in this chapter.

The *Tenants' Guarantee* reminds housing associations of their responsibility to provide accommodation for "those who are inadequately housed or homeless, and for whom suitable housing is not available at prices within their means" (paragraph A1). They must also consult relevant local authorities and voluntary and community groups, and make provision for tenants' needs for mobility (paragraphs A3, A4). As with local authorities, housing associations must publish their rules for the allocation of tenancies and applicants must have access to information about them held by an association (paragraph B).

Tenancy agreements should be in writing and tenants should generally be given long term security of tenure: "assured shorthold tenancies should only be used in exceptional circumstances" (paragraph C3). Where an association is offering a tenancy to an existing tenant of a local authority or of another housing association, the effect of the Housing Act 1988 should be explained since these tenants will be exchanging a secure or protected status for an assured status.

Associations are also expected to give their assured tenants "additional contractual rights" (paragraph C6). Effectively the additional rights are designed to give assured tenants much the same rights as are enjoyed by secure tenants of housing associations under Part IV of the Housing Act 1985. Thus they may have a *contractual* right to exchange tenancies with tenants of other associations, local authorities and New Towns subject to the consent of the association, which must not be unreasonably withheld. They may also have contractual rights to sublet or to take in a lodger (with the housing association's consent); to carry out improvements and certain repairs; and the right to be consulted about housing management changes.

Assured tenants have succession rights under s 17 of the 1988 Act. However this is limited to the tenants' spouse (see Chapter 3). Housing associations should consider granting additional contractual rights so that their assured tenants will have succession rights similar to those enjoyed by secure and protected tenants. The agreement should also explain the basis on which rents may be set and increased, and assured tenants should be informed of an association's policies on the fixing of rents (paragraph D). Agreements may also contain express terms dealing with a housing association's repairing obligations that are implied by statute. Assured tenants should also be informed of the association's procedures for repair and maintenance of the dwelling. In addition to these matters, tenants should be informed of the procedures for dealing with complaints, claims for compensation for failure to provide services and for assistance in applying for housing benefit (paragraph G).

A separate document will be produced for "fully mutual co-operative housing associations". These are housing associations in which tenants own nominal shares and therefore can take an active part in the running of the association's affairs (Alder & Handy, *op cit*, Chapter 2). The published guidance is likely to be in much the same terms as the *Tenants' Guarantee*. Such matters as tenancy agreements are likely to be similar. However, provision will have to be made to take account of the special characteristics of fully mutual co-operative housing associations since tenants of these associations must be members of the association, and only tenants or prospective tenants can be members (s 1(2) Housing Associations Act 1985). As a result, where an association selects new members, it is in effect choosing new tenants.

It is also important to note that a tenant of a fully mutual housing association cannot be an assured tenant (para 12(h), Sch 1 of the 1988 Act). Hence his security of tenure is only contractual in nature. However, it is likely that these associations will be expected to provide security of tenure "equivalent to the statutory protection given by the relevant provisions of the Housing Act 1988 to assured tenants" (draft guidance issued December 1988, paragraph C4.1). This would include security of tenure with specified grounds on which the co-operative might seek possession, and succession rights. The agreements will also make provision for subletting and improvements in the same way as other registered associations are required to do.

Only the guidance for registered housing associations has been approved. The document for co-operatives is expected to receive final approval in March 1989. By this time there will also be official guidance for shared housing and hostels, long leases and alms-houses. All of these documents will be used in the first instance by Housing for Wales. However, it is likely that Housing for Wales will amend the documentation in due course to take account of local conditions.

The standard tenancy agreement has been produced by the National Federation of Housing Associations. It has received qualified approval from the Housing Corporation (see circular HC/43/88). New tenants are to be given a copy of the *Tenants' Guarantee* with their tenancy agreement. The agreement gives a tenant rights similar to those enjoyed by secure tenants under the Housing Act 1985. For example, under the standard tenancy agreement, a tenant will have a *contractual* right to take in a lodger and to sublet with consent of the housing association; a right to exchange and transfer with consent of the housing association; a right to carry out certain repairs and improvements; and a right to be consulted over matters of housing management. On the death of the tenant the tenancy passes to his spouse. The agreement refers to a spouse. However, under s 17 of the 1988 Act, a "spouse" includes someone living with the deceased tenant at the time of his or her death. Obviously, the agreement cannot limit this statutory right.

On the other hand, the agreement gives assured tenants of housing associations wide succession rights. In effect, it give them rights similar to those enjoyed by secure tenants. If there is no surviving spouse, then a member of the deceased's family, who lived with him for at least twelve months before his death, will succeed if the premises were occupied as her/his principal home.

Under this agreement a housing association agrees to seek possession only on the grounds of rent arrears (ground 10, Sch 2 of the 1988 Act); breach of a term of the agreement (ground 12); damage to the premises (ground 13); nuisance and annoyance (ground 14); suitable alternative accommodation in limited cases (ground 9); and where the tenant dies without a successor (ground 7). Under the agreement a housing association will give no less than two months' notice of intended possession proceedings. However, under the 1988 Act, a claim under ground 7 must be preceded by not less than two months. The agreement does not make this clear.

5. An assessment

The legal position will be complex for many years. Housing associations may have tenants who are secure under the Housing Act 1985 or protected under the Rent Act 1977. In both cases the tenants have security of tenure and succession rights under the respective legislation. In both cases their rents are subject to the fair rent machinery of the Rent Act 1977. The position of these tenants is largely unaffected by the Housing Act 1988.

New lettings will generally be on assured lettings under the 1988 Act. These tenants will have security of tenure and succession rights under the 1988 Act. If associations use the standard tenancy agreement and follow the management guidance, assured tenants will have additional contractual rights. As a result they will have much the same security as secure and protected tenants.

However, their rents are not subject to the fair rent provisions. Because of the impending grants changes, it is likely that rents will be higher than fair rents registered uner the Rent Act 1977. However, they will on the whole be lower than the market rents for assured lets in the private sector.

The housing association movement will continue to expand, although fears have been expressed that the movement will not have the capacity for some time to cope with the volume of applications that may result from the continuing decline of council housing. The Government wants housing associations to increase the volume of new lets from its current level of 16,000 a year to 24,500 new units a year over the next three years (*The Economist*, 7–13 January 1989, page 20, column 3). However, the Government also plans to reduce grants from 100% to 75% for new building; the remainder must be raised from the private sector. Yet housing associations argue that at least 80% (90% in inner London) must remain grant-aided if rents are to be within the reach of their traditional clientèle (see *Rents, Risks, Rights*, National Federation of Housing Associations 1987, appendix 1).

Housing associations will also have a significant role in the change of landlord provisions in Part IV of the 1988 Act. This is considered in Chapters 10 and 11.

The Corporations have an expanded role. They will monitor the performance of housing associations to ensure compliance with their management guidance. The Corporations have extensive powers to intervene and regulate the performance of individual associations. For example they can carry out enquiries if they believe that there is mismanagement and they can withdraw registration (Alder & Handy, *op cit*, pages 162 to 172). In addition they can take account of the performance of an association when considering grant applications and in considering an application from an association for approval to take over council housing under Part IV of the Housing Act 1988.

Chapter 8

Housing action trusts: purposes and constitution

1. Introduction

One of the centre pieces of the 1988 Act is the set of provisions that enable Central Government to set up housing action trusts ("HATs"). In its White Paper, the Government claimed that some areas of local authority housing suffer such serious problems that direct action is needed to achieve improvements over a reasonable period (*Housing: The Government's Proposals*, 1987 Cmnd 214, paragraph 6.1).

HATs are modelled on "Urban Development Corporations" which were set up by the Local Government, Planning and Land Act 1980 to permit Central Government to intervene directly to regenerate the local economy in areas of urban deprivation. UDCs are free from the restraints of local authorities and are designed to attract private investment into local areas. (For an account see Parkinson 3 Local Economy 109 (1988)). The government believes that UDCs have been a success. HATs will be similar bodies, whose functions will be to improve housing in the worst areas of deprivation. Like UDCs, they will be set up by Central Government, who will fund them, define their tasks and appoint their members.

HATs will have a limited lifespan. They will take over local authority housing, renovate it and dispose of it to a range of different landlords. The procedures used in setting them up and their powers are broadly similar to those of UDCs as set out in the 1980 Act. However, criticisms have been levelled that reductions in local authority housing expenditure have made it impossible for some authorities to repair and improve their housing stock. Moreover, the worst housing stock is concentrated in the privately rented sector, yet HATs will focus on municipal rather than private rented housing. The Government was not persuaded by these arguments and it has pressed ahead with its plans to intervene directly with local authority housing, although at first HATs will be introduced on a small-scale and experimental basis.

The 1988 Act contains thirty three sections and six schedules that deal with HATs. However, it is difficult to determine how HATs will work simply by examining the legislative language. The Government has assumed very wide powers to set up a HAT in any part of the country and to allow it to take over part or all of the local authority responsibilities in the area affected. These powers *could* include housing, planning and public health functions, as well as such matters as highways. The Act allows Central Government to decide where HATs will be created and what powers they will have.

It is likely that individual HATs will differ significantly in the form they take and the powers they have. The creation of a HAT, the appointment of its officers, the designation of its powers and the transfer of local authority property will be brought about by statutory instrument. What Part III of the Act does is to list a series of broad powers exercisable by the Secretary of State and by the HATs. Thus the size of a HAT, its powers and role will depend on decisions taken by Central Government, who will also control its sphere of activity. In this sense then the HAT provisions may be regarded as primary legislation. The actual form they will take will depend on the terms of the statutory instruments that are laid before Parliament.

In considering this part of the Act, it is best to examine the various Government statements which identify its intentions and expectations. As has been mentioned, it is evident that the Government will use these powers on an experimental basis in the first instance: "the government is committed to establishing a pilot programme of HATs and it is expected that this will contain only a modest number of schemes" (*Housing Action Trusts: A Consultation Document*, 1987, paragraph 32). During the parliamentary debates, it was announced that six HATs will be created at first, with a commitment of £125 million over three years (Department of the Environment, news release, 11 July 1988). The first six HATs will be set up as follows:

- London Borough of Lambeth—two estates totalling 1,977 homes
- London Borough of Southwark—two estates totalling 2,705 homes
- London Borough of Tower Hamlets—five estates totalling 2,190 homes
- Leeds—three estates totalling 7,123 homes
- Sandwell—two estates totalling 3,930 homes
- Sunderland—three estates totalling 6,600 homes

This announcement led to widespread protests by the local authorities and council tenants affected. Particular concern was expressed over the plan to introduce HATs in these areas without the agreement of the tenants. In September 1988, the Secretary of State announced that he had commissioned consultants to carry out studies of the areas selected to enable him to make a final decision. Then in October 1988, the Opposition secured an amendment that requires the Secretary of State to ballot the tenants who will be affected. In November 1988, the Secretary of State announced that the Government accepted this amendment (Department of the Environment, news release, 6 November 1988). A HAT can now only be set up in an area if a majority of the tenants are in favour of it.

The Government's plans for HATs will become clearer once the results of its consultant's reports are available; a final decision is taken on the siting of the first HATs; and the necessary draft statutory instruments are laid before Parliament.

The remainder of this chapter examines how a HAT can be set up; the powers it will have; appointment of its members; its finances; and the sort of local authority functions that can be transferred to it.

2. Setting up a housing action trust

Section 60 of the Act allows the Secretary of State to designate an area a HAT where it is "expedient" to do so (s 60(1)). There are no limitations on the size or location of the area selected; indeed as the Act is drafted, one HAT could be set up for the whole of England and Wales! Once established a HAT has a corporate status with such local authority functions specified in ss 65 to 71 as are transferred to it. The area chosen will be known as a "designated area" (s 60(6)(a)). It may contain two or more pieces of land which need not be contiguous and which could be situated in more than one local authority area (s 60(2)). The designation order is made by statutory instrument which must be approved by a resolution of each House of Parliament (s 60(3)).

In deciding which areas to select, the Secretary of State is given an extremely wide discretion, since s 60(4) enjoins him to "have regard to such matters as he thinks fit". Among the matters to which he may have regard are the balance between rented and owner-occupied housing; the amount of and physical state of municipal housing in the area; the way local housing is managed; and the general conditions in the area (s 60(5)).

Apart from the Government enquiries that precede the making of an order, there is a statutory duty to consult the local authority that will be affected (s 61(1)). There is also a duty to publicise the proposal to persons appearing to the Secretary of State to be likely to be affected by the proposal (s 61(2)). However, the form the consultative process takes and the extent (if at all) to which the local authority views are taken into account is not specified. Nor is there any further elucidation as to how the proposal is to be publicised in the area and to whom. However, under s 61, no designation order can be made unless a majority of the tenants to be affected is in favour of it.

Several surveys of council tenants' views were carried out during the Parliamentary passage of the Act. For example, the National Consumer Council commissioned a survey of nearly one thousand council tenants. It found that 51% wanted to keep the local council as their landlord. However, 21% said that they would prefer a building society, housing association or tenants' co-operative, whilst 26% were uncommitted, many of them stating that they wanted more information before reaching a decision. Only 1% said that they would want a private landlord. This survey also found that the older the tenants are, the more likely they are to want to keep the local council as their landlord.

Other findings emerging from this report are that almost all tenants regard the prompt carrying out of repairs as important, and that they want a say in decisions affecting their homes. A majority also considered keeping any common areas in good condition as important, and they valued the right to carry out improvements. Predictably, most of the tenants were worried about possible rent increases if they were transferred to another landlord.

These findings emphasise the importance of the consultation procedures deployed in this Part and in Part IV of the Act.

In investigating an area the Secretary of State has powers to compel the local authority to disclose information to him. He can use this power before setting up the HAT and after, when deciding which functions to give it (s 90(3)(a) and (b)).

Once the HAT has been set up and its functions have been specified, the Secretary of State may require production of information to enable the HAT to carry out its functions (s 90(3)(c)). The only restriction on this widely drafted power is that the information must be relevant to the HAT's activities.

Another clue to the scope of this power appears in s 90(4). This states that among the information that might be required is that relating to the occupation of and interest in the local authority's land. Thus the local authority may be required to disclose information on its tenants as well as its use of land that is not used for residential letting. It also refers to information kept in a register kept under the Land Registration Act 1925 or the Land Charges Act 1925.

3. Status, functions and powers

Since a HAT has corporate status, it can hold property, enter into contracts and sue or be sued in its own name. A HAT will be given a name in the designation order (s 62(3)) and it may be established in the same statutory instrument as the one designating the area of land selected, or by a separate order. As an alternative, an existing HAT may (by order) be designated the HAT for that area (s 62(1)(b)). In this way a HAT might expand its activities into other areas. Where this occurs the name of the HAT may be altered to take account of its additional areas of activity (s 62(4)(b)).

Once tenants and their homes have been transferred, the HAT becomes their housing authority for the purposes of the Housing Act 1985. It is also added to the list of landlords in respect of whom a protected tenancy cannot be created under the Rent Act 1977 (s 62(7) of the 1988 Act).

The objects of a HAT are set out in s 63(1) which states that it will:

(a) secure the repair and maintenance of the housing it has acquired;
(b) manage this housing;
(c) encourage diversity of housing in the designated area;
(d) improve the social and living conditions as well as the general environment of the designated area.

Rather more specific objectives are contained in s 63(2) which refers to the provision and maintenance of housing and the facilitating of "shops, advice centres" and other facilities for the local community. These provisions then, express the general objectives set for HATs and they are supplemented by a broad statement of a HAT's powers in s 63(3). These include powers to hold, manage and dispose of land (and other property); the carrying out of building; seeking the provision of water, gas, electricity and other services; and the carrying on of "any business or undertaking". A HAT is also empowered to do anything necessary or expedient in carrying out its objectives or using its powers. To protect organisations or individuals dealing with a HAT, any transaction falling outside these provisions will not be invalidated for this reason only.

Following concessions made during the House of Commons Committee stage, the Government added another object by making s 71 of the Race Relations Act 1976 applicable to HATs. A HAT will therefore have duties to promote equality of opportunity and to eliminate racial discrimination.

4. Appointment of officers and staff

The manner in which a HAT's officers should be appointed was the subject of lively Parliamentary debate. The Opposition argued that residents should elect the members, or that, at the very least, the members should be drawn from people living in the locality. It was also argued that members might have a financial interest in the activities of a HAT giving rise to conflicts of interest.

Although the Government made some concessions, the basic principle of Central Government control over the appointments procedure remains intact. However, amendments were made at the Report Stage and in the House of Lords. In appointing members, the Secretary of State will have to consider people with special knowledge of the area and of the needs of the chronically sick and the disabled.

Schedule 7 deals with appointment of members and other constitutional matters. A fundamental difference between a HAT and a local authority housing committee is that the members of the latter are elected and the committee's proceedings are open to the public. In the case of a HAT, it is for the Secretary of State to appoint its members. A HAT will have a membership of between five and eleven, one of whom will be appointed to the chair (para 1, Sch 7).

In appointing the members preference must be given to people living in or having special knowledge of the area in which the HAT is situated. Before making appointments the Secretary of State must consult the relevant local authority (para 2(1), Sch 7). He must also satisfy himself that a member will have no financial or other interest which is "likely to affect prejudicially the exercise of his functions" (paragraph 2(2)). In assessing this, he may require a prospective member to give him such information "as he considers necessary for that purpose" (ibid.). It is possible for tenants of a HAT to be appointed; the fact that a prospective member is a tenant does not disqualify him from appointment (para 2(3)).

A member can be removed from office by the Secretary of State in cases of bankruptcy, illness, or unauthorised absence from meetings for longer than three consecutive months. There is also power to remove in the far less specific cases of "unfitness" or "unsuitability" (para 6). The terms and conditions of a member's appointment are, under paras 8, 9 and 10 of Sch 7, to be fixed by the Secretary of State. The levels of remuneration must also meet with Treasury approval.

Arrangements for meetings (including their quorum and their frequency) are a matter for the membership to determine, but this is subject to any directions they may receive from the Secretary of State (para 13). Unlike local authority housing committee meetings, HAT meetings are not open to members of the public. Nor do the provisions of the Local Government (Access to Information) Act 1985 apply. However, the Government gave an undertaking at the Report Stage that the Secretary of State will use his powers to give directions to ensure that residents will be able to attend meetings, unless confidential matters are under consideration.

The members of a HAT will have responsibilities similar to those of a local authority housing committee. Obviously, their precise obligations will depend on the functions transferred to them from the local authority.

To carry out the daily work of the HAT the members have power to appoint staff. They will have to recruit a chief executive and such other staff as are approved by the Secretary of State (para 11). Levels of remuneration will be a matter for the individual HAT (in negotiation, presumably, with relevant trade unions). The permanent staff will obviously be people with expertise in housing management and finance. Presumably staff from local authorities will apply for these positions although the consultative document stated that "while local authority staff clearly have relevant skills, they will not have any particular rights to employment with a HAT over and above other possible applicants" (para 29). However, a rather more positive statement was made by the Government during the House of Commons Committee Stage, stating that HATs will be expected to give preference to local authority staff.

5. A housing action trust's proposals for its area

Once it has been set up, a HAT must prepare a statement of its proposals for the designated area. This must be done "as soon as practicable" (s 64(1)). In preparing this statement the HAT must consult the relevant local authority and the local residents (s 64(2), (3)). However, the manner of its consultations with the local authority is not specified. Consultations with the residents is of obvious importance. A HAT will have to publicise its proposals and give residents an opportunity to comment.

Section 64 requires a HAT to "take such steps as it considers appropriate" to give publicity to its plans; make residents aware that they can make representations to the HAT on these plans; and to give them an "adequate opportunity" to make representations (s 64(3)). The HAT must then give consideration to the representations made. After this consultation exercise, the HAT must send to the Secretary of State a copy of its proposals, a report of the consultations and of the consideration it gave to the representations made (s 64(4)). Section 64 does not require the HAT to obtain Central Government approval of its proposals for the area. However, given the Secretary of State's considerable powers of intervention, Government will clearly have influence over the HAT's plans. A HAT may also prepare further statements and it may be directed to do so by Central Government. In this event the same consultation process must be undertaken (s 64(5)). This whole process is of critical importance to the residents and the local authority in whose area the HAT is situated. This is the stage when details of the HAT's operations will become apparent. Whilst HATs are given a considerable degree of latitude in the way they carry out the consultation and in their final decisions, their plans may be challenged by use of judicial review. This is considered in Chapter 9.

6. Financial matters

A HAT will be expected to attract private capital into the designated area. In addition it will receive Central Government funding. It will have a rental income from the housing it manages and it is possible that a local authority may have been required to make a payment on the transfer of its properties if they had a "negative value". Eventually, a HAT will receive capital payments on the sale of the housing to other landlords and where a tenant exercises the right to buy.

A HAT will have to borrow money to finance much of its operations. Borrowing powers and other financial matters are regulated by Sch 8 of the Act. It can borrow money from the Government or, with Government consent, from other sources. The Government can also guarantee a loan negotiated by a HAT. Details of these guarantees must be laid before Parliament (para 5, Sch 8).

The way a HAT's accounts are to be maintained and audited is regulated by part 3 of Sch 8. In addition to the usual auditing and accounting procedures, s 6 of the National Audit Act 1983 applies to a HAT. Thus a HAT is subject to an examination of its activities in terms of its efficiency and effectiveness. A copy of its financial reports must be laid before Parliament (para 13(3), Sch 8).

7. Functions of a housing action trust

Some of the local authority functions referred to in ss 65 to 71 are more likely to be transferred than others. For example, following the transfer of local authority properties, HATs will of necessity be given housing management powers under the Housing Act 1985. It is also likely that they will be given a number of planning functions (as has happened with Urban Development Corporations; see Telling: *Planning Law and Procedure*, 7th ed 1986, pages 18–19).

However, some local authority functions such as those under the Public Health Acts and the repairs notices procedures in the 1985 Act, may stay with the local authority. The Government will keep these as reserve powers to be transferred if it considers that a local authority is being obstructive. The various tasks that *may* be transferred to a HAT are now considered in turn.

8. Acquisition of housing

In the designated area local authority properties will be compulsorily transferred to the HAT. Section 74 empowers the Secretary of State, by statutory instrument, to order the transfer of the property. Included in the transfer can be :

(a) part or all of the local authority housing in the designated area; and

(b) other land held in connection with that housing.

In addition, there is a far more vaguely worded power to transfer any other land in the designated area; that is to say land that is not held in connection with housing. This land can be transferred if the Secretary of State is satisfied that it is needed by the HAT in connection with its work (s 74(2)). The order may also include other property held by the local authority in connection with its housing (s 74(3)).

How will local authorities be compensated for the loss of their property? The references in the Act to compensation are vague and give considerable powers to Central Government. In fact, s 74(4) leaves it very much to the Secretary of State to decide whether *any* compensation is payable and if so how much. It states that the transfer "shall be on such terms, including financial terms, as the Secretary of State thinks fit".

Not only does the compulsory acquisition fail to give automatic compensation, but the local authority may be ordered to make a payment to the HAT if the property has a "negative value" (s 74(5)). According to the Government, this could happen where the property to be transferred is in a very poor state of repair. Thus the local authority could lose some of its housing stock (and other property) and have to make a payment to the HAT. The Government believes that this is justified since the local authority would have had to expend monies on the properties anyway.

Negotiations will obviously take place before a transfer order is made, although of course a local authority may feel that it is not in a very strong bargaining position. Indeed, s 75(2) imposes a statutory duty on the Secretary of State to consult the local authority about the property included in the transfer order and the terms of the transfer. In addition, the proposed transfer must be brought to the attention of all of the secure tenants who will be affected, as well as any other person (such as a lessor, lessee, mortgagor or mortgagee) having an interest in the property.

Although s 75 requires consultation, the Secretary of State can reach decisions on the terms of the compulsory transfer over the objections of the local authority. There is no provision for (say) disputes over the level of compensation or payments to be made by the local authority to be referred to an independent valuer.

Although the primary purpose of a HAT is to acquire, manage and renovate local authority housing, it will also have compulsory powers to acquire private housing and land. Section 77 empowers a HAT to acquire property in the designated area either by agreement or (with Government approval) compulsorily. In addition it may acquire property in another area (which need not be adjacent to the HAT's area of operation) in order to carry out its work. In the absence of agreement it may compulsorily purchase such property subject to Government approval (s 77(2)). However, the general principles of compensation contained in the Acquisition of Land Act 1981 apply to these acquisitions (s 77(4)). In addition, the usual planning procedures, such as those dealing with the rights of the owner to object, apply to these acquisitions as they do to local authorities exercising powers of compulsory purchase. These matters are dealt with in ss 77(4), 78 and Sch 10 of the 1988 Act.

Other planning and compulsory purchase powers that are exercisable by local authorities (and Urban Development Corporations) may be exercisable by a HAT when it is acquiring property. For example, land held by a statutory undertaking (such as water or gas authorities) may be acquired by a HAT unless it is used for the purposes of the statutory duties (s 76 and

Sch 9). In addition a HAT will have subsidiary powers (similar to local authority planning and compulsory purchase powers) dealing with rights of way, easements and open spaces (Sch 10).

9. Housing management powers

The transfer of local authority housing to a HAT will necessarily involve the transfer of housing management obligations under the Housing Act 1985. During its period of ownership, a HAT will act as landlord of the tenants affected, who will remain secure tenants. In effect, it will have much the same role as does the local authority as a landlord under the Housing Act 1985 (for an account of this role see Hughes: *Public Sector Housing Law*, 2nd ed (1987) Chapters 3, 4 and part 2). The relationship between a HAT and the transferred tenants, and the transfer of the tenants to new landlords, is covered in Chapter 9.

The Housing Act 1985 contains a wide range of local authority powers and duties, from the provision of housing to dealing with overcrowding and slum clearance. Not all of these provisions will be transferred. In practice the specific role of a HAT and the extent of its powers will be shaped by factors such as its size, scale of operation and its relationship with the relevant local authority. Thus a HAT created in a small area, with a modest stock of housing, may be limited to managing and renovating this stock with a view to its ultimate disposal. With the co-operation of the local authority it would not need to take on other roles such as those under the public health legislation or enforcement of the overcrowding provisions in relation to the properties it has acquired. However, a large HAT designed to renovate a large area may be given a far wider role.

The full range of local authority functions that *may* be given to a HAT is considered below, and the HAT's potential role as a housing authority is examined here. As before, the Government has wide powers to determine the actual content of an individual HAT's housing role. Under s 65 of the 1988 Act, a HAT may be given any of the following housing functions:

(a) provision of housing accommodation, including powers of management (Part II Housing Act 1985);

(b) inspection of properties to see whether they comply with standards of fitness and the service (and enforcement) of repairs notices under Part VI of the 1985 Act. In *R* v

Cardiff City Council ex parts Cross (1983) it was held that these procedures cannot be invoked by a local authority's environmental health department in relation to that authority's housing stock. The same reasoning could be applied in the (unlikely) event of a HAT's trying to use the repairs notice procedures in relation to its own properties. However it will be open to its tenants to use these procedures by seeking the assistance of the local authority (the authority can be required to carry out an inspection and if it finds the property unfit it must serve a repairs notice on the HAT—see *R* v *Kerrier District Council ex parte Guppys (Bridport) Ltd (no 1)* (1976));

(c) service and enforcement of improvement notices under Part VII of the 1985 Act;

(d) slum clearance, overcrowding, houses in multiple occupation and the common lodging houses provisions contained in Parts IX, X, XI and XII of the Housing Act 1985;

(e) assistance for owners of defective housing under Part XVI of the 1985 Act.

Under Part II of the Housing Associations Act 1985, housing associations may apply to a local authority for a loan, and local authorities have powers and duties to promote housing associations (see Alder & Handy: *Housing Associations Law* (1987) Chapter 9). These powers may also be conferred on a HAT (s 65(2)(b)). Given the HAT's objective of diversifying types of landlord and the Government's expectation that housing associations will expand, considerable use of s 65(2)(b) is probable.

An occupier may lose his home as a result of compulsory purchase, a closing order made as a result of the repairs notice procedures described above, and other public actions. When this occurs, a local authority has duties to rehouse the displaced occupier and (in some circumstances) to pay "home loss" or "disturbance" payments (see ss 39 to 41 of the Land Compensation Act 1973 and Arden: *Manual of Housing Law*, 3rd ed (1986) pages 224 to 227). These powers may also be given to a HAT (s 65(2)(c)). Since a HAT will be renovating and developing housing it is likely that they will be given these powers.

When a HAT is established there will be several questions relating to its relationship with the local authority (or local authorities) from which it has acquired houses. This issue is to some extent addressed in s 65(3). Once established the functions transferred to a HAT can be exercisable *either* by the HAT or by the HAT concurrently with the local authority. This implies that local authority action is possible in the event of non-compliance by the HAT. However, s 65(4) provides that the transferred functions are to have effect in relation to the HAT and "where the trust is to have the function concurrently with another authority, in relation to that authority". Taken together, the effect of these subsections suggests that the Government may provide that some or certain functions are to be exercised exclusively by the HAT and others concurrently with the local authority.

In connection with repairs notices, this leads to three possibilities. First, that the repairs notice procedure (and other procedures applying in cases of unfitness) will remain with the local authority. In this event the local authority could serve and enforce the notices against the HAT. Second, that these procedures will be completely transferred to the HAT. Here, it is argued the HAT could not be compelled to enforce the procedures (and it is unlikely that a HAT would choose to do so). Third, that the procedures will be shared. This would enable the local authority to use the procedures but the potential for disputes between it and the HAT are obvious.

One would expect to find most housing management functions transferred to a HAT along with the local authority housing to which these responsibilities relate. However, it would be unfortunate if (say) the repairs notice function were transferred exclusively since this would make them unenforceable.

10. Planning functions

As with Urban Development Corporations, HATs are likely to be given planning functions. The Act makes two provisions for this, in s 66 and 67, which are considered in turn.

(a) Planning control

As part of its activities, a HAT will have the power, independently of the local authority (or other local planning authority), to develop land within the designated area. Before doing so, it must submit its development proposals to the Secretary of State for his approval. Before reaching a decision, the Secretary of State must consult any local authority (which will obviously include the planning authority concerned) affected. Approval may be given with or without modifications (s 66(1)).

Similar powers have been used by UDCs. In the Merseyside and London Docklands urban development areas, the special development order procedure has been used (Town & Country Planning (Merseyside Urban Development Area) Special Development Order 1981, SI 1981 No. 560; Town & Country Planning (London Docklands Urban Development Area) Special Development Order 1981, SI No. 1082). Both private and public development has been approved by the Secretary of State for these areas.

Under the Town and Country Planning (General Development) Order 1988 (SI 1988 No 1813), many developments do not require planning permission. For example, certain improvements and other works within the curtilage of an individual dwelling, and certain changes of use in a retail business, do not require planning permission.

In addition, a "special development order" may be made (ss 66(2) of the 1988 Act). A special development order can be made under s 24 of the Town and Country Planning Act 1971. This empowers the Secretary of State to grant planning permission for a specific development.

To summarise, a HAT, as part of its plans for the designated area, may submit development proposals to the Secretary of State. Following consultations with the local planning authority, approval may be given with or without modification of the proposal. In common with planning decisions of this sort the Minister must ensure that buildings with special architectural or historical features are preserved. This provision appears in s 66(3) of the 1988 Act which also refers to the full list of protected buildings contained in s 54(1) of the 1971 Act. In addition, a special development order can be made. The effect of this is that automatic planning permission may be given for developments of the type contained in the HAT's proposal. This may be subject to any conditions appearing in the order, such as a requirement that details of the development be submitted to the local planning authority. In consequence the local planning authority is relieved of all responsibility for developments of the type covered by the special development order.

All of this assumes that the HAT's development plans are within the scope of this form of permitted development. If its plans go beyond this it would have to obtain planning permission from the local authority. The Act empowers Central Government to circumvent this by making the HAT the planning authority for part or all of the designated area. Again this power is similar to that relating to UDCs under the Local Government Planning and Land Act 1980.

(b) The housing action trust as a planning authority

During the House of Commons committee stage of the Act, the Government indicated that the power to transfer planning functions in their entirety would, as with public health powers, be used as a reserve power for use where the Government believes that the local authority planning authority is being obstructive. Much will also depend on plans of an individual HAT, which may find that it has sufficient planning powers under s 66 of the 1988 Act.

However, the Secretary of State can, by order, declare the HAT to be the planning authority for part or all of the designated area. Section 67 of the Act allows transfer of the local authority planning functions contained in Part III of the Town and Country Planning Act 1971. In effect, a HAT could by order become the local planning authority for development control purposes under Part III of the 1971 Act. If this happens, applications for planning permission within the designated area would have to be made to the HAT rather than the local authority. Appeals against the HAT's decisions would lie to the Secretary of State (as they do in the case of local authority planning decisions). An order vesting these planning functions in a HAT is made by statutory instrument (s 67(7) of the 1988 Act). (For an account of the procedures under the Town & Country Planning Act 1971 see Telling, *op cit*).

In Committee, the Government gave an undertaking that HATs would be directed to hold meetings dealing with planning functions in public. This was in response to the criticism that HATs, unlike local authority planning committees, could reach planning decisions in secret. There can be little doubt that the transfer of planning functions to HATs (and to UDCs) diminishes the authority and functions of local authorities in the areas concerned.

11. Public Health Act functions

Under s 68, the Secretary of State may order the transfer to a HAT of a number of functions under the Public Health Acts. If these were transferred a HAT would become responsible for a number of public health matters in the designated area (or part of the designated area). The power to order the transfer of public health functions is exercisable by statutory instrument (s 68(6)). There are four categories of power that may be transferred.

First are those contained in ss 83 and 84 of the Public Health Act 1936 (as amended by s 35 of the Public Health Act 1961). These include the power to serve notices on the owner or occupier of premises which are in "such a filthy or unwholesome state" as to be prejudicial to health. These procedures also apply to premises found to be "verminous" (s 83(1) of the 1936 Act). The notice served has to state what steps will have to be taken to remedy the condition. This could include cleaning and removal of wallpaper. Where the premises are used for human habitation, the notice can also require the premises to be prepared, painted or distempered. Failure to comply with the notice is a criminal offence. (For a fuller account of these procedures see Hughes, op cit, pages 232 to 233).

A related power that could also be transferred is defined in s 84 of the 1936 Act. This would arise where either a medical officer of health or a sanitary inspector certifies that articles found on the premises are filthy or verminous. In this event the HAT would have to clean, purify or destroy the article as directed by the certificate. Another power dealing with "filthy or verminous" premises is found in s 36 Public Health Act 1961. This is a power to require the affected premises to be vacated if the local authority has to carry out fumigation.

Within the second category are the powers of local authorities to deal with statutory nuisances and offensive trades under Part III of the 1936 Act. The statutory nuisance procedure, in particular, has proved to be an important remedy in cases of disrepair. Local authorities have a duty to inspect properties in their area to ensure that they are not in such a condition as to be a nuisance or likely to cause prejudice to health. Where premises are in such a condition the local authority must serve a notice on the owner requiring him to take steps to abate the nuisance. In the event of non-compliance the local authority may take proceedings in a magistrates' court. If the matters complained of are proved, the magistrates may issue an abatement notice enforceable by a daily fine. The proceedings are criminal in nature (*R* v *Newham East Justices, ex parte Hunt* (1976)). Thus the local authority carries the burden of proof which must be established beyond a reasonable doubt.

These procedures may be used where premises suffer from condensation even when the structure is unaffected (see *Dover District Council* v *Farrar* (1980)). Magistrates have wide powers in relation to the works they can order to be carried out. For example they can order installation of ventilation, insulation and heating systems (see *Greater London Council* v *Tower Hamlets London Borough Council* (1984)). Local authorities *may* carry out the remedial works in the event of non-compliance and they may then recover the cost from the person responsible for the condition complained of.

The third set of powers that may be transferred to a HAT are those found in Part XII of the 1936 Act. Part XII deals with a number of matters relating to the enforcement of the Act, for example, the service of notices; powers enabling local authorities to enter premises; and the prosecution procedures. These powers will have to be transferred if a HAT is given responsibilities under the Public Health Acts.

The fourth set of powers that could be transferred are those in Part I of the Prevention of Damage by Pests Act 1949. Here local authorities have duties to ensure that premises in their area are free of vermin and they have powers to rid premises of such vermin.

The problem of a HAT's enforcing notices against its own properties were reviewed earlier (see pages 154–155). Exactly the same difficulties apply to the service of public health notices. Thus if exclusive responsibility for public health matters is given to a HAT, it could not be compelled to enforce these provisions. However it could be forced to use the powers against properties in the designated area that it does not own, or in relation to properties that it has sold.

In addition, private action can be taken by a tenant whose premises are unfit in the way defined in the Public Health Acts. The courts have held that an individual can take action under s 99 of the 1936 Act (see *R* v *Epping (Waltham Abbey) Justices, ex parte Burlinson* (1948)). As a result, a tenant of a HAT could take action to get certain repairs carried out under the statutory nuisance procedures.

The Secretary of State may order that these powers are to be exercised by the HAT alone, or concurrently by the HAT and the local authority.

12. Highways

Section 69 of the 1988 Act deals with the situation where street works have been carried out in a private street in the HAT's designated area. Where this happens the HAT will be able to serve a notice on the local street authority (usually the local authority) requiring it to declare the street to be a highway maintainable at public expense. This would result in this street authority becoming responsible for the maintenance of the street under the Highways Act 1980. If the authority objects, it may appeal to the Secretary of State. The grounds for objection may relate to the construction, design, layout or state of maintenance of the street (s 69(2)). Any appeal must be lodged within two months of the date of service of the notice. The Secretary of State may confirm or set aside the notice. In confirming the notice he may modify it and he could also impose financial and other conditions on the HAT (s 69(3) and (4)). This is but a general application of provisions relating to private street works under the 1980 Act; for a fuller account see Cross & Bailey *Cross on Local Government Law* 1986, Chapter 14.

13. Homelessness

Throughout the Parliamentary debate, the Government was pressed to impose duties on HATs under the homelessness provisions contained in Part III of the Housing Act 1985. The Opposition pointed to statistics showing an increase in the volume of people becoming homeless and to the mounting costs that local authorities face in keeping the homeless in bed and breakfast accommodation. Many authorities, it was said, face serious difficulties in discharging their duties to the homeless because of the reductions in Central Government funding and the restrictions on their use of capital receipts arising from the exercise of the right to buy.

The Government was unpersuaded by these arguments. It stated that it would be inappropriate for such duties to be imposed on a body that would have a limited lifespan. Moreover it claimed that the Act will, in the longer term, result in more rented accommodation becoming available and for a greater use of local authority properties that are currently unoccupied.

Under Part III of the 1985 Act a local authority owes a number of duties to persons who are homeless and who have a priority need. In particular, it must offer temporary accommodation (in practice often bed and breakfast) whilst it carries out certain enquiries. After this stage a local authority must offer permanent accommodation unless it considers that the applicant was intentionally homeless; has a local connection with another local authority; or if it is proved on enquiry that the applicant does not have a priority need. An applicant dissatisfied with the decision may seek judicial review, and there have been several cases where the courts have reviewed this type of local authority decision-making.

These statutory duties (or functions) will not be imposed on HATs. Instead, they will have duties to co-operate with local authorities when they are dealing with the homeless. At present, an authority can request another local authority, a housing association or a social services authority to assist them. This power appears in s 72 of the Housing Act 1985. The authority to whom the request is made "shall co-operate" by giving such assistance "as is reasonable in the circumstances". Section 72 of the 1985 Act is amended to enable an authority to seek the assistance of a HAT (s 70 of the 1988 Act). The precise scope of this duty to assist is unclear. In *Robinson* v *Torbay Borough Council* (1982) it was held that it is reasonable for an authority to ask a housing association not to evict one of its tenants. Beyond this it is difficult to escape the conclusion that s 72 of the 1985 Act "is so vague as to make it of little value" (Hughes, op cit, page 175).

14. Financial assistance

A HAT will be able to give financial assistance in order to carry out its functions. In Parliament, the Opposition sought unsuccessfully to restrict this to a power to give assistance to local authorities or to a charity. HATs will therefore have powers to offer financial assistance similar to those possessed by local authorities.

Subject to the approval of the Secretary of State, a HAT can give assistance to any person (s 71(1) of the 1988 Act). This assistance can take the form of grants, loans and guarantees. It can also consist of the HAT's incurring expenditure for any person and the purchase of loan or share capital in a company (s 71(2)). The conditions on which this form of assistance is given is a matter for the HAT. However, any conditions imposed will need the approval of the Secretary of State who will also have to seek Treasury approval (s 71(3), (4)). A HAT can make conditions as to repayment and recovery out of the proceeds of sale of a property in respect of which financial assistance was given (s 71(5)).

This provision implements the government objective of encouraging HATs to work in conjunction with the private sector in improving properties in the designated area.

15. Transfer of functions from a housing action trust

Not only is the Secretary of State empowered to transfer local authority housing and other functions to a HAT, he can also transfer these functions from one HAT to another HAT in a different area, or to an entirely new HAT. He may do this if it appears expedient to him to do so (s 73(1)). As with other powers of this sort, it is exercisable by the statutory instrument procedure (s 73(4)). The effect of such an order would be to hand over a HAT's powers, properties and so on to another HAT. The original HAT would then be dissolved as a result of the same order. The HAT to whom the transfer was made would be treated as established for both its own original designated area and the acquired designated areas (s 73(2)(a)). Its name may be altered to take account of its new responsibilities (s 73(2)(b)).

Before making an order under s 73, the Secretary of State must consult the HAT which is to be wound up, as well as the HAT to which its functions are to be transferred (assuming that a new HAT is not being set up). However, neither the local authority nor residents have to be consulted.

This power of transfer again illustrates the degree of Central Government controls over local authorities and HATs.

16. Agents

Under s 87 of the 1988 Act, a HAT may transfer functions relating to its housing stock (or other land) to "any person" (s 87(1)). In other words, a HAT may enter into an agreement whereby parts of its housing work are given to another body or individual. Before doing this the Secretary of State's approval of the agreement must be obtained and approval may be given subject to conditions (s 87(4)). Amongst other things the agreement may allow for the functions transferred to be performed by a committee or officer of the transferee body (s 87(3)). What would be the position of the tenants if (say) housing management functions were transferred? Since ownership of the properties remains with the HAT, and the transferee body is acting as the HAT's agent, the tenants remain secure tenants.

A more difficult situation might arise on dissolution of a HAT. This is considered in the passage following.

17. Dissolution

The Government expectation that a HAT will carry out its objects quickly is captured in s 88 which states that "a housing action trust shall use its best endeavours to secure that its objects are achieved as soon as practicable". Once this stage has been reached the dissolution procedures in s 88 will apply.

It is for the HAT to decide whether its objects "have been substantially achieved" (s 88(2)). Once it has taken this decision, it has two final responsibilities. First, it must dispose of its remaining properties and any remaining rights or liabilities arising from its functions (s 88(2)(a)). Second, it must submit proposals for its dissolution to the Secretary of State. This submission must address the following matters:

(a) the dissolution of the HAT;
(b) how any remaining property (rights and liabilities) may be disposed of (that is, any that the HAT has been unable to deal with); and
(c) the transfer of its functions, including transfer to an agent appointed under s 87.

Once again, considerable powers are given to the Secretary of State, since he can wind up the HAT and dispose of its remaining properties and obligations either in accordance with the HAT's suggestions, a modification of these suggestions "or otherwise" (s 88(3)). Moreover, he can transfer functions or dispose of rights or liabilities "on such terms as he thinks fit" (s 88(4)(a)). In addition he can, amongst other things, create a corporate body to take over functions, rights and so on (s 88(4)(b)).

The order winding up a HAT and dealing with its remaining

rights and obligations is made by statutory instrument subject to annulment following a resolution of either House of Parliament (s 88(4)(c)).

Chapter 9

The housing action trust as landlord

Although the Government hopes that HATs will improve living conditions in the designated areas, their introduction is likely to cause anxiety and confusion for many residents. Will their rents be increased? To whom do they bring their complaints? Will they have any say when the HAT transfers them to a new landlord? Who is responsible for repairs? This chapter deals with the relationship between a HAT and its tenants and with the procedures governing transfer of the tenants to new landlords. It also considers the ways in which a decision of a HAT may be challenged.

1. A tenant's position whilst the property is owned by a housing action trust

A council tenant whose home has been transferred to a HAT will remain a secure tenant under the Housing Act 1985 so long as the HAT retains ownership. Section 83 of the 1988 Act makes the necessary amendments to the 1985 Act. Thus s 80(1) of the 1985 Act, which lists landlords whose tenancies qualify as secure tenancies, is amended so as to include HATs (s 83(2) of the 1988 Act).

The other provisions of the 1985 Act that are amended in this way are ss 108, 114 and 171. These deal respectively with the making of heating charges; lists of landlords who must consult and provide information on housing allocation; and landlords to whom the "right to buy" applies. These duties and obligations are extended to HATs by s 83(3), (4) and (5). Principles dealing with qualifying periods and discounts relating to the right to buy are extended to HATs (s 83(7) of the 1988 Act).

Under the Housing Act 1985, a tenant's position is different in several respects if the letting was made in consequence of his employment. Some tenancies of this sort cannot be secure (para 2(1), Sch 1 of the 1985 Act). For those that are secure, there are special grounds for possession; additional grounds for withholding consent to assignments; and exceptions to the right to buy. This will continue to apply where tenancies of this sort are transferred to a HAT (s 83(6) of the 1988 Act).

2. Secure tenants

The legal position of council tenants, and that of tenants of other public bodies, was transformed by the Housing Act 1980. Before this Act, council tenants had no statutory security of tenure. The 1980 Act gave them security of tenure similar to that enjoyed by private tenants under the Rent Acts. They were given other statutory rights such as the controversial right to buy. These provisions now appear in the Housing Act 1985 which has been amended in several respects by the Housing and Planning Act 1986 and apply now to secure tenants of a HAT.

A secure tenant has security of tenure similar to that enjoyed by protected tenants and by assured tenants under Part I of the 1988 Act. In the case of a fixed term let, a periodic tenancy comes into being at the end of that term unless another secure tenancy is given to the tenant (s 86 of the 1985 Act). The more common periodic let can be brought to an end only by court order on proof of one or more of the grounds set out in Sch 2 of the Housing Act 1985. Unlike proceedings brought against protected or assured tenants, all of the grounds are either discretionary or require suitable alternative accommodation to be given to the tenant.

No possession proceedings can be started unless a notice (in a prescribed form) is served on the tenant setting out the ground or grounds on which possession may be sought (s 83). The notice must also contain particulars of these ground(s) (s 83(2)(c)). Failure to comply with these requirements renders the notice invalid: *Torridge District Council* v *Jones* (1985), where the local authority failed to specify the rent arrears alleged. If possession is ordered, enforcement of it may be suspended or postponed in the same way as orders made against protected or assured tenants (s 85 of the 1985 Act).

Apart from security of tenure, secure tenants have a number of other statutory rights. On the death of a secure tenant, the tenancy passes (once) to his surviving spouse. If there is no surviving spouse it can pass to a member of the deceased tenant's family who had been living with him for at least twelve months before his death (ss 87, 88, 89 of the 1985 Act).

A secure tenant also has a right to sublet or part with possession if he has the landlord's consent (s 93(1)(b) of the 1985 Act). This consent must not be unreasonably withheld (s 94 of the 1985 Act). A secure tenant also has an unqualified right to allow someone else to live in the property as a "lodger" (s 93(1)(a) of the 1985 Act). However, a secure tenant who parts with possession or sublets the whole loses the secure tenancy and he cannot subsequently become a secure tenant of the premises (s 93(2) of the 1985 Act).

Assignment of a secure tenancy is generally prohibited. However, there is the right to exchange with another secure tenant provided the landlord agrees (s 92 and Sch 3 of the 1985 Act). Assignment is also allowed to a person who would succeed to the tenancy on the secure tenant's death; and following a transfer order made by a divorce court under s 24 of the Matrimonial Causes Act 1973 (s 91(3)) of the 1985 Act).

Section 96 of the 1985 Act gives secure tenants the right to carry out certain repairs (see also SI 1985 No 1493 and DoE circular 23/85). On the whole, this applies to the repairs that are the landlord's responsibility under the Landlord and Tenant Act 1985. This scheme is designed to assist tenants who experience delays in having repairs carried out. It enables a secure tenant to carry out the repairs and recoup the cost from the landlord. However, there are detailed provisions relating to obtaining the landlord's consent and dealing with the recovery of costs. This remedy is not without its problems. For example, if the repairs are carried out negligently the tenant might be liable to pay damages to the landlord. Apart from repairs, a secure tenant may also carry out improvements with the written consent of the landlord (s 97 of the 1985 Act). The consent must not be unreasonably withheld (s 97(3)).

A HAT will also have the same obligations as local authorities to consult, and to provide information to, its tenants. Section 104 of the 1985 Act requires local authorities and other public landlords to publish information explaining the terms of the tenancy, the right to buy and the landlord's repairing obligations. A secure tenant must, on request, be supplied with a copy of this information as well as a copy of the tenancy agreement (s 104(2) of the 1985 Act).

As to consultation, s 105 of the 1985 Act requires landlords to consult those tenants who are likely to be affected by any matter of "housing management". The landlord has to inform the tenants of its proposals, allow them to make representations and consider any representations before reaching a decision (s 105(1)). Landlords are given considerable discretion as to the manner in which they carry out the consultation since they are to "maintain such arrangements as it considers appropriate" to consult (s 105(1)). Matters of "housing management" are those which "in the opinions of the landlord" relate to management, repair etc of a property or to the provision of services or amenities provided under the terms of the tenancy (s 105(2)). However there is no duty to consult tenants over rents (s 105(2)). There is also an obligation to consult over new maintenance, improvement or demolition programmes or a change in the landlord's practice or policies. Again it is for the landlord to decide whether there are in fact new programmes etc and whether they are "likely to substantially" affect its tenants or a group of them (s 105(3)).

Landlords must publish details of their consultative arrangements and make their copies available for inspection (s 105(5)). Once tenants are transferred to a HAT they lose their right to complain to the local authority (except in relation to fitness standards where the local authority retains or shares responsibilities for enforcement). As a result, the statutory duties to consult and to provide information under the 1985 Act, which will apply to HATs whilst they are landlords, will take on a new significance.

3. Management terms introduced by the Housing Act 1988

(a) Rents

Section 84(1) of the 1988 Act provides:

> "A housing action trust may make such reasonable charges as it may determine for the tenancy or occupation of housing accommodation for the time being held by it."

In addition, a HAT must carry out periodic reviews of the rents it is charging (s 84(2)).

This is similar to the powers and duties possessed by local authorities under the similarly worded s 24 of the Housing Act 1985. There have been several challenges in the courts to this level of local authority decision making. It has been consistently held by the courts that there is jurisdiction to review these decisions, although in only one case has a challenge been successful. This concerned a device used by a local authority to avoid the provisions of the Housing Finance Act 1972 (*Backhouse* v *Lambeth London Borough Council* (1972)).

In the cases where local authority rent fixing has been challenged, the courts have developed a number of principles. However, much of the reasoning in these cases is based on the nature of local authority housing finance and its duty to consider the interests of both the tenants and the general body of rate payers (see *Belcher* v *Reading Corporation* (1950)). As a consequence, few of the local authority cases are directly relevant to HATs.

Some tenants who are transferred to a HAT may not have a secure status. For example, temporary accommodation for the homeless provided under Part III of the 1985 Act and certain student lettings are not secure (see Sch 1 Housing Act 1985). As with non-secure lettings by local authorities, there is a special provision for increasing the rent. Section 86 of the 1988 Act relates to a periodic letting which is not secure. It allows the HAT to increase the rent by service of a written notice giving the tenant at least four weeks' notice of the increase and informing him of his right to terminate the tenancy (s 86(3)). The purpose of this provision is to allow service of a notice of increase without having to terminate the let in a case where the tenancy agreement makes no provision for rent review.

There can be little doubt that HATs will increase rents. As the consultative paper noted "rents may have to rise to allow the improvements to be maintained." (*Housing Action Trusts: A Consultative Document*, 1987, paragraph 21).

(b) Complaints

Local authority tenants have the right to attend meetings of the housing committee. They also have rights to information under the Local Government (Access to Information) Act 1985, the Access to Personal Files Act 1977 and the Data Protection Act 1984 (see Harrison: *Access to Information In Local Government Act*, 1988). The 1985 Act is of specific significance to council tenants.

During the Parliamentary debates, the Government was pressed to change the provisions relating to the constitution of HATs, to ensure that tenants will enjoy the same rights as they did when they were council tenants. The Government declined to do this, but it gave an undertaking that HATs will be directed to hold their meetings in public. This will be done under the Secretary of State's general power to give directions under s 72 of the Act (see Hansard, 14 June 1988, column 454). In addition, the Government will expect HATs to set up "non-statutory fora" to enable tenants to be consulted and for them to express their views (see Hansard, 14 June 1988, column 440).

4. Transfer of secure tenants by a housing action trust

The primary task of a HAT is to renovate and improve the properties with a view to selling them to a range of different landlords. Whilst a HAT is improving the properties, it will be the landlord of the tenants concerned. The position of the tenants during this time has just been considered.

A key concern to tenants will be the identity of the new landlord, the implications of losing their secure status and the terms of a tenancy offered by the new landlord. A tenant will retain the right to purchase his home and it is possible that some tenants will wish to exercise this right once their home has been improved, although the improvements will increase the purchase price. The tenants will also have the right to transfer to a landlord of their choice under Part IV of the 1988 Act (see Chapters 10 and 11).

In its consultative document on HATs, the Government canvassed a number of options. These included a transfer of the tenants to "housing associations or private landlords and the creation of tenants' co-operatives" (op cit, paragraph 23). Considerable concern has been expressed over the transfer provisions. How will the potential landlords be selected? Will they be vetted? To what extent will the wishes of the tenants be taken into account?

The Government made a number of changes to its original proposals in an attempt to meet these concerns. A major change is the requirement that tenants can be transferred only to landlords who have been approved by the Housing Corporation. The Corporation will also have the power to offer legal assistance to transferred tenants in certain cases.

There are three stages to complete before transfer. These are:

(a) consultation with the tenants and relevant local authorities;
(b) approval of the proposed landlord by the Housing Corporation;
(c) approval by the Secretary of State of the transfer of the tenants to the new landlord.

These individual steps are now considered in turn.

Except in the case of a sale to a secure tenant under the right to buy provisions of the 1985 Act, a HAT may sell the property to a landlord approved by the Housing Corporation or to a local authority only (s 79(2)). The Secretary of State, who may give "any directions", must consent to the sale (s 79(1)). Subject to this a HAT may sell to "such persons, in such manner and on such terms as it considers expedient for the purpose of achieving its objects" (s 79(1)).

The consultative exercise is dealt with in s 84. First, a HAT must serve a notice on the local authority in whose area the property is situated. If the property was in fact transferred from a different local authority that other authority must also be served with a copy of the notice. This deals with the case where the property is situated in one local authority area but was previously owned by another local authority.

The purpose of this procedure is to give the authority (or authorities) the opportunity of bidding for the property. Thus the notice must describe the property concerned and give the authority at least twenty-eight days to respond (s 84(2)). However, the notice does not have to describe any bid the HAT has had from another potential purchaser. The local authority has (a minimum) of twenty-eight days then to notify the HAT whether or not it is interested in purchasing the property. If it is interested, it must, in its notice, inform the HAT of what s 84(3) describes as "the likely consequences for the tenant if the house were to be acquired by the authority". This is presumably a reference to such matters as the rent that the authority will charge if it buys the property. However, many local authorities may find it difficult to purchase a renovated property that was previously taken from them, particularly if they were paid no compensation or had to make a payment to the HAT on the transfer. Other local authorities may no longer wish to be involved in the provision of rented housing.

After consulting the local authority, the HAT must then inform the tenants affected, in writing, of the proposed sale and of the identity of the person to whom the property is to be sold. The notice must also:

(a) explain the effect of the sale on their position as secure tenants (including the right to buy). Unless the sale is to be to a local authority the notice ought to describe the loss of security of tenure and other statutory rights under the 1985 Act. It ought also to describe the consequences of becoming an assured or assured shorthold tenant. None of these matters are required by s 84(4), although the HAT's notice may contain "such other details of the disposal as seem to the trust to be appropriate" (s 84(4)(b));

(b) tell the tenant whether or not the local authority has decided to bid for the property;

(c) where a local authority bid has been received, contain the information that has to be supplied as to the consequences of the local authority becoming the landlord;

(d) tell the tenant of his right to make representations. The tenant must be allowed at least twenty-eight days to do so.

By this stage the HAT will have details of its proposed sale, any local authority bid and the views of the tenants affected. It must then consider the views of the tenants (s 84(5)). If "it considers it appropriate" it may then reconsider its proposals and if it does so it must serve on the tenants a further notice under s 83(4) allowing the tenants to make further representations (s 84(5)).

This concludes the consultative stage. It is clear that the HAT is not bound to accept any bid it has received from a local authority. Nor is it bound to comply with the wishes of the tenants. As a result tenants cannot insist on being returned to local authority landlordship as secure tenants. Nor can they elect to return to the local authority under the change of landlord provisions in Part IV of the Act since these procedures do not apply to local authorities. The consultative procedures appear in this respect inconsistent with the policy of widening tenant choice that is said to underlie the Act.

After consultation, Government consent must be obtained. Copies of the s 84 notices; any representations received; and a statement of the HAT's consideration of any views received, must be sent to the Secretary of State. Apart from his general powers of approval and so on under s 72, he could at this stage direct the HAT to carry out further consultations and to inform him of the outcome (s 84(7)). This means that a dissatisfied party or his advisors (potential landlords as well as tenants) could urge the Secretary of State to give further directions.

Any proposed purchaser, other than a local authority, must be approved by the Housing Corporation, or Housing for Wales, either under Part III or Part IV of the 1988 Act (s 79(2)). Criteria are to be established by the Corporation setting the standards they will be applying (s 79)). These criteria will probably be very similar to those the Corporation has produced for the change of landlord provisions under Part IV and which are considered in Chapter 10.

There is another reference to criteria in s 79(6). The Corporation may not approve a purchaser who is a public sector landlord (or a county council). Nor may it approve a body which is "not independent of such a landlord or council" (s 79(6)). In making this assessment, the Corporation may examine whether the applicant is, or appears likely to be, under the control of, or subject to the influence of, the members or officers of a public landlord (or council). These broadly-drawn provisions are designed to stop local authorities from exercising indirect control over the new landlord. For the purposes of this assessment a "public landlord" means a local authority, a new town corporation or the Development Board for Wales (s 79(7)).

The Secretary of State may give consent subject to conditions (s 79(4)). In particular, conditions may be imposed concerning the sale price and any discount offered (s 79(5)).

To summarise, before a HAT can sell a property that is occupied by a secure tenant the following procedures must be followed:

(a) unless the proposed sale is to a local authority, obtain approval of the proposed purchaser from the Housing Corporation;

(b) serve notice on the relevant local authority (or authorities);

(c) serve notice on the tenants(s);

(d) consider representations from the tenants and local authority;

(e) obtain approval from the Secretary of State.

These procedures do not apply to a tenant exercising his right to buy. Under 80, a sale made without this consent is void, unless it is a sale of an individual property to a private individual (or two or more individuals). Such an individual does not have to make enquiries as to whether the consent has been obtained. The purpose of this provision is to protect an individual who purchases a property from a HAT where the HAT failed to obtain consent under s 79.

In most cases it is likely that sales will be to someone other than a local authority. If the property is sold to a housing association or a private landlord, the tenant will lose his status as a secure tenant, since the "landlord condition" will no longer apply (see s 80 Housing Act 1985 as amended by s 35 of the 1988 Act). The tenant cannot become a protected tenant or a secure tenant of a housing association, because of the "phasing out" provisions in the 1988 Act (see page 28). The expectation is that the tenant will be offered an assured tenancy by the new landlord, since it is otherwise difficult to see how the new landlord could be approved by the Housing Corporation or how the sale could be approved by the Secretary of State.

This deals with a sale by a HAT to an approved landlord. Section 81 deals with a subsequent sale or other disposal by the new landlord. A HAT must ensure that the conveyance contains a provision that the landlord obtains the Secretary of State's approval before selling the property (s 81(1)). After transfer, the landlord must usually obtain approval from the Secretary of State, who may give approval subject to conditions (s 81(3)). The landlord must satisfy the Secretary of State that he has consulted any tenants who will be affected and that he has taken account of their views (s 81(5)). Consent need not be sought in the case of "exempt disposals", the most important of which are right to buy sales, mortgaging a property or granting a new tenancy (s 81(8)).

Fears were expressed during the Parliamentary passage of the Act that tenants might be harassed or otherwise exploited by a landlord anxious to obtain vacant possession. In response, the Government introduced a new provision which empowers the Housing Corporation or Housing for Wales to provide assistance to tenants after the sale. Under s 82, a tenant, or if he has died, his surviving spouse, may apply for assistance to settle "any dispute" between himself and the purchaser. The Corporation has power to offer legal assistance where it believes that the dispute raises a "question of principle"; or where, because of the complexity of the case, it is unreasonable to expect the tenant to deal with it without assistance; or "by reason of any other special consideration" (s 82(2)). The assistance given can take a variety of forms. These include the giving of advice or endeavouring to settle the dispute; the provision of advice and representation by solicitor or counsel and "any other form of assistance which the Corporation may consider appropriate" (s 82(3)). As with a case where legal aid has been provided, the Corporation has a statutory charge on any costs or damages recovered by the tenant.

5. Regulating housing action trusts

(a) Central Government controls

The Secretary of State is closely involved at all stages from the creation of a HAT to its dissolution, and this involvement can be summarised in the following way:

Stage 1: it is for the Secretary of State to decide where to site a HAT, and what specific functions it will have. In doing this he has to consult relevant local authorities and inform the residents who will be affected. Assuming that a majority of the residents affected agree, he orders the transfer of local property to the HAT and must settle the terms of the transfer in consultation with the authority affected. The appointment of the members of the HAT is also a matter for the Secretary of State.

Stage 2: Following its creation, the members appoint staff and prepare a statement of its plans for the Secretary of State's approval. Preparation of this plan must include consultation with the local authority and local residents. A HAT will receive Central Government funding. It may also borrow money and in some cases it may receive payments from the local authority if the properties transferred have a negative value.

Stage 3: A HAT has a limited life span. The exact area of its activities will depend on its size, funding, plans and the functions it is given. At a minimum, it will manage the properties given to it. Here it will have powers and obligations under the Housing Act 1985. During this period the tenants who were transferred retain their rights under the 1985 Act. The HAT is to renovate the properties and encourage different forms of landlord. The Secretary of State's approval is needed before certain activities can be undertaken. In addition, the Secretary of State has powers. A list of any directions given by the Secretary of State must be published. He may also transfer a HAT's functions to another HAT and he has power to remove a member of a HAT.

Stage 4: The HAT must sell the property either to a local authority or to another landlord who has been approved by the Housing Corporation. Before selling, it must consult the local authority and the tenants affected *and* obtain the Secretary of State's consent. Most subsequent disposals by an approved landlord must be approved by the Secretary of State.

Stage 5: Following various procedures and consents the HAT will be wound up.

(b) Local controls

Residents in a designated area have consultation rights and may attend meetings of a HAT. A tenant of a HAT has rights as a secure tenant, including the right to be consulted over matters of housing management.

(c) Judicial review

It may be possible to challenge a decision of a HAT by using the procedure of judicial review. This procedure is governed by Order 53 of the Supreme Court Rules. An applicant must show that he has a sufficient interest in the matter of which he seeks judicial review. In assessing this, the court must consider the issue in the context of the general merits of the application (*R* v *I.R.C. ex parte National Federation of Self-Employed & Small Businesses Ltd* (1982)). A resident or a local authority will often have an interest in decisions taken by a HAT.

As to whether the courts have jurisdiction to review decisions taken by a body such as a HAT, a relevant Court of Appeal decision is *R* v *Panel on Take-Overs and Mergers ex parte Datafin* (1987). This concerned a decision taken by the Panel, which is a self-regulating unincorporated association, which administers a code of conduct that regulates the take-over of public companies. It has no direct statutory, prerogative or common law powers. The Court of Appeal held that its decisions *are* subject to judicial review. It held that a court is not limited to examining the sources of a body's powers; it must look at the nature of these powers. If a body is exercising public law functions, a court has jurisdiction to review its decisions.

On this reasoning, a HAT is also subject to judicial review. It has powers and duties imposed by statute; it exercises several public law functions; and its reports are laid before Parliament. The Government evidently believes that a HAT is subject to judicial review since during discussion of a HAT's duty to co-operate with a local authority in accommodating the homeless, the Government stated that a HAT could be challenged in the court. This was one of reasons given for not giving a HAT statutory duties under the homelessness provisions in the Housing Act 1985 (Hansard, House of Commons, Standing Committee, 16 February 1988, column 900).

It is difficult to summarise the basis on which the courts will review a decision and also difficult to predict the outcome in any particular case (see generally, Baldwin & McCrudden: *Regulation and Public Law*, 1987, Chapter 4). However, in a recent case, the House of Lords reformulated the general grounds on which the courts will review a public law decision (*Council of Civil Service Unions* v *Minister for the Civil Services* (1987)). Here Lord Diplock classified under three heads the grounds on which the courts may intervene. These grounds are "illegality, irrationality and procedural impropriety". By "illegality" he meant that the decision-maker must correctly understand the law applicable to his powers of decision-making and must give effect to it. As to "irrationality", Lord Diplock referred to "a decision that is so outrageous in its defiance of logic or of accepted moral standards that no sensible person who applied his mind to the question to be decided could have arrived at it". "Procedural impropriety" indicates failure to act with procedural fairness or in breach of the rules of natural justice. As illustrated in this chapter and in the previous chapter, a HAT will have to take a number of major decisions, many of which involve consultation. As a result, a resident, a local authority, or other person may challenge HAT decisions by means of judicial review.

Central Government decisions may also be challenged by judicial review; many of the decisions summarised in (*a*) above (see page 176) are capable of challenge under this procedure.

Chapter 10

Change of landlord: principles

Under Part IV of the 1988 Act, private landlords can compulsorily purchase council housing. These provisions are amongst the most contentious under the new legislation; the procedures governing the balloting of the council tenants in particular attracted much criticism (see page 183). Before the Act, local authorities had been given powers to sell parts or all of their housing stock. These are examined first.

1. Transfers under the Housing Act 1985

Under s 32 of the Housing Act 1985, a local authority has power to dispose of property that it holds for the provision of housing under Part II of the 1985 Act. This is separate from its powers to grant secure tenancies of the dwellings that it owns. It is also different from sales under the right to buy. Thus the s 32 powers and procedures do not in general affect secure lettings or the right to buy.

Before a local authority can sell housing under s 32, it must obtain the approval of the Secretary of State. He may give consent to local authorities generally or to a particular local authority or description of authority (s 34(2)(a)). Consent may relate to a particular property or to a description of property and it may be subject to conditions such as conditions as to the price or discount (s 34(2)(b), (3) and (4)).

A local authority has a limited power under s 33 to impose covenants or other conditions on the sale. Some conditions or covenants may be introduced only with Government consent. These include a condition limiting the price payable on a subsequent sale (s 33(2)). There are restrictions on the sale of properties in National Parks and in other areas of natural beauty (s 37).

The Secretary of State, in granting consent, has treated these sales as on the same footing as sales under the right to buy (Circular 21/84). Many local authorities have made extensive use of these powers to dispose of whole estates and tracts of housing (Hughes: *Public Sector Housing Law*, 2nd ed 1987, page 76).

(a) Changes introduced by the Housing and Planning Act 1986

This privatisation of council housing has been accelerated by provisions in the Housing and Planning Act 1986 which amends the Housing Act 1985 by inserting additional sections and schedules. Under new 106A and new Sch 3A, an authority wishing to sell dwellings occupied by secure tenants must obtain the views of these tenants. Before considering whether to approve such a transfer the Secretary of State must be satisifed that the transfer carries the support of the tenants. Consent must not be given if a majority of the tenants are opposed to the transfer (para 5(1), Sch 3A of the Housing Act 1985). Tenants transferred in this way cease to be secure tenants if they are taken over by a private landlord. However they retain their right to buy. This is effected by the insertion of a new sections 171A, B, C, D, E, F, G and H into the 1985 Act.

Before the 1988 Act, a tenant transferred to a private landlord could become a protected tenant under the Rent Act 1977. A local authority was able to obtain a certificate of fair rent for the property from a rent officer (new s 69(1)(A) Rent Act 1977 introduced by s 7 of the 1986 Act). A secure tenant would then become a tenant of the new private landlord and protected under the Rent Act 1977. With the phasing out of the Rent Acts, this procedure will gradually disappear.

Sales of council housing are also facilitated by the 1986 Act in another way. Local authorities are given a new ground for possession if they decide to carry out certain types of development. This change is achieved by inserting a new ground 10A into Sch 2 of the 1985 Act which contains the grounds for possession against secure tenants. A new part I is added to that schedule setting out a procedure whereby a local authority can obtain approval of its development scheme.

The 1986 Act also extended the powers of local authorities to enter into management agreements whereby it delegates part of its responsibilities for management of its housing (new s 27 inserted into the Housing Act 1985).

(b) Changes introduced by the Housing Act 1988

Many local authorities have tried to use these powers to sell housing stock to housing associations set up or influenced by themselves. However, the Department of the Environment has stated that these transfers may not meet with approval. The Department published a paper on this subject in June 1988 (*Large Scale Voluntary Transfers of Local Authority Housing to Private Bodies*). It noted that a "number of local housing authorities are considering selling all or much of their housing stock to new landlords" (para 1).

The Department wants to be satisfied that the body to which the housing is sold is independent of the local authority. Specifically, council membership or shareholding should not exceed 20%; neither the council nor the new landlord should provide each other with services, and the new landlord should be able to select staff at its own discretion (para 4). In other words, the council cannot make it a term of the sale that the landlord takes over part of its housing functions or its staff. Nor would the new landlord be independent of the council if the council retains nomination rights for the housing concerned (ibid). However a contract may be agreed under which the new landlord accommodates persons for whom the council is responsible under the homelessness provisions in Part III of the Housing Act 1985.

The Government also indicated that it will not usually agree to more than five thousand to ten thousand properties passing to a single landlord. An authority owning fewer than five thousand properties should also consider transfer to more than one landlord. The object of this is to avoid "large public housing monopolies" being converted into large private housing monopolies (para 6).

Section 132 of the 1988 Act makes further changes to disposals under the Housing Act 1985. The Secretary of State will have regard to the degree of local authority influence or control of the proposed purchaser when considering whether to approve a sale. He may also give directions as to the use of the capital monies received by the local authority. In addition his consent must be obtained to any further sale by the body that purchased the housing from the local authority (s 133 of the 1988 Act).

Summary

Under the Housing Act 1985, local authorities may, with Central Government approval, sell part or all of its housing stock. These powers have been extended by the Housing and Planning Act 1966 and by the Housing Act 1988. Sales may be permitted even though the housing is occupied by secure tenants, provided a majority of these tenants agree with the transfer. To facilitate disposals, local authorities may obtain vacant possession of properties in order to carry out approved development. A local authority may be prevented from selling if the proposed purchaser is under its control or influence.

2. Introduction to Part IV Housing Act 1988

Sales of council homes under the Housing Act 1985 will occur only if the local authority decides to divest itself of part or all of its housing stock. Many authorities are using this power. However, there are also several housing authorities who remain committed to the provision of council housing and are opposed to selling their stock.

During the 1987 general election campaign, the Conservative Party announced its plans to introduce "tenants' choice" procedures under which council tenants can opt for a private landlord. After their return to Government, this idea was expounded in the White Paper preceding the Housing Bill; in a consultative document; and in a later paper produced in June 1988 (*Tenants' Choice*).

The original idea has changed considerably during this period although the basic policy is the same. It will force unwilling local authorities to sell parts or all of their housing stock to private landlords. Tenants may take the initiative by seeking out a landlord to take over their estate. However, in many cases it will be the landlord who takes the initiative by approaching a local authority.

During the Parliamentary passage of the Bill, surveys of council tenants indicated that there will in many cases be opposition to being transferred to a private landlord. In the *Tenants' Choice* paper, the Government stated that a transfer will go ahead unless "a majority of qualifying tenants had voted to continue as tenants of their current landlord" (paragraph 34). In other words when tenants are asked to vote on a proposal to transfer them to a private landlord, a majority must vote *against* the proposal in order to defeat it. If there is no absolute majority against, the proposal will go ahead however small the number supporting it. This anomalous method of conducting a ballot has attracted more criticism than anything else in Part IV of the 1988 Act.

The Housing Corporation and Housing for Wales have important functions in administering the change of landlord procedures. They will offer advice and assistance to council tenants and to landlords seeking to acquire council housing compulsorily. They will approve and offer a degree of regulation of these new landlords.

The advice-giving functions commenced on 15 January 1989. However Part IV of the Act will not be brought fully into force until towards the middle of 1989. The reason for this is that regulations dealing with consultation and other matters will not be ready until that time. Consultation papers have been issued on these subjects and they are examined in this and the next chapter.

The way in which the Government envisages these procedures working was set out in the *Tenants' Choice* document and in statements made during the Parliamentary debates. It believes that the statutory procedures will, in most cases, be preceded by informal consultations supervised by the Corporation. Tenants interested in considering a transfer to a new landlord will be put in touch with a range of organisations. This was described by the Government in Parliament as a "marriage-broking service" (Hansard, 17 January 1988, column 60).

Assuming that more than one potential applicant is involved, a preliminary consultation will be arranged to enable the tenants to discover what the applicants have on offer. This was described by the Government as a "preliminary beauty contest" (Hansard, ibid, column 61). If at the end of the "preliminary beauty contest" the tenants express a clear preference, the preferred applicant will proceed to the statutory phase of the procedure. The other potential applicants will not be allowed to proceed.

Under the statutory procedure, the applicant is entitled to information about the properties and the tenants he is considering taking over. The local authority and the applicant are to agree the terms of the transfer. Arbitration will be used to deal with any disputes over these matters. Following these preliminary matters, the tenants are to be consulted. Unless a majority of them vote against transfer, the local authority will be forced to sell the properties.

The remainder of this chapter considers the preliminary factors. These include the identification of housing authorities which can be forced to sell their housing stock; which tenants will be affected; the timing of the procedures; properties that may be excluded; approval of applicants and the initial procedures.

3. Authorities affected by Part IV Housing Act 1988

Only housing owned by a "public sector landlord" can be acquired under Part IV of the 1988 Act. A "public sector landlord" is a local housing authority, a new town corporation, a housing action trust and the Development Board for Wales (s 93(2)). For the sake of simplicity, further references will be to local authorities only.

4. Properties

Under s 93 of the Act, an approved person has the right to acquire from a public sector landlord:

(a) the freehold of any building consisting of a residential dwelling or a number of dwellings, occupied by "qualifying tenants"; and
(b) the freehold of any other property "which is reasonably required for occupation with the buildings referred to in (a) above.

However, some property may be excluded for one or more of the following reasons:

(a) Buildings that are not wholly used for residential purposes

Local authorities may own property that is used in whole or in part for purposes other than residential use. These properties are exempt from s 93 where the building (or part of it) is occupied or intended for occupation otherwise than for residential purposes (s 95(1)(a)), providing the non-residential occupation extends to at least 50% of the available floor area of the whole building excluding any common parts or facilities; see s 95(1)(b). The Secretary of State has power to alter this percentage (s 95(7)).

Section 95(2) deals with property that would not ordinarily be considered as being for residential use and provides that property which is used *with* a dwelling-house is to be treated as residential for the purposes of the calculation in s 95(1) (s 95(2)(a)). The same applies to a building owned by a local authority which is used to provide services to a dwelling in the same building (s 95(2)(b)).

(b) Blocks of flats

A building containing two or more dwellings may also be exempt from s 93. This is so where the individual dwellings are occupied by secure tenants who are not "qualifying tenants" for the purposes of Part IV of the 1988 Act (s 95(3)) (see page 186 below—in summary, a tenant who is subject to a possession order or a tenant who does not have the right to buy is not a qualifying tenant). In addition, the number of dwellings occupied by tenants who are not qualifying tenants must exceed 50% of the total number of dwellings in the building (s 95(3)(b)). The purpose of this exemption is to exclude a building where the local authority is entitled to possession of most of the flats, or where most of the tenants do not have the right to buy.

(c) Individual houses

A house is exempt if it is occupied by a tenant who is not a "qualifying tenant" in the way described in the previous paragraph. It is also exempt if it is occupied by someone who is not a secure tenant, as in the case of, for example, accommodation for the homeless (s 95(4)).

(d) Buildings subject to an application to purchase under Part IV

If a person has already applied to buy council property, any building that is the subject of that application is also excluded until the application is disposed of (s 95(5)). Thus a local authority will not have to deal with applications by different persons in relation to the same buildings simultaneously, at the statutory stage of the procedures.

(e) Miscellaneous

Under s 95(6), land held for pleasure grounds under s 164 of the Public Health Act 1875 or open spaces and burial grounds under s 10 Open Spaces Act 1906 are excluded.

5. Qualifying tenants

Only property occupied by qualifying tenants can be purchased under s 93. A tenant is not a qualifying tenant if he must give up possession as a result of a court order either immediately or at a date specified in the possession order (s 93(4)(a)). This includes, therefore, cases where both immediate and suspended possession orders have been made. As will be explained in Chapter 11, the Secretary of State will, by regulations to be promulgated, extend the definition of "qualifying tenant" to others. This is likely to include a successor of a qualifying tenant who has died, and a tenant under a suspended possession order who has arranged for the order to be rescinded. Tenants who do not have the right to buy are not qualifying tenants.

6. The "relevant date"

Questions of whether a property is exempt and whether a tenant is a qualifying tenant must be considered at the "relevant date". This is the date the applicant lodged his application with the local authority. The importance of this will become apparent once the balloting of tenants procedures is considered. Broadly speaking, a local authority cannot seek exemption by changing the use of properties after it has received an application. Nor, generally, can any tenant who is moved into the properties after the date of the application be a qualifying tenant. He will be ineligible to vote in the ballot.

7. Eligibility to buy

Only a person or organisation approved by the Housing Corporation or Housing for Wales may seek to exercise rights under Part IV of the Act. An individual, group of individuals or a company may seek approval. The only groups that cannot be approved are public sector landlords, a county council and any other body "which the Corporation have reason to believe might not be independent" of a public landlord or county council (s 94(1)). Thus, as with sales under the 1985 and 1986 Acts, there cannot be a transfer to a body controlled by the local authority. Under s 94(2) a body is not independent if it is "or appears likely to be under the control of, or subject to influence from" such a landlord or council "or particular members or officers of such a landlord or council" (s 94(2)). This is not as precise as the criteria relating to the independence of transferee bodies under voluntary disposals. However, the Corporations will have to have an identifiable basis for a determination that the applicant is not independent. Factors such as ownership of shares and the membership of the transferee body are obviously relevant. Under s 94(3) the Housing Corporation must establish criteria, which can be varied from time to time, that it must use in considering applications. A copy of the published criteria appears as appendix 5 to this book (see page 443) and sheds further light on the question of the independence of applicants for approval.

Section 94(4) contains other matters governing applications for approval. Subject to approval of the Secretary of State, a fee may be charged on the making of an application. The Corporation may consider applications for approval from an individual or from "persons of a particular description" (s 94(4)(b)). There is also a discretion in relation to the types of bid that the applicant intends to make. Thus approval may be limited to one or more particular acquisitions by the applicant or to acquisitions generally (s 94(4)(c)). Further, approval may be limited to acquisition in a particular area or within a specific period (ibid). For example, a general approval might be given to a registered housing association with considerable experience in providing accommodation. In the case of an individual or a company whose experience is limited, approval may be limited in the first instance. As with applications for registration of a housing association, the Corporation may require the applicant to give undertakings as a condition of granting approval. There is no definition of the sorts of undertaking that may be required. Section 94(4)(d) refers to "such undertakings as may be specified by the Corporation". The Secretary of State may give directions to the Corporation as to the exercise of its functions (s 76 Housing Associations Act 1985). He may invoke this power to give directions in relation to applications for approval.

As with applications for registration by housing associations, there is no right of appeal against a refusal to approve an applicant under s 94. Another similarity with registration is the power to revoke approval. This power is contained in s 94(5) and the Corporation is given a very wide discretion. Approval may be withdrawn "if it appears to the Corporation appropriate to do so" (s 94(5) of the 1988 Act). The only qualification is that approval may be withdrawn for a failure to honour an undertaking, or to meet the criteria or "any other reason" (ibid). There is no requirement that the Corporation gives the approved body an opportunity to respond to criticisms. Again, the Secretary of State may, under s 76 Housing Associations Act 1985, give directions to the Corporation about the discharge of this function.

If the Corporation decides to revoke approval, it must notify the approved person in writing and the revocation is provisional for a period specified in the notice, which must not be less than fourteen days (s 94(5)(a)). This gives the approved person the opportunity to respond, although there is no requirement that the notice particularises the basis on which revocation is intended. The notice of revocation may be withdrawn during the period specified. If it is withdrawn approval will be treated as if it has not been revoked (s 95(5)(b)). During the period of the notice, the approved person may not exercise rights under Part IV of the 1988 Act. However, this does not affect any transaction completed before service of the notice (s 94(5)(c)). If it appears to the Corporation that an approved body does not have a registered office and that it has ceased to exist or to operate, the notice may be served at the last known principal business address of that body. Unlike removal from the register of housing associations, there is no right of appeal to the High Court against a revocation of approval.

Since revocation does not affect any pre-notice transaction, tenants previously transferred remain with the formerly approved landlord. There is no power to transfer the properties and tenants back to the relevant local authority. Nor will the Corporation have the supervisory powers to monitor and intervene that it has with housing associations (except of course where the approved landlord is a registered housing association). The Corporation must maintain a public register of approved persons and the extent of their approval. These registers are open to public inspection (s 94(7)).

Chapter 11

Change of landlord: procedure

Although the change of landlord provisions have been heralded as "tenants' choice", the tenants concerned will be balloted only after negotiations between the applicant and the local authority. These negotiations are likely to be protracted. A local authority that is willing to sell its housing will use the procedures under the 1985 and 1986 Acts. The 1988 procedures pre-suppose that a local authority is unwilling to sell. The "initial procedures" involve an applicant bidding for housing and obtaining information concerning the housing. There are also mechanisms for resolving disputes over property that should be exempt from the sale and over the terms of the sale. The latter, in particular, are likely to be the subject of disagreement. These procedures assume, of course, that the applicant has been approved by the Housing Corporation under s 94 of the Act. The different elements of these initial procedures are considered in turn. In most cases, these statutory procedures will have been preceded by an informal consultation between proposed applicants, supervised by the Corporations.

1. The application to purchase

The applicant must apply to the local authority, in a prescribed form, indicating his desire to purchase council housing. In addition to specifying the properties he wishes to buy, the applicant must also lodge a plan with the local authority which shows the property he wants to buy (s 96(1)). This, under s 93(1), may include property other than housing where that other property is "reasonably required for occupation" with the housing.

There are additional requirements where the housing is the subject of an "approved co-operative management agreement". Under s 10 of the Housing and Planning Act 1986, local authorities have power to delegate management of properties to a housing co-operative. Where a building contains a dwelling which is the subject of such an agreement, the application must also particularise any other buildings which are the subject of this agreement and which are owned by the local authority (s 96(2)). Where an applicant applies to buy properties subject to an approved management agreement, he may not bid for any other properties (s 96(2)(b)).

2. The local authority's duty to provide information and access

The local authority has four weeks to provide information on the properties and on the tenants. It must serve a notice on the applicant within four weeks of the "relevant date", that is, the date on which the application is made (s 93(5)). Their notice must disclose the name and address of every tenant or licensee who occupies a dwelling in any of the properties the applicant wants to buy, as well as the "general nature of" the tenancies or licences (s 97(1)). This rather vague reference appears to refer to the status of the occupant. The information to be provided could also include information on any suspended possession orders. The local authority is under a duty to disclose this information regardless of its or its tenants' wishes.

Four weeks after the applicant has received the s 97 notice he acquires a number of statutory rights over the properties he wants to buy. He will have the right of access to any property that is not subject to a tenancy (s 97(2)(a)). Curiously, this subsection does not refer to a property that is subject to a licence. If a property is occupied by a licensee, he can be a secure tenant under s 79 of the Housing Act 1985. However a licence granted as a temporary expedient, to a person who originally entered the property as a squatter, cannot be a secure tenancy. On a literal interpretation, the applicant could not seek access to a property occupied by a former squatter. On the other hand the spirit of s 97 implies that access is to be allowed to properties that are not occupied for residential purposes. Indeed in the *Tenant's Choice* paper referred to earlier, reference was made in this context to "common parts and ancillary buildings etc" (para 16).

This right of access can only be exercised at reasonable times and on the giving of reasonable notice (s 97(2)(a)). The expression "reasonable" is not further defined, with the result that there may be disputes between local authorities and applicants.

The applicant also acquires statutory rights to documents, described as any document "sight of which is reasonably required for the purpose of pursuing the application" (s 97(3)(a)). However, there is an important qualification to this. The documents must be of a type a vendor would have to disclose to a purchaser on a voluntary sale (s 97(3)(b)). For example an authority could be forced to disclose information on any notices that affect the property, reports on the property and the title deeds.

An applicant might seek information about the state of repair of the buildings. He might also seek additional information about the occupants, such as the records of rent payments. Many authorities will resist imparting confidential information on their tenants. If the information is stored on computer (as will often be the case) the authority would be committing an offence under the Data Protection Act 1984. The purpose of providing an applicant with information is basically to enable him to formulate a bid for the properties. Information on the physical condition of the property and the legal nature of the occupancies is relevant; information concerning individuals is not. The applicant has the right, on reasonable notice, to be provided with a list of the documents he considers that he is entitled to (s 97(2)(b)). Again there is no further definition of what is "reasonable notice". He also has the right to inspect and to copy documents (on payment of a reasonable fee—s 97(2)(c), (d)). The word "document" carries the same meaning as in Part I of the Civil Evidence Act 1968. In s 10 of this Act there is a lengthy list which includes maps, plans, graphs or drawings, photographs and so on. There is again potential for disputes about the applicant's entitlement to documents.

3. Determining which properties can be included

As indicated at page 184 above, some properties are exempt from sale under s 93. Under s 98, the local authority must serve notice on the applicant within twelve weeks of the date on which it received the original application. The notice must specify which properties, in the view of the local authority, fall into the exempt category under s 93, and identify any other property it needs to retain because of factors listed in s 98 (see below). In addition, an authority may contend that the applicant does not "reasonably" require any non-residential property applied for under s 93(1). There is obviously scope for disagreements between local authorities and applicants on this question.

The converse is that some authorities may consider that properties other than those contained in the application should also be sold. For example it may believe that if the sale goes ahead, it would be difficult to manage or maintain adjacent property. If an authority is of this view, it can specify in the notice other properties which it wants included in the sale (s 98(1)(d)). However, it cannot list properties that are excluded under either s 98 or s 96(2)(b). For example, a building excluded because it is occupied by non-qualifying tenants cannot be purchased by the applicant and cannot be added to the application by the local authority. Of course there may be a dispute over whether the building can properly be categorised in this way. An applicant might include it in his list and the local authority might resist this, arguing that it is exempt.

If a local authority seeks to add properties to the application, the applicant acquires the right of access to any such property that is not tenanted (s 98(3)).

An authority may need to retain some rights over the properties listed by the applicant. It may need these rights to enable it to manage and maintain the properties it retains. For example, if the applicant wants to take over part of a council estate, the authority might need access to common parts to run the rest of the estate. If this is the case, it must state which rights it wishes to retain (s 98(1)(e)).

Apart from any disagreement over properties to be included, the local authority must set out its proposals for the terms of the conveyance and "such other particulars as may be prescribed" (s 98(1)(f), (g)). Four weeks after receipt of the local authority's notice, the applicant must notify the authority of any matters in their notice "which he does not accept" (s 98(4)).

It will be surprising if there are not disputes between an applicant and a local authority that does not wish to dispose of its housing stock. Many of the disputes will involve complex issues of fact and of law. The county court might be the best forum under a summary procedure. However, the Government decided that these disputes should be settled by arbitration. If the parties cannot agree on a person to act as arbitrator, one will be appointed by the Secretary of State (s 98(5)(a)). Regulations will be published dealing with procedural matters, including costs (s 98(5)(b)).

4. Determining the purchase price

It will be for the local authority to propose the sale price. However, the price is regulated by a number of assumptions in s 99. If the parties cannot agree a price, the matter will be settled by the district valuer.

Under s 99, the local authority must, within eight weeks of service of its notice, serve another notice proposing a price (or the disposal cost). If there is a dispute about the first notice, the period for service of the second notice will be eight weeks of the determination of the dispute. The reference to "disposal cost" is to situations where the property has a "negative value" and the authority is required to hand over the property *and* a sum of money to the applicant (see below, page 195).

Apart from arriving at a figure based on the assumptions in s 99, the price (or disposal cost) proposed is also subject to the following restraints:

(a) the effect of the local authority's retaining ownership of any dwelling occupied by a tenant who wishes to stay with the authority (under a procedure set out in s 100) must be left out of account. The same factor is to be disregarded where a disposal cost is proposed. The explanation for this is that it will not be known at this stage which tenants wish to stay;

(b) where the property includes houses, the figure must deal with an amount attributable to those houses as set out in s 100(4). In the case of property consisting solely of houses, any house that will remain in local authority ownership because the tenant wishes to remain a council tenant must be disregarded. However, where the property consists of houses and other properties a different calculation must be made. This in turn relates to the assumptions that regulate the purchase price or disposal cost (see further page (196)). Whatever figure is arrived at, it must exclude the value of any house. Even without the assumptions in s 92 this is a complicated calculation.

In summary, the local authority must specify a price for the property including any dwellings it will retain because a tenant wants to remain a council tenant. If the property consists of houses the value of those remaining in local authority ownership must also be included. The same factors apply to a disposal cost.

This brings one to the assumptions that regulate the price or the disposal cost. There are listed in s 99(2) and disposal costs are the subject of s 99(3). The valuation is that payable on the relevant date, that is the date of the original application. This will benefit the applicant in most cases. If (which is likely) there is a dispute over which properties are to be affected, or over the other matters in s 98, it may be several months before the date of service of the s 99 notice. Thus the applicant will benefit, not having to pay for any inflation in property prices during this period. (The converse will hold true if there is a drop in prices during this period, although the applicant could, in this event, withdraw his application).

The price must reflect any tenancies existing at the date of the original application (s 99(2)(a)). This also works to the advantage of the applicant. A sale with a sitting tenant will depress the purchase price. There is another benefit as well since the tenancies to be considered are those at the date of the original application. If a tenant leaves during the intervening period, the calculation must still be on the basis of a sale with a sitting tenant. Thus the applicant will not have to pay for what would otherwise be an inflationary factor in the calculation.

The next assumption is that the property is sold "with the same rights and subject to the same burdens as it would be in pursuance of the right of acquisition" (s 99(2)(b)). The most obvious burden will be any outstanding loan on the property and the most obvious right will be the tenant's preserved right to buy. Again both of these factors will depress the purchase price.

A third assumption is that the only bidders in the market are those approved by the Corporations or those who fulfil the approval criteria under s 94 (s 99(2)(c)). During the period immediately after commencement of these provisions, there will obviously be few approved bidders, a factor that will depress the price, although an assessment of other potential bidders who will meet the approval criteria will mitigate this factor. Thus, if a number of housing associations were persuaded to join in the pre-statutory "preliminary beauty contest", this could persuade a valuer that there is a significant market. Moreover, a statement by an association that was not selected by the Corporation as an applicant, that it would have bid at a higher price, might also influence the valuation.

Where the property is in a state of disrepair, it is assumed that the applicant will carry out the repairs "in a reasonable period" (s 99(2)(d)). This once again will depress the purchase price.

The final assumption relates to the possibility that some of the tenants will elect to remain council tenants. If they occupy a flat, the applicant will have to grant a lease to the local authority after completion of the sale, enabling the authority to grant a sub-lease or subtenancy to the tenant concerned. However, it is assumed for the purposes of the purchase price that no leases will be granted.

Taken together, these assumptions will considerably reduce the genuine market value of the properties being sold. If some or all of the properties are in a poor state of repair, the price may be a negative one. Hence the references to "disposal costs". A disposal cost is the difference between the value of the property on the assumptions in s 99(2) and the value if the repairs had been carried out.

The s 99 notice must show how the has authority arrived at the price or disposal cost, taking account of all of the matters described. If the property consists of any houses, the addresses and the number of rooms in each house must also be stated in the notice (s 99(4)).

Under the new régime, therefore, local authorities face the prospect of compulsory purchase of their housing stock and having to make a cash payment to the applicant in some cases. This presents a major investment opportunity for applicants, but it will be a traumatic experience for local authorities, who will retain responsibilities for the homeless.

It seems almost inevitable that authorities and applicants will disagree over the purchase price or disposal cost. The applicant has four weeks to notify the authority in writing if he disagrees with anything in their s 99 notice. Continuing disputes will be settled by the district valuer in accordance with regulations to be prescribed (s 99(6)).

5. Tenants continuing to be council tenants

Tenants can decide to remain council tenants even if the ballot result favours the applicant. However this option is available only to a qualifying tenant, that is a tenant in occupation at the time of the application (s 100(2)(a)). These tenants must notify their local authority of their wishes after the balloting procedure, which is discussed later; see pages 200 to 202. Regulations will be made dealing with these matters and other matters contained in s 100. The effect is that where a tenant decides to remain a council tenant, the house or flat he occupies will be excluded from the sale. In the case of flats, there will be situations where only some of the flats become owned by the applicant. The tenants of these flats will lose their status as secure tenants (except for the right to buy) and they will become assured tenants paying market rents. Tenants electing to remain council tenants will continue to be secure tenants. The local authority will continue to have discretion in the fixing of their rents. However, the new landlord will be charging the local authority a rent under the lease he must grant to it in relation to the flats excluded from the sale. Thus the authority will face the prospect of passing on this rent to the remaining tenants. If it maintains the rents at their original level and it is paying the new landlord more than it is receiving from the tenants, the shortfall must be met out of the housing revenue account. In other words, it would be passed on to the general body of tenants. Under the Government's plans to change housing revenue accounts, this will not be permissible.

Section 100 also makes allowance for any properties that are excluded from the sale. Under regulations to be made, there will have to be a calculation of "the sum referable to excluded houses" (s 100(3)(a)). This calculation is based on the number of habitable rooms in the houses. This expression is defined in s 114(1) as a room used (or intended for use) as a bedroom, living room, dining room or kitchen. A total must be made of the number of the rooms in the houses that are excluded from the sale and a separate total is taken for *all* of the houses which are the subject of the sale. The first total is then expressed as a proportion of the second. The "sum referable to excluded houses" is arrived at by reference to this proportion (s 100(3)(a)). Thus if the first total is 25 habitable rooms and the total for all of the houses is 100, the proportion is 25%. This proportion must then be applied to the purchase price or disposal cost as the case may be. If the applicant is paying a price, there will be a deduction made to reflect the fact that he is not acquiring all of the properties he originally bid for. In the example given above, the basic purchase determined under s 99 is reduced by

25% (s 100(3)(b)). If the transfer is accompanied by a payment by the local authority, the starting point is the disposal cost estimated under s 99. This will be increased, using the same example, by 25%. The calculation may be expressed in the following formula:

$$\frac{\text{Number of habitable rooms in excluded houses}}{\text{Total habitable rooms in all of the houses bid for}} \times \text{sum calculated under s 99}$$

This may appear to be an arbitrary and unnecessarily complicated way of adjusting the purchase price to take account of houses that become excluded from the transfer. Would it not have been simpler to value the excluded houses separately and deduct this from the sale price (or add it to the disposal costs)? The Government felt that a second valuation would be "administratively and procedurally burdensome, and would involve avoidable delay to the proceedings" (*Tenants' Choice*, appendix B).

How will excluded flats be accounted for in the sale? The answer derives from the fact the local authority will be conveying the freehold of a block of flats together with the tenancies of the occupants who have opted for the applicant. Under regulations to be produced under s 100, the new owner will have to lease back those flats occupied by tenants who decide to stay with the council. It will be the terms of this lease that will permit an adjustment to the price (or disposal costs). The local authority will not have to pay a premium for this lease. However the new owner will be able to impose rents and service charges linked to those payable by his new tenants. Thus the new landlord will not be affected by having two classes of tenant living in the same block. He will, overall, receive the same rental income from the tenants occupying under assured tenancies and from the local authority under the terms of the lease-back. As noted earlier, local authorities will have to consider passing on this rent to the secure tenants in the block. If they do, these tenants who voted against transferring to the applicant for fear that their rents would increase will feel aggrieved. If the local authority passes on the increased rents to the general body of tenants in their area, they too may complain.

6. Tenants who move in after the relevant date

Subject to 9(c) below (pages 201 to 202) only tenants in occupation at the date of the application can participate in these procedures and choices. A tenant who moves into a dwelling that is subject to the transfer will not be involved. Section 101 makes some additional provisions which affect these tenants (or licensees). The same applies to a property that a local authority adds, under 98(1)(d), to the applicant's list of properties to be acquired, assuming that the applicant agrees to the addition or that the addition was made after a determination by arbitration.

The most important feature of s 101 is that it prevents tenants or licensees acquiring any statutory protection if they move in after the relevant date (or after the property was added to the applicant's list). In particular, these occupants cannot become secure tenants of the local authority (s 101(2)(a)), nor can they become assured tenants of the applicants. The provisions of the Landlord and Tenant Act 1954 and legislation affecting lettings to agricultural workers are also excluded.

These tenancies (or licences) can be brought to an end by either the local authority or the tenant on four weeks' notice. This is so even if a fixed term is granted and, in the case of a periodic let, regardless of the period. Thus the local authority cannot create any secure tenancies after the date of the application. Nor can it grant an effective fixed term to the tenant. The authority is entitled to possession after terminating such a tenancy on four weeks' notice. The tenant cannot enjoy any of the rights of a secure tenant. He does not have to be consulted over the proposed transfer and he cannot take part in the ballot. He faces eviction on or after the completion of the transfer unless his authority offers him other accommodation or the applicant offers him an assured tenancy.

The Secretary of State has power to make regulations under s 101. For example, he can make provision for tenants to be treated differently if they move in after the relevant date. Regulations may also require the authority to give notice to the applicant if it grants a tenancy after the relevant date, and that notice is given to the tenant of the effect of s 101. In addition the regulations may make the authority responsible for giving vacant possession of properties that become tenanted after the relevant date. There may also be provision enabling the applicant to sue the authority for any expenses and losses consequent on its failure to give vacant possession.

The regulations will also deal with the position of these occupiers if the applicant does not proceed. Presumably, there will be provision for them to become secure tenants if they satisfy the qualifying conditions in Part IV of the Housing Act 1985.

7. Extending the periods for service of notices

Section 110 makes provision for the various time periods to be extended. If either the applicant or the local authority finds it difficult to make a particular deadline, the party concerned may extend the period, simply by serving a written notice on the other party before the deadline expires. For example, the applicant might ask the local authority to extend his time to serve notice under s 99 of the Act (see page 193). If the authority agrees, it must notify the applicant in writing. Obviously if the local authority is unwilling to extend the time, the applicant will have to meet the deadline, otherwise his application will fail. The notice must fix a new deadline and this may in turn be extended by written notice.

There is a specific application of this procedure to a case where the Housing Corporation or Housing for Wales has served a revocation notice under s 94 (see page 188) and later withdraws the notice. Once the notice is served, the applicant cannot take any further steps with his application. He might therefore find that a deadline will expire during the period when the revocation notice is provisional. This potential difficulty is resolved by s 110(3). If a provisional revocation notice is withdrawn, the applicant's time for service is automatically extended by a period equal to the period of the currency of the notice.

If during the course of an application, the applicant fails to meet a deadline, this application is treated as withdrawn. However he can make another application (s 110(4)).

8. Summary of preliminary procedure

These initial statutory procedures may be summarised as follows:

(a) The applicant lodges his application.

(b) Four weeks later he becomes entitled to information on the properties he wants to purchase and acquires the right of access to some of the properties.

(c) Within twelve weeks of the application the authority must serve a notice on the applicant detailing properties it considers should be excluded or added (and other miscellaneous matters).

(d) The applicant must notify the authority if he disagrees with its notice within four weeks of receiving it.

(e) This dispute will be resolved by arbitration if the parties remain in disagreement.

(f) Eight weeks after the determination of this dispute the authority must serve a notice proposing a purchase price or disposal cost.

(g) The applicant must notify the authority if he disputes its figures.

(h) This dispute is to be resolved by the district valuer.

(i) Only tenants in occupation at the date of the application are involved in the procedure.

These different deadlines can be extended by using the s 110 procedure.

If there are disagreements over the properties to be included and the price, it may be several months before the initial procedures are completed. Where the statutory procedures were preceded by an informal phase, the tenants will have early notice of the proposed application. However under the statutory phase, the consultation procedures are not set in train until after the basic details of the transfer have been settled. The final procedures consist of this statutory consultation procedure, followed by the applicant's notifying the local authority if he is able to proceed and the final transfer of the properties. These matters are now considered in turn.

9. The consultation procedure

There is relatively little in the Act itself on the consultation procedure. Section 102 makes provision for these procedures to be introduced by statutory instrument. It also states that the period for consultation starts at the time the district valuer notifies the applicant of his decision where there has been a dispute over the purchase price or other terms of the transfer (s 102(1)(a)). In the unlikely event of there being no dispute, the period starts from the date the landlord served notice under s 99 proposing the price and other terms of the transfer (s 102(1)(b)). Other details will appear in regulations introduced by statutory instrument. The Government's thinking on these remaining matters was set out in a consultative document published in December 1988 (*Tenants' Choice: Consultation and Voting*). This document deals with the period of consultation, how it is to be carried out and the additional categories of tenant who are to be consulted.

(a) Period of consultation

Starting with the date referred to in s 102(1), the Government envisages consultation extending over a period of thirteen weeks. Up to seven weeks will be allowed for the applicant to prepare and distribute material containing details of his offer of a new tenancy. The general form that the offer takes will be dealt with in the regulations. It will have to be submitted to the Corporation for the details to be checked against the details of the applicant's approval. As will be seen later in this chapter, tenants will be deemed to have accepted the terms of this offer unless they cast a vote against it.

There is no reference to a local authority preparing a reply, although authorities will obviously do so. About six weeks will be left for the balloting material to be distributed and for the results to be collated.

(b) How the consultation will be carried out

As one of the conditions of being granted approval, the applicant will have to pay for an independent teller to collect the votes cast and to certify the outcome. The teller should be contracted to call on non-voters and those who have returned spoilt or incomplete ballot papers to assist them in casting a valid vote. A standard contract will be drawn up in order to safeguard the independence of the teller.

(c) Eligibility to be consulted and to vote

The basic category is qualifying tenants. As noted on page 186, these are secure tenants of the local authority who were living in their homes when the original offer was made (subject to the exceptions in s 93(4)). However s 102 allows the Secretary of State to add other categories by statutory instrument. The consultative document identified the following additional categories:

(i) qualifying tenants whose homes were added to the

applicant's list under s 98(1)(d) because the authority considered that it could not otherwise reasonably manage or maintain them;

(ii) a tenant who has succeeded to the tenancy after the date of the application (or under s 98(1)(d) above) to a tenancy held by a qualifying tenant who occupied the dwelling at that time;

(iii) a tenant who was at the relevant date subject to a possession order which has since been withdrawn (for example where a tenant has complied with the terms of a suspended possession order which is then rescinded).

These additional categories of tenant will be entitled to vote and to remain council tenants if they choose to. However it is likely that voting rights will be extended to other tenants who will not have the right to stay with the local authority. The consultation paper identified two categories: first, tenants who have bought and who own a long lease on the relevant date; and second, tenants with business lets.

Many council homes are occupied by joint tenants. However under s 103(3) they are regarded as a single tenant and entitled to cast one vote only. The voting procedure is anomalous in another respect. Whether the application can proceed depends on the outcome of the vote. At least 50% of tenants must cast a vote. If they do not, the application fails. However, assuming that 50% do cast a vote, more than 50% must have voted *against* the proposals for it to fail. In other words, unless 50% of the qualified tenants vote to stay council tenants, the proposal succeeds however small the number in favour of it. Thus if there are one hundred tenants qualified to cast a vote, 51 of them will have to vote against the proposal to defeat it. Otherwise the proposal succeeds, however few of the tenants voted in favour.

Assuming that at least one half of the eligible tenants cast their votes, and that fewer than one half have voted to remain council tenants, the applicant may then proceed to complete the transfer.

10. Notice of intention to proceed

If, following the consultation process, the applicant is entitled to proceed with the application, he must serve a notice on the local authority within two weeks of the close of the consultation exercise. This notice must contain the applicant's final specification of the tenants and properties to be transferred and related matters. Under s 103(4) the notice must contain a list of the names and the addresses of the tenants who have given notice of their decision to remain tenants of the local authority. Where these tenants live in flats, the applicant must lease back the flats to the local authority. The applicant must list in his notice the flats concerned and a statement of his proposals for the terms of the leases (s 103(4)(c)). He must also list any houses that are excluded from the transfer under s 100 (see page 185). This deals with the lists of tenants and properties that remain with the local authority and with the lease-back arrangements. The notice must also contain information which explains how the lists have been established and it must specify the purchase price (s 103(4)(d), (e)).

The local authority may disagree with matters contained in the list. It may, for example, not accept the proposed terms of the lease-back arrangements. If it disagrees with this or any other matter in the list, it must notify the applicant in writing within two weeks of receipt of the applicant's notice.

The applicant's notice has another important function. Once it has been served, the terms of the assured tenancies offered to the tenants will have effect (s 103(6)). Thus every tenant who has not notified the applicant of his wish to remain a council tenant will be taken to have accepted and to have given consideration for the offer made by the applicant during the consultation period. This is the case even if the tenant did not vote. During the consultation period, the applicant will have offered assured tenancies and will have explained the terms of the let, including the rent. Unless these terms change during the consultation period as a result of negotiations, they become the terms of the assured lettings which come into effect on completion of the transfer.

11. Completion of the transfer

The local authority will be bound to transfer the properties at the close of the procedures mentioned in the previous section. Once the applicant's notice has been served and any remaining disputes are settled, the local authority "shall make . . . a grant of the property . . . in fee simple" to the applicant, which will be subject to any rights it retains in these properties. At the same time, the applicant must grant leases of any properties that will be retained by the local authority. If either party fails to comply with this duty they can be compelled to do so by injunction (s 104(3)). What is the position if any of the tenants who are being transferred owe rent to the local authority. The Government concluded that "the debt should remain as a matter between the former tenant who accumulated it and the landlord which had allowed it to accrue" (*Tenant's Choice* paragraph 39). This is implemented in s 104(4). Any debts owing to the local authority before the date of the transfer can be recovered by the local authority only.

Registration of title is dealt with in Sch 12. The most salient points relate to the special characteristics of these transfers. The local authority must state in the conveyance that it is a transfer under s 104(1)(a) of the Act and it must pass all of the relevant deeds and other documents to the applicant (para 2, Sch 12). There will be additional regulations published requiring the local authority to produce information to the Land Registry when a lease granted to it under s 104(1)(b) comes to an end (para 3).

12. Later disposals

After acquisition of the property, the new landlord may not, usually, sell or dispose of it without the consent of the Secretary of State (s 105(1)). "Disposing" of any of the properties includes, for these purposes, entering into a contract for sale or granting an option to purchase (s 105(8)). Before considering the procedures that govern seeking this consent, it is necessary to summarise cases where consent is not required. These are called "exempt disposals" and they are listed in s 101(7). The most important examples are a grant of a lease to the local authority under s 104(1)(b); a sale to a tenant exercising his right to buy; and the creation of a mortgage. If a mortgagee seeks to enforce rights under the mortgage, it will also have to obtain consent (s 105(2)). For example, the new landlord might borrow money and mortgage one of the properties he has acquired. If he defaults on the loan, the mortgagee will seek to exercise a power of sale to recover the outstanding loan. Consent will be needed before the property may be sold by the mortgagee.

The purpose of this consent procedure is to ensure that the tenants are consulted. However, this consultation process is different from the one that precedes the transfer from the local authority. On a later transfer, it is left to the Secretary of State to "satisfy himself" that all of the tenants have been consulted by the person seeking to buy the property (s 105(4)(a)). He must also take account of the views of these tenants (s 105(4)(b)). There is no requirement that the person seeking to buy the property is approved by the Corporation. The only possible exception to this is a sale by a housing association which originally acquired the property from a local authority. Most sales by a housing association require consent of the Corporation (s 9 Housing Associations Act 1985). If a housing association wishes to sell property acquired from a local authority under s 104 of the 1988 Act, it has to obtain the consent of the Secretary of State, as would any landlord in these circumstances. However in the case of a housing association the Secretary of State must consult the Corporation as well as the tenants who are affected (s 105(5)). Once this is done, there is no further requirement that the association seek approval of the Corporation (s 105(6)). It is possible that the Secretary of State and the Corporation will take steps to appraise the individual or body wishing to purchase, although there is no statutory requirement that this is done.

13. The role of the Housing Corporation and of Housing for Wales

The additional functions given to the Corporations were examined in Chapters 7 and 10. They will have additional responsibilities for funding and supervising housing associations. They are also responsible for approving landlords who intend bidding for local authority housing under Part IV of the Act. In addition, they are to provide information, advice and assistance in connection with Part IV. They also have power to offer legal assistance, similar to their powers under Part III where a housing action trust sells council housing to a private landlord.

(a) Information, advice and assistance

The Government wants the Corporations to take a leading role in promoting the change of landlord provisions (*Tenants' Choice*). Applicants for approval under s 94 of the Act can look to the Corporation for information or advice and assistance in connection with Part IV. This facility is also available to approved landlords. In either case the Corporations may make charges for this service.

Council tenants and tenants of other public landlords can also look to the Corporations for information, advice and assistance, which must be offered to tenants free of charge. As noted earlier in this chapter, the Government expects that council tenants will contact the Corporations in order to be put in touch with a range of new landlords. However, tenants who are worried about an impending takeover of their homes by a private landlord may also seek advice. If this occurs, the Corporation may be placed in a difficult position – it will be asked for advice by tenants in relation to a landlord it has approved. It is difficult to see how it can avoid a conflict of interest in some situations.

(b) Legal assistance

The power to offer legal assistance is very similar to the Corporations' powers under s 82 where it can provide legal assistance to tenants after a sale by a housing action trust to a private landlord. This form of assistance may be given to a tenant in relation to a dispute concerning an acquisition, a proposed acquisition or after a transfer, if the tenant is a party to the proceedings or prospective proceedings (s 107). As under s 82, the Corporation will have to be satisfied that the dispute raises a question of principle; that the complexity of the case warrants assistance, or that there is "any special reason" (s 107(1)). "Legal assistance" can consist of advice; attempts at arriving at a settlement; legal representation in court proceedings or "any other form of assistance which the Corporation may consider appropriate" (s 107(3)). If costs or compensation are recovered on behalf of a tenant, the Corporation will have a first charge on them (s 107(4)).

Similar problems of conflicts of interest may arise. It is difficult to see how the Corporations can offer this service to tenants in dispute with their new landlord or prospective landlord whom the Corporation has approved and whom it may have been advising under s 106.

14. Conclusion

The general effect of the Act on county court jurisdiction was considered in Chapter 2. Under Part IV of the Act the court has jurisdiction over disputes except for those that are to be resolved by arbitration or by the district valuer (s 113). As a result, two of the most difficult issues—exempt properties and the terms of the transfer—will not fall within the remit of the county court. Section 113 also deals with questions of costs where proceedings were started in the High Court when they should have been begun in the county court. This was considered in Chapter 2.

As observed in this and the previous chapter, many important issues will not be settled until a number of detailed regulations appear. Consultation arrangements and the terms of lease-backs, for example, will be regulated by statutory instruments. The regulations and prescribed forms will be introduced subject to the annulment procedure (ss 111 and 112).

Since a large proportion of council housing is in good condition and well managed, transfer to a new landlord may not be a high priority for many tenants. The likely candidates to take over housing under Part IV of the Act are established housing associations. However, they may not relish the prospect of a bitter "take-over" battle with an authority with which they have a working relationship. As the National Federation of Housing Associations has put it "it is not possible for us to envisage housing associations in open conflict with local authorities, attempting to take on the ownership and management of council property in the face of sustained opposition by the municipal authority" (*Rents, Risks, Rights*, 1988, page 19). There are also indications that the voluntary housing movement would not be willing to take over without clear indications that the tenants wish this to happen (ibid, page 13). Where a majority of tenants express the desire to remain council tenants, it is unlikely that a housing association would attempt to take them over by relying on the anomalies of the balloting procedure. On the other hand, larger housing associations operating on a regional basis may have fewer qualms about invoking the Part IV Procedures.

There may also be cases where local authorities advise tenants on a particular estate, or part of an estate, to exercise their rights under Part IV. However, with this degree of co-operation and given the complexities of Part IV, the parties would be more likely to use the voluntary transfer procedures in the Housing Act 1985.

This leaves the possibility of other private investors moving into rented accommodation through the vehicle of Part IV. Concern was expressed throughout the Parliamentary passage of the Act that Part IV will attract investors who, far from being committed to long term provision of rented housing, will view Part IV as an opportunity for speculative gain, and the Act could be exploited in this way. An investor could gamble on obtaining the property at a substantial discount or with payment of a disposal cost by the local authority. Use of the various grounds for possession against assured tenants for (say) rent arrears could enable such an investor to obtain vacant possession of the property. The investor's approval might be withdrawn, but this would not affect the original transfer of the properties to him.

The Government argues that the supervisory role of the Corporations will ensure that only responsible applicants with a proven record of housing provision will be selected. Moreover the Government's own powers under Part IV will ensure that landlords do not abuse these new procedures. It remains to be seen whether the Corporations have the necessary powers and the resources to monitor Part IV effectively.

As has been argued earlier in this book, Part IV will have more impact on local housing than will the HAT provisions. Even so, its impact may be modest in the short term if the predictions in the previous paragraphs prove to be correct. Along with the voluntary procedures in the Housing Act 1985, Part IV will form part of the background to negotiations designed to advance the privatisation of council housing. In the longer term transfer to a new landlord may become more attractive to council tenants if their rents continue to increase. As noted in Chapter 1, the Government is committed to major changes to local authority housing revenue accounts in its Local Government and Housing Bill 1989. An inevitable consequence will be further council rent increases from 1990 onwards. Once this happens compulsory acquisition under the Part IV procedures may start to have an appreciable effect on public housing.

Appendix 1

Housing Act 1988

1988 CHAPTER 50

An Act to make further provision with respect to dwelling-houses let on tenancies or occupied under licences; to amend the Rent Act 1977 and the Rent (Agriculture) Act 1976; to establish a body, Housing for Wales, having functions relating to housing associations; to amend the Housing Associations Act 1985 and to repeal and re-enact with amendments certain provisions of Part II of that Act; to make provision for the establishment of housing action trusts for areas designated by the Secretary of State; to confer on persons approved for the purpose the right to acquire from public sector landlords certain dwelling-houses occupied by secure tenants; to make further provision about rent officers, the administration of housing benefit and rent allowance subsidy, the right to buy, repair notices and certain disposals of land and the application of capital money arising thereon; to make provision consequential upon the Housing (Scotland) Act 1988; and for connected purposes. [15th November 1988]

BE IT ENACTED by the Queen's most Excellent Majesty, by and with the advice and consent of the Lords Spiritual and Temporal, and Commons, in this present Parliament assembled, and by the authority of the same, as follows:—

PART I
RENTED ACCOMMODATION

CHAPTER I
ASSURED TENANCIES

Meaning of assured tenancy etc.

1.—(1) A tenancy under which a dwelling-house is let as a separate dwelling is for the purposes of this Act an assured tenancy if and so long as— Assured tenancies.

PART I

(a) the tenant or, as the case may be, each of the joint tenants is an individual; and

(b) the tenant or, as the case may be, at least one of the joint tenants occupies the dwelling-house as his only or principal home; and

(c) the tenancy is not one which, by virtue of subsection (2) or subsection (6) below, cannot be an assured tenancy.

(2) Subject to subsection (3) below, if and so long as a tenancy falls within any paragraph in Part I of Schedule 1 to this Act, it cannot be an assured tenancy; and in that Schedule—

(a) "tenancy" means a tenancy under which a dwelling-house is let as a separate dwelling;

(b) Part II has effect for determining the rateable value of a dwelling-house for the purposes of Part I; and

(c) Part III has effect for supplementing paragraph 10 in Part I.

(3) Except as provided in Chapter V below, at the commencement of this Act, a tenancy—

(a) under which a dwelling-house was then let as a separate dwelling, and

1980 c. 51.

(b) which immediately before that commencement was an assured tenancy for the purposes of sections 56 to 58 of the Housing Act 1980 (tenancies granted by approved bodies),

shall become an assured tenancy for the purposes of this Act.

(4) In relation to an assured tenancy falling within subsection (3) above—

(a) Part I of Schedule 1 to this Act shall have effect, subject to subsection (5) below, as if it consisted only of paragraphs 11 and 12; and

(b) sections 56 to 58 of the Housing Act 1980 (and Schedule 5 to that Act) shall not apply after the commencement of this Act.

(5) In any case where—

(a) immediately before the commencement of this Act the landlord under a tenancy is a fully mutual housing association, and

(b) at the commencement of this Act the tenancy becomes an assured tenancy by virtue of subsection (3) above,

then, so long as that association remains the landlord under that tenancy (and under any statutory periodic tenancy which arises on the coming to an end of that tenancy), paragraph 12 of Schedule 1 to this Act shall have effect in relation to that tenancy with the omission of sub-paragraph (1)(h).

(6) If, in pursuance of its duty under—

1985 c. 68.

(a) section 63 of the Housing Act 1985 (duty to house pending inquiries in case of apparent priority need),

(b) section 65(3) of that Act (duty to house temporarily person found to have priority need but to have become homeless intentionally), or

(c) section 68(1) of that Act (duty to house pending determination whether conditions for referral of application are satisfied),

a local housing authority have made arrangements with another person to provide accommodation, a tenancy granted by that other person in pursuance of the arrangements to a person specified by the authority cannot be an assured tenancy before the expiry of the period of twelve months beginning with the date specified in subsection (7) below unless, before the expiry of that period, the tenant is notified by the landlord (or, in the case of joint landlords, at least one of them) that the tenancy is to be regarded as an assured tenancy.

(7) The date referred to in subsection (6) above is the date on which the tenant received the notification required by section 64(1) of the Housing Act 1985 (notification of decision on question of homelessness or threatened homelessness) or, if he received a notification under section 68(3) of that Act (notification of which authority has duty to house), the date on which he received that notification. 1985 c. 68.

Letting of a dwelling-house together with other land.

2.—(1) If, under a tenancy, a dwelling-house is let together with other land, then, for the purposes of this Part of this Act,—

(a) if and so long as the main purpose of the letting is the provision of a home for the tenant or, where there are joint tenants, at least one of them, the other land shall be treated as part of the dwelling-house; and

(b) if and so long as the main purpose of the letting is not as mentioned in paragraph (a) above, the tenancy shall be treated as not being one under which a dwelling-house is let as a separate dwelling.

(2) Nothing in subsection (1) above affects any question whether a tenancy is precluded from being an assured tenancy by virtue of any provision of Schedule 1 to this Act.

Tenant sharing accommodation with persons other than landlord.

3.—(1) Where a tenant has the exclusive occupation of any accommodation (in this section referred to as "the separate accommodation") and—

(a) the terms as between the tenant and his landlord on which he holds the separate accommodation include the use of other accommodation (in this section referred to as "the shared accommodation") in common with another person or other persons, not being or including the landlord, and

(b) by reason only of the circumstances mentioned in paragraph (a) above, the separate accommodation would not, apart from this section, be a dwelling-house let on an assured tenancy,

the separate accommodation shall be deemed to be a dwelling-house let on an assured tenancy and the following provisions of this section shall have effect.

(2) For the avoidance of doubt it is hereby declared that where, for the purpose of determining the rateable value of the separate accommodation, it is necessary to make an apportionment under Part II of Schedule 1 to this Act, regard is to be had to the circumstances mentioned in subsection (1)(a) above.

PART I

(3) While the tenant is in possession of the separate accommodation, any term of the tenancy terminating or modifying, or providing for the termination or modification of, his right to the use of any of the shared accommodation which is living accommodation shall be of no effect.

(4) Where the terms of the tenancy are such that, at any time during the tenancy, the persons in common with whom the tenant is entitled to the use of the shared accommodation could be varied or their number could be increased, nothing in subsection (3) above shall prevent those terms from having effect so far as they relate to any such variation or increase.

(5) In this section "living accommodation" means accommodation of such a nature that the fact that it constitutes or is included in the shared accommodation is sufficient, apart from this section, to prevent the tenancy from constituting an assured tenancy of a dwelling-house.

Certain sublettings not to exclude any part of sub-lessor's premises from assured tenancy.

4.—(1) Where the tenant of a dwelling-house has sub-let a part but not the whole of the dwelling-house, then, as against his landlord or any superior landlord, no part of the dwelling-house shall be treated as excluded from being a dwelling-house let on an assured tenancy by reason only that the terms on which any person claiming under the tenant holds any part of the dwelling-house include the use of accommodation in common with other persons.

(2) Nothing in this section affects the rights against, and liabilities to, each other of the tenant and any person claiming under him, or of any two such persons.

Security of tenure

Security of tenure.

5.—(1) An assured tenancy cannot be brought to an end by the landlord except by obtaining an order of the court in accordance with the following provisions of this Chapter or Chapter II below or, in the case of a fixed term tenancy which contains power for the landlord to determine the tenancy in certain circumstances, by the exercise of that power and, accordingly, the service by the landlord of a notice to quit shall be of no effect in relation to a periodic assured tenancy.

(2) If an assured tenancy which is a fixed term tenancy comes to an end otherwise than by virtue of—

(a) an order of the court, or

(b) a surrender or other action on the part of the tenant,

then, subject to section 7 and Chapter II below, the tenant shall be entitled to remain in possession of the dwelling-house let under that tenancy and, subject to subsection (4) below, his right to possession shall depend upon a periodic tenancy arising by virtue of this section.

(3) The periodic tenancy referred to in subsection (2) above is one—

(a) taking effect in possession immediately on the coming to an end of the fixed term tenancy;

(b) deemed to have been granted by the person who was the landlord under the fixed term tenancy immediately before it came to an end to the person who was then the tenant under that tenancy;

(c) under which the premises which are let are the same dwelling-house as was let under the fixed term tenancy;

(d) under which the periods of the tenancy are the same as those for which rent was last payable under the fixed term tenancy; and

(e) under which, subject to the following provisions of this Part of this Act, the other terms are the same as those of the fixed term tenancy immediately before it came to an end, except that any term which makes provision for determination by the landlord or the tenant shall not have effect while the tenancy remains an assured tenancy.

(4) The periodic tenancy referred to in subsection (2) above shall not arise if, on the coming to an end of the fixed term tenancy, the tenant is entitled, by virtue of the grant of another tenancy, to possession of the same or substantially the same dwelling-house as was let to him under the fixed term tenancy.

(5) If, on or before the date on which a tenancy is entered into or is deemed to have been granted as mentioned in subsection (3)(b) above, the person who is to be the tenant under that tenancy—

(a) enters into an obligation to do any act which (apart from this subsection) will cause the tenancy to come to an end at a time when it is an assured tenancy, or

(b) executes, signs or gives any surrender, notice to quit or other document which (apart from this subsection) has the effect of bringing the tenancy to an end at a time when it is an assured tenancy,

the obligation referred to in paragraph (a) above shall not be enforceable or, as the case may be, the surrender, notice to quit or other document referred to in paragraph (b) above shall be of no effect.

(6) If, by virtue of any provision of this Part of this Act, Part I of Schedule 1 to this Act has effect in relation to a fixed term tenancy as if it consisted only of paragraphs 11 and 12, that Part shall have the like effect in relation to any periodic tenancy which arises by virtue of this section on the coming to an end of the fixed term tenancy.

(7) Any reference in this Part of this Act to a statutory periodic tenancy is a reference to a periodic tenancy arising by virtue of this section.

Fixing of terms of statutory periodic tenancy.

6.—(1) In this section, in relation to a statutory periodic tenancy,—

(a) "the former tenancy" means the fixed term tenancy on the coming to an end of which the statutory periodic tenancy arises; and

(b) "the implied terms" means the terms of the tenancy which have effect by virtue of section 5(3)(e) above, other than terms as to the amount of the rent;

but nothing in the following provisions of this section applies to a statutory periodic tenancy at a time when, by virtue of paragraph 11 or paragraph 12 in Part 1 of Schedule 1 to this Act, it cannot be an assured tenancy.

(2) Not later than the first anniversary of the day on which the former tenancy came to an end, the landlord may serve on the tenant, or the tenant may serve on the landlord, a notice in the prescribed form proposing terms of the statutory periodic tenancy different from the

PART I implied terms and, if the landlord or the tenant considers it appropriate, proposing an adjustment of the amount of the rent to take account of the proposed terms.

(3) Where a notice has been served under subsection (2) above,—

(a) within the period of three months beginning on the date on which the notice was served on him, the landlord or the tenant, as the case may be, may, by an application in the prescribed form, refer the notice to a rent assessment committee under subsection (4) below; and

(b) if the notice is not so referred, then, with effect from such date, not falling within the period referred to in paragraph (a) above, as may be specified in the notice, the terms proposed in the notice shall become terms of the tenancy in substitution for any of the implied terms dealing with the same subject matter and the amount of the rent shall be varied in accordance with any adjustment so proposed.

(4) Where a notice under subsection (2) above is referred to a rent assessment committee, the committee shall consider the terms proposed in the notice and shall determine whether those terms, or some other terms (dealing with the same subject matter as the proposed terms), are such as, in the committee's opinion, might reasonably be expected to be found in an assured periodic tenancy of the dwelling-house concerned, being a tenancy—

(a) which begins on the coming to an end of the former tenancy; and

(b) which is granted by a willing landlord on terms which, except in so far as they relate to the subject matter of the proposed terms, are those of the statutory periodic tenancy at the time of the committee's consideration.

(5) Whether or not a notice under subsection (2) above proposes an adjustment of the amount of the rent under the statutory periodic tenancy, where a rent assessment committee determine any terms under subsection (4) above, they shall, if they consider it appropriate, specify such an adjustment to take account of the terms so determined.

(6) In making a determination under subsection (4) above, or specifying an adjustment of an amount of rent under subsection (5) above, there shall be disregarded any effect on the terms or the amount of the rent attributable to the granting of a tenancy to a sitting tenant.

(7) Where a notice under subsection (2) above is referred to a rent assessment committee, then, unless the landlord and the tenant otherwise agree, with effect from such date as the committee may direct—

(a) the terms determined by the committee shall become terms of the statutory periodic tenancy in substitution for any of the implied terms dealing with the same subject matter; and

(b) the amount of the rent under the statutory periodic tenancy shall be altered to accord with any adjustment specified by the committee;

but for the purposes of paragraph (b) above the committee shall not direct a date earlier than the date specified, in accordance with subsection (3)(b) above, in the notice referred to them.

(8) Nothing in this section requires a rent assessment committee to continue with a determination under subsection (4) above if the landlord and tenant give notice in writing that they no longer require such a determination or if the tenancy has come to an end.

Orders for possession.

7.—(1) The court shall not make an order for possession of a dwelling-house let on an assured tenancy except on one or more of the grounds set out in Schedule 2 to this Act; but nothing in this Part of this Act relates to proceedings for possession of such a dwelling-house which are brought by a mortgagee, within the meaning of the Law of Property Act 1925, who has lent money on the security of the assured tenancy.

1925 c. 20.

(2) The following provisions of this section have effect, subject to section 8 below, in relation to proceedings for the recovery of possession of a dwelling-house let on an assured tenancy.

(3) If the court is satisfied that any of the grounds in Part I of Schedule 2 to this Act is established then, subject to subsection (6) below, the court shall make an order for possession.

(4) If the court is satisfied that any of the grounds in Part II of Schedule 2 to this Act is established, then, subject to subsection (6) below, the court may make an order for possession if it considers it reasonable to do so.

(5) Part III of Schedule 2 to this Act shall have effect for supplementing Ground 9 in that Schedule and Part IV of that Schedule shall have effect in relation to notices given as mentioned in Grounds 1 to 5 of that Schedule.

(6) The court shall not make an order for possession of a dwelling-house to take effect at a time when it is let on an assured fixed term tenancy unless—

(a) the ground for possession is Ground 2 or Ground 8 in Part I of Schedule 2 to this Act or any of the grounds in Part II of that Schedule, other than Ground 9 or Ground 16; and

(b) the terms of the tenancy make provision for it to be brought to an end on the ground in question (whether that provision takes the form of a provision for re-entry, for forfeiture, for determination by notice or otherwise).

(7) Subject to the preceding provisions of this section, the court may make an order for possession of a dwelling-house on grounds relating to a fixed term tenancy which has come to an end; and where an order is made in such circumstances, any statutory periodic tenancy which has arisen on the ending of the fixed term tenancy shall end (without any notice and regardless of the period) on the day on which the order takes effect.

Notice of proceedings for possession.

8.—(1) The court shall not entertain proceedings for possession of a dwelling-house let on an assured tenancy unless—

(a) the landlord or, in the case of joint landlords, at least one of them has served on the tenant a notice in accordance with this section and the proceedings are begun within the time limits stated in the notice in accordance with subsections (3) and (4) below; or

(b) the court considers it just and equitable to dispense with the requirement of such a notice.

PART I

(2) The court shall not make an order for possession on any of the grounds in Schedule 2 to this Act unless that ground and particulars of it are specified in the notice under this section; but the grounds specified in such a notice may be altered or added to with the leave of the court.

(3) A notice under this section is one in the prescribed form informing the tenant that—

(a) the landlord intends to begin proceedings for possession of the dwelling-house on one or more of the grounds specified in the notice; and

(b) those proceedings will not begin earlier than a date specified in the notice which, without prejudice to any additional limitation under subsection (4) below, shall not be earlier than the expiry of the period of two weeks from the date of service of the notice; and

(c) those proceedings will not begin later than twelve months from the date of service of the notice.

(4) If a notice under this section specifies, in accordance with subsection (3)(a) above, any of Grounds 1, 2, 5 to 7, 9 and 16 in Schedule 2 to this Act (whether with or without other grounds), the date specified in the notice as mentioned in subsection (3)(b) above shall not be earlier than—

(a) two months from the date of service of the notice; and

(b) if the tenancy is a periodic tenancy, the earliest date on which, apart from section 5(1) above, the tenancy could be brought to an end by a notice to quit given by the landlord on the same date as the date of service of the notice under this section.

(5) The court may not exercise the power conferred by subsection (1)(b) above if the landlord seeks to recover possession on Ground 8 in Schedule 2 to this Act.

(6) Where a notice under this section—

(a) is served at a time when the dwelling-house is let on a fixed term tenancy, or

(b) is served after a fixed term tenancy has come to an end but relates (in whole or in part) to events occurring during that tenancy,

the notice shall have effect notwithstanding that the tenant becomes or has become tenant under a statutory periodic tenancy arising on the coming to an end of the fixed term tenancy.

Extended discretion of court in possession claims.

9.—(1) Subject to subsection (6) below, the court may adjourn for such period or periods as it thinks fit proceedings for possession of a dwelling-house let on an assured tenancy.

(2) On the making of an order for possession of a dwelling-house let on an assured tenancy or at any time before the execution of such an order, the court, subject to subsection (6) below, may—

(a) stay or suspend execution of the order, or

(b) postpone the date of possession,

for such period or periods as the court thinks just.

(3) On any such adjournment as is referred to in subsection (1) above or on any such stay, suspension or postponement as is referred to in subsection (2) above, the court, unless it considers that to do so would cause exceptional hardship to the tenant or would otherwise be unreasonable, shall impose conditions with regard to payment by the tenant of arrears of rent (if any) and rent or payments in respect of occupation after the termination of the tenancy (mesne profits) and may impose such other conditions as it thinks fit.

(4) If any such conditions as are referred to in subsection (3) above are complied with, the court may, if it thinks fit, discharge or rescind any such order as is referred to in subsection (2) above.

(5) In any case where—

(a) at a time when proceedings are brought for possession of a dwelling-house let on an assured tenancy, the tenant's spouse or former spouse, having rights of occupation under the Matrimonial Homes Act 1983, is in occupation of the dwelling-house, and 1983 c. 19.

(b) the assured tenancy is terminated as a result of those proceedings,

the spouse or former spouse, so long as he or she remains in occupation, shall have the same rights in relation to, or in connection with, any such adjournment as is referred to in subsection (1) above or any such stay, suspension or postponement as is referred to in subsection (2) above, as he or she would have if those rights of occupation were not affected by the termination of the tenancy.

(6) This section does not apply if the court is satisfied that the landlord is entitled to possession of the dwelling-house—

(a) on any of the grounds in Part I of Schedule 2 to this Act; or

(b) by virtue of subsection (1) or subsection (4) of section 21 below.

Special provisions applicable to shared accommodation.

10.—(1) This section applies in a case falling within subsection (1) of section 3 above and expressions used in this section have the same meaning as in that section.

(2) Without prejudice to the enforcement of any order made under subsection (3) below, while the tenant is in possession of the separate accommodation, no order shall be made for possession of any of the shared accommodation, whether on the application of the immediate landlord of the tenant or on the application of any person under whom that landlord derives title, unless a like order has been made, or is made at the same time, in respect of the separate accommodation; and the provisions of section 6 above shall have effect accordingly.

(3) On the application of the landlord, the court may make such order as it thinks just either—

(a) terminating the right of the tenant to use the whole or any part of the shared accommodation other than living accommodation; or

(b) modifying his right to use the whole or any part of the shared accommodation, whether by varying the persons or increasing the number of persons entitled to the use of that accommodation or otherwise.

PART I

(4) No order shall be made under subsection (3) above so as to effect any termination or modification of the rights of the tenant which, apart from section 3(3) above, could not be effected by or under the terms of the tenancy.

Payment of removal expenses in certain cases.

11.—(1) Where a court makes an order for possession of a dwelling-house let on an assured tenancy on Ground 6 or Ground 9 in Schedule 2 to this Act (but not on any other ground), the landlord shall pay to the tenant a sum equal to the reasonable expenses likely to be incurred by the tenant in removing from the dwelling-house.

(2) Any question as to the amount of the sum referred to in subsection (1) above shall be determined by agreement between the landlord and the tenant or, in default of agreement, by the court.

(3) Any sum payable to a tenant by virtue of this section shall be recoverable as a civil debt due from the landlord.

Compensation for misrepresentation or concealment.

12. Where a landlord obtains an order for possession of a dwelling-house let on an assured tenancy on one or more of the grounds in Schedule 2 to this Act and it is subsequently made to appear to the court that the order was obtained by misrepresentation or concealment of material facts, the court may order the landlord to pay to the former tenant such sum as appears sufficient as compensation for damage or loss sustained by that tenant as a result of the order.

Rent and other terms

Increases of rent under assured periodic tenancies.

13.—(1) This section applies to—

(a) a statutory periodic tenancy other than one which, by virtue of paragraph 11 or paragraph 12 in Part I of Schedule 1 to this Act, cannot for the time being be an assured tenancy; and

(b) any other periodic tenancy which is an assured tenancy, other than one in relation to which there is a provision, for the time being binding on the tenant, under which the rent for a particular period of the tenancy will or may be greater than the rent for an earlier period.

(2) For the purpose of securing an increase in the rent under a tenancy to which this section applies, the landlord may serve on the tenant a notice in the prescribed form proposing a new rent to take effect at the beginning of a new period of the tenancy specified in the notice, being a period beginning not earlier than—

(a) the minimum period after the date of the service of the notice; and

(b) except in the case of a statutory periodic tenancy, the first anniversary of the date on which the first period of the tenancy began; and

(c) if the rent under the tenancy has previously been increased by virtue of a notice under this subsection or a determination under section 14 below, the first anniversary of the date on which the increased rent took effect.

(3) The minimum period referred to in subsection (2) above is—

(a) in the case of a yearly tenancy, six months;

(b) in the case of a tenancy where the period is less than a month, one month; and

(c) in any other case, a period equal to the period of the tenancy.

(4) Where a notice is served under subsection (2) above, a new rent specified in the notice shall take effect as mentioned in the notice unless, before the beginning of the new period specified in the notice,—

(a) the tenant by an application in the prescribed form refers the notice to a rent assessment committee; or

(b) the landlord and the tenant agree on a variation of the rent which is different from that proposed in the notice or agree that the rent should not be varied.

(5) Nothing in this section (or in section 14 below) affects the right of the landlord and the tenant under an assured tenancy to vary by agreement any term of the tenancy (including a term relating to rent).

Determination of rent by rent assessment committee.

14.—(1) Where, under subsection (4)(a) of section 13 above, a tenant refers to a rent assessment committee a notice under subsection (2) of that section, the committee shall determine the rent at which, subject to subsections (2) and (4) below, the committee consider that the dwelling-house concerned might reasonably be expected to be let in the open market by a willing landlord under an assured tenancy—

(a) which is a periodic tenancy having the same periods as those of the tenancy to which the notice relates;

(b) which begins at the beginning of the new period specified in the notice;

(c) the terms of which (other than relating to the amount of the rent) are the same as those of the tenancy to which the notice relates; and

(d) in respect of which the same notices, if any, have been given under any of Grounds 1 to 5 of Schedule 2 to this Act, as have been given (or have effect as if given) in relation to the tenancy to which the notice relates.

(2) In making a determination under this section, there shall be disregarded—

(a) any effect on the rent attributable to the granting of a tenancy to a sitting tenant;

(b) any increase in the value of the dwelling-house attributable to a relevant improvement carried out by a person who at the time it was carried out was the tenant, if the improvement—

(i) was carried out otherwise than in pursuance of an obligation to his immediate landlord, or

(ii) was carried out pursuant to an obligation to his immediate landlord being an obligation which did not relate to the specific improvement concerned but arose by reference to consent given to the carrying out of that improvement; and

(c) any reduction in the value of the dwelling-house attributable to a failure by the tenant to comply with any terms of the tenancy.

PART I

(3) For the purposes of subsection (2)(b) above, in relation to a notice which is referred by a tenant as mentioned in subsection (1) above, an improvement is a relevant improvement if either it was carried out during the tenancy to which the notice relates or the following conditions are satisfied, namely—

(a) that it was carried out not more than twenty-one years before the date of service of the notice; and

(b) that, at all times during the period beginning when the improvement was carried out and ending on the date of service of the notice, the dwelling-house has been let under an assured tenancy; and

(c) that, on the coming to an end of an assured tenancy at any time during that period, the tenant (or, in the case of joint tenants, at least one of them) did not quit.

(4) In this section "rent" does not include any service charge, within
1985 c. 70. the meaning of section 18 of the Landlord and Tenant Act 1985, but, subject to that, includes any sums payable by the tenant to the landlord on account of the use of furniture or for any of the matters referred to in subsection (1)(a) of that section, whether or not those sums are separate from the sums payable for the occupation of the dwelling-house concerned or are payable under separate agreements.

(5) Where any rates in respect of the dwelling-house concerned are borne by the landlord or a superior landlord, the rent assessment committee shall make their determination under this section as if the rates were not so borne.

(6) In any case where—

(a) a rent assessment committee have before them at the same time the reference of a notice under section 6(2) above relating to a tenancy (in this subsection referred to as "the section 6 reference") and the reference of a notice under section 13(2) above relating to the same tenancy (in this subsection referred to as "the section 13 reference"), and

(b) the date specified in the notice under section 6(2) above is not later than the first day of the new period specified in the notice under section 13(2) above, and

(c) the committee propose to hear the two references together,

the committee shall make a determination in relation to the section 6 reference before making their determination in relation to the section 13 reference and, accordingly, in such a case the reference in subsection (1)(c) above to the terms of the tenancy to which the notice relates shall be construed as a reference to those terms as varied by virtue of the determination made in relation to the section 6 reference.

(7) Where a notice under section 13(2) above has been referred to a rent assessment committee, then, unless the landlord and the tenant otherwise agree, the rent determined by the committee (subject, in a case where subsection (5) above applies, to the addition of the appropriate amount in respect of rates) shall be the rent under the tenancy with effect from the beginning of the new period specified in the notice or, if it appears to the rent assessment committee that that would cause undue hardship to the tenant, with effect from such later date (not being later than the date the rent is determined) as the committee may direct.

(8) Nothing in this section requires a rent assessment committee to continue with their determination of a rent for a dwelling-house if the landlord and tenant give notice in writing that they no longer require such a determination or if the tenancy has come to an end.

Limited prohibition on assignment etc. without consent.

15.—(1) Subject to subsection (3) below, it shall be an implied term of every assured tenancy which is a periodic tenancy that, except with the consent of the landlord, the tenant shall not—

(a) assign the tenancy (in whole or in part); or

(b) sub-let or part with possession of the whole or any part of the dwelling-house let on the tenancy.

(2) Section 19 of the Landlord and Tenant Act 1927 (consents to assign not to be unreasonably withheld etc.) shall not apply to a term which is implied into an assured tenancy by subsection (1) above. 1927 c. 36.

(3) In the case of a periodic tenancy which is not a statutory periodic tenancy subsection (1) above does not apply if—

(a) there is a provision (whether contained in the tenancy or not) under which the tenant is prohibited (whether absolutely or conditionally) from assigning or sub-letting or parting with possession or is permitted (whether absolutely or conditionally) to assign, sub-let or part with possession; or

(b) a premium is required to be paid on the grant or renewal of the tenancy.

(4) In subsection (3)(b) above "premium" includes—

(a) any fine or other like sum;

(b) any other pecuniary consideration in addition to rent; and

(c) any sum paid by way of deposit, other than one which does not exceed one-sixth of the annual rent payable under the tenancy immediately after the grant or renewal in question.

Access for repairs.

16. It shall be an implied term of every assured tenancy that the tenant shall afford to the landlord access to the dwelling-house let on the tenancy and all reasonable facilities for executing therein any repairs which the landlord is entitled to execute.

Miscellaneous

Succession to assured periodic tenancy by spouse.

17.—(1) In any case where—

(a) the sole tenant under an assured periodic tenancy dies, and

(b) immediately before the death, the tenant's spouse was occupying the dwelling-house as his or her only or principal home, and

(c) the tenant was not himself a successor, as defined in subsection (2) or subsection (3) below,

then, on the death, the tenancy vests by virtue of this section in the spouse (and, accordingly, does not devolve under the tenant's will or intestacy).

(2) For the purposes of this section, a tenant is a successor in relation to a tenancy if—

(a) the tenancy became vested in him either by virtue of this section or under the will or intestacy of a previous tenant; or

PART I

(b) at some time before the tenant's death the tenancy was a joint tenancy held by himself and one or more other persons and, prior to his death, he became the sole tenant by survivorship; or

(c) he became entitled to the tenancy as mentioned in section 39(5) below.

(3) For the purposes of this section, a tenant is also a successor in relation to a tenancy (in this subsection referred to as "the new tenancy") which was granted to him (alone or jointly with others) if—

(a) at some time before the grant of the new tenancy, he was, by virtue of subsection (2) above, a successor in relation to an earlier tenancy of the same or substantially the same dwelling-house as is let under the new tenancy; and

(b) at all times since he became such a successor he has been a tenant (alone or jointly with others) of the dwelling-house which is let under the new tenancy or of a dwelling-house which is substantially the same as that dwelling-house.

(4) For the purposes of this section, a person who was living with the tenant as his or her wife or husband shall be treated as the tenant's spouse.

(5) If, on the death of the tenant, there is, by virtue of subsection (4) above, more than one person who fulfils the condition in subsection (1)(b) above, such one of them as may be decided by agreement or, in default of agreement, by the county court shall be treated as the tenant's spouse for the purposes of this section.

Provisions as to reversions on assured tenancies.

18.—(1) If at any time—

(a) a dwelling-house is for the time being lawfully let on an assured tenancy, and

(b) the landlord under the assured tenancy is himself a tenant under a superior tenancy; and

(c) the superior tenancy comes to an end,

then, subject to subsection (2) below, the assured tenancy shall continue in existence as a tenancy held of the person whose interest would, apart from the continuance of the assured tenancy, entitle him to actual possession of the dwelling-house at that time.

(2) Subsection (1) above does not apply to an assured tenancy if the interest which, by virtue of that subsection, would become that of the landlord, is such that, by virtue of Schedule 1 to this Act, the tenancy could not be an assured tenancy.

(3) Where, by virtue of any provision of this Part of this Act, an assured tenancy which is a periodic tenancy (including a statutory periodic tenancy) continues beyond the beginning of a reversionary tenancy which was granted (whether before, on or after the commencement of this Act) so as to begin on or after—

(a) the date on which the previous contractual assured tenancy came to an end, or

(b) a date on which, apart from any provision of this Part, the periodic tenancy could have been brought to an end by the landlord by notice to quit,

the reversionary tenancy shall have effect as if it had been granted subject to the periodic tenancy.

(4) The reference in subsection (3) above to the previous contractual assured tenancy applies only where the periodic tenancy referred to in that subsection is a statutory periodic tenancy and is a reference to the fixed-term tenancy which immediately preceded the statutory periodic tenancy.

19.—(1) Subject to subsection (2) below, no distress for the rent of any dwelling-house let on an assured tenancy shall be levied except with the leave of the county court; and, with respect to any application for such leave, the court shall have the same powers with respect to adjournment, stay, suspension, postponement and otherwise as are conferred by section 9 above in relation to proceedings for possession of such a dwelling-house. Restriction on levy of distress for rent.

(2) Nothing in subsection (1) above applies to distress levied under section 102 of the County Courts Act 1984. 1984 c. 28.

CHAPTER II

ASSURED SHORTHOLD TENANCIES

20.—(1) Subject to subsection (3) below, an assured shorthold tenancy is an assured tenancy— Assured shorthold tenancies.

(a) which is a fixed term tenancy granted for a term certain of not less than six months; and

(b) in respect of which there is no power for the landlord to determine the tenancy at any time earlier than six months from the beginning of the tenancy; and

(c) in respect of which a notice is served as mentioned in subsection (2) below.

(2) The notice referred to in subsection (1)(c) above is one which—

(a) is in such form as may be prescribed;

(b) is served before the assured tenancy is entered into;

(c) is served by the person who is to be the landlord under the assured tenancy on the person who is to be the tenant under that tenancy; and

(d) states that the assured tenancy to which it relates is to be a shorthold tenancy.

(3) Notwithstanding anything in subsection (1) above, where—

(a) immediately before a tenancy (in this subsection referred to as "the new tenancy") is granted, the person to whom it is granted or, as the case may be, at least one of the persons to whom it is granted was a tenant under an assured tenancy which was not a shorthold tenancy, and

(b) the new tenancy is granted by the person who, immediately before the beginning of the tenancy, was the landlord under the assured tenancy referred to in paragraph (a) above,

the new tenancy cannot be an assured shorthold tenancy.

(4) Subject to subsection (5) below, if, on the coming to an end of an assured shorthold tenancy (including a tenancy which was an assured shorthold but ceased to be assured before it came to an end), a new tenancy of the same or substantially the same premises comes into being

PART I

under which the landlord and the tenant are the same as at the coming to an end of the earlier tenancy, then, if and so long as the new tenancy is an assured tenancy, it shall be an assured shorthold tenancy, whether or not it fulfils the conditions in paragraphs (a) to (c) of subsection (1) above.

(5) Subsection (4) above does not apply if, before the new tenancy is entered into (or, in the case of a statutory periodic tenancy, takes effect in possession), the landlord serves notice on the tenant that the new tenancy is not to be a shorthold tenancy.

(6) In the case of joint landlords—

(a) the reference in subsection (2)(c) above to the person who is to be the landlord is a reference to at least one of the persons who are to be joint landlords; and

(b) the reference in subsection (5) above to the landlord is a reference to at least one of the joint landlords.

(7) Section 14 above shall apply in relation to an assured shorthold tenancy as if in subsection (1) of that section the reference to an assured tenancy were a reference to an assured shorthold tenancy.

Recovery of possession on expiry or termination of assured shorthold tenancy.

21.—(1) Without prejudice to any right of the landlord under an assured shorthold tenancy to recover possession of the dwelling-house let on the tenancy in accordance with Chapter I above, on or after the coming to an end of an assured shorthold tenancy which was a fixed term tenancy, a court shall make an order for possession of the dwelling-house if it is satisfied—

(a) that the assured shorthold tenancy has come to an end and no further assured tenancy (whether shorthold or not) is for the time being in existence, other than a statutory periodic tenancy; and

(b) the landlord or, in the case of joint landlords, at least one of them has given to the tenant not less than two months' notice stating that he requires possession of the dwelling-house.

(2) A notice under paragraph (b) of subsection (1) above may be given before or on the day on which the tenancy comes to an end; and that subsection shall have effect notwithstanding that on the coming to an end of the fixed term tenancy a statutory periodic tenancy arises.

(3) Where a court makes an order for possession of a dwelling-house by virtue of subsection (1) above, any statutory periodic tenancy which has arisen on the coming to an end of the assured shorthold tenancy shall end (without further notice and regardless of the period) on the day on which the order takes effect.

(4) Without prejudice to any such right as is referred to in subsection (1) above, a court shall make an order for possession of a dwelling-house let on an assured shorthold tenancy which is a periodic tenancy if the court is satisfied—

(a) that the landlord or, in the case of joint landlords, at least one of them has given to the tenant a notice stating that, after a date specified in the notice, being the last day of a period of the tenancy and not earlier than two months after the date the notice was given, possession of the dwelling-house is required by virtue of this section; and

Part I

(b) that the date specified in the notice under paragraph (a) above is not earlier than the earliest day on which, apart from section 5(1) above, the tenancy could be brought to an end by a notice to quit given by the landlord on the same date as the notice under paragraph (a) above.

Reference of excessive rents to rent assessment committee.

22.—(1) Subject to section 23 and subsection (2) below, the tenant under an assured shorthold tenancy in respect of which a notice was served as mentioned in section 20(2) above may make an application in the prescribed form to a rent assessment committee for a determination of the rent which, in the committee's opinion, the landlord might reasonably be expected to obtain under the assured shorthold tenancy.

(2) No application may be made under this section if—

(a) the rent payable under the tenancy is a rent previously determined under this section; or

(b) the tenancy is an assured shorthold tenancy falling within subsection (4) of section 20 above (and, accordingly, is one in respect of which notice need not have been served as mentioned in subsection (2) of that section).

(3) Where an application is made to a rent assessment committee under subsection (1) above with respect to the rent under an assured shorthold tenancy, the committee shall not make such a determination as is referred to in that subsection unless they consider—

(a) that there is a sufficient number of similar dwelling-houses in the locality let on assured tenancies (whether shorthold or not); and

(b) that the rent payable under the assured shorthold tenancy in question is significantly higher than the rent which the landlord might reasonably be expected to be able to obtain under the tenancy, having regard to the level of rents payable under the tenancies referred to in paragraph (a) above.

(4) Where, on an application under this section, a rent assessment committee make a determination of a rent for an assured shorthold tenancy—

(a) the determination shall have effect from such date as the committee may direct, not being earlier than the date of the application;

(b) if, at any time on or after the determination takes effect, the rent which, apart from this paragraph, would be payable under the tenancy exceeds the rent so determined, the excess shall be irrecoverable from the tenant; and

(c) no notice may be served under section 13(2) above with respect to a tenancy of the dwelling-house in question until after the first anniversary of the date on which the determination takes effect.

(5) Subsections (4), (5) and (8) of section 14 above apply in relation to a determination of rent under this section as they apply in relation to a determination under that section and, accordingly, where subsection (5) of that section applies, any reference in subsection (4)(b) above to rent is a reference to rent exclusive of the amount attributable to rates.

PART I

Termination of rent assessment committee's functions.

23.—(1) If the Secretary of State by order made by statutory instrument so provides, section 22 above shall not apply in such cases or to tenancies of dwelling-houses in such areas or in such other circumstances as may be specified in the order.

(2) An order under this section may contain such transitional, incidental and supplementary provisions as appear to the Secretary of State to be desirable.

(3) No order shall be made under this section unless a draft of the order has been laid before, and approved by a resolution of, each House of Parliament.

CHAPTER III

ASSURED AGRICULTURAL OCCUPANCIES

Assured agricultural occupancies.

24.—(1) A tenancy or licence of a dwelling-house is for the purposes of this Part of this Act an "assured agricultural occupancy" if—

(a) it is of a description specified in subsection (2) below; and

(b) by virtue of any provision of Schedule 3 to this Act the agricultural worker condition is for the time being fulfilled with respect to the dwelling-house subject to the tenancy or licence.

(2) The following are the tenancies and licences referred to in subsection (1)(a) above—

(a) an assured tenancy which is not an assured shorthold tenancy;

(b) a tenancy which does not fall within paragraph (a) above by reason only of paragraph 3 or paragraph 7 of Schedule 1 to this Act (or of both of those paragraphs); and

(c) a licence under which a person has the exclusive occupation of a dwelling-house as a separate dwelling and which, if it conferred a sufficient interest in land to be a tenancy, would be a tenancy falling within paragraph (a) or paragraph (b) above.

(3) For the purposes of Chapter I above and the following provisions of this Chapter, every assured agricultural occupancy which is not an assured tenancy shall be treated as if it were such a tenancy and any reference to a tenant, a landlord or any other expression appropriate to a tenancy shall be construed accordingly; but the provisions of Chapter I above shall have effect in relation to every assured agricultural occupancy subject to the provisions of this Chapter.

(4) Section 14 above shall apply in relation to an assured agricultural occupancy as if in subsection (1) of that section the reference to an assured tenancy were a reference to an assured agricultural occupancy.

Security of tenure.

25.—(1) If a statutory periodic tenancy arises on the coming to an end of an assured agricultural occupancy—

(a) it shall be an assured agricultural occupancy as long as, by virtue of any provision of Schedule 3 to this Act, the agricultural worker condition is for the time being fulfilled with respect to the dwelling-house in question; and

(b) if no rent was payable under the assured agricultural occupancy which constitutes the fixed term tenancy referred to in subsection (2) of section 5 above, subsection (3)(d) of that section shall apply as if for the words "the same as those for which rent was last payable under" there were substituted "monthly beginning on the day following the coming to an end of".

(2) In its application to an assured agricultural occupancy, Part II of Schedule 2 to this Act shall have effect with the omission of Ground 16.

(3) In its application to an assured agricultural occupancy, Part III of Schedule 2 to this Act shall have effect as if any reference in paragraph 2 to an assured tenancy included a reference to an assured agricultural occupancy.

(4) If the tenant under an assured agricultural occupancy gives notice to terminate his employment then, notwithstanding anything in any agreement or otherwise, that notice shall not constitute a notice to quit as respects the assured agricultural occupancy.

(5) Nothing in subsection (4) above affects the operation of an actual notice to quit given in respect of an assured agricultural occupancy.

Rehousing of agricultural workers etc. 1976 c. 80.

26. In section 27 of the Rent (Agriculture) Act 1976 (rehousing: applications to housing authority)—

(a) in subsection (1)(a) after "statutory tenancy" there shall be inserted "or an assured agricultural occupancy"; and

(b) at the end of subsection (3) there shall be added "and assured agricultural occupancy has the same meaning as in Chapter III of Part I of the Housing Act 1988".

CHAPTER IV

PROTECTION FROM EVICTION

Damages for unlawful eviction.

27.—(1) This section applies if, at any time after 9th June 1988, a landlord (in this section referred to as "the landlord in default") or any person acting on behalf of the landlord in default unlawfully deprives the residential occupier of any premises of his occupation of the whole or part of the premises.

(2) This section also applies if, at any time after 9th June 1988, a landlord (in this section referred to as "the landlord in default") or any person acting on behalf of the landlord in default—

(a) attempts unlawfully to deprive the residential occupier of any premises of his occupation of the whole or part of the premises, or

(b) knowing or having reasonable cause to believe that the conduct is likely to cause the residential occupier of any premises—

(i) to give up his occupation of the premises or any part thereof, or

(ii) to refrain from exercising any right or pursuing any remedy in respect of the premises or any part thereof,

does acts likely to interfere with the peace or comfort of the residential occupier or members of his household, or persistently withdraws or withholds services reasonably required for the occupation of the premises as a residence,

and, as a result, the residential occupier gives up his occupation of the premises as a residence.

PART I (3) Subject to the following provisions of this section, where this section applies, the landlord in default shall, by virtue of this section, be liable to pay to the former residential occupier, in respect of his loss of the right to occupy the premises in question as his residence, damages assessed on the basis set out in section 28 below.

(4) Any liability arising by virtue of subsection (3) above—

(a) shall be in the nature of a liability in tort; and

(b) subject to subsection (5) below, shall be in addition to any liability arising apart from this section (whether in tort, contract or otherwise).

(5) Nothing in this section affects the right of a residential occupier to enforce any liability which arises apart from this section in respect of his loss of the right to occupy premises as his residence; but damages shall not be awarded both in respect of such a liability and in respect of a liability arising by virtue of this section on account of the same loss.

(6) No liability shall arise by virtue of subsection (3) above if—

(a) before the date on which proceedings to enforce the liability are finally disposed of, the former residential occupier is reinstated in the premises in question in such circumstances that he becomes again the residential occupier of them; or

(b) at the request of the former residential occupier, a court makes an order (whether in the nature of an injunction or otherwise) as a result of which he is reinstated as mentioned in paragraph (a) above;

and, for the purposes of paragraph (a) above, proceedings to enforce a liability are finally disposed of on the earliest date by which the proceedings (including any proceedings on or in consequence of an appeal) have been determined and any time for appealing or further appealing has expired, except that if any appeal is abandoned, the proceedings shall be taken to be disposed of on the date of the abandonment.

(7) If, in proceedings to enforce a liability arising by virtue of subsection (3) above, it appears to the court—

(a) that, prior to the event which gave rise to the liability, the conduct of the former residential occupier or any person living with him in the premises concerned was such that it is reasonable to mitigate the damages for which the landlord in default would otherwise be liable, or

(b) that, before the proceedings were begun, the landlord in default offered to reinstate the former residential occupier in the premises in question and either it was unreasonable of the former residential occupier to refuse that offer or, if he had obtained alternative accommodation before the offer was made, it would have been unreasonable of him to refuse that offer if he had not obtained that accommodation,

the court may reduce the amount of damages which would otherwise be payable to such amount as it thinks appropriate.

(8) In proceedings to enforce a liability arising by virtue of subsection (3) above, it shall be a defence for the defendant to prove that he believed, and had reasonable cause to believe—

(a) that the residential occupier had ceased to reside in the premises in question at the time when he was deprived of occupation as mentioned in subsection (1) above or, as the case may be, when the attempt was made or the acts were done as a result of which he gave up his occupation of those premises; or

(b) that, where the liability would otherwise arise by virtue only of the doing of acts or the withdrawal or withholding of services, he had reasonable grounds for doing the acts or withdrawing or withholding the services in question.

(9) In this section—

(a) "residential occupier", in relation to any premises, has the same meaning as in section 1 of the 1977 Act;

(b) "the right to occupy", in relation to a residential occupier, includes any restriction on the right of another person to recover possession of the premises in question;

(c) "landlord", in relation to a residential occupier, means the person who, but for the occupier's right to occupy, would be entitled to occupation of the premises and any superior landlord under whom that person derives title;

(d) "former residential occupier", in relation to any premises, means the person who was the residential occupier until he was deprived of or gave up his occupation as mentioned in subsection (1) or subsection (2) above (and, in relation to a former residential occupier, "the right to occupy" and "landlord" shall be construed accordingly).

The measure of damages.

28.—(1) The basis for the assessment of damages referred to in section 27(3) above is the difference in value, determined as at the time immediately before the residential occupier ceased to occupy the premises in question as his residence, between—

(a) the value of the interest of the landlord in default determined on the assumption that the residential occupier continues to have the same right to occupy the premises as before that time; and

(b) the value of that interest determined on the assumption that the residential occupier has ceased to have that right.

(2) In relation to any premises, any reference in this section to the interest of the landlord in default is a reference to his interest in the building in which the premises in question are comprised (whether or not that building contains any other premises) together with its curtilage.

(3) For the purposes of the valuations referred to in subsection (1) above, it shall be assumed—

(a) that the landlord in default is selling his interest on the open market to a willing buyer;

(b) that neither the residential occupier nor any member of his family wishes to buy; and

(c) that it is unlawful to carry out any substantial development of any of the land in which the landlord's interest subsists or to demolish the whole or part of any building on that land.

PART I

(4) In this section "the landlord in default" has the same meaning as in section 27 above and subsection (9) of that section applies in relation to this section as it applies in relation to that.

1985 c. 68.

(5) Section 113 of the Housing Act 1985 (meaning of "members of a person's family") applies for the purposes of subsection (3)(b) above.

(6) The reference in subsection (3)(c) above to substantial development of any of the land in which the landlord's interest subsists is a reference to any development other than—

(a) development for which planning permission is granted by a general development order for the time being in force and which is carried out so as to comply with any condition or limitation subject to which planning permission is so granted; or

(b) a change of use resulting in the building referred to in subsection (2) above or any part of it being used as, or as part of, one or more dwelling-houses;

1971 c. 78.

and in this subsection "general development order" has the same meaning as in section 43(3) of the Town and Country Planning Act 1971 and other expressions have the same meaning as in that Act.

Offences of harassment.

29.—(1) In section 1 of the 1977 Act (unlawful eviction and harassment of occupier), with respect to acts done after the commencement of this Act, subsection (3) shall have effect with the substitution, for the word "calculated", of the word "likely".

(2) After that subsection there shall be inserted the following subsections—

"(3A) Subject to subsection (3B) below, the landlord of a residential occupier or an agent of the landlord shall be guilty of an offence if—

(a) he does acts likely to interfere with the peace or comfort of the residential occupier or members of his household, or

(b) he persistently withdraws or withholds services reasonably required for the occupation of the premises in question as a residence,

and (in either case) he knows, or has reasonable cause to believe, that that conduct is likely to cause the residential occupier to give up the occupation of the whole or part of the premises or to refrain from exercising any right or pursuing any remedy in respect of the whole or part of the premises.

(3B) A person shall not be guilty of an offence under subsection (3A) above if he proves that he had reasonable grounds for doing the acts or withdrawing or withholding the services in question.

(3C) In subsection (3A) above "landlord", in relation to a residential occupier of any premises, means the person who, but for—

(a) the residential occupier's right to remain in occupation of the premises, or

(b) a restriction on the person's right to recover possession of the premises,

would be entitled to occupation of the premises and any superior landlord under whom that person derives title."

Variation of scope of 1977 ss. 3 and 4.

30.—(1) In section 3 of the 1977 Act (prohibition of eviction without due process of law), in subsection (1) for the words "not a statutorily protected tenancy" there shall be substituted "neither a statutorily protected tenancy nor an excluded tenancy".

(2) After subsection (2A) of that section there shall be inserted the following subsections—

"(2B) Subsections (1) and (2) above apply in relation to any premises occupied as a dwelling under a licence, other than an excluded licence, as they apply in relation to premises let as a dwelling under a tenancy, and in those subsections the expressions "let" and "tenancy" shall be construed accordingly.

(2C) References in the preceding provisions of this section and section 4(2A) below to an excluded tenancy do not apply to—

(a) a tenancy entered into before the date on which the Housing Act 1988 came into force, or

(b) a tenancy entered into on or after that date but pursuant to a contract made before that date,

but, subject to that, "excluded tenancy" and "excluded licence" shall be construed in accordance with section 3A below."

(3) In section 4 of the 1977 Act (special provisions for agricultural employees) after subsection (2) there shall be inserted the following subsection—

"(2A) In accordance with section 3(2B) above, any reference in subsections (1) and (2) above to the tenant under the former tenancy includes a reference to the licensee under a licence (other than an excluded licence) which has come to an end (being a licence to occupy premises as a dwelling); and in the following provisions of this section the expressions "tenancy" and "rent" and any other expressions referable to a tenancy shall be construed accordingly."

Excluded tenancies and licences.

31. After section 3 of the 1977 Act there shall be inserted the following section—

"Excluded tenancies and licences.

3A.—(1) Any reference in this Act to an excluded tenancy or an excluded licence is a reference to a tenancy or licence which is excluded by virtue of any of the following provisions of this section.

(2) A tenancy or licence is excluded if—

(a) under its terms the occupier shares any accommodation with the landlord or licensor; and

PART I

(b) immediately before the tenancy or licence was granted and also at the time it comes to an end, the landlord or licensor occupied as his only or principal home premises of which the whole or part of the shared accommodation formed part.

(3) A tenancy or licence is also excluded if—

(a) under its terms the occupier shares any accommodation with a member of the family of the landlord or licensor;

(b) immediately before the tenancy or licence was granted and also at the time it comes to an end, the member of the family of the landlord or licensor occupied as his only or principal home premises of which the whole or part of the shared accommodation formed part; and

(c) immediately before the tenancy or licence was granted and also at the time it comes to an end, the landlord or licensor occupied as his only or principal home premises in the same building as the shared accommodation and that building is not a purpose-built block of flats.

(4) For the purposes of subsections (2) and (3) above, an occupier shares accommodation with another person if he has the use of it in common with that person (whether or not also in common with others) and any reference in those subsections to shared accommodation shall be construed accordingly, and if, in relation to any tenancy or licence, there is at any time more than one person who is the landlord or licensor, any reference in those subsections to the landlord or licensor shall be construed as a reference to any one of those persons.

(5) In subsections (2) to (4) above—

(a) "accommodation" includes neither an area used for storage nor a staircase, passage, corridor or other means of access;

(b) "occupier" means, in relation to a tenancy, the tenant and, in relation to a licence, the licensee; and

(c) "purpose-built block of flats" has the same meaning as in Part III of Schedule 1 to the Housing Act 1988;

and section 113 of the Housing Act 1985 shall apply to determine whether a person is for the purposes of subsection (3) above a member of another's family as it applies for the purposes of Part IV of that Act.

(6) A tenancy or licence is excluded if it was granted as a temporary expedient to a person who entered the premises in question or any other premises as a trespasser (whether or not, before the beginning of that tenancy or licence, another tenancy or licence to occupy the premises or any other premises had been granted to him).

(7) A tenancy or licence is excluded if— PART I

(a) it confers on the tenant or licensee the right to occupy the premises for a holiday only; or

(b) it is granted otherwise than for money or money's worth.

(8) A licence is excluded if it confers rights of occupation in a hostel, within the meaning of the Housing Act 1985, which is provided by—

(a) the council of a county, district or London Borough, the Common Council of the City of London, the Council of the Isles of Scilly, the Inner London Education Authority, a joint authority within the meaning of the Local Government Act 1985 or a residuary body within the meaning of that Act;

(b) a development corporation within the meaning of the New Towns Act 1981;

(c) the Commission for the New Towns;

(d) an urban development corporation established by an order under section 135 of the Local Government, Planning and Land Act 1980;

(e) a housing action trust established under Part III of the Housing Act 1988;

(f) the Development Board for Rural Wales;

(g) the Housing Corporation or Housing for Wales;

(h) a housing trust which is a charity or a registered housing association, within the meaning of the Housing Associations Act 1985; or

(i) any other person who is, or who belongs to a class of person which is, specified in an order made by the Secretary of State.

(9) The power to make an order under subsection (8)(i) above shall be exercisable by statutory instrument which shall be subject to annulment in pursuance of a resolution of either House of Parliament."

32.—(1) In section 5 of the 1977 Act (validity of notices to quit) at the beginning of subsection (1) there shall be inserted the words "Subject to subsection (1B) below". Notice to quit etc.

(2) After subsection (1) of that section there shall be inserted the following subsections—

"(1A) Subject to subsection (1B) below, no notice by a licensor or a licensee to determine a periodic licence to occupy premises as a dwelling (whether the licence was granted before or after the passing of this Act) shall be valid unless—

(a) it is in writing and contains such information as may be prescribed, and

(b) it is given not less than 4 weeks before the date on which it is to take effect.

PART I

(1B) Nothing in subsection (1) or subsection (1A) above applies to—

(a) premises let on an excluded tenancy which is entered into on or after the date on which the Housing Act 1988 came into force unless it is entered into pursuant to a contract made before that date; or

(b) premises occupied under an excluded licence."

Interpretation of Chapter IV and the 1977 Act.

33.—(1) In this Chapter "the 1977 Act" means the Protection from Eviction Act 1977.

1977 c. 43.

(2) In section 8 of the 1977 Act (interpretation) at the end of subsection (1) (statutory protected tenancy) there shall be inserted—

"(e) an assured tenancy or assured agricultural occupancy under Part I of the Housing Act 1988."

(3) At the end of that section there shall be added the following subsections—

"(4) In this Act "excluded tenancy" and "excluded licence" have the meaning assigned by section 3A of this Act.

(5) If, on or after the date on which the Housing Act 1988 came into force, the terms of an excluded tenancy or excluded licence entered into before that date are varied, then—

(a) if the variation affects the amount of the rent which is payable under the tenancy or licence, the tenancy or licence shall be treated for the purposes of sections 3(2C) and 5(1B) above as a new tenancy or licence entered into at the time of the variation; and

(b) if the variation does not affect the amount of the rent which is so payable, nothing in this Act shall affect the determination of the question whether the variation is such as to give rise to a new tenancy or licence.

(6) Any reference in subsection (5) above to a variation affecting the amount of the rent which is payable under a tenancy or licence does not include a reference to—

(a) a reduction or increase effected under Part III or Part VI of the Rent Act 1977 (rents under regulated tenancies and housing association tenancies), section 78 of that Act (power of rent tribunal in relation to restricted contracts) or sections 11 to 14 of the Rent (Agriculture) Act 1976; or

(b) a variation which is made by the parties and has the effect of making the rent expressed to be payable under the tenancy or licence the same as a rent for the dwelling which is entered in the register under Part IV or section 79 of the Rent Act 1977."

CHAPTER V

PHASING OUT OF RENT ACTS AND OTHER TRANSITIONAL PROVISIONS

New protected tenancies and agricultural occupancies restricted to special cases.

34.—(1) A tenancy which is entered into on or after the commencement of this Act cannot be a protected tenancy, unless—

(a) it is entered into in pursuance of a contract made before the commencement of this Act; or

(b) it is granted to a person (alone or jointly with others) who, immediately before the tenancy was granted, was a protected or statutory tenant and is so granted by the person who at that time was the landlord (or one of the joint landlords) under the protected or statutory tenancy; or

(c) it is granted to a person (alone or jointly with others) in the following circumstances—

(i) prior to the grant of the tenancy, an order for possession of a dwelling-house was made against him (alone or jointly with others) on the court being satisfied as mentioned in section 98(1)(a) of, or Case 1 in Schedule 16 to, the Rent Act 1977 or Case 1 in Schedule 4 to the Rent (Agriculture) Act 1976 (suitable alternative accommodation available); and 1977 c. 42. 1976 c. 80.

(ii) the tenancy is of the premises which constitute the suitable alternative accommodation as to which the court was so satisfied; and

(iii) in the proceedings for possession the court considered that, in the circumstances, the grant of an assured tenancy would not afford the required security and, accordingly, directed that the tenancy would be a protected tenancy; or

(d) it is a tenancy in relation to which subsections (1) and (3) of section 38 below have effect in accordance with subsection (4) of that section.

(2) In subsection (1)(b) above "protected tenant" and "statutory tenant" do not include—

(a) a tenant under a protected shorthold tenancy;

(b) a protected or statutory tenant of a dwelling-house which was let under a protected shorthold tenancy which ended before the commencement of this Act and in respect of which at that commencement either there has been no grant of a further tenancy or any grant of a further tenancy has been to the person who, immediately before the grant, was in possession of the dwelling-house as a protected or statutory tenant;

and in this subsection "protected shorthold tenancy" includes a tenancy which, in proceedings for possession under Case 19 in Schedule 15 to the Rent Act 1977, is treated as a protected shorthold tenancy.

(3) In any case where—

(a) by virtue of subsections (1) and (2) above, a tenancy entered into on or after the commencement of this Act is an assured tenancy, but

(b) apart from subsection (2) above, the effect of subsection (1)(b) above would be that the tenancy would be a protected tenancy, and

PART I

(c) the landlord and the tenant under the tenancy are the same as at the coming to an end of the protected or statutory tenancy which, apart from subsection (2) above, would fall within subsection (1)(b) above,

the tenancy shall be an assured shorthold tenancy (whether or not it fulfils the conditions in section 20(1) above) unless, before the tenancy is entered into, the landlord serves notice on the tenant that it is not to be a shorthold tenancy.

(4) A licence or tenancy which is entered into on or after the commencement of this Act cannot be a relevant licence or relevant tenancy for the purposes of the Rent (Agriculture) Act 1976 (in this subsection referred to as "the 1976 Act") unless—

1976 c. 80.

(a) it is entered into in pursuance of a contract made before the commencement of this Act; or

(b) it is granted to a person (alone or jointly with others) who, immediately before the licence or tenancy was granted, was a protected occupier or statutory tenant, within the meaning of the 1976 Act, and is so granted by the person who at that time was the landlord or licensor (or one of the joint landlords or licensors) under the protected occupancy or statutory tenancy in question.

(5) Except as provided in subsection (4) above, expressions used in this section have the same meaning as in the Rent Act 1977.

1977 c. 42.

Removal of special regimes for tenancies of housing associations etc.

35.—(1) In this section "housing association tenancy" has the same meaning as in Part VI of the Rent Act 1977.

(2) A tenancy which is entered into on or after the commencement of this Act cannot be a housing association tenancy unless—

(a) it is entered into in pursuance of a contract made before the commencement of this Act; or

(b) it is granted to a person (alone or jointly with others) who, immediately before the tenancy was granted, was a tenant under a housing association tenancy and is so granted by the person who at that time was the landlord under that housing association tenancy; or

(c) it is granted to a person (alone or jointly with others) in the following circumstances—

(i) prior to the grant of the tenancy, an order for possession of a dwelling-house was made against him (alone or jointly with others) on the court being satisfied as mentioned in paragraph (b) or paragraph (c) of subsection (2) of section 84 of the Housing Act 1985; and

1985 c. 68.

(ii) the tenancy is of the premises which constitute the suitable accommodation as to which the court was so satisfied; and

(iii) in the proceedings for possession the court directed that the tenancy would be a housing association tenancy; or

(d) it is a tenancy in relation to which subsections (1) and (3) of section 38 below have effect in accordance with subsection (4) of that section.

(3) Where, on or after the commencement of this Act, a registered housing association, within the meaning of the Housing Associations Act 1985, grants a secure tenancy pursuant to an obligation under section 554(2A) of the Housing Act 1985 (as set out in Schedule 17 to this Act) then, in determining whether that tenancy is a housing association tenancy, it shall be assumed for the purposes only of section 86(2)(b) of the Rent Act 1977 (tenancy would be a protected tenancy but for section 15 or 16 of that Act) that the tenancy was granted before the commencement of this Act.

PART I

1985 c. 69.

1985 c. 68.

1977 c. 42.

(4) A tenancy or licence which is entered into on or after the commencement of this Act cannot be a secure tenancy unless—

(a) the interest of the landlord belongs to a local authority, a new town corporation or an urban development corporation, all within the meaning of section 80 of the Housing Act 1985, a housing action trust established under Part III of this Act or the Development Board for Rural Wales; or

(b) the interest of the landlord belongs to a housing co-operative within the meaning of section 27B of the Housing Act 1985 (agreements between local housing authorities and housing co-operatives) and the tenancy or licence is of a dwelling-house comprised in a housing co-operative agreement falling within that section; or

(c) it is entered into in pursuance of a contract made before the commencement of this Act; or

(d) it is granted to a person (alone or jointly with others) who, immediately before it was entered into, was a secure tenant and is so granted by the body which at that time was the landlord or licensor under the secure tenancy; or

(e) it is granted to a person (alone or jointly with others) in the following circumstances—

(i) prior to the grant of the tenancy or licence, an order for possession of a dwelling-house was made against him (alone or jointly with others) on the court being satisfied as mentioned in paragraph (b) or paragraph (c) of subsection (2) of section 84 of the Housing Act 1985; and

(ii) the tenancy or licence is of the premises which constitute the suitable accommodation as to which the court was so satisfied; and

(iii) in the proceedings for possession the court considered that, in the circumstances, the grant of an assured tenancy would not afford the required security and, accordingly, directed that the tenancy or licence would be a secure tenancy; or

(f) it is granted pursuant to an obligation under section 554(2A) of the Housing Act 1985 (as set out in Schedule 17 to this Act).

(5) If, on or after the commencement of this Act, the interest of the landlord under a protected or statutory tenancy becomes held by a housing association, a housing trust, the Housing Corporation or Housing for Wales, nothing in the preceding provisions of this section shall prevent the tenancy from being a housing association tenancy or a secure tenancy and, accordingly, in such a case section 80 of the Housing

Part I

Act 1985 (and any enactment which refers to that section) shall have effect without regard to the repeal of provisions of that section effected by this Act.

(6) In subsection (5) above "housing association" and "housing trust" have the same meaning as in the Housing Act 1985.

1985 c. 68.

New restricted contracts limited to transitional cases.

36.—(1) A tenancy or other contract entered into after the commencement of this Act cannot be a restricted contract for the purposes of the Rent Act 1977 unless it is entered into in pursuance of a contract made before the commencement of this Act.

(2) If the terms of a restricted contract are varied after this Act comes into force then, subject to subsection (3) below,—

(a) if the variation affects the amount of the rent which, under the contract, is payable for the dwelling in question, the contract shall be treated as a new contract entered into at the time of the variation (and subsection (1) above shall have effect accordingly); and

(b) if the variation does not affect the amount of the rent which, under the contract, is so payable, nothing in this section shall affect the determination of the question whether the variation is such as to give rise to a new contract.

(3) Any reference in subsection (2) above to a variation affecting the amount of the rent which, under a contract, is payable for a dwelling does not include a reference to—

(a) a reduction or increase effected under section 78 of the Rent Act 1977 (power of rent tribunal); or

(b) a variation which is made by the parties and has the effect of making the rent expressed to be payable under the contract the same as the rent for the dwelling which is entered in the register under section 79 of the Rent Act 1977.

(4) In subsection (1) of section 81A of the Rent Act 1977 (cancellation of registration of rent relating to a restricted contract) paragraph (a) (no cancellation until two years have elapsed since the date of the entry) shall cease to have effect.

(5) In this section "rent" has the same meaning as in Part V of the Rent Act 1977.

No further assured tenancies under Housing Act 1980.

1980 c. 51.

37.—(1) A tenancy which is entered into on or after the commencement of this Act cannot be an assured tenancy for the purposes of sections 56 to 58 of the Housing Act 1980 (in this section referred to as a "1980 Act tenancy").

(2) In any case where—

(a) before the commencement of this Act, a tenant under a 1980 Act tenancy made an application to the court under section 24 of the Landlord and Tenant Act 1954 (for the grant of a new tenancy), and

1954 c. 56.

(b) at the commencement of this Act the 1980 Act tenancy is continuing by virtue of that section or of any provision of Part IV of the said Act of 1954,

section 1(3) of this Act shall not apply to the 1980 Act tenancy.

(3) If, in a case falling within subsection (2) above, the court makes an order for the grant of a new tenancy under section 29 of the Landlord and Tenant Act 1954, that tenancy shall be an assured tenancy for the purposes of this Act. 1954 c. 56.

(4) In any case where—

(a) before the commencement of this Act a contract was entered into for the grant of a 1980 Act tenancy, but

(b) at the commencement of this Act the tenancy had not been granted,

the contract shall have effect as a contract for the grant of an assured tenancy (within the meaning of this Act).

(5) In relation to an assured tenancy falling within subsection (3) above or granted pursuant to a contract falling within subsection (4) above, Part I of Schedule 1 to this Act shall have effect as if it consisted only of paragraphs 11 and 12; and, if the landlord granting the tenancy is a fully mutual housing association, then, so long as that association remains the landlord under that tenancy (and under any statutory periodic tenancy which arises on the coming to an end of that tenancy), the said paragraph 12 shall have effect in relation to that tenancy with the omission of sub-paragraph (1)(h).

(6) Any reference in this section to a provision of the Landlord and Tenant Act 1954 is a reference only to that provision as applied by section 58 of the Housing Act 1980. 1980 c. 51.

Transfer of existing tenancies from public to private sector.

38.—(1) The provisions of subsection (3) below apply in relation to a tenancy which was entered into before, or pursuant to a contract made before, the commencement of this Act if,—

(a) at that commencement or, if it is later, at the time it is entered into, the interest of the landlord is held by a public body (within the meaning of subsection (5) below); and

(b) at some time after that commencement, the interest of the landlord ceases to be so held.

(2) The provisions of subsection (3) below also apply in relation to a tenancy which was entered into before, or pursuant to a contract made before, the commencement of this Act if,—

(a) at the commencement of this Act or, if it is later, at the time it is entered into, it is a housing association tenancy; and

(b) at some time after that commencement, it ceases to be such a tenancy.

(3) On and after the time referred to in subsection (1)(b) or, as the case may be, subsection (2)(b) above—

(a) the tenancy shall not be capable of being a protected tenancy, a protected occupancy or a housing association tenancy;

(b) the tenancy shall not be capable of being a secure tenancy unless (and only at a time when) the interest of the landlord under the tenancy is (or is again) held by a public body; and

(c) paragraph 1 of Schedule 1 to this Act shall not apply in relation to it, and the question whether at any time thereafter it becomes (or remains) an assured tenancy shall be determined accordingly.

PART I

(4) In relation to a tenancy under which, at the commencement of this Act or, if it is later, at the time the tenancy is entered into, the interest of the landlord is held by a new town corporation, within the meaning of section 80 of the Housing Act 1985, subsections (1) and (3) above shall have effect as if any reference in subsection (1) above to the commencement of this Act were a reference to—

1985 c. 68.

- (a) the date on which expires the period of two years beginning on the day this Act is passed; or
- (b) if the Secretary of State by order made by statutory instrument within that period so provides, such other date (whether earlier or later) as may be specified by the order for the purposes of this subsection.

(5) For the purposes of this section, the interest of a landlord under a tenancy is held by a public body at a time when—

- (a) it belongs to a local authority, a new town corporation or an urban development corporation, all within the meaning of section 80 of the Housing Act 1985; or
- (b) it belongs to a housing action trust established under Part III of this Act; or
- (c) it belongs to the Development Board for Rural Wales; or
- (d) it belongs to Her Majesty in right of the Crown or to a government department or is held in trust for Her Majesty for the purposes of a government department.

(6) In this section—

- (a) "housing association tenancy" means a tenancy to which Part VI of the Rent Act 1977 applies;

1977 c. 42.

- (b) "protected tenancy" has the same meaning as in that Act; and

1976 c. 80.

- (c) "protected occupancy" has the same meaning as in the Rent (Agriculture) Act 1976.

Statutory tenants: succession.

39.—(1) In section 2(1)(b) of the Rent Act 1977 (which introduces the provisions of Part I of Schedule 1 to that Act relating to statutory tenants by succession) after the words "statutory tenant of a dwelling-house" there shall be inserted "or, as the case may be, is entitled to an assured tenancy of a dwelling-house by succession".

(2) Where the person who is the original tenant, within the meaning of Part I of Schedule 1 to the Rent Act 1977, dies after the commencement of this Act, that Part shall have effect subject to the amendments in Part I of Schedule 4 to this Act.

(3) Where subsection (2) above does not apply but the person who is the first successor, within the meaning of Part I of Schedule 1 to the Rent Act 1977, dies after the commencement of this Act, that Part shall have effect subject to the amendments in paragraphs 5 to 9 of Part I of Schedule 4 to this Act.

(4) In any case where the original occupier, within the meaning of section 4 of the Rent (Agriculture) Act 1976 (statutory tenants and tenancies) dies after the commencement of this Act, that section shall have effect subject to the amendments in Part II of Schedule 4 to this Act.

(5) In any case where, by virtue of any provision of— PART I

(a) Part I of Schedule 1 to the Rent Act 1977, as amended in accordance with subsection (2) or subsection (3) above, or 1977 c. 42.

(b) section 4 of the Rent (Agriculture) Act 1976, as amended in accordance with subsection (4) above, 1976 c. 80.

a person (in the following provisions of this section referred to as "the successor") becomes entitled to an assured tenancy of a dwelling-house by succession, that tenancy shall be a periodic tenancy arising by virtue of this section.

(6) Where, by virtue of subsection (5) above, the successor becomes entitled to an assured periodic tenancy, that tenancy is one—

(a) taking effect in possession immediately after the death of the protected or statutory tenant or protected occupier (in the following provisions of this section referred to as "the predecessor") on whose death the successor became so entitled;

(b) deemed to have been granted to the successor by the person who, immediately before the death of the predecessor, was the landlord of the predecessor under his tenancy;

(c) under which the premises which are let are the same dwelling-house as, immediately before his death, the predecessor occupied under his tenancy;

(d) under which the periods of the tenancy are the same as those for which rent was last payable by the predecessor under his tenancy;

(e) under which, subject to sections 13 to 15 above, the other terms are the same as those on which, under his tenancy, the predecessor occupied the dwelling-house immediately before his death; and

(f) which, for the purposes of section 13(2) above, is treated as a statutory periodic tenancy;

and in paragraphs (b) to (e) above "under his tenancy", in relation to the predecessor, means under his protected tenancy or protected occupancy or in his capacity as a statutory tenant.

(7) If, immediately before the death of the predecessor, the landlord might have recovered possession of the dwelling-house under Case 19 in Schedule 15 to the Rent Act 1977, the assured periodic tenancy to which the successor becomes entitled shall be an assured shorthold tenancy (whether or not it fulfils the conditions in section 20(1) above).

(8) If, immediately before his death, the predecessor was a protected occupier or statutory tenant within the meaning of the Rent (Agriculture) Act 1976, the assured periodic tenancy to which the successor becomes entitled shall be an assured agricultural occupancy (whether or not it fulfils the conditions in section 24(1) above).

(9) Where, immediately before his death, the predecessor was a tenant under a fixed term tenancy, section 6 above shall apply in relation to the assured periodic tenancy to which the successor becomes entitled on the predecessor's death subject to the following modifications—

(a) for any reference to a statutory periodic tenancy there shall be substituted a reference to the assured periodic tenancy to which the successor becomes so entitled;

PART I

(b) in subsection (1) of that section, paragraph (a) shall be omitted and the reference in paragraph (b) to section 5(3)(e) above shall be construed as a reference to subsection (6)(e) above; and

(c) for any reference to the coming to an end of the former tenancy there shall be substituted a reference to the date of the predecessor's death.

(10) If and so long as a dwelling-house is subject to an assured tenancy to which the successor has become entitled by succession, section 7 above and Schedule 2 to this Act shall have effect subject to the modifications in Part III of Schedule 4 to this Act; and in that Part "the predecessor" and "the successor" have the same meaning as in this section.

CHAPTER VI

GENERAL PROVISIONS

Jurisdiction of county courts.

40.—(1) A county court shall have jurisdiction to hear and determine any question arising under any provision of—

(a) Chapters I to III and V above, or

(b) sections 27 and 28 above,

other than a question falling within the jurisdiction of a rent assessment committee by virtue of any such provision.

1984 c. 28.

(2) Subsection (1) above has effect notwithstanding that the damages claimed in any proceedings may exceed the amount which, for the time being, is the county court limit for the purposes of the County Courts Act 1984.

(3) Where any proceedings under any provision mentioned in subsection (1) above are being taken in a county court, the court shall have jurisdiction to hear and determine any other proceedings joined with those proceedings, notwithstanding that, apart from this subsection, those other proceedings would be outside the court's jurisdiction.

(4) If any person takes any proceedings under any provision mentioned in subsection (1) above in the High Court, he shall not be entitled to recover any more costs of those proceedings than those to which he would have been entitled if the proceedings had been taken in a county court: and in such a case the taxing master shall have the same power of directing on what county court scale costs are to be allowed, and of allowing any item of costs, as the judge would have had if the proceedings had been taken in a county court.

(5) Subsection (4) above shall not apply where the purpose of taking the proceedings in the High Court was to enable them to be joined with any proceedings already pending before that court (not being proceedings taken under any provision mentioned in subsection (1) above).

Rent assessment committees: procedure and information powers.
1977 c. 42.

41.—(1) In section 74 of the Rent Act 1977 (regulations made by the Secretary of State) at the end of paragraph (b) of subsection (1) (procedure of rent officers and rent assessment committees) there shall be added the words "whether under this Act or Part I of the Housing Act 1988".

PART I

(2) The rent assessment committee to whom a matter is referred under Chapter I or Chapter II above may by notice in the prescribed form served on the landlord or the tenant require him to give to the committee, within such period of not less than fourteen days from the service of the notice as may be specified in the notice, such information as they may reasonably require for the purposes of their functions.

(3) If any person fails without reasonable excuse to comply with a notice served on him under subsection (2) above, he shall be liable on summary conviction to a fine not exceeding level 3 on the standard scale.

(4) Where an offence under subsection (3) above committed by a body corporate is proved to have been committed with the consent or connivance of, or to be attributable to any neglect on the part of, any director, manager or secretary or other similar officer of the body corporate or any person who was purporting to act in any such capacity, he as well as the body corporate shall be guilty of that offence and shall be liable to be proceeded against and punished accordingly.

Information as to determinations of rents.

42.—(1) The President of every rent assessment panel shall keep and make publicly available, in such manner as is specified in an order made by the Secretary of State, such information as may be so specified with respect to rents under assured tenancies and assured agricultural occupancies which have been the subject of references or applications to, or determinations by, rent assessment committees.

(2) A copy of any information certified under the hand of an officer duly authorised by the President of the rent assessment panel concerned shall be receivable in evidence in any court and in any proceedings.

(3) An order under subsection (1) above—

(a) may prescribe the fees to be charged for the supply of a copy, including a certified copy, of any of the information kept by virtue of that subsection; and

(b) may make different provision with respect to different cases or descriptions of case, including different provision for different areas.

(4) The power to make an order under subsection (1) above shall be exercisable by statutory instrument which shall be subject to annulment in pursuance of a resolution of either House of Parliament.

Powers of local authorities for purposes of giving information.

1977 c. 42.

43. In section 149 of the Rent Act 1977 (which, among other matters, authorises local authorities to publish information for the benefit of landlords and tenants with respect to their rights and duties under certain enactments), in subsection (1)(a) after sub-paragraph (iv) there shall be inserted—

"(v) Chapters I to III of Part I of the Housing Act 1988".

Application to Crown Property.

44.—(1) Subject to paragraph 11 of Schedule 1 to this Act and subsection (2) below, Chapters I to IV above apply in relation to premises in which there subsists, or at any material time subsisted, a Crown interest as they apply in relation to premises in relation to which no such interest subsists or ever subsisted.

PART I

(2) In Chapter IV above—

(a) sections 27 and 28 do not bind the Crown; and

1977 c. 43.

(b) the remainder binds the Crown to the extent provided for in section 10 of the Protection from Eviction Act 1977.

(3) In this section "Crown interest" means an interest which belongs to Her Majesty in right of the Crown or of the Duchy of Lancaster or to the Duchy of Cornwall, or to a government department, or which is held in trust for Her Majesty for the purposes of a government department.

(4) Where an interest belongs to Her Majesty in right of the Duchy of Lancaster, then, for the purposes of Chapters I to IV above, the Chancellor of the Duchy of Lancaster shall be deemed to be the owner of the interest.

Interpretation of Part I.

45.—(1) In this Part of this Act, except where the context otherwise requires,—

"dwelling-house" may be a house or part of a house;

"fixed term tenancy" means any tenancy other than a periodic tenancy;

1985 c. 69.

"fully mutual housing association" has the same meaning as in Part I of the Housing Associations Act 1985;

"landlord" includes any person from time to time deriving title under the original landlord and also includes, in relation to a dwelling-house, any person other than a tenant who is, or but for the existence of an assured tenancy would be, entitled to possession of the dwelling-house;

"let" includes "sub-let";

"prescribed" means prescribed by regulations made by the Secretary of State by statutory instrument;

1976 c. 70.

"rates" includes water rates and charges but does not include an owner's drainage rate, as defined in section 63(2)(a) of the Land Drainage Act 1976;

1985 c. 68.

"secure tenancy" has the meaning assigned by section 79 of the Housing Act 1985;

"statutory periodic tenancy" has the meaning assigned by section 5(7) above;

"tenancy" includes a sub-tenancy and an agreement for a tenancy or sub-tenancy; and

"tenant" includes a sub-tenant and any person deriving title under the original tenant or sub-tenant.

(2) Subject to paragraph 11 of Schedule 2 to this Act, any reference in this Part of this Act to the beginning of a tenancy is a reference to the day on which the tenancy is entered into or, if it is later, the day on which, under the terms of any lease, agreement or other document, the tenant is entitled to possession under the tenancy.

(3) Where two or more persons jointly constitute either the landlord or the tenant in relation to a tenancy, then, except where this Part of this Act otherwise provides, any reference to the landlord or to the tenant is a reference to all the persons who jointly constitute the landlord or the tenant, as the case may require.

PART I

(4) For the avoidance of doubt, it is hereby declared that any reference in this Part of this Act (however expressed) to a power for a landlord to determine a tenancy does not include a reference to a power of re-entry or forfeiture for breach of any term or condition of the tenancy.

(5) Regulations under subsection (1) above may make different provision with respect to different cases or descriptions of case, including different provision for different areas.

PART II

HOUSING ASSOCIATIONS

Housing for Wales

Housing for Wales.

46.—(1) There shall be a body known as Housing for Wales.

(2) Schedule 5 to this Act shall have effect with respect to the constitution and proceedings of, and other matters relating to, Housing for Wales.

(3) Housing for Wales shall have the functions conferred on it by the Housing Associations Act 1985 (in this Part referred to as "the 1985 Act") as amended in accordance with section 59 below. 1985 c. 69.

(4) All property in Wales which, immediately before the day appointed for the coming into force of this section, is held by the Housing Corporation shall on that day be transferred to and vest in Housing for Wales.

(5) Any question whether any property has been transferred to Housing for Wales by virtue of subsection (4) above shall be determined by the Secretary of State.

Transfer to Housing for Wales of regulation etc. of housing associations based in Wales.

47.—(1) Every registered housing association which, immediately before the appointed day,—

(a) is a society registered under the 1965 Act and has its registered office for the purposes of that Act in Wales, or

(b) is a registered charity and has its address for the purposes of registration by the Charity Commissioners in Wales,

shall on the appointed day cease to be registered in the register maintained by the Housing Corporation under section 3 of the 1985 Act and, by virtue of this subsection, be deemed to be registered in the register maintained by Housing for Wales under that section.

(2) Not later than one month before the appointed day, the Secretary of State shall notify every registered housing association which appears to him to be one which on that day will be deemed to be registered as mentioned in subsection (1) above of that fact and of the effect of that subsection.

(3) As soon as may be after the appointed day, Housing for Wales shall give notice of any registration effected by virtue of subsection (1) above,—

(a) if the housing association is a registered charity, to the Charity Commissioners; and

(b) if the housing association is a society registered under the 1965 Act, to the Chief Registrar of friendly societies.

PART II

(4) All rights, liabilities and obligations to which, immediately before the appointed day, the Housing Corporation was entitled or subject in relation to—

(a) any registered housing association to which subsection (1) above applies, and

(b) land in Wales held by an unregistered housing association,

shall on that day become rights, liabilities and obligations of Housing for Wales.

(5) Any question whether any rights, liabilities or obligations have become rights, liabilities or obligations of Housing for Wales by virtue of subsection (4) above shall be determined by the Secretary of State.

(6) In this section—

1965 c. 12.

"the 1965 Act" means the Industrial and Provident Societies Act 1965; and

"the appointed day" means the day appointed for the coming into force of this section.

Registration and issue of guidance

Permissible purposes, objects or powers.

48.—(1) For subsections (3) and (4) of section 4 (eligibility for registration) of the 1985 Act there shall be substituted the following subsections—

"(3) The permissible additional purposes or objects are—

(a) providing land, amenities or services, or providing, constructing, repairing or improving buildings, for the benefit of the association's residents, either exclusively or together with other persons;

(b) acquiring, or repairing and improving, or creating by the conversion of houses or other property, houses to be disposed of on sale, on lease or on shared ownership terms;

(c) constructing houses to be disposed of on shared ownership terms;

(d) managing houses which are held on leases or other lettings (not being houses falling within subsection (2)(a) or (b)) or blocks of flats;

(e) providing services of any description for owners or occupiers of houses in arranging or carrying out works of maintenance, repair or improvement, or encouraging or facilitating the carrying out of such works;

(f) encouraging and giving advice on the formation of other housing associations or providing services for, and giving advice on the running of, such associations and other voluntary organisations concerned with housing, or matters connected with housing.

(4) A housing association shall not be ineligible for registration by reason only that its powers include power—

(a) to acquire commercial premises or businesses as an incidental part of a project or series of projects undertaken for purposes or objects falling within subsection (2) or (3);

PART II

(b) to repair, improve or convert any commercial premises acquired as mentioned in paragraph (a) or to carry on, for a limited period, any business so acquired;

(c) to repair or improve houses, or buildings in which houses are situated, after the tenants have exercised, or claimed to exercise, acquisition rights;

(d) to acquire houses to be disposed of at a discount to tenants to whom section 58 of the Housing Act 1988 applies (tenants of charitable housing associations etc.).

(5) In this section—

"acquisition right" means—

(a) in England and Wales, the right to buy or the right to be granted a shared ownership lease under Part V of the Housing Act 1985;

(b) in Scotland, a right to purchase under section 61 of the Housing (Scotland) Act 1987;

"block of flats" means a building—

(a) containing two or more flats which are held on leases or other lettings; and

(b) occupied or intended to be occupied wholly or mainly for residential purposes;

"disposed of on shared ownership terms" means—

(a) in England and Wales, disposed of on a shared ownership lease;

(b) in Scotland, disposed of under a shared ownership agreement;

"letting" includes the grant—

(a) in England and Wales, of a licence to occupy;

(b) in Scotland, of a right or permission to occupy;

"residents", in relation to a housing association, means the persons occupying the houses or hostels provided or managed by the association;

"voluntary organisation" means an organisation whose activities are not carried on for profit."

(2) The Secretary of State may by order made by statutory instrument amend the subsections substituted by subsection (1) above, but not so as to restrict or limit the permissible purposes, objects or powers.

(3) An order under subsection (2) above may contain such incidental, supplemental or transitional provisions as the Secretary of State thinks fit.

(4) A statutory instrument containing an order under subsection (2) above shall be subject to annulment in pursuance of a resolution of either House of Parliament.

PART II

Guidance as to management of accommodation by registered housing associations.

49. After section 36 of the 1985 Act there shall be inserted the following section—

"Issue of guidance by the Corporation.

36A.—(1) In accordance with the provisions of this section, the Corporation may issue guidance with respect to the management of housing accommodation by registered housing associations and, in considering under the preceding provisions of this Part whether action needs to be taken to secure the proper management of an association's affairs or whether there has been mismanagement, the Corporation may have regard (among other matters) to the extent to which any such guidance is being or has been followed.

(2) Guidance issued under this section may make different provision in relation to different cases and, in particular, in relation to different areas, different descriptions of housing accommodation and different descriptions of registered housing associations.

(3) Without prejudice to the generality of subsections (1) and (2), guidance issued under this section may relate to—

(a) the housing demands for which provision should be made and the means of meeting those demands;

(b) the allocation of housing accommodation between individuals;

(c) the terms of tenancies and the principles upon which the levels of rent should be determined;

(d) standards of maintenance and repair and the means of achieving these standards; and

(e) consultation and communication with tenants.

(4) Guidance issued under this section may be revised or withdrawn but, before issuing or revising any guidance under this section, the Corporation—

(a) shall consult such bodies appearing to it to be representative of housing associations as it considers appropriate; and

(b) shall submit a draft of the proposed guidance or, as the case may be, the proposed revision to the Secretary of State for his approval.

(5) If the Secretary of State gives his approval to a draft submitted to him under subsection (4)(b), the Corporation shall issue the guidance or, as the case may be, the revision concerned in such manner as the Corporation considers appropriate for bringing it to the notice of the housing associations concerned."

Grants: functions of Corporation

50.—(1) The Housing Corporation and Housing for Wales may make grants to registered housing associations in respect of expenditure incurred or to be incurred by them in connection with housing activities; and any reference in the following provisions of this section to "the Corporation" shall be construed accordingly. **Housing association grants.**

(2) As respects grants under this section the following, namely—

(a) the procedure to be followed in relation to applications for grant;

(b) the circumstances in which grant is or is not to be payable;

(c) the method for calculating, and any limitations on, the amount of grant; and

(d) the manner in which, and time or times at which, grant is to be paid,

shall be such as may be specified by the Corporation, acting in accordance with such principles as it may from time to time determine.

(3) In making a grant under this section, the Corporation may provide that the grant is conditional on compliance by the association with such conditions as it may specify.

(4) On such terms as it may, with the appropriate approval, specify, the Corporation may appoint a local housing authority which is willing to do so to act as its agent in connection with the assessment and payment of grant under this section; and, where such an appointment is made, the local housing authority shall act as such an agent in accordance with the terms of their appointment.

(5) In subsection (4) above, "the appropriate approval" means the approval of the Secretary of State given with the consent of the Treasury.

(6) Where—

(a) a grant under this section is payable to an association, and

(b) at any time property to which the grant relates becomes vested in, or is leased for a term of years to, or reverts to, some other registered housing association, or trustees for some other such association,

this section (including this subsection) shall have effect after that time as if the grant, or such proportion of it as is specified or determined under subsection (7) below, were payable to that other association.

(7) The proportion referred to in subsection (6) above is that which, in the circumstances of the particular case—

(a) the Corporation, acting in accordance with such principles as it may from time to time determine, may specify as being appropriate; or

(b) the Corporation may determine to be appropriate.

(8) Where one of the associations mentioned in subsection (6) above is registered by the Housing Corporation and another is registered by Housing for Wales, the determination mentioned in subsection (7) above shall be such as shall be agreed between the two Corporations.

PART II

Revenue deficit grants.

51.—(1) The Housing Corporation or, as the case may be, Housing for Wales may make a grant to a registered housing association if—

(a) in relation to all housing activities of the association,

(b) in relation to housing activities of the association of a particular description, or

(c) in relation to particular housing activities of the association,

the association's expenditure as calculated by the Corporation concerned for any period (including a period which is wholly or partly a future period) exceeds its income as so calculated for that period.

(2) In calculating an association's expenditure or income for the purposes of subsection (1) above, the Housing Corporation or, as the case may be, Housing for Wales—

(a) shall act in accordance with such principles as it may from time to time determine; and

(b) may act on such assumptions (whether or not borne out or likely to be borne out by events) as it may from time to time determine.

(3) Subsections (2) and (3) of section 50 above shall apply for the purposes of this section as they apply for the purposes of that section.

Recovery etc. of grants.

52.—(1) Where a grant to which this section applies, that is to say—

(a) a grant under section 50 or 51 above, or

(b) a grant under section 41 of the 1985 Act or any enactment replaced by that section, or

1988 c. 43.

(c) a grant under section 2(2) of the Housing (Scotland) Act 1988,

has been made to a registered housing association, the powers conferred by subsection (2) below are exercisable in such events (including the association not complying with any conditions) as the Corporation may from time to time determine (in this section referred to as "relevant events").

(2) The Corporation, acting in accordance with such principles as it may from time to time determine, may—

(a) reduce the amount of, or of any payment in respect of, the grant;

(b) suspend or cancel any instalment of the grant; or

(c) direct the association to pay to it an amount equal to the whole, or such proportion as it may specify, of the amount of any payment made to the association in respect of the grant,

and a direction under paragraph (c) above requiring the payment of any amount may also require the payment of interest on that amount in accordance with subsections (7) to (9) below.

(3) Where, after a grant to which this section applies has been made to an association, a relevant event occurs, the association shall notify the Corporation and, if so required by written notice of the Corporation, shall furnish it with such particulars of and information relating to the event as are specified in the notice.

(4) Where a grant to which this section applies (other than one falling within subsection (1)(c) above) has been made to an association, the Chief Land Registrar may furnish the Corporation with such particulars and information as it may reasonably require for the purpose of ascertaining

whether a relevant event has occurred; but this subsection shall cease to have effect on the day appointed under section 3(2) of the Land Registration Act 1988 for the coming into force of that Act. 1988 c. 3.

(5) Where—

(a) a grant to which this section applies has been made to an association, and

(b) at any time property to which the grant relates becomes vested in, or is leased for a term of years to, or reverts to, some other registered housing association, or trustees for some other such association,

this section (including this subsection) shall have effect after that time as if the grant, or such proportion of it as is specified or determined under subsection (6) below, had been made to that other association.

(6) The proportion referred to in subsection (5) above is that which, in the circumstances of the particular case,—

(a) the Corporation, acting in accordance with such principles as it may from time to time determine, may specify as being appropriate; or

(b) the Corporation may determine to be appropriate.

(7) A direction under subsection (2)(c) above requiring the payment of interest on the amount directed to be paid to the Corporation shall specify, in accordance with subsection (9) below,—

(a) the rate or rates of interest (whether fixed or variable) which is or are applicable;

(b) the date from which interest is payable, being not earlier than the date of the relevant event; and

(c) any provision for suspended or reduced interest which is applicable.

(8) In subsection (7)(c) above—

(a) the reference to a provision for suspended interest is a reference to a provision whereby, if the amount which is directed to be paid to the Corporation is paid before a date specified in the direction, no interest will be payable for any period after the date of the direction; and

(b) the reference to a provision for reduced interest is a reference to a provision whereby, if that amount is so paid, any interest payable will be payable at a rate or rates lower than the rate or rates which would otherwise be applicable.

(9) The matters specified in a direction as mentioned in paragraphs (a) to (c) of subsection (7) above shall be either—

(a) such as the Corporation, acting in accordance with such principles as it may from time to time determine, may specify as being appropriate, or

(b) such as the Corporation may determine to be appropriate in the particular case.

Determinations under Part II.

53.—(1) A general determination may either—

(a) make the same provision for all cases; or

PART II

(b) make different provision for different cases or descriptions of cases, including different provision for different areas or for different descriptions of housing associations or housing activities;

and for the purposes of this subsection descriptions may be framed by reference to any matters whatever, including in particular, in the case of housing activities, the manner in which they are financed.

(2) The Corporation shall not make a determination under the foregoing provisions of this Part except with the approval of the Secretary of State given, in the case of a general determination, with the consent of the Treasury.

(3) Before making a general determination, the Corporation shall consult such bodies appearing to it to be representative of housing associations as it considers appropriate; and after making such a determination, the Corporation shall publish the determination in such manner as it considers appropriate for bringing the determination to the notice of the associations concerned.

(4) In this section "general determination" means a determination under any provision of sections 50 to 52 above, other than a determination relating solely to a particular case.

Grants: functions of Secretary of State

Tax relief grants.

54.—(1) If a housing association makes a claim to the Secretary of State in respect of a period and satisfies him that throughout the period it was a housing association to which this section applies and its functions either—

(a) consisted exclusively of the function of providing or maintaining housing accommodation for letting or hostels and activities incidental to that function, or

(b) included that function and activities incidental to that function,

the Secretary of State may make grants to the association for affording relief from tax chargeable on the association.

(2) This section applies to a housing association at any time if, at that time—

(a) it is registered;

(b) it does not trade for profit; and

1988 c. 1.

(c) it is not approved for the purposes of section 488 of the Income and Corporation Taxes Act 1988 (tax treatment of co-operative housing associations).

(3) References in this section to tax chargeable on an association are to income tax (other than income tax which the association is entitled to deduct on making any payment) and corporation tax.

(4) A grant under this section may be made—

(a) in a case falling within subsection (1)(a) above, for affording relief from any tax chargeable on the association for the period in respect of which the claim is made; and

(b) in a case falling within subsection (1)(b) above, for affording relief from such part of any tax so chargeable as the Secretary of State considers appropriate having regard to the other functions of the association;

and in any case shall be of such amount, shall be made at such times and shall be subject to such conditions as the Secretary of State thinks fit.

(5) The conditions may include conditions for securing the repayment in whole or in part of a grant made to an association—

(a) in the event of tax in respect of which it was made being found not to be chargeable; or

(b) in such other events (including the association beginning to trade for profit) as the Secretary of State may determine.

(6) A claim under this section shall be made in such manner and shall be supported by such evidence as the Secretary of State may direct.

(7) The Commissioners of Inland Revenue and their officers may disclose to the Secretary of State such particulars as he may reasonably require for determining whether a grant should be made on a claim or whether a grant should be repaid or the amount of such grant or repayment.

(8) In this section "letting" includes—

(a) in England and Wales, the grant of a shared ownership lease or a licence to occupy;

(b) in Scotland, disposal under a shared ownership agreement or the grant of a right or permission to occupy.

Surplus rental income.

55.—(1) An association to which this section applies, that is to say, a registered housing association which has at any time received a payment in respect of—

(a) a grant under section 50 above, or

(b) a grant under section 41 of the 1985 Act or any enactment replaced by that section, or

(c) a grant under section 2(2) of the Housing (Scotland) Act 1988, 1988 c. 43.

(in this section referred to as a "relevant grant") shall show separately in its accounts for any period ending after the coming into force of this section the surpluses arising from increased rental income during that period from such housing activities to which the grant relates as the Secretary of State may from time to time determine.

(2) The surpluses shall be shown by each association in a fund to be known as its rent surplus fund; and the method of constituting that fund and of showing it in the association's accounts shall be as required by order of the Secretary of State under section 24 of the 1985 Act (general requirements as to accounts) and, notwithstanding anything in subsection (5) of that section, such an order may make provision applying to any period to which this section applies.

(3) The surpluses in respect of a period shall be calculated in such manner as the Secretary of State may from time to time determine; and a determination under this subsection may provide that, in calculating surpluses, an association shall act on such assumptions (whether or not borne out or likely to be borne out by events) as may be specified in the determination.

(4) A determination under subsection (1) or (3) above may—

(a) make the same provision for all cases; or

(b) make different provision for different cases or descriptions of cases, including different provision for different areas or for different descriptions of housing associations or housing activities;

and for the purposes of this subsection descriptions may be framed by reference to any matters whatever, including in particular, in the case of housing activities, the manner in which they are financed.

(5) Before making a determination under subsection (1) or (3) above, the Secretary of State shall consult such bodies appearing to him to be representative of housing associations as he considers appropriate; and after making such a determination, the Secretary of State shall publish it in such manner as he considers appropriate for bringing it to the notice of the associations concerned.

(6) The Secretary of State may from time to time give notice to an association to which this section applies requiring it to pay to him, with interest if demanded, or to apply or appropriate for purposes he specifies, any sums standing in its rent surplus fund at the end of a period of account.

(7) Any interest demanded by such a notice is payable—

(a) at the rate or rates (whether fixed or variable) previously determined by the Secretary of State, with the consent of the Treasury, for housing associations generally and published by him or, if no such determination has been made, at the rate or rates (whether fixed or variable) specified with the consent of the Treasury in the notice; and

(b) either from the date of the notice or from such other date, not earlier than the end of the period of account, as may be specified in the notice.

(8) A notice under subsection (6) above demanding interest may with the consent of the Treasury provide that, if the sums required by the notice to be paid to the Secretary of State are paid before a date specified in the notice—

(a) no interest shall be payable for any period after the date of the notice; and

(b) any interest payable shall be payable at a rate or rates lower than the rate or rates given by subsection (7) above.

(9) The Secretary of State may from time to time give notice—

(a) to all associations to which this section applies,

(b) to associations to which this section applies of a particular description, or

(c) to particular associations to which this section applies,

requiring them to furnish him with such information as he may reasonably require in connection with the exercise of his functions under this section; and a notice under paragraph (a) or (b) above may be given by publication in such manner as the Secretary of State considers appropriate for bringing it to the attention of the associations concerned.

(10) Where—

(a) an association has received a payment in respect of a relevant grant, and

(b) at any time property to which the grant relates becomes vested in, or is leased for a term of years to, or reverts to, some other registered housing association, or trustees for some other such association,

this section (including this subsection) shall have effect in relation to periods after that time as if the payment, or such proportion of it as may be determined by the Secretary of State to be appropriate, had been made to that other association.

Miscellaneous and supplemental

Duty of Housing Corporation and Housing for Wales in relation to racial discrimination.

56. At the end of section 75 of the 1985 Act (general functions of the Corporation) there shall be added the following subsection—

"(5) Section 71 of the Race Relations Act 1976 (local authorities: general statutory duty) shall apply to the Corporation as it applies to a local authority."

Delegation of certain functions.

57. The Secretary of State may delegate to the Corporation, to such extent and subject to such conditions as he may specify, any of his functions under—

(a) section 54 or 55 above;

(b) sections 53 (recoupment of surplus rental income), 54 to 57 (deficit grants) and 62 (grants for affording tax relief) of the 1985 Act, so far as continuing in force after the passing of this Act; and

(c) Parts I and II of Schedule 5 to the 1985 Act (residual subsidies);

and where he does so, references to him in those provisions shall be construed accordingly.

Application of Housing Acts to certain transactions.
1985 c. 68.

58.—(1) This section applies to any tenant of a publicly-funded house who, but for paragraph 1 of Schedule 5 to the Housing Act 1985 (no right to buy where landlord a charitable housing trust or housing association), would have the right to buy under Part V of the Housing Act 1985.

(2) A house is publicly-funded for the purposes of subsection (1) above if a grant under section 50 above, or a grant under section 41 of the 1985 Act or any enactment replaced by that section, has been paid in respect of a project which included—

(a) the acquisition of the house;

(b) the acquisition of a building and the provision of the house by means of the conversion of the building; or

(c) the acquisition of land and the construction of the house on the land.

(3) Where a registered housing association contracts for the acquisition of a house and, without taking the conveyance, grant or assignment, disposes of its interest at a discount to a tenant to whom this section applies, the provisions mentioned in subsection (4) below shall have effect as if the association first acquired the house and then disposed of it to the tenant.

PART II

(4) The said provisions are—

section 4 of the 1985 Act (eligibility for registration);

section 8 of that Act (disposal of land by registered housing associations);

section 9 of that Act (consent of Corporation to disposals);

section 79(2) of that Act (power of Corporation to lend to person acquiring interest from registered housing association);

Schedule 2 to that Act (covenants for repayments of discount on early disposal and restricting disposal of houses in National Parks etc.); and

1985 c. 68.

section 130 of the Housing Act 1985 (reduction of discount on exercise of right to buy where previous discount given).

Interpretation of Part II and amendments of Housing Associations Act 1985.

1985 c. 69.

59.—(1) In this Part of this Act—

(a) "the 1985 Act" means the Housing Associations Act 1985; and

(b) except as provided in section 50(1) above, "the Corporation" and other expressions used in this Part have the same meaning as in the 1985 Act.

(2) The 1985 Act shall have effect subject to the amendments in Schedule 6 to this Act, being amendments—

(a) extending the supervisory powers conferred by Part I of the 1985 Act;

1988 c. 43.

(b) making provision incidental to and consequential upon the establishment by this Part of this Act of Housing for Wales and the establishment by the Housing (Scotland) Act 1988 of Scottish Homes;

(c) making provision incidental to and consequential upon other provisions of this Part of this Act and the provisions of Part IV of this Act; and

(d) varying the grounds on which the Secretary of State may remove a member of the Housing Corporation from office.

(3) In Schedule 6 to this Act,—

(a) Part I contains amendments of Part I of the 1985 Act, including amendments which reproduce the effect of amendments made by Schedule 3 to the Housing (Scotland) Act 1988 with respect to Scottish Homes; and

(b) Parts II and III contain amendments of Parts II and III respectively of the 1985 Act.

(4) Without prejudice to the operation of Schedule 3 to the Housing (Scotland) Act 1988 in relation to anything done before the day appointed for the coming into force of this section, for the purpose of giving effect to the amendments in Part I of Schedule 6 to this Act, the said Schedule 3 shall be deemed never to have come into force.

PART III

HOUSING ACTION TRUST AREAS

Areas and trusts

60.—(1) Subject to section 61 below, the Secretary of State may by order designate an area of land for which, in his opinion, it is expedient that a corporation, to be known as a housing action trust, having the functions specified in this Part of this Act, should be established. **Housing action trust areas.**

(2) The area designated by an order under this section may comprise two or more parcels of land which—

(a) need not be contiguous; and

(b) need not be in the district of the same local housing authority.

(3) An order under this section shall be made by statutory instrument but no such order shall be made unless a draft of it has been laid before, and approved by a resolution of, each House of Parliament.

(4) In deciding whether to make an order under this section designating any area of land, the Secretary of State shall have regard to such matters as he thinks fit.

(5) Without prejudice to the generality of subsection (4) above, among the matters to which the Secretary of State may have regard in deciding whether to include a particular area of land in an order under this section, are—

(a) the extent to which the housing accommodation in the area as a whole is occupied by tenants or owner-occupiers and the extent to which it is local authority housing;

(b) the physical state and design of the housing accommodation in the area and any need to repair or improve it;

(c) the way in which the local authority housing in the area is being managed; and

(d) the living conditions of those who live in the area and the social conditions and general environment of the area.

(6) An area designated by an order under this section shall be known as a housing action trust area and in the following provisions of this Part of this Act—

(a) such an area is referred to as a "designated area"; and

(b) an order under this section is referred to as a "designation order".

61.—(1) Before making a designation order, the Secretary of State shall consult every local housing authority any part of whose district is to be included in the proposed designated area. **Consultation and publicity.**

(2) Where the Secretary of State is considering a proposal to make a designation order, he shall use his best endeavours to secure that notice of the proposal is given to all tenants of houses in the area proposed to be designated who are either secure tenants or tenants of such description as may be prescribed by regulations.

(3) After having taken the action required by subsection (2) above, the Secretary of State shall either—

(a) make arrangements for such independent persons as appear to him to be appropriate to conduct, in such manner as seems best to them, a ballot or poll of the tenants who have been given notice of the proposal as mentioned in that subsection with a view to establishing their opinions about the proposal to make a designation order; or

(b) if it seems appropriate to him to do so, arrange for the conduct of a ballot or poll of those tenants in such manner as appears to him best suited to establish their opinions about the proposal.

(4) If it appears from a ballot or poll conducted as mentioned in subsection (3) above that a majority of the tenants who, on that ballot or poll, express an opinion about the proposal to make the designation order are opposed to it, the Secretary of State shall not make the order proposed.

(5) The power to make regulations under subsection (2) above shall be exercisable by the Secretary of State by statutory instrument which shall be subject to annulment in pursuance of a resolution of either House of Parliament.

(6) Consultation undertaken before the passing of this Act shall constitute as effective compliance with subsection (1) above as if undertaken after that passing.

Housing action trusts.

62.—(1) Subject to subsection (2) below, where the Secretary of State makes a designation order, he shall, in that order or by a separate order, either—

(a) establish a housing action trust for the designated area; or

(b) specify as the housing action trust for the designated area a housing action trust already established for another designated area.

(2) Such a separate order as is referred to in subsection (1) above shall be made by statutory instrument but no such order shall be made unless a draft of it has been laid before, and approved by a resolution of, each House of Parliament.

(3) Subject to subsection (4) below, a housing action trust shall be a body corporate by such name as may be prescribed by the order establishing it.

(4) Where the Secretary of State makes the provision referred to in subsection (1)(b) above,—

(a) the housing action trust specified in the order shall, by virtue of the order, be treated as established for the new designated area (as well as for any designated area for which it is already established); and

(b) the order may alter the name of the trust to take account of the addition of the new designated area.

(5) Schedule 7 to this Act shall have effect with respect to the constitution of housing action trusts and Schedule 8 to this Act shall have effect with respect to their finances.

(6) It is hereby declared that a housing action trust is not to be regarded as the servant or agent of the Crown or as enjoying any status, immunity or privilege of the Crown and that the trust's property is not to be regarded as the property of, or property held on behalf of, the Crown.

(7) At the end of section 4 of the Housing Act 1985 (descriptions of authority) there shall be added— 1985 c. 68.

"(f) "housing action trust" means a housing action trust established under Part III of the Housing Act 1988";

and at the end of section 14 of the Rent Act 1977 (landlord's interest belonging to local authority etc.) there shall be added— 1977 c. 42.

"(h) a housing action trust established under Part III of the Housing Act 1988".

Objects and general powers of housing action trusts.

63.—(1) The primary objects of a housing action trust in relation to the designated area for which it is established shall be—

(a) to secure the repair or improvement of housing accommodation for the time being held by the trust;

(b) to secure the proper and effective management and use of that housing accommodation;

(c) to encourage diversity in the interests by virtue of which housing accommodation in the area is occupied and, in the case of accommodation which is occupied under tenancies, diversity in the identity of the landlords; and

(d) generally to secure or facilitate the improvement of living conditions in the area and the social conditions and general environment of the area.

(2) Without prejudice to subsection (1) above, a housing action trust may—

(a) provide and maintain housing accommodation; and

(b) facilitate the provision of shops, advice centres and other facilities for the benefit of the community or communities who live in the designated area.

(3) For the purpose of achieving its objects and exercising the powers conferred on it by subsection (2) above, a housing action trust may—

(a) acquire, hold, manage, reclaim and dispose of land and other property;

(b) carry out building and other operations;

(c) seek to ensure the provision of water, electricity, gas, sewerage and other services; and

(d) carry on any business or undertaking;

and may generally do anything necessary or expedient for the purposes of those objects and powers or for purposes incidental thereto.

(4) For the avoidance of doubt it is hereby declared that subsection (3) above relates only to the capacity of a housing action trust as a statutory corporation; and nothing in this section authorises such a trust to disregard any enactment or rule of law.

PART III

1976 c. 74.

(5) Section 71 of the Race Relations Act 1976 (local authorities: general statutory duty) shall apply to a housing action trust as it applies to a local authority.

(6) A transaction between any person and a housing action trust shall not be invalidated by reason of any failure by the trust to observe the objects in subsection (1) above or the requirement that the trust shall exercise the powers conferred by subsections (2) and (3) above for the purpose referred to in that subsection.

The housing action trust's proposals for its area.

64.—(1) As soon as practicable after a housing action trust has been established for a designated area, the trust shall prepare a statement of its proposals with regard to the exercise of its functions in the area.

(2) The trust shall consult every local housing authority or county council, any part of whose area lies within the designated area, with regard to the proposals contained in the statement prepared under subsection (1) above.

(3) A housing action trust shall take such steps as it considers appropriate to secure—

(a) that adequate publicity is given in the designated area to the proposals contained in the statement prepared under subsection (1) above;

(b) that those who live in the designated area are made aware that they have an opportunity to make, within such time as the trust may specify, representations to the trust with respect to those proposals; and

(c) that those who live in the designated area are given an adequate opportunity of making such representations;

and the trust shall consider any such representations as may be made within the time specified.

(4) As soon as may be after a housing action trust has complied with the requirements of subsections (1) to (3) above it shall send to the Secretary of State a copy of the statement prepared under subsection (1) above together with a report of—

(a) the steps the trust has taken to consult as mentioned in subsection (2) above and to secure the matters referred to in subsection (3) above; and

(b) the consideration it has given to points raised in the course of consultation and to representations received.

(5) At such times as a housing action trust considers appropriate or as it may be directed by the Secretary of State, the trust shall prepare a further statement of its proposals with regard to the exercise of its functions in its area; and subsections (2) to (4) above shall again apply as they applied in relation to the first statement.

Functions

Housing action trust as housing authority etc.

65.—(1) If the Secretary of State so provides by order, in a designated area or, as the case may be, in such part of the area as may be specified in the order, the housing action trust for the area shall have such of the functions described in subsection (2) below as may be so specified.

(2) The functions referred to in subsection (1) above are— PART III

(a) the functions conferred on a local housing authority by Parts II, VI, VII and IX to XII and XVI of the Housing Act 1985 and section 3(1) of the Chronically Sick and Disabled Persons Act 1970; 1985 c. 68. 1970 c. 44.

(b) the functions conferred by Part II of the Housing Associations Act 1985 on a local authority, within the meaning of that Act; and 1985 c. 69.

(c) the functions conferred by sections 39 to 41 of the Land Compensation Act 1973 on the authority which is "the relevant authority" for the purposes of section 39 of that Act. 1973 c. 26.

(3) As respects the designated area or part thereof to which an order under this section applies, on the coming into force of the order, any function conferred on a housing action trust by the order shall, according to the terms of the order, be exercisable either—

(a) by the trust instead of by the authority by which, apart from the order, the function would be exercisable; or

(b) by the trust concurrently with that authority.

(4) Any enactment under which a housing action trust is to exercise a function by virtue of an order under this section shall have effect—

(a) in relation to the trust, and

(b) where the trust is to have the function concurrently with another authority, in relation to that authority,

subject to such modifications (if any) as may be specified in the order.

(5) Where a housing action trust is to exercise functions conferred on a local housing authority by any of Parts VI, VII, IX and XI of the Housing Act 1985, section 36 of the Local Government Act 1974 (recovery by local authorities of establishment charges) shall apply to the housing action trust as if it were a local authority within the meaning of that section. 1974 c. 7.

(6) Such (if any) of the provisions of Parts XVII and XVIII of the Housing Act 1985 (compulsory purchase, land acquisition and general provisions) as may be specified in an order under this section shall have effect in relation to a housing action trust subject to such modifications as may be specified in the order.

(7) An order under this section—

(a) may contain such savings and transitional and supplementary provisions as appear to the Secretary of State to be appropriate; and

(b) shall be made by statutory instrument which shall be subject to annulment in pursuance of a resolution of either House of Parliament.

66.—(1) A housing action trust may submit to the Secretary of State proposals for the development of land within its designated area and the Secretary of State, after consultation with the local planning authority within whose area the land is situated and with any other local authority which appears to him to be concerned, may approve any such proposals either with or without modification. Planning control.

PART III

(2) Without prejudice to the generality of the powers conferred by section 24 of the 1971 Act, a special development order made by the Secretary of State under that section with respect to a designated area may grant permission for any development of land in accordance with proposals approved under subsection (1) above, subject to such conditions, if any (including conditions requiring details of any proposed development to be submitted to the local planning authority), as may be specified in the order.

(3) The Secretary of State shall give to a housing action trust such directions with regard to the disposal of land held by it and with respect to the development by it of such land as appear to him to be necessary or expedient for securing, so far as practicable, the preservation of any features of special architectural or historical interest and, in particular, of any buildings included in any list compiled or approved or having effect as if compiled or approved under section 54(1) of the 1971 Act (which relates to the compilation or approval by the Secretary of State of lists of buildings of special architectural or historical interest).

(4) Any reference in this section to the local planning authority,—

(a) in relation to land in Greater London or a metropolitan county, is a reference to the authority which is the local planning authority as ascertained in accordance with section 1 of the 1971 Act; and

(b) in relation to other land, is a reference to the district planning authority and also (in relation to proposals for any development which is a county matter, as defined in paragraph 32 of Schedule 16 to the Local Government Act 1972) to the county planning authority.

1972 c. 70.

Housing action trust as planning authority.

67.—(1) If the Secretary of State so provides by order, for such purposes of Part III of the 1971 Act and in relation to such kinds of development as may be specified in the order, a housing action trust shall be the local planning authority for the whole or such part as may be so specified of its designated area in place of any authority which would otherwise be the local planning authority.

(2) An order under subsection (1) above may provide—

(a) that any enactment relating to local planning authorities shall not apply to the trust; and

(b) that any such enactment which applies to the trust shall apply to it subject to such modifications as may be specified in the order.

(3) An order made by the Secretary of State may provide—

(a) that, subject to any modifications specified in the order, a housing action trust specified in the order shall have, in the whole or any part of its designated area and in place of any authority (except the Secretary of State) which would otherwise have them, such of the functions conferred by Parts IV, V and XV of the 1971 Act as may be so specified; and

(b) that such of the provisions of Part IX and sections 212 and 214 of the 1971 Act as are mentioned in the order shall have effect, in relation to the housing action trust specified in the order and to land in the trust's area, subject to the modifications there specified.

PART III

(4) An order under subsection (3) above may provide that, for the purposes of any of the provisions specified in the order, any enactment relating to local planning authorities shall apply to the housing action trust specified in the order subject to such modifications as may be so specified.

(5) In relation to a housing action trust which, by virtue of an order under subsection (1) above, is the local planning authority for the whole or part of its area, section 270 of the 1971 Act (application to local planning authorities of provisions as to planning control and enforcement) shall have effect for the purposes of Part III of the 1971 Act prescribed by that order, and in relation to the kinds of development so prescribed, as if—

(a) in subsection (1) the reference to the development by local authorities of land in respect of which they are the local planning authorities included a reference to the development by the trust of land in respect of which it is the local planning authority;

(b) in subsection (2),—

(i) in paragraph (a) for the words "such an authority" there were substituted "housing action trust" and for the words "local planning authority" there were substituted "housing action trust"; and

(ii) in paragraph (b) for the words "local planning authority" there were substituted "housing action trust".

(6) If, by virtue of an order under subsection (1) above, a housing action trust is the local planning authority in relation to all kinds of development for the whole or part of its area, it shall be the hazardous substances authority for that area or, as the case may be, that part for the purposes of the 1971 Act.

(7) Any power to make an order under this section shall be exercisable by statutory instrument which shall be subject to annulment in pursuance of a resolution of either House of Parliament; and any such order shall have effect subject to such savings and transitional provisions as may be specified in the order.

Public health.

68.—(1) The Secretary of State may by order provide that, in relation to premises comprising or consisting of housing accommodation, a housing action trust shall have in its designated area (or in such part of its designated area as may be specified in the order) the functions conferred on a local authority—

(a) by sections 83 and 84 of the Public Health Act 1936 (the "1936 Act") and section 36 of the Public Health Act 1961 (all of which relate to filthy or verminous premises or articles); 1936 c. 49. 1961 c. 64.

(b) by any enactment contained in Part III (nuisances and offensive trades) of the 1936 Act;

(c) by so much of Part XII of the 1936 Act as relates to any of the enactments mentioned in paragraphs (a) and (b) above; and

(d) by Part I of the Prevention of Damage by Pests Act 1949 (rats and mice). 1949 c. 55.

PART III (2) On the order coming into force, the trust shall have the functions conferred in relation to the designated area (or part) instead of or concurrently with any such authority, depending on the terms of the order.

(3) The order may provide that any enactment under which the trust is to exercise functions by virtue of the order shall have effect in relation to the trust and, where the trust is to have any function concurrently with another authority, in relation to that authority, as modified by the order.

(4) Where an order under this section provides that a housing action trust shall have the functions conferred upon a local authority by Part III of the 1936 Act, section 36 of the Local Government Act 1974 (recovery by local authorities of establishment charges) shall apply to the housing action trust as if it were a local authority within the meaning of that section.

1974 c. 7.

(5) The order shall have effect subject to such savings and transitional and supplementary provisions as may be specified in the order.

(6) The power to make an order under this section shall be exercisable by statutory instrument which shall be subject to annulment in pursuance of a resolution of either House of Parliament.

Highways.

69.—(1) When any street works have been executed in a private street (or part of a private street) in a designated area, the housing action trust may serve a notice on the street works authority requiring it to declare the street (or part) to be a highway which for the purposes of the Highways Act 1980 is a highway maintainable at the public expense.

1980 c. 66.

(2) Within the period of two months beginning on the date of the service of a notice under subsection (1) above, the street works authority may appeal against the notice to the Secretary of State on grounds relating to all or any of the following matters—

(a) the construction of the street (or part);

(b) its design;

(c) its layout; and

(d) the state of its maintenance.

(3) After considering any representations made to him by the housing action trust and the street works authority, the Secretary of State shall determine an appeal under subsection (2) above by setting aside or confirming the notice under subsection (1) above (with or without modifications).

(4) Where, under subsection (3) above, the Secretary of State confirms a notice,—

(a) he may at the same time impose conditions (including financial conditions) upon the housing action trust with which the trust must comply in order for the notice to take effect, and

(b) the highway (or part) shall become a highway maintainable at the public expense with effect from such date as the Secretary of State may specify.

(5) Where a street works authority neither complies with the notice under subsection (1) above, nor appeals under subsection (2) above, the street (or part) concerned shall become a highway maintainable at the public expense upon the expiry of the period of two months referred to in subsection (2) above.

(6) In this section "private street" and "street works authority" have the same meanings as in Part XI of the Highways Act 1980. 1980 c. 66.

Co-operation on homelessness between local housing authorities and housing action trusts.

1985 c. 68.

70. In paragraph (a) of section 72 of the Housing Act 1985 (which provides that, on a request by a local housing authority for assistance in the discharge of certain statutory functions relating to homelessness, or threatened homelessness, a body of a description specified in the paragraph shall co-operate in rendering such assistance as is reasonable in the circumstances) after the words "a registered housing association" there shall be inserted "a housing action trust"; and in the words following paragraph (c) of that section after the word "authority" there shall be inserted "or other body".

Power to give financial assistance.

71.—(1) For the purpose of achieving its objects a housing action trust may, with the consent of the Secretary of State, give financial assistance to any person.

(2) Financial assistance under subsection (1) above may be given in any form and, in particular, may be given by way of—

(a) grants,

(b) loans,

(c) guarantees,

(d) incurring expenditure for the benefit of the person assisted, or

(e) purchasing loan or share capital in a company.

(3) Financial assistance under subsection (1) above may be given on such terms as the housing action trust, with the consent of the Secretary of State, considers appropriate.

(4) Any consent under this section—

(a) may be given either unconditionally or subject to conditions; and

(b) may be given in relation to a particular case or in relation to such description of cases as may be specified in the consent;

and the reference in subsection (3) above to the consent of the Secretary of State is a reference to his consent given with the approval of the Treasury.

(5) The terms referred to in subsection (3) above may, in particular, include provision as to—

(a) the circumstances in which the assistance must be repaid or otherwise made good to the housing action trust and the manner in which that is to be done; or

(b) the circumstances in which the housing action trust is entitled to recover the proceeds or part of the proceeds of any disposal of land or buildings in respect of which assistance was provided.

(6) Any person receiving assistance under subsection (1) above shall comply with the terms on which it is given and compliance may be enforced by the housing action trust.

PART III

Directions as to exercise of functions.

72.—(1) In the exercise of its functions, a housing action trust shall comply with any directions given by the Secretary of State.

(2) Directions given by the Secretary of State may be of a general or particular character and may be varied or revoked by subsequent directions.

(3) The Secretary of State shall publish any direction given under this section.

(4) A transaction between any person and a housing action trust acting in purported exercise of its powers under this Part of this Act shall not be void by reason only that the transaction was carried out in contravention of a direction given under this section; and a person dealing with a housing action trust shall not be concerned to see or enquire whether a direction under this section has been given or complied with.

Transfer of functions.

73.—(1) If, in the case of any designated area, it appears to the Secretary of State that it is expedient that the functions of a housing action trust established for the area should be transferred—

(a) to the housing action trust established for another designated area, or

(b) to a new housing action trust to be established for the area,

he may by order provide for the dissolution of the first-mentioned trust and for the transfer of its functions, property, rights and liabilities to the trust referred to in paragraph (a) above, or, as the case may be, to a new housing action trust established for the area by the order.

(2) Where an order under this section provides for the functions of a housing action trust established for a designated area to be transferred to the housing action trust established for another designated area—

(a) the latter trust shall, by virtue of the order, be treated as established for the first-mentioned designated area (as well as the area referred to in subsection (1)(a) above); and

(b) the order may alter the name of the latter trust in such manner as appears to the Secretary of State to be expedient.

(3) Before making an order under this section the Secretary of State shall consult the housing action trust whose functions are to be transferred and also, in a case falling within subsection (1)(a) above, the housing action trust to whom the functions are to be transferred.

(4) An order under this section shall be made by statutory instrument but no such order shall be made unless a draft of it has been laid before, and approved by a resolution of, each House of Parliament.

Transfer of housing accommodation etc.

Transfer of land and other property to housing action trusts.

74.—(1) The Secretary of State may by order provide for the transfer from a local housing authority to a housing action trust of—

(a) all or any of the authority's local authority housing situated in the designated area; and

(b) any other land held or provided in connection with that local authority housing.

(2) Without prejudice to the powers under subsection (1) above, if in the opinion of the Secretary of State a housing action trust requires for the purposes of its functions any land which, though not falling within that subsection, is situated in the designated area and held (for whatever purpose) by a local authority, the Secretary of State may by order provide for the transfer of that land to the trust. PART III

(3) The Secretary of State may by order transfer from a local housing authority or other local authority to a housing action trust so much as appears to him to be appropriate of any property which is held or used by the authority in connection with any local authority housing or other land transferred to the trust under subsection (1) or subsection (2) above; and for this purpose "property" includes chattels of any description and rights and liabilities, whether arising by contract or otherwise.

(4) A transfer of any local authority housing or other land or property under the preceding provisions of this section shall be on such terms, including financial terms, as the Secretary of State thinks fit; and an order under this section may provide that, notwithstanding anything in section 141 of the Law of Property Act 1925 (rent and benefit of lessee's covenants to run with the reversion), any rent or other sum which— 1925 c. 20.

(a) arises under a tenancy of any local authority housing or other land transferred to the housing action trust under subsection (1) or subsection (2) above, and

(b) falls due before the date of the transfer,

shall continue to be recoverable by the local housing authority or, as the case may be, the local authority to the exclusion of the trust and of any other person in whom the reversion on the tenancy may become vested.

(5) Without prejudice to the generality of subsection (4) above, the financial terms referred to in that subsection may include provision for payments by a local authority (as well as or instead of payments to a local authority); and the transfer from a local housing authority or other local authority of any local authority housing or other land or property by virtue of this section shall not be taken to give rise to any right to compensation.

(6) Where an order is made under this section—

(a) payments made by a local authority as mentioned in subsection (5) above shall be prescribed expenditure for the purposes of Part VIII of the Local Government, Planning and Land Act 1980 (capital expenditure of local authorities); and 1980 c. 65.

(b) unless the order otherwise provides, payments made to a local authority as mentioned in subsection (5) above shall be regarded for the purposes of that Part as sums received by the authority in respect of a disposal falling within section 75(2) of that Act.

(7) Any power to make an order under this section shall be exercisable by statutory instrument which shall be subject to annulment in pursuance of a resolution of either House of Parliament.

(8) In this section "local authority" means any of the following—

(a) a local housing authority;

(b) the council of a county;

(c) the Inner London Education Authority;

PART III

1985 c. 51.

(d) an authority established by an order under section 10(1) of the Local Government Act 1985 (waste disposal);

(e) a joint authority established by Part IV of that Act; and

(f) a residuary body established by Part VII of that Act.

Supplementary provisions as to transfer orders.

75.—(1) In this section a "transfer order" means an order under any of subsections (1) to (3) of section 74 above and, in relation to a transfer order, "the transferor authority" means the local housing authority or other local authority from whom local authority housing or other land or property is or is to be transferred by the order.

(2) Before making a transfer order, the Secretary of State shall consult the transferor authority with respect to—

(a) the local authority housing or other land or property which it is proposed should be transferred by the order; and

(b) the terms of the proposed transfer.

(3) Before making a transfer order with respect to any local authority housing or other land, the Secretary of State shall take such steps as appear to him to be appropriate to bring the proposed transfer to the attention of any secure tenant or other person (other than a local authority) having an interest in the property proposed to be transferred as lessor, lessee, mortgagor or mortgagee.

(4) In connection with any transfer made by it, a transfer order may contain such incidental, consequential, transitional or supplementary provisions as appear to the Secretary of State to be necessary or expedient and, in particular, may—

(a) apply, with or without modification, any provision made by or under any enactment; and

(b) modify the operation of any provision made by or under any enactment.

Vesting and acquisition of land

Vesting by order in housing action trust.

76.—(1) Subject to subsections (2) and (3) below, the Secretary of State may by order provide that land specified in the order which is vested in statutory undertakers or any other public body or in a wholly-owned subsidiary of a public body shall vest in a housing action trust established or to be established for the designated area in which the land is situated.

(2) An order under this section may not specify land vested in statutory undertakers which is used for the purpose of carrying on their statutory undertakings or which is held for that purpose.

(3) In the case of land vested in statutory undertakers, the power to make an order under this section shall be exercisable by the Secretary of State and the appropriate Minister.

(4) Part I of Schedule 9 to this Act shall have effect for supplementing the preceding provisions of this section.

1981 c. 66.

(5) An order under this section shall have the same effect as a declaration under the Compulsory Purchase (Vesting Declarations) Act 1981 except that, in relation to such an order, the enactments mentioned in Part II of Schedule 9 to this Act shall have effect subject to the modifications specified in that Part.

(6) Compensation under the Land Compensation Act 1961, as applied by subsection (5) above and Part II of Schedule 9 to this Act, shall be assessed by reference to values current on the date the order under this section comes into force. **PART III** 1961 c. 33.

(7) An order under this section shall be made by statutory instrument but no such order shall be made unless a draft of it has been laid before, and approved by a resolution of, each House of Parliament.

Acquisition by housing action trust.

77.—(1) For the purposes of achieving its objects (and performing any of its functions), a housing action trust may acquire land within its designated area by agreement or, on being authorised to do so by the Secretary of State, compulsorily.

(2) A housing action trust may acquire (by agreement or, on being authorised to do so by the Secretary of State, compulsorily)—

(a) land adjacent to the designated area which the trust requires for purposes connected with the discharge of its functions in the area; and

(b) land outside the designated area (whether or not adjacent to it) which the trust requires for the provision of services in connection with the discharge of its functions in the area.

(3) Where a housing action trust exercises its powers under subsection (1) or subsection (2) above in relation to land which forms part of a common or open space or fuel or field garden allotment, the trust may acquire (by agreement or, on being authorised to do so by the Secretary of State, compulsorily) land for giving in exchange for the land acquired.

(4) Subject to section 78 below, the Acquisition of Land Act 1981 shall apply in relation to the compulsory acquisition of land in pursuance of the preceding provisions of this section. 1981 c. 67.

(5) A housing action trust may be authorised by the Secretary of State, by means of a compulsory purchase order, to purchase compulsorily such new rights as are specified in the order—

(a) being rights over land in the designated area and which the trust requires for the purposes of its functions;

(b) being rights over land adjacent to the designated area and which the trust requires for purposes connected with the discharge of its functions in the area; and

(c) being rights over land outside the designated area (whether or not adjacent to it) and which the trust requires for the provision of services in connection with the discharge of its functions in the area.

(6) In subsection (5) above—

(a) "new rights" means rights which are not in existence when the order specifying them is made; and

(b) "compulsory purchase order" has the same meaning as in the Acquisition of Land Act 1981;

and Schedule 3 to that Act shall apply to a compulsory purchase of a right by virtue of subsection (5) above.

PART III

1965 c. 56.

1978 c. 30.

(7) The provisions of Part I of the Compulsory Purchase Act 1965 (so far as applicable), other than section 31, shall apply in relation to the acquisition of land by agreement under this section; and in that Part as so applied "land" has the meaning given by the Interpretation Act 1978.

Supplementary provisions as to vesting, acquisition and compensation.
1981 c. 67.

78.—(1) The Acquisition of Land Act 1981, as applied by section 77 above, shall have effect subject to the modifications in Part I of Schedule 10 to this Act.

(2) The supplementary provisions in Parts II and III of that Schedule shall have effect, being,—

(a) as to those in Part II, provisions about land vested in or acquired by a housing action trust under this Part of this Act; and

(b) as to those in Part III, provisions about the acquisition by a housing action trust of rights over land under section 77(5) above.

1961 c. 33.

1980 c. 65.

(3) In Schedule 1 to the Land Compensation Act 1961 (actual or prospective development which is not to be taken into account in assessing compensation in certain cases or the effect of which is to reduce compensation in certain cases of adjacent land in the same ownership), the following paragraph shall be added after the paragraph 4A inserted by section 145 of the Local Government, Planning and Land Act 1980:

"4B. Where any of the relevant land forms part of a housing action trust area established under Part III of the Housing Act 1988.	Development of any land other than the relevant land in the course of the development or re-development of the area as a housing action trust area."

(4) In section 6 of the Land Compensation Act 1961 (disregard of actual or prospective development in certain cases) in subsection (1)(b) for "4A" there shall be substituted "4B".

Disposals of land

Disposal of land by housing action trusts.

79.—(1) Subject to subsection (2) below and any directions given by the Secretary of State, a housing action trust may, with the consent of the Secretary of State, dispose of any land for the time being held by it to such persons, in such manner and on such terms as it considers expedient for the purpose of achieving its objects.

(2) A housing action trust may not dispose of a house which is for the time being subject to a secure tenancy except—

(a) to a person who is for the time being approved by the Corporation either under this section or under section 94 below, or

(b) to a local housing authority or other local authority in accordance with section 84 below;

1985 c. 68.

but this subsection does not apply to a disposal under Part V of the Housing Act 1985 (the right to buy).

(3) The reference in subsection (1) above to disposing of land includes a reference to granting an interest in or right over land and, in particular, the granting of an option to purchase the freehold of, or any other interest in, land is a disposal for the purposes of that subsection; and a consent under that subsection given to such a disposal extends to a disposal made in pursuance of the option. PART III

(4) The consent of the Secretary of State referred to in subsection (1) above may be given—

(a) either generally to all housing action trusts or to a particular trust or description of trust;

(b) either in relation to particular land or in relation to land of a particular description; and

(c) subject to conditions.

(5) Without prejudice to the generality of subsection (4)(c) above, consent under subsection (1) above may, in particular, be given subject to conditions as to the price, premium or rent to be obtained by the housing action trust on the disposal, including conditions as to the amount by which, on the disposal of a house by way of sale or by the grant or assignment of a lease at a premium, the price or premium is to be, or may be, discounted by the housing action trust.

(6) The Corporation shall not under this section approve—

(a) a public sector landlord; or

(b) the council of a county; or

(c) any other body which the Corporation have reason to believe might not be independent of such a landlord or council;

and, for the purposes of paragraph (c) above, a body shall not be regarded as independent of a public sector landlord or the council of a county if the body is or appears likely to be under the control of, or subject to influence from, such a landlord or council or particular members or officers of such a landlord or council.

(7) In subsection (6) above "public sector landlord" means—

(a) a local housing authority;

(b) a new town corporation within the meaning of section 4(b) of the Housing Act 1985; and 1985 c. 68.

(c) the Development Board for Rural Wales.

(8) The Corporation shall establish (and may from time to time vary) criteria to be satisfied by a person seeking approval under this section and, in deciding whether to give such approval, the Corporation shall have regard to whether the person satisfies the criteria.

(9) Subject to any directions under section 76 of the Housing Associations Act 1985 (directions by the Secretary of State),— 1985 c. 69.

(a) an approval under this section shall not be given except to a person making an application accompanied by such fee as the Corporation, with the consent of the Secretary of State, may specify; and

(b) an approval under this section may be made conditional upon the person or persons concerned entering into such undertakings as may be specified by the Corporation; and

PART III

(c) if it appears to the Corporation appropriate to do so (whether by reason of a failure to honour an undertaking or to meet any criteria or for any other reason) the Corporation may revoke an approval given under this section by notice in writing served on the approved person, but such a revocation shall not affect any transaction completed before the service of the notice;

and different fees may be specified under paragraph (a) above for different descriptions of cases.

(10) The Housing Corporation and Housing for Wales shall each maintain a register of persons for the time being approved by it under this section; and each register so maintained shall be open to inspection at the head office of the Corporation by which it is maintained at all reasonable times.

1985 c. 68. (11) In section 45(2)(b) of the Housing Act 1985 (which defines "public sector authority" for the purposes of provisions of that Act restricting service charges payable after disposal of a house) after the entry "an urban development corporation" there shall be inserted "a housing action trust".

(12) A housing action trust shall be treated as a local authority for the
1985 c. 70. purposes of sections 18 to 30 of the Landlord and Tenant Act 1985 (service charges).

(13) The provisions of Schedule 11 to this Act shall have effect in the case of certain disposals of houses by a housing action trust.

Disposals made without consent.

80.—(1) Any disposal of a house by a housing action trust which is made without the consent required by section 79(1) above is void unless—

(a) the disposal is to an individual (or to two or more individuals); and

(b) the disposal does not extend to any other house.

(2) Subject to subsection (1) above,—

(a) a disposal of any land made by a housing action trust shall not be invalid by reason only that it is made without the consent required by section 79(1) above; and

(b) a person dealing with a housing action trust or with a person claiming under such a trust shall not be concerned to see or enquire whether any consent required by section 79(1) above has been obtained.

Consent required for certain subsequent disposals.

81.—(1) If, by a material disposal, a housing action trust disposes of a house which is for the time being subject to a secure tenancy to such a person as is mentioned in section 79(2)(a) above (in this section referred to as an "approved person"), the conveyance shall contain a statement that the requirement of this section as to consent applies to a subsequent disposal of the house by the approved person.

(2) For the purposes of this section a "material disposal" is—

(a) the transfer of the fee simple;

(b) the transfer of an existing lease; or

(c) the grant of a new lease; PART III

and "the conveyance" means the instrument by which such a disposal is effected.

(3) An approved person who acquires a house on a material disposal falling within subsection (1) above shall not dispose of it except with the consent of the Secretary of State which may be given either unconditionally or subject to conditions; but nothing in this subsection shall apply in relation to an exempt disposal as defined in subsection (8) below.

(4) Where an estate or interest in a house acquired by an approved person as mentioned in subsection (3) above has been mortgaged or charged, the prohibition in that subsection applies also to a disposal by the mortgagee or chargee in exercise of a power of sale or leasing, whether or not the disposal is in the name of the approved person; and in any case where—

(a) by operation of law or by virtue of an order of a court, property which has been acquired by an approved person passes or is transferred to another person, and

(b) that passing or transfer does not constitute a disposal for which consent is required under subsection (3) above,

this section (including, where there is more than one such passing or transfer, this subsection) shall apply as if the other person to whom the property passes or is transferred were the approved person.

(5) Before giving consent in respect of a disposal to which subsection (3) above applies, the Secretary of State—

(a) shall satisfy himself that the person who is seeking the consent has taken appropriate steps to consult every tenant of any house proposed to be disposed of; and

(b) shall have regard to the responses of any such tenants to that consultation.

(6) If, apart from subsection (7) below, the consent of the Corporation would be required under section 9 of the Housing Associations Act 1985 (control of dispositions of land by housing associations) for a disposal to which subsection (3) above applies, the Secretary of State shall consult the Corporation before giving his consent in respect of the disposal for the purposes of this section. 1985 c. 69.

(7) No consent shall be required under the said section 9 for any disposal in respect of which consent is given in accordance with subsection (6) above.

(8) In this section an "exempt disposal" means—

(a) the disposal of a dwelling-house to a person having the right to buy it under Part V of the Housing Act 1985 (whether the disposal is in fact made under that Part or otherwise); 1985 c. 68.

(b) a compulsory disposal, within the meaning of Part V of the Housing Act 1985;

(c) the disposal of an easement or rentcharge;

(d) the disposal of an interest by way of security for a loan;

PART III

1985 c. 68.

(e) the grant of a secure tenancy or what would be a secure tenancy but for any of paragraphs 2 to 12 of Schedule 1 to the Housing Act 1985;

(f) the grant of an assured tenancy or an assured agricultural occupancy, within the meaning of Part I of this Act, or what would be such a tenancy or occupancy but for any of paragraphs 4 to 8 of Schedule 1 to this Act; and

(g) the transfer of an interest held on trust for any person where the disposal is made in connection with the appointment of a new trustee or in connection with the discharge of any trustee.

(9) Where the title of a housing action trust to a house which is disposed of by a material disposal falling within subsection (1) above is not registered—

1925 c. 21.

(a) section 123 of the Land Registration Act 1925 (compulsory registration of title) applies in relation to the conveyance whether or not the house is in an area in which an Order in Council under section 120 of that Act (areas of compulsory registration) is in force;

(b) the housing action trust shall give the approved person a certificate stating that it is entitled to make the disposal subject only to such encumbrances, rights and interests as are stated in the conveyance or summarised in the certificate; and

(c) for the purpose of registration of title, the Chief Land Registrar shall accept such a certificate as evidence of the facts stated in it, but if as a result he has to meet a claim against him under the Land Registration Acts 1925 to 1986 the housing action trust is liable to indemnify him.

(10) On an application being made for registration of a disposition of registered land or, as the case may be, of the approved person's title under a disposition of unregistered land, if the conveyance contains the statement required by subsection (1) above, the Chief Land Registrar shall enter in the register a restriction stating the requirement of this section as to consent to a subsequent disposal.

(11) In this section references to disposing of a house include references to—

(a) granting or disposing of any interest in the house;

(b) entering into a contract to dispose of the house or to grant or dispose of any such interest; and

(c) granting an option to acquire the house or any such interest;

and any reference to a statement or certificate is a reference to a statement or, as the case may be, certificate in a form approved by the Chief Land Registrar.

Power of Corporation to provide legal assistance to tenants after disposal.

82.—(1) This section applies where a house has been disposed of by a disposal falling within section 79(2) above and, in relation to a house which has been so disposed of, a "transferred tenant" means a tenant of it who either—

(a) was the secure tenant of the house immediately before the disposal; or

(b) is the widow or widower of the person who was then the secure tenant of it.

(2) On an application by a transferred tenant of a house who is a party or a prospective party to proceedings or prospective proceedings to determine any dispute between himself and the person who acquired the house on the disposal referred to in subsection (1) above, the Corporation may give assistance to the transferred tenant if it thinks fit to do so—

(a) on the ground that the case raises a question of principle; or

(b) on the ground that it is unreasonable, having regard to the complexity of the case, or to any other matter, to expect the transferred tenant to deal with it without assistance; or

(c) by reason of any other special consideration.

(3) Assistance given by the Corporation under this section may include—

(a) giving advice;

(b) procuring or attempting to procure the settlement of the matter in dispute;

(c) arranging for the giving of advice or assistance by a solicitor or counsel;

(d) arranging for representation by a solicitor or counsel, including such assistance as is usually given by a solicitor or counsel in the steps preliminary or incidental to any proceedings, or in arriving at or giving effect to a compromise to avoid or bring to an end any proceedings; and

(e) any other form of assistance which the Corporation may consider appropriate;

but paragraph (d) above does not affect the law and practice regulating the descriptions of persons who may appear in, conduct, defend and address the court in any proceedings.

(4) In so far as expenses are incurred by the Corporation in providing a transferred tenant with assistance under this section, the recovery of those expenses (as taxed or assessed in such manner as may be prescribed by rules of court) shall constitute a first charge for the benefit of the Corporation—

(a) on any costs which (whether by virtue of a judgment or order of a court or an agreement or otherwise) are payable to the tenant by any other person in respect of the matter in connection with which the assistance was given, and

(b) so far as relates to any costs, on his rights under any compromise or settlement arrived at in connection with that matter to avoid or bring to an end any proceedings;

but subject to any charge under the Legal Aid Act 1988 and to any provision of that Act for payment of any sum to the Legal Aid Board. 1988 c. 34.

Secure tenancies and right to buy

Application of Parts IV and V of Housing Act 1985. 1985 c. 68.

83.—(1) Parts IV and V of the Housing Act 1985 (secure tenancies and the right to buy) shall be amended in accordance with this section.

PART III

(2) In section 80(1) (which lists the landlords whose tenancies can qualify as secure tenancies), after the entry specifying a new town corporation there shall be inserted—

"a housing action trust".

(3) In section 108 (heating charges to secure tenants), in paragraph (a) of subsection (5) (the definition of "heating authority") after the words "housing authority" there shall be inserted "or housing action trust".

(4) In section 114 (meaning of "landlord authority" for the purposes of that Part), in each of subsections (1) and (2), after the entry specifying a development corporation, there shall be inserted—

"a housing action trust".

(5) In section 171 (power to extend right to buy where certain bodies hold an interest in a dwelling-house), in subsection (2), after the entry specifying a new town corporation there shall be inserted—

"a housing action trust".

(6) In each of the following provisions (all of which relate to cases where premises are or were let to a person in consequence of employment), namely—

(a) paragraph 2(1) of Schedule 1 (tenancies which are not secure tenancies),

(b) Grounds 7 and 12 of Schedule 2 (grounds for possession of dwelling-houses let under secure tenancies),

(c) Ground 5 of Schedule 3 (grounds for withholding consent to assignment by way of exchange), and

(d) paragraph 5 of Schedule 5 (exceptions to the right to buy),

after the entry specifying a new town corporation there shall be inserted—

"a housing action trust".

(7) In Schedule 4 (qualifying period for right to buy and discount), in paragraph 7 (the landlord condition) after the entry specifying a new town corporation there shall be inserted—

"a housing action trust".

Provisions applicable to disposals of dwelling-houses subject to secure tenancies.

84.—(1) The provisions of this section apply in any case where a housing action trust proposes to make a disposal of one or more houses let on secure tenancies which would result in a person who, before the disposal, is a secure tenant of the trust becoming, after the disposal, the tenant of another person.

(2) Before applying to the Secretary of State for consent to the proposed disposal or serving notice under subsection (4) below, the housing action trust shall serve notice in writing—

(a) on any local housing authority in whose area any houses falling within subsection (1) above are situated, and

(b) if any such houses were transferred to the trust from another local housing authority or other local authority under section 74 above, on that authority, PART III

informing the authority of the proposed disposal, specifying the houses concerned, and requiring the authority within such period, being not less than 28 days, as may be specified in the notice, to serve on the trust a notice under subsection (3) below.

(3) A notice by a local housing authority or other local authority under this subsection shall inform the housing action trust, with respect to each of the houses specified in the notice under subsection (2) above which is in the authority's area or, as the case may be, which was transferred from the authority as mentioned in paragraph (b) of that subsection,—

(a) that the authority wishes to acquire the house or is considering its acquisition; or

(b) that the authority does not wish to acquire the house;

and where the authority serves notice as mentioned in paragraph (a) above with respect to any house, the notice shall give information as to the likely consequences for the tenant if the house were to be acquired by the authority.

(4) Before applying to the Secretary of State for consent to the proposed disposal, and after the expiry of the period specified in the notice under subsection (2) above, the housing action trust shall serve notice in writing on the secure tenant—

(a) informing him of the proposed disposal and of the name of the person to whom the disposal is to be made;

(b) containing such other details of the disposal as seem to the trust to be appropriate;

(c) informing him of the likely consequences of the disposal on his position as a secure tenant and, if appropriate, of the effect of sections 171A to 171H of the Housing Act 1985 (preservation of right to buy on disposal to private sector landlord); 1985 c. 68.

(d) informing him, with respect to the house of which he is tenant, of the wishes of the local housing authority and of any other authority which has served a notice under subsection (3) above;

(e) if an authority has served notice under paragraph (a) of subsection (3) above with respect to that house, informing him (in accordance with the information given in the notice) of the likely consequences for him if the house were to be acquired by that authority and also, if he wishes to become a tenant of that authority, of his right to make representations to that effect under paragraph (f) below; and

(f) informing him of his right to make representations to the trust with respect to the proposed disposal within such period, being not less than 28 days, as may be specified in the notice.

(5) The housing action trust shall consider any representations made to it in accordance with subsection (4)(f) above and, if it considers it appropriate having regard to—

(a) any representations so made, and

PART III

(b) any further information which may be provided by an authority which served a notice under subsection (3)(a) above that it was considering the acquisition of a house,

the trust may amend its proposals with respect to the disposal and, in such a case, shall serve a further notice under subsection (4) above (in relation to which this subsection will again apply).

(6) When applying to the Secretary of State for consent to the proposed disposal (as amended, where appropriate, by virtue of subsection (5) above) the housing action trust shall furnish to him—

(a) a copy of any notice served on it under subsection (3) above or served by it under subsection (4) above;

(b) a copy of any representations received by the trust; and

(c) a statement of the consideration given by the trust to those representations.

(7) Without prejudice to the generality of section 72 above, where an application is made to the Secretary of State for consent to a disposal to which this section applies, the Secretary of State may, by a direction under that section, require the housing action trust—

(a) to carry out such further consultation with respect to the proposed disposal as may be specified in the direction; and

(b) to furnish to him such information as may be so specified with respect to the results of that consultation.

1985 c. 68.

(8) Notwithstanding the application to a housing action trust of Part IV of the Housing Act 1985 (secure tenancies) a disposal falling within subsection (1) above shall be treated as not being a matter of housing management to which section 105 of that Act applies.

Rents

Rents generally.

85.—(1) A housing action trust may make such reasonable charges as it may determine for the tenancy or occupation of housing accommodation for the time being held by it.

(2) A housing action trust shall from time to time review rents and make such changes, either of rents generally or of particular rents, as circumstances may require.

Increase of rent where tenancy not secure.

86.—(1) This section applies where a dwelling-house is let by a housing action trust on a periodic tenancy which is not a secure tenancy.

(2) The rent payable under the tenancy may, without the tenancy being terminated, be increased with effect from the beginning of a rental period by a written notice of increase given by the housing action trust to the tenant.

(3) A notice under subsection (2) above is not effective unless—

(a) it is given at least four weeks before the first day of the rental period, or any earlier day on which the payment of rent in respect of that period falls to be made;

(b) it tells the tenant of his right to terminate the tenancy and of the steps to be taken by him if he wishes to do so; and

(c) it gives him the dates by which, if (by virtue of subsection (4) below) the increase is not to be effective, a notice to quit must be received by the trust and the tenancy be made to terminate.

(4) Where a notice is given under subsection (2) above specifying an increase in rent with effect from the beginning of a rental period and the tenancy continues into that period, the notice shall not have effect if—

(a) the tenancy is terminated by notice to quit given by the tenant in accordance with the provisions (express or implied) of the tenancy;

(b) the notice to quit is given before the expiry of the period of two weeks beginning on the day following the date on which the notice of increase is given, or before the expiry of such longer period as may be allowed by the notice of increase; and

(c) the date on which the tenancy is made to terminate is not later than the earliest day on which the tenancy could be terminated by a notice to quit given by the tenant on the last day of that rental period.

(5) In this section "rental period" means a period in respect of which a payment of rent falls to be made.

Agency and dissolution

Agency agreements.

87.—(1) With the approval of the Secretary of State, a housing action trust may enter into an agreement with another person whereby, in relation to any housing accommodation or other land held by the trust which is specified in the agreement, that other person shall exercise, as agent of the trust, such of the functions of the trust as are so specified.

(2) An agreement under subsection (1) above shall set out the terms on which the functions of the housing action trust are exercisable by the person who, under the agreement, is the agent of the trust (in this Part of this Act referred to as "the agent").

(3) Where the agent is a body or association, an agreement under subsection (1) above may provide that the functions of the agent under the agreement may be performed by a committee or sub-committee, or by an officer, of the body or association.

(4) The approval of the Secretary of State under subsection (1) above may be given unconditionally or subject to conditions.

(5) References in this section to the functions of a housing action trust in relation to housing accommodation or other land include—

(a) functions conferred by any statutory provision, and

(b) the powers and duties of the trust as holder of an estate or interest in the housing accommodation or land in question.

Dissolution of housing action trust.

88.—(1) A housing action trust shall use its best endeavours to secure that its objects are achieved as soon as practicable.

PART III

(2) Where it appears to a trust that its objects have been substantially achieved, it shall—

(a) so far as practicable, dispose or arrange to dispose of any remaining property, rights or liabilities of the trust in accordance with the preceding provisions of this Part of this Act; and

(b) submit proposals to the Secretary of State for—

(i) the dissolution of the trust;

(ii) the disposal to any person of any remaining property, rights or liabilities of the trust which it has not been able to dispose of or arrange to dispose of under paragraph (a) above; and

(iii) the transfer of any function exercisable by the trust to another person (including, where appropriate, a person with whom the trust has entered into an agreement under section 87 above).

(3) The Secretary of State may by order provide for the dissolution of a housing action trust and for any such disposal or transfer as is mentioned in subsection (2)(b) above, whether by way of giving effect (with or without modifications) to any proposals submitted to him under subsection (2) above or otherwise.

(4) Any order under this section—

(a) where it provides for any such disposal or transfer as is mentioned in subsection (2)(b) above, may be on such terms, including financial terms, as the Secretary of State thinks fit and may create or impose such new rights or liabilities in respect of what is transferred as appear to him to be necessary or expedient;

(b) may contain such supplementary and transitional provisions as the Secretary of State thinks necessary or expedient, including provisions amending any enactment or any instrument made under any enactment or establishing new bodies corporate to receive any functions, property, rights or liabilities transferred by the order; and

(c) shall be made by statutory instrument which shall be subject to annulment in pursuance of a resolution of either House of Parliament.

Miscellaneous and general

Supply of goods and services.
1980 c. 65.
1970 c. 39.

89.—(1) A housing action trust and an urban development corporation established by an order under section 135 of the Local Government, Planning and Land Act 1980, may enter into any agreement with each other for all or any of the purposes set out in section 1(1) of the Local Authorities (Goods and Services) Act 1970, as if they were local authorities within the meaning of section 1 of that Act.

(2) Without prejudice to subsection (1) above, in section 1(4) of the Local Authorities (Goods and Services) Act 1970 (supply of goods and services by local authorities to public bodies), after the words ""public body" means any local authority" there shall be inserted "housing action trust established under Part III of the Housing Act 1988".

PART III

Information.

90.—(1) If required to do so by notice in writing given by the Secretary of State for any of the purposes mentioned in subsection (3) below, a local authority,—

(a) at such time and place as may be specified in the notice, shall produce any document; or

(b) within such period as may be so specified, or such longer period as the Secretary of State may allow, shall furnish a copy of any document or supply any information;

being a document, copy or information of a description specified in the notice.

(2) Where notice is given to a local authority under subsection (1) above, any officer of the authority—

(a) who has the custody or control of any document to which the notice relates, or

(b) who is in a position to give information to which the notice relates,

shall take all reasonable steps to ensure that the notice is complied with.

(3) The purposes referred to in subsection (1) above are—

(a) determining whether the Secretary of State should make a designation order in respect of any area;

(b) where a designation order is to be or has been made, determining whether, and to what extent, he should exercise any of his other powers under this Part of this Act; and

(c) enabling him to provide information to a housing action trust the better to enable it to carry out its functions.

(4) Without prejudice to the generality of subsection (1) above, among the information which may be required by a notice under that subsection is information with respect to the interests in, and the occupation of, land held by a local authority and, in particular, information with respect to any matter entered in a register kept under the Land Registration Act 1925 or the Land Charges Act 1972. 1925 c. 21. 1972 c. 61.

(5) To any extent to which, apart from this subsection, he would not be able to do so, the Secretary of State may use, for any of the purposes mentioned in subsection (3) above, any information obtained by him under, or in connection with his functions under, the Housing Act 1985 or any other enactment. 1985 c. 68.

(6) If the Secretary of State considers it necessary or desirable to do so in order the better to enable a housing action trust to carry out its functions, he may disclose to the trust any information originally obtained by him for a purpose falling within paragraph (a) or paragraph (b) of subsection (3) above as well as information obtained for the purpose referred to in paragraph (c) of that subsection.

(7) In this section "local authority" has the same meaning as in section 74 above.

Service of notices.

91.—(1) This section has effect in relation to any notice required or authorised by this Part of this Act to be served on any person by a housing action trust.

PART III

(2) Any such notice may be served on the person in question either by delivering it to him, or by leaving it at his proper address, or by sending it by post to him at that address.

(3) Any such notice may—

(a) in the case of a body corporate, be given to or served on the secretary or clerk of that body; and

(b) in the case of a partnership, be given to or served on a partner or a person having the control or management of the partnership business.

1978 c. 30.

(4) For the purposes of this section and of section 7 of the Interpretation Act 1978 (service of documents by post) in its application to this section, the proper address of any person to or on whom a notice is to be given or served shall be his last known address, except that—

(a) in the case of a body corporate or its secretary or clerk, it shall be the address of the registered or principal office of that body; and

(b) in the case of a partnership or a person having the control or management of the partnership business, it shall be that of the principal office of the partnership;

and for the purposes of this subsection the principal office of a company registered outside the United Kingdom or of a partnership carrying on business outside the United Kingdom shall be its principal office within the United Kingdom.

(5) If the person to be given or served with any notice mentioned in subsection (1) above has specified an address within the United Kingdom other than his proper address within the meaning of subsection (4) above as the one at which he or someone on his behalf will accept documents of the same description as that notice, that address shall also be treated for the purposes of this section and section 7 of the Interpretation Act 1978 as his proper address.

(6) If the name or address of any owner, lessee or occupier of land to or on whom any notice mentioned in subsection (1) above is to be served cannot after reasonable inquiry be ascertained, the document may be served either by leaving it in the hands of a person who is or appears to be resident or employed on the land or by leaving it conspicuously affixed to some building or object on the land.

Interpretation of Part III.

92.—(1) In this Part of this Act, except where the context otherwise requires,—

(a) "designated area" and "designation order" have the meaning assigned by section 60(6) above;

(b) any reference to a "house" includes a reference to a flat and to any yard, garden, outhouses and appurtenances belonging to the house or flat or usually enjoyed with it;

(c) "housing accommodation" includes flats, lodging-houses and hostels;

1985 c. 68.

(d) "local housing authority" has the same meaning as in the Housing Act 1985 and section 2 of that Act (the district of a local housing authority) has effect in relation to this Part of this Act as it has effect in relation to that Act;

(e) "local authority housing" means housing accommodation provided by a local housing authority (whether in its own district or not); PART III

(f) "secure tenancy" has the meaning assigned by section 79 of the Housing Act 1985 and "secure tenant" shall be construed accordingly; and 1985 c. 68.

(g) "the 1971 Act" means the Town and Country Planning Act 1971. 1971 c. 78.

(2) In this Part of this Act "the Corporation" means the Housing Corporation or Housing for Wales but—

(a) an approval given by the Housing Corporation shall not have effect in relation to buildings or other property in Wales; and

(b) an approval given by Housing for Wales shall not have effect in relation to buildings or other property in England.

PART IV

CHANGE OF LANDLORD: SECURE TENANTS

Preliminary

93.—(1) This Part has effect for the purpose of conferring on any person who has been approved under section 94 below the right to acquire from a public sector landlord, subject to and in accordance with the provisions of this Part— Right conferred by Part IV.

(a) the fee simple estate in any buildings each of which comprises or contains one or more dwelling-houses which on the relevant date are occupied by qualifying tenants of the public sector landlord; and

(b) the fee simple estate in any other property which is reasonably required for occupation with buildings falling within paragraph (a) above.

(2) The following are public sector landlords for the purposes of this Part, namely—

(a) a local housing authority within the meaning of section 1 of the Housing Act 1985 (in this Part referred to as "the 1985 Act");

(b) a new town corporation within the meaning of section 4(b) of that Act;

(c) a housing action trust within the meaning of Part III of this Act; and

(d) the Development Board for Rural Wales.

(3) Subject to subsection (4) below, a secure tenant of a public sector landlord is a qualifying tenant for the purposes of this Part if (and only if) his secure tenancy is held directly from the landlord as owner of the fee simple estate and, in relation to any acquisition or proposed acquisition under this Part, any reference in the following provisions of this Part to qualifying tenant is a reference only to a qualifying tenant of the public sector landlord from whom the acquisition is or is proposed to be made.

PART IV

(4) A secure tenant is not a qualifying tenant for the purposes of this Part if—

(a) he is obliged to give up possession of the dwelling-house in pursuance of an order of the court or will be so obliged at a date specified in such an order; or

(b) the circumstances are as set out in any of paragraphs 5 to 11 of Schedule 5 to the 1985 Act (exceptions to right to buy).

(5) In this Part "the relevant date", in relation to an acquisition or proposed acquisition under this Part, means the date on which is made the application under section 96 below claiming to exercise the right conferred by this Part.

Persons by whom right may be exercised.

94.—(1) The right conferred by this Part shall not be exercisable except by a person who is for the time being approved by the Corporation under this section; and neither a public sector landlord nor the council of a county nor any other body which the Corporation have reason to believe might not be independent of such a landlord or council may be approved under this section.

(2) For the purposes of subsection (1) above, a body shall not be regarded as independent of a public sector landlord or the council of a county if the body is or appears likely to be under the control of, or subject to influence from, such a landlord or council or particular members or officers of such a landlord or council.

(3) The Corporation shall establish (and may from time to time vary) criteria to be satisfied by a person seeking approval under this section and, without prejudice to subsections (1) and (2) above, in deciding whether to give such approval, the Corporation shall have regard to whether the person satisfies those criteria.

1985 c. 69.

(4) Subject to any directions under section 76 of the Housing Associations Act 1985 (directions by the Secretary of State), an approval under this section—

(a) shall not be given except to a person making an application accompanied by such fee as the Corporation, with the consent of the Secretary of State, may specify; and

(b) may be given to a particular person or to persons of a particular description; and

(c) may apply either in relation to acquisitions generally or in relation to a particular acquisition or acquisitions or in relation to acquisitions made in a particular area or within a particular period; and

(d) may be made conditional upon the person or persons concerned entering into such undertakings as may be specified by the Corporation;

and different fees may be specified under paragraph (a) above for different descriptions of cases.

(5) Subject to any directions under section 76 of the Housing Associations Act 1985, if it appears to the Corporation appropriate to do so (whether by reason of a failure to honour an undertaking or to meet any criteria or for any other reason), the Corporation may revoke an approval given under this section by notice in writing served on the approved person; and where such a notice of revocation is served—

(a) the revocation shall be provisional until the expiry of such period, being not less than 14 days, as may be specified in the notice;

(b) if the Corporation withdraws the notice at any time during the specified period, the approval shall be treated as never having been revoked; and

(c) subject to paragraph (b) above, after the date of service of the notice, the person concerned may not take any steps in connection with a claim to exercise the right conferred by this Part;

but the service of a notice under this subsection shall not affect any transaction completed before the service of the notice.

(6) In the case of a body which has been approved under this section which does not have a registered office (at which documents can be served) and which appears to the Corporation to have ceased to exist or not to operate, notice under subsection (5) above shall be deemed to be served on the body if it is served at the address last known to the Corporation to be the principal place of business of the body.

(7) The Housing Corporation and Housing for Wales shall each maintain a register of persons for the time being approved by it under this section, specifying the extent of the approval given in each case; and each register so maintained shall be open to inspection at the head office of the Corporation by which it is maintained at all reasonable times.

Property excluded from right.

95.—(1) A building shall be excluded from an acquisition under this Part if on the relevant date—

(a) any part or parts of the building is or are occupied or intended to be occupied otherwise than for residential purposes; and

(b) the internal floor area of that part or those parts (taken together) exceeds 50 per cent. of the internal floor area of the building (taken as a whole);

and for the purposes of this subsection the internal floor area of any common parts or common facilities shall be disregarded.

(2) In the application of subsection (1) above to property falling within section 93(1)(b) above, a building or part of a building which, apart from this subsection, would not be regarded as occupied for residential purposes shall be so regarded if—

(a) it is or is intended to be occupied together with a dwelling-house and used for purposes connected with the occupation of the dwelling-house; or

(b) it is or is intended to be used for the provision of services to a dwelling-house which is comprised in a building falling within section 93(1)(a) above.

(3) A building shall be excluded from an acquisition under this Part if—

(a) it contains two or more dwelling-houses which on the relevant date are occupied by secure tenants who are not qualifying tenants; and

(b) the number of dwelling-houses which on that date are occupied by such tenants exceeds 50 per cent. of the total number of dwelling-houses in the building.

PART IV

(4) A dwelling-house shall be excluded from an acquisition under this Part if it is a house and it is occupied on the relevant date by—

(a) a secure tenant who is precluded from being a qualifying tenant by section 93(4)(b) above; or

(b) a tenant who is not a secure tenant.

(5) A building or other property shall be excluded from an acquisition under this Part if—

(a) it was specified in some other application made under section 96 below made before the relevant date; and

(b) that other application has not been disposed of.

(6) Except to the extent that it comprises or is let together with a dwelling-house, property shall be excluded from an acquisition under this Part if it is land held—

1875 c. 55. (a) for the purposes of section 164 of the Public Health Act 1875 (pleasure grounds); or

1906 c. 25. (b) in accordance with section 10 of the Open Spaces Act 1906 (duty of local authority to maintain open spaces and burial grounds).

(7) The Secretary of State may by order substitute for the percentage for the time being specified in subsection (1)(b) above such other percentage as is specified in the order.

Initial procedures

Application to exercise right.

96.—(1) An application claiming to exercise the right conferred by this Part—

(a) shall be made in the prescribed form to the public sector landlord concerned; and

(b) shall specify and be accompanied by a plan which shows—

(i) the buildings proposed to be acquired by virtue of paragraph (a) of subsection (1) of section 93 above; and

(ii) the property proposed to be acquired by virtue of paragraph (b) of that subsection.

(2) Where an application claiming to exercise the right conferred by this Part specifies, as a building proposed to be acquired by virtue of section 93(1)(a) above, a building containing a dwelling-house which is subject to an approved co-operative management agreement, the application—

(a) shall specify all the buildings which contain dwelling-houses subject to the agreement and in which the public sector landlord has the fee simple estate; and

(b) shall not specify (by virtue of paragraph (a) or paragraph (b) of subsection (1) of section 93 above) any building which contains dwelling-houses if none of them is subject to the agreement.

(3) For the purposes of subsection (2) above, an approved co-operative management agreement is an agreement—

1985 c. 68.
1986 c. 63.

(a) which is made with the approval of the Secretary of State under section 27 of the Housing Act 1985, either as originally enacted or as substituted by section 10 of the Housing and Planning Act 1986; and

(b) under which the body exercising functions of the local housing authority is a society, company or body of trustees approved by the Secretary of State for the purposes of subsection (2) above.

Information etc. for applicant.

97.—(1) Within four weeks of the relevant date, the landlord shall serve on the applicant a notice specifying—

(a) the name and address of every tenant or licensee of a dwelling-house which the buildings proposed to be acquired by virtue of section 93(1)(a) above comprise or contain; and

(b) the general nature of his tenancy or licence.

(2) As from four weeks after that date, the applicant shall have the following rights, namely—

(a) a right of access, at any reasonable time and on giving reasonable notice, to any property proposed to be acquired which is not subject to a tenancy;

(b) a right, on giving reasonable notice, to be provided with a list of any documents to which subsection (3) below applies;

(c) a right to inspect, at any reasonable time and on giving reasonable notice, any documents to which that subsection applies; and

(d) a right, on payment of a reasonable fee, to be provided with a copy of any documents inspected under paragraph (c) above.

(3) This subsection applies to any document in the possession of the landlord—

(a) sight of which is reasonably required for the purpose of pursuing the application; and

(b) which, on a proposed sale by a willing vendor to a willing purchaser of the property proposed to be acquired, the landlord, as vendor, would be expected to make available to the purchaser (whether at or before contract or completion).

(4) In this section "document" has the same meaning as in Part I of the Civil Evidence Act 1968. 1968 c. 64.

Determination of property to be included.

98.—(1) Within twelve weeks of the relevant date, the landlord shall serve on the applicant a notice stating—

(a) which (if any) of the buildings proposed to be acquired by virtue of paragraph (a) of subsection (1) of section 93 above should be excluded from the acquisition on the ground that they do not comprise or contain one or more dwelling-houses which on the relevant date were occupied by qualifying tenants;

(b) which (if any) property proposed to be acquired by virtue of paragraph (b) of that subsection should be excluded from the acquisition on the ground that it is not reasonably required for occupation with any of the buildings proposed to be acquired by virtue of paragraph (a) of that subsection or that it is reasonably required for occupation with such of those buildings as should be excluded from the acquisition on the ground mentioned in paragraph (a) above;

PART IV

(c) which (if any) property proposed to be acquired by virtue of either paragraph of that subsection should be excluded from the acquisition on the ground that its inclusion is precluded by section 95 above or that it is reasonably required for occupation with property the inclusion of which is so precluded or that it is a building which is excluded from the acquisition by virtue of section 96(2)(b) above;

(d) which property (if any) the landlord desires to have included in the acquisition on the ground that it cannot otherwise be reasonably managed or maintained;

(e) which rights (if any) the landlord desires to retain over property included in the acquisition on the ground that they are necessary for the proper management or maintenance of land to be retained by the landlord;

(f) the other proposed terms of the conveyance; and

(g) such other particulars as may be prescribed.

(2) A building which is excluded from an acquisition by virtue of section 95 or section 96(2)(b) above may not be included by virtue of subsection (1)(d) above.

(3) Where a notice under subsection (1) above specifies property falling within paragraph (d) of that subsection, the applicant shall have a right of access, at any reasonable time and on giving reasonable notice, to any of that property which is not subject to a tenancy.

(4) Within four weeks of service of the notice under subsection (1) above, the applicant shall notify the landlord in writing of any matters stated in that notice which he does not accept.

(5) Any dispute as to any matters stated in a notice under subsection (1) above shall be determined—

(a) by a person agreed to by the parties or, in default of agreement, appointed by the Secretary of State; and

(b) in accordance with such provisions (including provisions as to costs) as may be prescribed.

(6) In relation to a proposed acquisition under this Part, any reference in the following provisions of this Part to the property to which the acquisition relates is a reference to the whole of the property which, in accordance with the provisions of this section, is to be acquired, disregarding the effect of any exclusion by virtue of regulations under section 100 below.

Determination of purchase price.

99.—(1) Within eight weeks of—

(a) if there is no dispute as to any of the matters stated in the notice under section 98(1) above, the service of that notice, or

(b) if there is such a dispute, the determination of the dispute,

the landlord shall serve on the applicant a notice specifying—

(i) the price which, disregarding sections 100(3) and 103(1) below, it considers should be payable for the property to be acquired or, as the case may be, the disposal cost which, disregarding section 100(3) below, is attributable to the property to be acquired by virtue of subsection (3) below; and

PART IV

(ii) if the property to which the acquisition relates includes dwelling-houses which are houses as well as other property, an amount which the landlord considers to be the amount attributable to houses as defined in section 100(4)(b) below.

(2) Subject to sections 100(3) and 103(1) below, the price payable for the property to be acquired shall be the price which on the relevant date the property to which the acquisition relates would realise if sold on the open market by a willing vendor on the following assumptions, namely—

(a) that it was sold subject to any tenancies subsisting on that date but otherwise with vacant possession;

(b) that it was to be conveyed with the same rights and subject to the same burdens as it would be in pursuance of the right of acquisition;

(c) that the only bidders in the market were persons who on that date either were approved under section 94 above or fulfilled the criteria for approval established under subsection (3) of that section;

(d) that the applicant would, within a reasonable period, carry out such works as are reasonably necessary to put the buildings included in the acquisition into the state of repair required by the landlord's repairing obligations; and

(e) that the applicant would not be required to grant any leases in pursuance of regulations made under section 100 below.

(3) Subject to section 100(3) below, there is a disposal cost attributable to the property to be acquired if, having regard to the expense likely to be incurred in carrying out the works referred to in paragraph (d) of subsection (2) above, the property to which the acquisition relates would not realise any price in the circumstances specified in that subsection; and that disposal cost is the amount by which the expense likely to be so incurred exceeds what would be determined under that subsection as the price if those works had already been carried out.

(4) The notice under subsection (1) above shall contain sufficient information to enable the applicant to see how the price or, as the case may be, disposal cost and any amount referred to in sub-paragraphs (i) and (ii) of subsection (1) above were arrived at and, if the property to which the acquisition relates consists of or includes any dwelling-houses which are houses, the notice shall also contain a list of the addresses of the houses together with the number of habitable rooms in each of them.

(5) Within four weeks of service of the notice under subsection (1) above, the applicant shall notify the landlord in writing of any matters stated in that notice which he does not accept.

(6) Any dispute as to any matters stated in a notice under subsection (1) above shall be determined by the district valuer, in accordance with such provisions (including provisions as to costs) as may be prescribed.

Special cases

Tenants continuing as tenants of landlord.

100.—(1) The Secretary of State shall make regulations imposing the following requirements in relation to any acquisition under this Part, namely—

PART IV

(a) that any dwelling-house which is a house and is occupied by a tenant to whom subsection (2) below applies shall be excluded from the acquisition; and

(b) that a lease of any dwelling-house which is a flat and is occupied by a tenant to whom subsection (2) below applies or by a tenant of a description prescribed for the purposes of this paragraph shall be granted by the applicant to the landlord immediately after the acquisition.

(2) This subsection applies—

(a) to any qualifying tenant whose tenancy commenced before the relevant date, and

(b) to any tenant of a description prescribed for the purposes of this subsection,

being, in either case, a tenant who, before the end of the period mentioned in section 102 below and in response to the consultation under that section, gives notice as mentioned in section 103(2) below of his wish to continue as a tenant of the landlord.

(3) If, by virtue of regulations under this section, any houses fall to be excluded from the acquisition—

(a) there shall be determined the sum (in this subsection referred to as "the sum referable to excluded houses") which represents that proportion of the amount attributable to houses which the number of habitable rooms in the houses which fall to be so excluded bears to the number of habitable rooms in all of the houses comprised in the property to which the acquisition relates; and

(b) if the amount attributable to houses is a price, the sum referable to excluded houses shall be applied as a deduction from any price payable for the property to be acquired, as determined under section 99 above, and as an increase in any disposal cost attributable to that property; and

(c) if the amount attributable to houses is a disposal cost, the sum referable to excluded houses shall be applied as an increase in any price payable for the property to be acquired, as determined under section 99 above, and as a deduction from any disposal cost attributable to that property.

(4) In section 99(1)(ii) and subsection (3) above, "the amount attributable to houses", in relation to an acquisition under this Part, means,—

(a) if the property to which the acquisition relates consists of dwelling-houses which are houses and no other property, the price or, as the case may be, disposal cost specified in accordance with section 99(1)(i) above; and

(b) in any other case, the price or disposal cost which, under subsection (2) or subsection (3) of section 99 above, would be payable for, or attributable to, the property to which the acquisition relates if there were excluded from that property all property other than dwelling-houses which are houses.

Tenancies granted after relevant date.

101.—(1) Subject to subsection (4)(a) below, this section applies to any tenancy of or licence to occupy any part of the property proposed to be acquired, being a tenancy or licence commencing,—

(a) in the case of property falling within paragraph (d) of subsection (1) of section 98 above, after the date of the notice under that subsection;

(b) in any other case, after the relevant date.

(2) Notwithstanding anything in any enactment, a tenancy or licence to which this section applies—

(a) shall not be a secure tenancy, and

(b) shall not be capable of becoming an assured tenancy or an assured agricultural occupancy,

and neither Part II of the Landlord and Tenant Act 1954 (business tenancies) nor Parts III to VI of the Agricultural Holdings Act 1986 (tenancies of agricultural holdings, including market gardens and smallholdings) shall apply to a tenancy or licence to which this section applies.

1954 c. 56.
1986 c. 75.

(3) Every tenancy or licence to which this section applies shall be determinable by the landlord or licensor by giving not less than four weeks notice to quit expiring at any time during the tenancy; and this subsection has effect whether or not the tenancy or licence is periodic and, if it is periodic, regardless of the length of the period.

(4) The Secretary of State may make regulations—

(a) excluding from the tenancies and licences to which this section applies a tenancy or licence of a description specified in the regulations;

(b) requiring the public sector landlord to give notice to the applicant of the grant of any tenancy or licence to which this section applies;

(c) requiring the public sector landlord to give notice of the effect of this section to any tenant or licensee under a tenancy or licence to which this section applies;

(d) for securing that, on the transfer of the property included in the acquisition to the applicant, the public sector landlord gives vacant possession of any property subject to a tenancy or licence to which this section applies;

(e) that, in so far as vacant possession is not so given, any costs or expenses attributable to the recovery of vacant possession by the applicant and any losses consequent upon the failure of the public sector landlord to give vacant possession are recoverable by the applicant from that landlord as a simple contract debt; and

(f) making provision for and in connection with the disapplication of this section in any case where the applicant does not proceed with the acquisition.

Final procedures

Consultations by applicant.

102.—(1) During such period as may be prescribed beginning with,—

(a) if there is a determination by the district valuer under section 99 above, notification to the applicant of that determination,

PART IV

(b) if there is no such determination, service of the landlord's notice under that section,

the applicant shall consult, in accordance with such provisions as may be prescribed, tenants to whom this section applies.

(2) This section applies—

(a) to any qualifying tenant, or tenant under a long tenancy, who on the relevant date occupied a dwelling-house proposed to be included in the acquisition and continued to occupy the dwelling during the period referred to in subsection (1) above; and

(b) to any tenant of a description prescribed for the purposes of section 100(2) above; and

(c) to any tenant of a description prescribed for the purposes of this section.

Notice by applicant of intention to proceed.

103.—(1) Subject to subsection (2) below, the applicant may, within two weeks of the end of the period mentioned in section 102 above, serve on the landlord notice of his intention to proceed with the acquisition; and in that notice the applicant, in such circumstances as may be prescribed, may inform the landlord—

(a) that he wishes to enter into a prescribed covenant to make payments to the landlord on the occasion of any prescribed disposal (occurring after the date of the acquisition) of a dwelling-house comprised in the property to be acquired; and

(b) that he requires the value of that covenant to be taken into account in reducing the price which would otherwise be payable for the property to be acquired.

(2) The applicant shall not be entitled to serve a notice under subsection (1) above if, in response to the consultation under section 102 above,—

(a) less than 50 per cent. of the tenants to whom that section applies have given notice of their wishes in such manner as may be prescribed; or

(b) the number of tenants to whom that section applies who have given notice in that manner of their wish to continue as tenants of the landlord exceeds 50 per cent. of the total number of tenants to whom that section applies.

(3) In any case where a tenancy is held by two or more persons jointly, those persons shall be regarded as a single tenant for the purposes of subsection (2) above and, accordingly, any notice given in response to the consultation under section 102 above shall be of no effect for the purposes of subsection (2) above unless it is given by or on behalf of all the joint tenants.

(4) A notice under subsection (1) above shall contain—

(a) a list of the names and addresses of tenants to whom section 102 above applies (if any) who have given notice as mentioned in subsection (2)(b) above;

(b) a list of the houses (if any) which are, by virtue of regulations under section 100 above, to be excluded from the acquisition;

PART IV

(c) a list of flats (if any) of which the applicant is required, by virtue of such regulations, to grant leases to the landlord and a statement of the proposed terms of those leases;

(d) such information as may be necessary to show how the lists mentioned in paragraphs (a), (b) and (c) above were established; and

(e) the price payable for the property to be acquired (disregarding any reduction by virtue of such a covenant as is referred to in subsection (1) above) or, as the case may be, the disposal cost attributable to that property.

(5) Within two weeks of service of the notice under subsection (1) above, the landlord shall notify the applicant in writing of any matters stated in that notice which it does not accept.

(6) Where a notice has been served under subsection (1) above, every tenant to whom section 102 above applies and who has not given notice as mentioned in subsection (2)(b) above shall be taken to have accepted, and to have given consideration for, any offer which—

(a) relates to the terms on which, after the acquisition, he is to occupy the dwelling-house occupied by him on the relevant date;

(b) was made to him by the applicant either in the course of the consultation required by subsection (1) of section 102 above or otherwise before the end of the period referred to in that subsection; and

(c) was neither withdrawn by the applicant nor rejected by the tenant before the end of that period.

(7) Regulations prescribing any of the matters referred to in subsection (1) above shall also make provision with respect to the determination of the amounts which are to be payable on the occasion of prescribed disposals; and the amount of any reduction in the price payable for the property to be acquired which is attributable to such a covenant as is referred to in that subsection shall be determined by the district valuer.

Duty to complete and consequences of completion.

104.—(1) Where the applicant has served on the landlord a notice under section 103(1) above, then, as soon as any dispute as to any matters stated in that notice has been determined and, where appropriate, any determination has been made under section 103(7) above—

(a) the landlord shall make to the applicant a grant of the property included in the acquisition for an estate in fee simple absolute, but subject to any rights to be retained by the landlord; and

(b) the applicant shall grant to the landlord leases of any flats of which he is required to grant leases by regulations under section 100 above.

(2) The terms of any grant or lease under subsection (1) above shall comply with such requirements as may be prescribed.

(3) The duties imposed by the preceding provisions of this section are enforceable by injunction.

(4) Notwithstanding anything in section 141 of the Law of Property Act 1925 (rent and benefit of lessee's covenants to run with the reversion) any rent or other sum which— 1925 c. 20.

PART IV

(a) arises under a tenancy of any property included in the acquisition, and

(b) falls due before the date of the grant under subsection (1) above,

shall continue to be recoverable by the landlord to the exclusion of the applicant and of any other person in whom the reversion on the tenancy may become vested.

1980 c. 65.

(5) Without prejudice to the application of Part VIII of the Local Government, Planning and Land Act 1980 (capital expenditure of local authorities) to the price received by the landlord on the disposal (as mentioned in subsection (1)(a) above) of the property included in the acquisition, where there is a disposal cost attributable to that property any payments made by the landlord in respect of that cost shall be prescribed expenditure for the purposes of that Part.

Subsequent disposals

Consent required for subsequent disposals.

105.—(1) A person who acquires any property under this Part (in this section referred to as "the new landlord") shall not dispose of it except with the consent of the Secretary of State; but nothing in this subsection shall apply in relation to an exempt disposal, as defined in subsection (7) below.

(2) Where an estate or interest in property acquired by the new landlord has been mortgaged or charged, the prohibition in subsection (1) above on disposal of the property without consent applies also to a disposal by the mortgagee or chargee in exercise of a power of sale or leasing, whether or not the disposal is in the name of the new landlord.

(3) In any case where—

(a) by operation of law or by virtue of an order of a court property which has been acquired by the new landlord passes or is transferred to another person, and

(b) that passing or transfer does not constitute a disposal for which consent is required under subsection (1) above,

this section (including, where there is more than one such passing or transfer, this subsection) shall apply as if the other person to whom the property passes or is transferred were the new landlord.

(4) Any consent for the purposes of subsection (1) above may be given either unconditionally or subject to conditions; but, before giving any such consent, the Secretary of State—

(a) shall satisfy himself that the person who is seeking the consent has taken appropiate steps to consult every tenant of the whole or any part of the property proposed to be disposed of; and

(b) shall have regard to the responses of any such tenants to that consultation.

(5) If, apart from subsection (6) below, the consent of the Housing Corporation or Housing for Wales would be required under section 9 of the Housing Associations Act 1985 (control of dispositions of land by housing associations) for a disposal to which subsection (1) above applies, the Secretary of State shall consult that body before giving his consent in respect of that disposal for the purposes of that subsection.

1985 c. 69.

(6) No consent shall be required under the said section 9 for any disposal in respect of which consent is given in accordance with subsection (5) above.

(7) In this section an "exempt disposal" means—

(a) the grant of a lease pursuant to such a requirement as is referred to in section 100(1)(b) above;

(b) the disposal of a dwelling-house to a person having the right to buy it under Part V of the 1985 Act (whether the disposal is in fact made under that Part or otherwise);

(c) a compulsory disposal, within the meaning of Part V of the 1985 Act;

(d) the disposal of an easement or rentcharge;

(e) the disposal of an interest by way of security for a loan;

(f) the grant of a secure tenancy or what would be a secure tenancy but for any of paragraphs 2 to 12 of Schedule 1 to the 1985 Act;

(g) the grant of an assured tenancy, within the meaning of Part I of this Act, or what would be such a tenancy but for any of paragraphs 4 to 8 of Schedule 1 to this Act; and

(h) the transfer of an interest which is held on trust where the disposal is made in connection with the appointment of a new trustee or in connection with the discharge of any trustee.

(8) In this section references to disposing of property include references to—

(a) granting or disposing of any interest in property;

(b) entering into a contract to dispose of property or to grant or dispose of any such interest; and

(c) granting an option to acquire property or any such interest.

Supplemental

Service of information, advice and assistance.

106.—(1) The Corporation may provide in connection with this Part a service of information, advice and assistance to, and for the benefit of,—

(a) persons who have been approved or are considering applying for approval under section 94 above; and

(b) persons who are tenants of public sector landlords.

(2) The Corporation may make charges for information, advice and assistance provided under this section otherwise than to persons falling within subsection (1)(b) above.

(3) The powers conferred on the Corporation by this section may be exercised by the Housing Corporation and Housing for Wales acting jointly.

Power of Corporation to provide legal assistance to tenants in relation to acquisitions.

107.—(1) On an application by the tenant of a dwelling-house who is a party or a prospective party to proceedings or prospective proceedings falling within subsection (2) below, the Corporation may give assistance to the tenant if it thinks fit to do so—

(a) on the ground that the case raises a question of principle; or

PART IV

(b) on the ground that it is unreasonable, having regard to the complexity of the case, or to any other matter, to expect the tenant to deal with it without assistance; or

(c) by reason of any other special consideration.

(2) The proceedings referred to in subsection (1) above are—

(a) proceedings to determine any question arising in relation to an acquisition or proposed acquisition under this Part; and

(b) proceedings to determine any dispute arising after an acquisition under this Part between a transferred tenant of a dwelling-house included in the acquisition and the body by which the acquisition was made;

and for the purposes of paragraph (b) above a tenant of a dwelling-house is a transferred tenant of it if he was the qualifying tenant of it at the time of the acquisition or is the widow or widower of the person who was then the qualifying tenant of it.

(3) Assistance given by the Corporation under this section may include—

(a) giving advice;

(b) procuring or attempting to procure the settlement of the matter in dispute;

(c) arranging for the giving of advice or assistance by a solicitor or counsel;

(d) arranging for representation by a solicitor or counsel, including such assistance as is usually given by a solicitor or counsel in the steps preliminary or incidental to any proceedings, or in arriving at or giving effect to a compromise to avoid or bring to an end any proceedings; and

(e) any other form of assistance which the Corporation may consider appropriate;

but paragraph (d) above does not affect the law and practice regulating the descriptions of persons who may appear in, conduct, defend and address the court in any proceedings.

(4) In so far as expenses are incurred by the Corporation in providing the tenant with assistance under this section, the recovery of those expenses (as taxed or assessed in such manner as may be prescribed by rules of court) shall constitute a first charge for the benefit of the Corporation—

(a) on any costs which (whether by virtue of a judgment or order of a court or an agreement or otherwise) are payable to the tenant by any other person in respect of the matter in connection with which the assistance was given; and

(b) so far as relates to any costs, on his rights under any compromise or settlement arrived at in connection with that matter to avoid or bring to an end any proceedings;

1988 c. 34.

but subject to any charge under the Legal Aid Act 1988 and to any provision of that Act for payment of any sum to the Legal Aid Board.

Registration of title and related matters.

108. Schedule 12 to this Act shall have effect with respect to registration of title and related matters arising on acquisitions of property under this Part and disposals of property so acquired.

Public open space etc.

109.—(1) To the extent that any land held—

(a) for the purposes of section 164 of the Public Health Act 1875 (pleasure grounds), or 1875 c. 55.

(b) in accordance with section 10 of the Open Spaces Act 1906 (duty of local authority to maintain open spaces and burial grounds), 1906 c. 25.

is included in an acquisition under this Part, it shall be deemed to be freed from any trust arising solely by virtue of its being land held in trust for enjoyment by the public in accordance with that section.

(2) Nothing in section 5 of the Green Belt (London and Home Counties) Act 1938 (restrictions on alienation of land by local authorities) applies in relation to a disposal of land included in an acquisition under this Part. 1938 c. xciii.

Extension etc. of relevant periods.

110.—(1) In this section "relevant period" means any period within which anything is required by this Part to be done by either of the parties, that is to say, the applicant and the landlord.

(2) At any time before the end of any relevant period, or any such period as previously extended under this subsection, the other party may, by a written notice served on the party to whom the requirement relates, extend or further extend that period.

(3) Where a notice of revocation of the applicant's approval is served under subsection (5) of section 94 above and subsequently withdrawn as mentioned in paragraph (b) of that subsection, any relevant period which, apart from this subsection, would have expired before the withdrawal shall be taken to be extended by a period equal to that beginning with the date of the service of the notice of revocation and ending on the date of the withdrawal.

(4) Where—

(a) the applicant is the party to whom the requirement relates, and

(b) the relevant period, or that period as extended under subsection (2) above, expires without his doing what he is required by this Part to do within that period,

his application claiming to exercise the right conferred by this Part shall be deemed to be withdrawn, but without prejudice to his making a further such application.

Power to prescribe forms etc.

111. The Secretary of State may by regulations prescribe—

(a) anything which by this Part is to be prescribed; and

(b) the form of any notice, statement or other document which is required or authorised to be used under or for the purposes of this Part.

Orders and regulations.

112.—(1) Any power of the Secretary of State to make orders or regulations under this Part shall be exercised by statutory instrument.

(2) A statutory instrument containing any order or regulations under this Part, other than regulations under section 111(b) above, shall be subject to annulment in pursuance of a resolution of either House of Parliament.

PART IV

(3) Orders or regulations under this Part may make different provision for different cases or circumstances or different areas and may contain such incidental, supplemental or transitional provisions as the Secretary of State thinks fit.

Jurisdiction of county court.

113.—(1) Subject to sections 98(5) and 99(6) above, a county court has jurisdiction—

(a) to entertain any proceedings brought under this Part; and

(b) to determine any question arising under this Part.

(2) The jurisdiction conferred by this section includes jurisdiction to entertain proceedings on any such question as is mentioned in subsection (1) above notwithstanding that no other relief is sought than a declaration.

(3) If a person takes in the High Court proceedings which, by virtue of this section, he could have taken in the county court, he shall not be entitled to recover any more costs of those proceedings than those to which he would have been entitled if the proceedings had been taken in a county court.

(4) In a case falling within subsection (3) above the taxing master shall have the same power of directing on what scale costs are to be allowed, and of allowing any item of costs, as the judge would have had if the proceedings had been taken in a county court.

Interpretation of Part IV.
1985 c. 68.

114.—(1) In this Part—

"the 1985 Act" means the Housing Act 1985;

"the Corporation" means the Housing Corporation or Housing for Wales but—

(a) an approval given by the Housing Corporation shall not have effect in relation to buildings or other property in Wales; and

(b) an approval given by Housing for Wales shall not have effect in relation to buildings or other property in England;

"qualifying tenant" shall be construed in accordance with subsections (3) and (4) of section 93 above;

"prescribed" means prescribed by regulations made by the Secretary of State;

"property" means land with or without buildings;

"public sector landlord" has the meaning given by section 93(2) above;

"the relevant date" has the meaning given by section 93(5) above; and

"habitable room", in relation to a house, means a room used, or intended for use, as a bedroom, living room, dining room or kitchen.

(2) Subject to subsection (1) above, in this Part expressions which are also used in Part V of the 1985 Act have the same meaning as in that Part.

PART V

MISCELLANEOUS AND GENERAL

Leases

115.—(1) With respect to— Premiums on long leases.

(a) any premium received or required to be paid after the commencement of this Act, or

(b) any loan required to be made after that commencement,

section 127 of the Rent Act 1977 (allowable premiums in relation to certain long tenancies) shall have effect subject to the amendments in subsections (2) and (3) below. 1977 c. 42.

(2) For subsections (2) and (3) there shall be substituted the following subsections—

"(2) The conditions mentioned in subsection (1)(a) above are—

(a) that the landlord has no power to determine the tenancy at any time within twenty years beginning on the date when it was granted; and

(b) that the terms of the tenancy do not inhibit both the assignment and the underletting of the whole of the premises comprised in the tenancy;

but for the purpose of paragraph (b) above there shall be disregarded any term of the tenancy which inhibits assignment and underletting only during a period which is or falls within the final seven years of the term for which the tenancy was granted.

(3) The reference in subsection (2) above to a power of the landlord to determine a tenancy does not include a reference to a power of re-entry or forfeiture for breach of any term or condition of the tenancy."

(3) Subsections (3C) and (3D) shall be omitted and in subsection (5) for "(2)(c)" there shall be substituted "(2)(b)".

(4) Expressions used in subsection (1) above have the same meaning as in Part IX of the Rent Act 1977.

116.—(1) In section 11 of the Landlord and Tenant Act 1985 (repairing obligations in short leases) after subsection (1) there shall be inserted the following subsections— Repairing obligations in short leases. 1985 c. 70.

"(1A) If a lease to which this section applies is a lease of a dwelling-house which forms part only of a building, then, subject to subsection (1B), the covenant implied by subsection (1) shall have effect as if—

(a) the reference in paragraph (a) of that subsection to the dwelling-house included a reference to any part of the building in which the lessor has an estate or interest; and

(b) any reference in paragraphs (b) and (c) of that subsection to an installation in the dwelling-house included a reference to an installation which, directly or indirectly, serves the dwelling-house and which either—

(i) forms part of any part of a building in which the lessor has an estate or interest; or

(ii) is owned by the lessor or under his control.

PART V

(1B) Nothing in subsection (1A) shall be construed as requiring the lessor to carry out any works or repairs unless the disrepair (or failure to maintain in working order) is such as to affect the lessee's enjoyment of the dwelling-house or of any common parts, as defined in section 60(1) of the Landlord and Tenant Act 1987, which the lessee, as such, is entitled to use."

(2) After subsection (3) of that section there shall be inserted the following subsection—

"(3A) In any case where—

(a) the lessor's repairing covenant has effect as mentioned in subsection (1A), and

(b) in order to comply with the covenant the lessor needs to carry out works or repairs otherwise than in, or to an installation in, the dwelling-house, and

(c) the lessor does not have a sufficient right in the part of the building or the installation concerned to enable him to carry out the required works or repairs,

then, in any proceedings relating to a failure to comply with the lessor's repairing covenant, so far as it requires the lessor to carry out the works or repairs in question, it shall be a defence for the lessor to prove that he used all reasonable endeavours to obtain, but was unable to obtain, such rights as would be adequate to enable him to carry out the works or repairs."

(3) At the end of section 14(4) of the said Act of 1985 (which excludes from section 11 certain leases granted to various bodies) there shall be added—

"a housing action trust established under Part III of the Housing Act 1988".

(4) The amendments made by this section do not have effect with respect to—

(a) a lease entered into before the commencement of this Act; or

(b) a lease entered into pursuant to a contract made before the commencement of this Act.

Certain tenancies excluded from bankrupt's estate.
1986 c. 45.

117.—(1) In section 283 of the Insolvency Act 1986 (definition of bankrupt's estate) at the end of subsection (3) (property excluded from the estate) there shall be inserted the following subsection—

"(3A) Subject to section 308A in Chapter IV, subsection (1) does not apply to—

(a) a tenancy which is an assured tenancy or an assured agricultural occupancy, within the meaning of Part I of the Housing Act 1988, and the terms of which inhibit an assignment as mentioned in section 127(5) of the Rent Act 1977, or

(b) a protected tenancy, within the meaning of the Rent Act 1977, in respect of which, by virtue of any provision of Part IX of that Act, no premium can lawfully be required as a condition of assignment, or

PART V

(c) a tenancy of a dwelling-house by virtue of which the bankrupt is, within the meaning of the Rent (Agriculture) Act 1976, a protected occupier of the dwelling-house, and the terms of which inhibit an assignment as mentioned in section 127(5) of the Rent Act 1977, or

(d) a secure tenancy, within the meaning of Part IV of the Housing Act 1985, which is not capable of being assigned, except in the cases mentioned in section 91(3) of that Act."

(2) After section 308 of that Act there shall be inserted the following section—

"Vesting in trustee of certain tenancies.

308A. Upon the service on the bankrupt by the trustee of a notice in writing under this section, any tenancy—

(a) which is excluded by virtue of section 283(3A) from the bankrupt's estate, and

(b) to which the notice relates,

vests in the trustee as part of the bankrupt's estate; and, except against a purchaser in good faith, for value and without notice of the bankruptcy, the trustee's title to that tenancy has relation back to the commencement of the bankruptcy."

(3) In section 309 of that Act (time-limit for certain notices) in subsection (1)(b)—

(a) after the words "section 308" there shall be inserted "or section 308A"; and

(b) after the words "the property" there shall be inserted "or tenancy".

(4) In section 315 of that Act (disclaimer (general power)), in subsection (4) after the words "reasonable replacement value)" there shall be inserted "or 308A".

Certain tenancies excluded from debtor's estate: Scotland.

1985 c. 66.

118.—(1) In section 31 of the Bankruptcy (Scotland) Act 1985 (vesting of debtor's estate at date of sequestration) in subsection (8) after the word "means" there shall be inserted the words ", subject to subsection (9) below,".

(2) After the said subsection (8) there shall be added the following subsections—

"(9) Subject to subsection (10) below, the "whole estate of the debtor" does not include any interest of the debtor as tenant under any of the following tenancies—

(a) a tenancy which is an assured tenancy within the meaning of Part II of the Housing (Scotland) Act 1988, or

(b) a protected tenancy within the meaning of the Rent (Scotland) Act 1984 in respect of which, by virtue of any provision of Part VIII of that Act, no premium can lawfully be required as a condition of the assignation, or

(c) a secure tenancy within the meaning of Part III of the Housing (Scotland) Act 1987.

PART V

(10) On the date on which the permanent trustee serves notice to that effect on the debtor, the interest of the debtor as tenant under any of the tenancies referred to in subsection (9) above shall form part of his estate and vest in the permanent trustee as if it had vested in him under section 32(6) of this Act."

Amendment of Landlord and Tenant Act 1987. 1987 c. 31.

119. The Landlord and Tenant Act 1987 shall have effect subject to the amendments in Schedule 13 to this Act.

Rent officers

Appointment etc. of rent officers. 1977 c. 42.

120. Section 63 of the Rent Act 1977 (schemes for the appointment of rent officers) shall have effect subject to the amendments in Part I of Schedule 14 to this Act and after section 64 of that Act there shall be inserted the sections set out in Part II of that Schedule.

Rent officers: additional functions relating to housing benefit etc.

121.—(1) The Secretary of State may by order require rent officers to carry out such functions as may be specified in the order in connection with housing benefit and rent allowance subsidy.

(2) An order under this section—

(a) shall be made by statutory instrument which, except in the case of the first order to be made, shall be subject to annulment in pursuance of a resolution of either House of Parliament;

(b) may make different provision for different cases or classes of case and for different areas; and

(c) may contain such transitional, incidental and supplementary provisions as appear to the Secretary of State to be desirable;

and the first order under this section shall not be made unless a draft of it has been laid before, and approved by a resolution of, each House of Parliament.

(3) In subsection (7) of section 63 of the Rent Act 1977 (expenditure arising in connection with rent officers etc.), in paragraph (a) after the words "this section" there shall be inserted "or an order under section 121 of the Housing Act 1988".

1986 c. 50.

(4) At the end of section 21(6) of the Social Security Act 1986 (regulations prescribing maximum family credit and maximum housing benefit) there shall be added the words "and regulations prescribing the appropriate maximum housing benefit may provide for benefit to be limited by reference to determinations made by rent officers in exercise of functions conferred under section 121 of the Housing Act 1988".

(5) In section 30 of that Act (housing benefit finance) at the end of subsection (2) there shall be added the words "and, in relation to rent allowance subsidy, the Secretary of State may exercise his discretion as to what is unreasonable for the purposes of paragraph (b) above by reference to determinations made by rent officers in exercise of functions conferred under section 121 of the Housing Act 1988".

(6) In section 51(1)(h) of that Act (regulations may require information etc. needed for determination of a claim) the reference to information or evidence needed for the determination of a claim includes a reference to information or evidence required by a rent officer for the purpose of a function conferred on him under this section.

(7) In this section "housing benefit" and "rent allowance subsidy" have the same meaning as in Part II of the Social Security Act 1986. 1986 c. 50

Right to buy etc. and grants to obtain accommodation

Variation of cost floor for right to buy discount. 1985 c. 68.

122.—(1) Section 131 of the Housing Act 1985 (limits on amount of discount in relation to the right to buy) shall be amended in accordance with subsections (2) and (3) below.

(2) In subsection (1) (the cost floor provision) for paragraph (a) there shall be substituted the following paragraph—

"(a) is to be treated as incurred at or after the beginning of that period of account of the landlord in which falls the date which is eight years, or such other period of time as may be specified in an order made by the Secretary of State, earlier than the relevant time, and".

(3) After subsection (1) there shall be inserted the following subsection—

"(1A) In subsection (1)(a) above "period of account", in relation to any costs, means the period for which the landlord made up those of its accounts in which account is taken of those costs."

(4) This section has effect in relation to the determination of discount in any case where—

(a) the relevant time falls on or after the date on which this section comes into force; or

(b) paragraph (a) above does not apply but the landlord has not before that date served on the tenant a notice complying with section 125 of the Housing Act 1985; or

(c) the tenant has before that date claimed to exercise the right to be granted a shared ownership lease but the landlord has not before that date served on the tenant a notice complying with section 147 of that Act; or

(d) the tenant has before that date served a notice under paragraph 1 of Schedule 8 to that Act (claiming to exercise the right to acquire an additional share under a shared ownership lease) but the landlord has not before that date served a notice under sub-paragraph (3) of that paragraph;

and, for the purposes of this subsection, no account shall be taken of any steps taken under section 177 of that Act (amendment or withdrawal and re-service of notice to correct mistakes).

(5) Expressions used in subsection (4) above have the same meaning as in Part V of the Housing Act 1985.

Amendment of Schedule 5 to Housing Act 1985.

123.—(1) Schedule 5 of the Housing Act 1985 (exceptions to the right to buy) shall be amended in accordance with this section.

(2) Paragraphs 6 and 8 shall be omitted.

(3) The repeal by this Act of paragraphs 6 and 8 of Schedule 5 shall not affect the operation of either of those paragraphs in any case where the tenant's notice claiming to exercise the right to buy was served before the repeal comes into force unless, at that time, no notice in response had been served under section 124 of the Housing Act 1985 (landlord's notice admitting or denying right to buy).

PART V

1985 c. 68.

(4) For the purposes of subsection (3) above, no account shall be taken of any steps taken under section 177 of the Housing Act 1985 (amendment or withdrawal and re-service of notice to correct mistakes).

Right to buy: tenant's sanction for landlord's delays.

124. After section 153 of the Housing Act 1985 there shall be inserted the following sections—

"Tenant's notices of delay.

153A.—(1) Where a secure tenant has claimed to exercise the right to buy, he may serve on his landlord a notice (in this section referred to as an "initial notice of delay") in any of the following cases, namely,—

(a) where the landlord has failed to serve a notice under section 124 within the period appropriate under subsection (2) of that section;

(b) where the tenant's right to buy has been established and the landlord has failed to serve a notice under section 125 within the period appropriate under subsection (1) of that section;

(c) where the tenant has claimed to exercise the right to be granted a shared ownership lease and the landlord has failed to serve a notice under section 146 within the period of the four weeks required by that section;

(d) where the tenant's right to a shared ownership lease has been established and the landlord has failed to serve a notice under section 147 within the period of the eight weeks required by that section; or

(e) where the tenant considers that delays on the part of the landlord are preventing him from exercising expeditiously his right to buy or his right to be granted a shared ownership lease;

and where an initial notice of delay specifies any of the cases in paragraphs (a) to (d), any reference in this section or section 153B to the default date is a reference to the end of the period referred to in the paragraph in question or, if it is later, the day appointed for the coming into force of section 124 of the Housing Act 1988.

(2) An initial notice of delay—

(a) shall specify the most recent action of which the tenant is aware which has been taken by the landlord pursuant to this Part of this Act; and

(b) shall specify a period (in this section referred to as "the response period"), not being less than one month, beginning on the date of service of the notice, within which the service by the landlord of a counter notice under subsection (3) will have the effect of cancelling the initial notice of delay.

(3) Within the response period specified in an initial notice of delay or at any time thereafter, the landlord may serve on the tenant a counter notice in either of the following circumstances—

(a) if the initial notice specifies any of the cases in paragraphs (a) to (d) of subsection (1) and the landlord has served, or is serving together with the counter notice, the required notice under section 124, section 125, section 146 or section 147, as the case may be; or

(b) if the initial notice specifies the case in subsection (1)(e) and there is no action under this Part which, at the beginning of the response period, it was for the landlord to take in order to allow the tenant expeditiously to exercise his right to buy or his right to be granted a shared ownership lease and which remains to be taken at the time of service of the counter notice.

(4) A counter notice under subsection (3) shall specify the circumstances by virtue of which it is served.

(5) At any time when—

(a) the response period specified in an initial notice of delay has expired, and

(b) the landlord has not served a counter notice under subsection (3),

the tenant may serve on the landlord a notice (in this section and section 153B referred to as an "operative notice of delay") which shall state that section 153B will apply to payments of rent made by the tenant on or after the default date or, if the initial notice of delay specified the case in subsection (1)(e), the date of the service of the notice.

(6) If, after a tenant has served an initial notice of delay, a counter notice has been served under subsection (3), then, whether or not the tenant has also served an operative notice of delay, if any of the cases in subsection (1) again arises, the tenant may serve a further initial notice of delay and the provisions of this section shall apply again accordingly.

Payments of rent attributable to purchase price etc.

153B.—(1) Where a secure tenant has served on his landlord an operative notice of delay, this section applies to any payment of rent which is made on or after the default date or, as the case may be, the date of the service of the notice and before the occurrence of any of the following events (and, if more than one event occurs, before the earliest to occur)—

(a) the service by the landlord of a counter notice under section 153A(3);

(b) the date on which the landlord makes to the tenant the grant required by section 138 or, as the case may be, section 150;

(c) the date on which the tenant serves notice under section 142(2) (claiming to be entitled to defer completion);

PART V

(d) the date on which the tenant withdraws or is deemed to have withdrawn the notice claiming to exercise the right to buy or, as the case may be, the notice claiming to exercise the right to be granted a shared ownership lease; and

(e) the date on which the tenant ceases to be entitled to exercise the right to buy.

(2) Except where this section ceases to apply on a date determined under any of paragraphs (c) to (e) of subsection (1), so much of any payment of rent to which this section applies as does not consist of—

(a) a sum due on account of rates, or

(b) a service charge (as defined in section 621A),

shall be treated not only as a payment of rent but also as a payment on account by the tenant which is to be taken into account in accordance with subsection (3).

(3) In a case where subsection (2) applies, the amount which, apart from this section, would be the purchase price or, as the case may be, the tenant's initial contribution for the grant of a shared ownership lease shall be reduced by an amount equal to the aggregate of—

(a) the total of any payments on account treated as having been paid by the tenant by virtue of subsection (2); and

(b) if those payments on account are derived from payments of rent referable to a period of more than twelve months, a sum equal to the appropriate percentage of the total referred to in paragraph (a).

(4) In subsection (3)(b) "the appropriate percentage" means 50 per cent. or such other percentage as may be prescribed."

Restriction on letting etc. of certain houses in National Parks etc.

1985 c. 68.

125.—(1) Section 37 of the Housing Act 1985 (restriction on disposals of dwelling-houses in National Parks etc.) shall be amended in accordance with this section.

(2) In subsection (2) (the covenanted limitation) after the word "his" there shall be inserted "(a)" and at the end there shall be added "and

(b) there will be no disposal by way of tenancy or licence without the written consent of the authority unless the disposal is to a person satisfying that condition or by a person whose only or principal home is and, throughout the duration of the tenancy or licence, remains the house".

(3) In subsection (3) (disposals limited to persons employed or living locally) after the words "application for consent" there shall be inserted the words "or, in the case of a disposal by way of tenancy or licence, preceding the disposal".

(4) At the end of subsection (4) (disposals in breach of covenant to be void) there shall be added "and, so far as it relates to disposals by way of tenancy or licence, such a covenant may be enforced by the local authority as if—

(a) the authority were possessed of land adjacent to the house concerned; and

(b) the covenant were expressed to be made for the benefit of such adjacent land".

(5) After subsection (4) there shall be inserted the following subsection—

"(4A) Any reference in the preceding provisions of this section to a disposal by way of tenancy or licence does not include a reference to a relevant disposal or an exempted disposal."

(6) This section has effect where the conveyance, grant or assignment referred to in subsection (1) of section 37 is executed on or after the commencement of this Act.

Restriction on disposal of dwelling-houses in National Parks etc. acquired under the right to buy.

1985 c. 68.

126.—(1) In Part V of the Housing Act 1985 (the right to buy), section 157 (restriction on disposal of dwelling-houses in National Parks etc.) shall be amended in accordance with this section.

(2) In subsection (2) (the covenanted limitation) after the word "his" there shall be inserted "(a)" and at the end there shall be added "and—

(b) there will be no disposal by way of tenancy or licence without the written consent of the landlord unless the disposal is to a person satisfying that condition or by a person whose only or principal home is and, throughout the duration of the tenancy or licence, remains the dwelling-house".

(3) In subsection (3) (disposals limited to persons employed or living locally) after the words "application for consent" there shall be inserted the words "or, in the case of a disposal by way of tenancy or licence, preceding the disposal".

(4) At the end of subsection (6) (disposals in breach of covenant to be void) there shall be added "and, so far as it relates to disposals by way of tenancy or licence, such a covenant may be enforced by the landlord as if—

(a) the landlord were possessed of land adjacent to the house concerned; and

(b) the covenant were expressed to be made for the benefit of such adjacent land".

(5) After subsection (6) there shall be inserted the following subsection—

"(6A) Any reference in the preceding provisions of this section to a disposal by way of tenancy or licence does not include a reference to a relevant disposal or an exempted disposal."

(6) This section has effect where the conveyance or grant referred to in subsection (1) of section 157 is executed on or after the commencement of this Act.

PART V
Preserved right to buy.
1985 c. 68.

127.—(1) In subsection (4) of section 171B of the Housing Act 1985 for paragraph (a) there shall be substituted the following paragraphs—

"(a) where the former secure tenancy was not a joint tenancy and, immediately before his death, the former secure tenant was tenant under an assured tenancy of a dwelling-house in relation to which he had the preserved right to buy, a member of the former secure tenant's family who acquired that assured tenancy under the will or intestacy of the former secure tenant;

(aa) where the former secure tenancy was not a joint tenancy, a member of the former secure tenant's family to whom the former secure tenant assigned his assured tenancy of a dwelling-house in relation to which, immediately before the assignment, he had the preserved right to buy".

(2) In subsection (2)(a) of section 171C of that Act after the word "paragraphs" there shall be inserted "1, 3 and".

(3) After subsection (4) of that section there shall be added the following subsection—

"(5) The disapplication by the regulations of paragraph 1 of Schedule 5 shall not be taken to authorise any action on the part of a charity which would conflict with the trusts of the charity."

Preservation of right to buy on disposal to private sector landlord: Scotland.
1987 c. 26.

128. After section 81 of the Housing (Scotland) Act 1987 there shall be inserted the following section—

"Preservation of right to buy on disposal to private sector landlord

Preservation of right to buy on disposal to private sector landlord.

81A.—(1) The right to buy provisions shall continue to apply where a person ceases to be a secure tenant of a house by reason of the disposal by the landlord of an interest in the house to a private sector landlord.

(2) The right to buy provisions shall not, however, continue to apply under subsection (1) in such circumstances as may be prescribed.

(3) The continued application under subsection (1) of the right to buy provisions shall be in accordance with and subject to such provision as is prescribed which may—

(a) include—

(i) such additions and exceptions to, and adaptations and modifications of, the right to buy provisions in their continued application by virtue of this section; and

(ii) such incidental, supplementary and transitional provisions;

as the Secretary of State considers appropriate;

(b) differ as between different cases or descriptions of case and as between different areas;

(c) relate to a particular disposal.

(4) Without prejudice to the generality of subsection (3), provision may be made by virtue of it— PART V

(a) specifying the persons entitled to the benefit of the right to buy provisions in their continued application by virtue of this section;

(b) preventing, except with the consent of the Secretary of State, the disposal by the private sector landlord of less than his whole interest in a house in relation to which the right to buy provisions continue to apply by virtue of this section;

(c) ensuring that where, under Ground 9 of Schedule 5 to the Housing (Scotland) Act 1988 (availability of suitable alternative accommodation), the sheriff makes an order for possession of a house in relation to which the right to buy provisions continue to apply by virtue of this section and the tenant would not have the right under this Part (other than this section) to buy the house which is or will be available by way of alternative accommodation, these provisions as so continued will apply in relation to the house which is or will be so available.

(5) In this section—

(a) "secure tenant" means a tenant under a secure tenancy;

(b) "private sector landlord" means a landlord other than one of those set out in sub-paragraphs (i) to (iv) and (viii) and (ix) of paragraph (a) of subsection (2) of section 61;

(c) the "right to buy provisions" means the provisions of this Act relating to the right of a tenant of a house to purchase it under this Part and to his rights in respect of a loan."

Schemes for payments to assist local housing authority tenants to obtain other accommodation.

129.—(1) In accordance with a scheme made by a local housing authority and approved by the Secretary of State under this section, the authority may make grants to or for the benefit of qualifying tenants or licensees of the authority with a view to assisting each person to whom or for whose benefit a grant is made to obtain accommodation otherwise than as a tenant or licensee of the authority either—

(a) by acquiring an interest in a dwelling-house; or

(b) by carrying out works to a dwelling-house to provide additional accommodation; or

(c) by both of those means.

(2) A scheme under this section shall contain such provisions as the local housing authority considers appropriate together with any which the Secretary of State may require as a condition of his approval and, without prejudice to the generality, a scheme may include provisions specifying, or providing for the determination of—

PART V

(a) the persons who are qualifying tenants or licensees for the purposes of the scheme;

(b) the interests which qualifying tenants or licensees may be assisted to acquire;

(c) the works for the carrying out of which grants may be made;

(d) the circumstances in which a grant may be made for the benefit of a qualifying tenant or licensee;

(e) the amount of the grant which may be made in any particular case and the terms on which it may be made;

(f) the limits on the total number and amount of grants which may be made; and

(g) the period within which the scheme is to apply.

(3) The Secretary of State may approve a scheme made by a local housing authority under this section with or without conditions and, where a scheme has been approved, the authority shall take such steps as it considers appropriate to bring the scheme to the attention of persons likely to be able to benefit from it and shall take such other steps (if any) as the Secretary of State may direct in any particular case to secure publicity for the scheme.

(4) The Secretary of State may revoke an approval of a scheme under this section by a notice given to the local housing authority concerned; and, where such a notice is given, the revocation shall not affect the operation of the scheme in relation to any grants made or agreed before the date of the notice.

(5) Any grant made pursuant to a scheme under this section—

(a) shall be regarded as a grant of a capital nature for the purposes of Part VIII of the Local Government, Planning and Land Act 1980 (capital expenditure of local authorities); and

1980 c. 65.

(b) shall be regarded as expenditure on management for the purposes of Part II of Schedule 14 to the Housing Act 1985 (debits to the Housing Revenue Account).

1985 c. 68.

(6) Where a scheme made by a local housing authority under this section has been approved, a person dealing with the authority shall not be concerned to see or enquire whether the terms of the scheme have been or are being complied with; and any failure to comply with the terms of a scheme shall not invalidate any grant purporting to be made in accordance with the scheme unless the person to whom the grant is made has actual notice of the failure.

(7) In this section—

(a) "local housing authority" has the meaning assigned by section 1 of the Housing Act 1985;

(b) "dwelling-house" has the meaning assigned by section 112 of that Act; and

(c) "tenant" does not include a tenant under a long tenancy, as defined in section 115 of that Act.

Repair notices and improvement grants

Repair notices.

130.—(1) Part VI of the Housing Act 1985 (repair notices) shall have effect subject to the amendments in Schedule 15 to this Act.

(2) In section 604 of that Act (fitness for human habitation) after subsection (1) there shall be inserted the following subsection—

"(1A) In the application, for the purposes of Part VI, of subsection (1) to premises consisting of a flat, within the meaning of that Part, regard shall be had not only to the condition of the flat itself but also to the condition of any other part of the building as it affects the flat and, accordingly, the flat may be deemed to be unfit by reference to the defective condition of a part of the building outside the flat (whether or not that part is itself used, or suitable for use, as a dwelling)."

(3) The amendments in subsection (2) above and Schedule 15 to this Act do not have effect in relation to any repair notice, within the meaning of the said Part VI, served before this section comes into force.

Letting conditions applicable to improvement grants etc.
1985 c. 68.

131.—(1) With respect to applications for grants approved after the commencement of this Act, Part XV of the Housing Act 1985 (grants for works of improvement, repair and conversion) shall have effect subject to the following provisions of this section.

(2) In each of the following provisions—

(a) section 464 (preliminary condition: certificates as to future occupation), in subsection (5) (certificate of availability for letting), and

(b) section 501 (condition as to availability for letting), in subsection (2) (the terms of the condition),

in paragraph (a) after the word "holiday" there shall be inserted "on a tenancy which is not a long tenancy and".

(3) After the words "Rent (Agriculture) Act 1976", in each place where they occur in—

(a) section 464(5),

(b) section 501(2), and

(c) subsection (2)(d) of section 503 (restriction on imposition of further conditions in relation to certain grants),

there shall be inserted "or is occupied under an assured agricultural occupancy, within the meaning of Part I of the Housing Act 1988".

(4) In section 504 (further conditions as to letting of dwelling), at the beginning of subsection (1) there shall be inserted the words "Subject to subsection (1A)"; in paragraph (a) of that subsection after the word "letting" there shall be inserted "on an assured tenancy which is not a long tenancy or"; and at the end of that subsection there shall be inserted the following subsection—

"(1A) Paragraphs (d) to (f) of subsection (1) do not apply in the case of a dwelling which is or is to be let or available for letting on an assured tenancy."

(5) In subsection (2) of section 504 (definitions) after the words "subsection (1)" there shall be inserted "and subsection (1A)" and before paragraph (a) there shall be inserted the following paragraph—

PART V

"(aa) "assured tenancy" means a tenancy which is an assured tenancy within the meaning of Part I of the Housing Act 1988 or would be such a tenancy if paragraphs 3, 6, 7 and 10 of Schedule 1 to that Act were omitted".

(6) In section 526 (index of defined expressions in Part XV), after the entry relating to "local housing authority" there shall be inserted—

"long tenancy .... section 115".

(7) Without prejudice to subsection (1) above, where an application for a grant—

(a) was made but not approved before the commencement of this Act, and

(b) was accompanied by a certificate of availability for letting in a form which does not take account of the amendments of section 464(5) by subsections (2) and (3) above,

the certificate shall be treated as if it were in a form which takes account of the amendments made by those subsections.

(8) Without prejudice to subsection (1) above, where a grant has been approved before the commencement of this Act and—

(a) section 501(2) applies to impose a condition of the grant, or

(b) conditions have been imposed in terms of section 504(1),

the condition or conditions shall have effect as if it or they were in a form which takes account of the amendments made by subsection (3) or, as the case may be, subsections (4) and (5) above.

Disposals of housing stock

Consents to disposals of housing stock and application of receipts. 1985 c. 68.

132.—(1) At the end of subsection (4) of section 34 of the Housing Act 1985 (consent to disposals of land held for the purposes of Part II—provision of housing accommodation) and at the end of subsection (4) of section 43 of that Act (consent for certain disposals of other houses) there shall be inserted the subsections set out in subsection (2) below.

(2) The subsections referred to in subsection (1) above and subsection (3) below are as follows—

"(4A) The matters to which the Secretary of State may have regard in determining whether to give consent and, if so, to what conditions consent should be subject shall include—

(a) the extent (if any) to which the person to whom the proposed disposal is to be made (in this subsection referred to as "the intending purchaser") is, or is likely to be, dependent upon, controlled by or subject to influence from the local authority making the disposal or any members or officers of that authority;

(b) the extent (if any) to which the proposed disposal would result in the intending purchaser becoming the predominant or a substantial owner in any area of housing accommodation let on tenancies or subject to licences;

(c) the terms of the proposed disposal; and

(d) any other matters whatsoever which he considers relevant.

(4B) Where the Secretary of State gives consent to a disposal by a local authority, he may give directions as to the purpose for which any capital money received by the authority in respect of the disposal is to be applied and, where any such directions are given, nothing in any enactment shall require his consent to be given for the application of the capital money concerned in accordance with the directions." PART V

(3) Section 13 of the Housing (Scotland) Act 1987 (power of Secretary of State to impose conditions in sale of local authority houses) shall be renumbered as subsection (1) of that section and after that subsection there shall be inserted as subsections (2) and (3) the subsections which are set out in subsection (2) above and there numbered (4A) and (4B). 1987 c. 26.

(4) In section 153 of the Local Government Act 1972 (application of capital money on disposal of land), in subsection (1) after the words "127(4) above" there shall be inserted "to any directions given in respect of the disposal under section 43(4B) of the Housing Act 1985". 1972 c. 70.

(5) In section 430 of the Housing Act 1985 (application of capital money received on disposal of land), in subsection (1) after the word "applied", in the first place where it occurs, there shall be inserted "in accordance with any directions given in respect of the disposal under section 34(4B) or section 43(4B) and, subject thereto". 1985 c. 68.

(6) In section 208 of the Housing (Scotland) Act 1987 (application of receipts from disposal of certain land), in subsection (2) there shall be inserted at the end the words "or has made directions under section 13(3)".

(7) In section 26 of the Local Government Act 1988 (provisions as to consents under section 25 for provision of financial assistance etc.), in subsection (5) (which excludes consent under various enactments where consent is given to a disposal of land under section 25) after the words "such a consent" there shall be inserted "then, if the consent given for the purposes of section 25 above so provides". 1988 c. 9.

(8) This section shall be deemed to have come into force on 9th June 1988.

Consent required for certain subsequent disposals.

133.—(1) Where consent is required for a disposal (in this section referred to as "the original disposal") by virtue of section 32 or section 43 of the Housing Act 1985 and that consent does not provide otherwise, the person who acquires the land or house on the disposal shall not dispose of it except with the consent of the Secretary of State; but nothing in this section shall apply in relation to an exempt disposal as defined in section 81(8) above.

(2) Where an estate or interest of the person who acquired the land or house on the original disposal has been mortgaged or charged, the prohibition in subsection (1) above applies also to a disposal by the mortgagee or chargee in exercise of a power of sale or leasing, whether or not the disposal is in the name of the person who so acquired the land or house; and in any case where—

(a) by operation of law or by virtue of an order of a court, the land or house which has been acquired passes or is transferred from the person who so acquired it to another person, and

PART V

(b) that passing or transfer does not constitute a disposal for which consent is required under this section,

this section (including, where there is more than one such passing or transfer, this subsection) shall apply as if the other person to whom the land or house passes or is transferred were the person who acquired it on the original disposal.

(3) Where subsection (1) above applies—

1985 c. 68.

(a) if section 34 of the Housing Act 1985 applies to the consent given to the original disposal, subsections (2)(b) and (3) to (4A) of that section shall also apply to any consent required by virtue of this section;

(b) if the consent to the original disposal was given under section 43 of that Act, subsections (2)(b) and (3) to (4A) of that section shall also apply to any consent required by virtue of this section;

(c) in the application of subsection (4A) of section 34 or section 43 to any consent required by virtue of this section, any reference to the local authority making the disposal shall be construed as a reference to the local authority making the original disposal; and

(d) the instrument by which the original disposal is effected shall contain a statement in a form approved by the Chief Land Registrar that the requirement of this section as to consent applies to a subsequent disposal of the land or house by the person to whom the original disposal was made.

(4) Subsection (4) of section 32 of the Housing Act 1985 or, as the case may be, subsection (5) of section 43 of that Act (options to purchase as disposals) applies for the purposes of this section.

(5) Before giving any consent required by virtue of this section, the Secretary of State—

(a) shall satisfy himself that the person who is seeking the consent has taken appropriate steps to consult every tenant of any land or house proposed to be disposed of; and

(b) shall have regard to the responses of any such tenants to that consultation.

1985 c. 69.

(6) If, apart from subsection (7) below, the consent of the Housing Corporation or Housing for Wales would be required under section 9 of the Housing Associations Act 1985 (control of dispositions of land by housing associations) for a disposal in respect of which, by virtue of subsection (1) above, the consent of the Secretary of State is required, the Secretary of State shall consult that body before giving his consent for the purposes of this section.

(7) No consent shall be required under the said section 9 for any disposal in respect of which consent is given in accordance with subsection (6) above.

1925 c. 21.

(8) Where the title of the authority to the land or house which is disposed of by the original disposal is not registered, and the original disposal is a conveyance, grant or assignment of a description mentioned in section 123 of the Land Registration Act 1925 (compulsory registration of title)—

(a) that section applies in relation to the instrument by which the original disposal is effected whether or not the land or house is in an area in which an Order in Council under section 120 of that Act (areas of compulsory registration) is in force;

(b) the authority shall give to the person to whom the original disposal is made a certificate in a form approved by the Chief Land Registrar stating that the authority is entitled to make the disposal subject only to such encumbrances, rights and interests as are stated in the instrument by which the original disposal is effected or summarised in the certificate; and

(c) for the purpose of registration of title, the Chief Land Registrar shall accept such a certificate as evidence of the facts stated in it, but if as a result he has to meet a claim against him under the Land Registration Acts 1925 to 1986 the authority by whom the original disposal was made is liable to indemnify him.

(9) On an application being made for registration of a disposition of registered land or, as the case may be, of the title under a disposition of unregistered land, if the instrument by which the original disposal is effected contains the statement required by subsection (3)(d) above, the Chief Land Registrar shall enter in the register a restriction stating the requirement of this section as to consent to a subsequent disposal.

(10) In every case where the consent of the Secretary of State is required for the original disposal by virtue of section 32 or section 43 of the Housing Act 1985 (whether or not consent is required under this section to a subsequent disposal), the authority by which the original disposal is made shall furnish to the person to whom it is made a copy of that consent. 1985 c. 68.

Consent required for certain subsequent disposals: Scotland.

134. In Part I of the Housing (Scotland) Act 1987 (provision of housing) after section 12 there shall be inserted the following section— 1987 c. 26.

"Consent of Secretary of State required for certain subsequent disposals.

12A.—(1) Where a person acquires any land or house from a local authority under section 12(1)(c) or (d) above and the consent of the Secretary of State is required under section 12(7) above to the local authority's disposal of the land or house to that person, that person shall not dispose of the land or house without the consent in writing of the Secretary of State.

(2) Any consent for the purposes of subsection (1) above may be given either in respect of a particular disposal or in respect of disposals of any class or description (including disposals in particular areas) and either unconditionally or subject to conditions.

(3) Before giving any consent for the purposes of subsection (1) above, the Secretary of State—

(a) shall satisfy himself that the person who is seeking the consent has taken appropriate steps to consult every tenant of any land or house proposed to be disposed of; and

(b) shall have regard to the responses of any such tenants to that consultation.

PART V

(4) The consent of Scottish Homes under section 9 of the Housing Associations Act 1985 (control of dispositions) is not required for any disposal, or disposals of any class or description, in respect of which consent is given under subsection (1) above.

(5) In this section references to disposing of property include references to—

(a) granting or disposing of any interest in property;

(b) entering into a contract to dispose of property or to grant or dispose of any such interest; and

(c) granting an option to acquire property or any such interest."

Consultation before disposal: Scotland.
1987 c. 26.

135.—(1) In Part III of the Housing (Scotland) Act 1987 (rights of public sector tenants) after section 81 there shall be inserted the following section—

"*Consultation before disposal to private sector landlord*

Consultation before disposal to private sector landlord.

81B. The provisions of Schedule 6A have effect with respect to the duties of—

(a) a local authority proposing to dispose of houses let on secure tenancies;

(b) the Secretary of State in considering whether to give his consent under section 12(7) to such a disposal,

to have regard to the views of tenants liable as a result of the disposal to cease to be secure tenants (that is to say, tenants under secure tenancies)."

(2) After Schedule 6 to the Housing (Scotland) Act 1987 there shall be inserted, as Schedule 6A, the Schedule set out in Schedule 16 to this Act.

(3) The amendments made by this section apply to disposals after the coming into force of this section.

Application of capital money to meet costs of disposals of land.
1985 c. 68.

136.—(1) At the end of section 430 of the Housing Act 1985 (application of capital money received on disposal of land) there shall be inserted the following subsection—

"(3) In the case of capital money received by a local authority in respect of—

(a) disposals of land held for the purposes of Part II (provision of housing), and

(b) any other disposals of land made by virtue of Part V (the right to buy) which do not fall within paragraph (a),

the reference in subsection (1) to any other purpose for which capital money may properly be applied includes a reference to the purpose of meeting the administrative costs of and incidental to such disposals; and, accordingly, the reference in subsection (2) to subsection (1) includes a reference to that subsection as extended by virtue of this subsection."

PART V

(2) In section 72 of the Local Government, Planning and Land Act 1980 (expenditure which authorities may make), in subsection (7) (net capital receipts for any year defined as the receipts which are capital receipts for the purposes of Part VIII of that Act, reduced by certain payments) after the words "reduced by" there shall be inserted— 1980 c. 65.

"(a) any amount of capital money which in that year is applied for the purpose specified in section 430(3) of the Housing Act 1985 (meeting administrative costs of and incidental to certain disposals of land); and

(b)".

Codes of practice

137.—(1) Section 47 of the Race Relations Act 1976 (codes of practice) shall be amended in accordance with the following provisions of this section. Codes of practice in field of rented housing. 1976 c. 74.

(2) In subsection (1) for the words "either or both" there shall be substituted the words "all or any" and at the end there shall be added the following paragraphs—

"(c) the elimination of discrimination in the field of housing let on tenancies or occupied under licences ("the field of rented housing");

(d) the promotion of equality of opportunity in the field of rented housing between persons of different racial groups".

(3) In subsection (3), after the words "code of practice" there shall be inserted "relating to the field of employment" and after that subsection there shall be inserted the following subsection—

"(3A) In the course of preparing any draft code of practice relating to the field of rented housing for eventual publication under subsection (2) the Commission shall consult with such organisations or bodies as appear to the Commission to be appropriate having regard to the content of the draft code."

(4) In subsection (4) for the words "the draft" there shall be substituted "a draft code of practice".

(5) In subsection (10) after the words "industrial tribunal" there shall be inserted "a county court or, in Scotland, a sheriff court" and after the words "the tribunal" there shall be inserted "or the court".

Supplementary

138.—(1) There shall be paid out of money provided by Parliament— Financial provisions.

(a) any sums required for the payment by the Secretary of State of grants under this Act;

(b) any sums required to enable the Secretary of State to make payments to housing action trusts established under Part III of this Act;

(c) any other expenses of the Secretary of State under this Act; and

(d) any increase attributable to this Act in the sums so payable under any other enactment.

PART V

(2) Any sums received by the Secretary of State under this Act, other than those required to be paid into the National Loans Fund, shall be paid into the Consolidated Fund.

Application to Isles of Scilly.

139.—(1) This Act applies to the Isles of Scilly subject to such exceptions, adaptations and modifications as the Secretary of State may by order direct.

(2) The power to make an order under this section shall be exercisable by statutory instrument which shall be subject to annulment in pursuance of a resolution of either House of Parliament.

Amendments and repeals.

1988 c. 43.

140.—(1) Schedule 17 to this Act, which contains minor amendments and amendments consequential on the provisions of this Act and the Housing (Scotland) Act 1988, shall have effect and in that Schedule Part I contains general amendments and Part II contains amendments consequential on the establishment of Housing for Wales.

(2) The enactments specified in Schedule 18 to this Act, which include some that are spent, are hereby repealed to the extent specified in the third column of that Schedule, but subject to any provision at the end of that Schedule and to any saving in Chapter V of Part I of or Schedule 17 to this Act.

Short title, commencement and extent.

141.—(1) This Act may be cited as the Housing Act 1988.

(2) The provisions of Parts II and IV of this Act and sections 119, 122, 124, 128, 129, 135 and 140 above shall come into force on such day as the Secretary of State may by order made by statutory instrument appoint, and different days may be so appointed for different provisions or for different purposes.

(3) Part I and this Part of this Act, other than sections 119, 122, 124, 128, 129, 132, 133, 134, 135 and 138 onwards, shall come into force at the expiry of the period of two months beginning on the day it is passed; and any reference in those provisions to the commencement of this Act shall be construed accordingly.

(4) An order under subsection (2) above may make such transitional provisions as appear to the Secretary of State necessary or expedient in connection with the provisions brought into force by the order.

(5) Parts I, III and IV of this Act and this Part, except sections 118, 128, 132, 134, 135 and 137 onwards, extend to England and Wales only.

(6) This Act does not extend to Northern Ireland.

SCHEDULES

SCHEDULE 1

Section 1.

TENANCIES WHICH CANNOT BE ASSURED TENANCIES

PART I

THE TENANCIES

Tenancies entered into before commencement

1. A tenancy which is entered into before, or pursuant to a contract made before, the commencement of this Act.

Tenancies of dwelling-houses with high rateable values

2. A tenancy under which the dwelling-house has for the time being a rateable value which,—

(a) if it is in Greater London, exceeds £1,500; and

(b) if it is elsewhere, exceeds £750.

Tenancies at a low rent

3.—(1) A tenancy under which either no rent is payable or the rent payable is less than two-thirds of the rateable value of the dwelling-house for the time being.

(2) In determining whether the rent under a tenancy falls within sub-paragraph (1) above, there shall be disregarded such part (if any) of the sums payable by the tenant as is expressed (in whatever terms) to be payable in respect of rates, services, management, repairs, maintenance or insurance, unless it could not have been regarded by the parties to the tenancy as a part so payable.

Business tenancies

4. A tenancy to which Part II of the Landlord and Tenant Act 1954 applies (business tenancies). 1954 c. 56.

Licensed premises

5. A tenancy under which the dwelling-house consists of or comprises premises licensed for the sale of intoxicating liquors for consumption on the premises.

Tenancies of agricultural land

6.—(1) A tenancy under which agricultural land, exceeding two acres, is let together with the dwelling-house.

(2) In this paragraph "agricultural land" has the meaning set out in section 26(3)(a) of the General Rate Act 1967 (exclusion of agricultural land and premises from liability for rating). 1967 c. 9.

Tenancies of agricultural holdings

7. A tenancy under which the dwelling-house—

(a) is comprised in an agricultural holding (within the meaning of the Agricultural Holdings Act 1986); and 1986 c. 5.

(b) is occupied by the person responsible for the control (whether as tenant or as servant or agent of the tenant) of the farming of the holding.

SCH. 1

Lettings to students

8.—(1) A tenancy which is granted to a person who is pursuing, or intends to pursue, a course of study provided by a specified educational institution and is so granted either by that institution or by another specified institution or body of persons.

(2) In sub-paragraph (1) above "specified" means specified, or of a class specified, for the purposes of this paragraph by regulations made by the Secretary of State by statutory instrument.

(3) A statutory instrument made in the exercise of the power conferred by sub-paragraph (2) above shall be subject to annulment in pursuance of a resolution of either House of Parliament.

Holiday lettings

9. A tenancy the purpose of which is to confer on the tenant the right to occupy the dwelling-house for a holiday.

Resident landlords

10.—(1) A tenancy in respect of which the following conditions are fulfilled—

(a) that the dwelling-house forms part only of a building and, except in a case where the dwelling-house also forms part of a flat, the building is not a purpose-built block of flats; and

(b) that, subject to Part III of this Schedule, the tenancy was granted by an individual who, at the time when the tenancy was granted, occupied as his only or principal home another dwelling-house which,—

(i) in the case mentioned in paragraph (a) above, also forms part of the flat; or

(ii) in any other case, also forms part of the building; and

(c) that, subject to Part III of this Schedule, at all times since the tenancy was granted the interest of the landlord under the tenancy has belonged to an individual who, at the time he owned that interest, occupied as his only or principal home another dwelling-house which,—

(i) in the case mentioned in paragraph (a) above, also formed part of the flat; or

(ii) in any other case, also formed part of the building; and

(d) that the tenancy is not one which is excluded from this sub-paragraph by sub-paragraph (3) below.

(2) If a tenancy was granted by two or more persons jointly, the reference in sub-paragraph (1)(b) above to an individual is a reference to any one of those persons and if the interest of the landlord is for the time being held by two or more persons jointly, the reference in sub-paragraph (1)(c) above to an individual is a reference to any one of those persons.

(3) A tenancy (in this sub-paragraph referred to as "the new tenancy") is excluded from sub-paragraph (1) above if—

(a) it is granted to a person (alone, or jointly with others) who, immediately before it was granted, was a tenant under an assured tenancy (in this sub-paragraph referred to as "the former tenancy") of the same dwelling-house or of another dwelling-house which forms part of the building in question; and

(b) the landlord under the new tenancy and under the former tenancy is the same person or, if either of those tenancies is or was granted by two or more persons jointly, the same person is the landlord or one of the landlords under each tenancy.

Crown tenancies SCH. 1

11.—(1) A tenancy under which the interest of the landlord belongs to Her Majesty in right of the Crown or to a government department or is held in trust for Her Majesty for the purposes of a government department.

(2) The reference in sub-paragraph (1) above to the case where the interest of the landlord belongs to Her Majesty in right of the Crown does not include the case where that interest is under the management of the Crown Estate Commissioners.

Local authority tenancies etc.

12.—(1) A tenancy under which the interest of the landlord belongs to—

(a) a local authority, as defined in sub-paragraph (2) below;

(b) the Commission for the New Towns;

(c) the Development Board for Rural Wales;

(d) an urban development corporation established by an order under section 135 of the Local Government, Planning and Land Act 1980; 1980 c. 65.

(e) a development corporation, within the meaning of the New Towns Act 1981; 1981 c. 64.

(f) an authority established under section 10 of the Local Government Act 1985 (waste disposal authorities); 1985 c. 51.

(g) a residuary body, within the meaning of the Local Government Act 1985;

(h) a fully mutual housing association; or

(i) a housing action trust established under Part III of this Act.

(2) The following are local authorities for the purposes of sub-paragraph (1)(a) above—

(a) the council of a county, district or London borough;

(b) the Common Council of the City of London;

(c) the Council of the Isles of Scilly;

(d) the Broads Authority;

(e) the Inner London Education Authority; and

(f) a joint authority, within the meaning of the Local Government Act 1985.

Transitional cases

13.—(1) A protected tenancy, within the meaning of the Rent Act 1977. 1977 c. 42.

(2) A housing association tenancy, within the meaning of Part VI of that Act.

(3) A secure tenancy.

(4) Where a person is a protected occupier of a dwelling-house, within the meaning of the Rent (Agriculture) Act 1976, the relevant tenancy, within the meaning of that Act, by virtue of which he occupies the dwelling-house. 1976 c. 80.

SCH. 1

PART II

RATEABLE VALUES

14.—(1) The rateable value of a dwelling-house at any time shall be ascertained for the purposes of Part I of this Schedule as follows—

(a) if the dwelling-house is a hereditament for which a rateable value is then shown in the valuation list, it shall be that rateable value;

(b) if the dwelling-house forms part only of such a hereditament or consists of or forms part of more than one such hereditament, its rateable value shall be taken to be such value as is found by a proper apportionment or aggregation of the rateable value or values so shown.

(2) Any question arising under this Part of this Schedule as to the proper apportionment or aggregation of any value or values shall be determined by the county court and the decision of that court shall be final.

15. Where, after the time at which the rateable value of a dwelling-house is material for the purposes of any provision of Part I of this Schedule, the valuation list is altered so as to vary the rateable value of the hereditament of which the dwelling-house consists (in whole or in part) or forms part and the alteration has effect from that time or from an earlier time, the rateable value of the dwelling-house at the material time shall be ascertained as if the value shown in the valuation list at the material time had been the value shown in the list as altered.

16. Paragraphs 14 and 15 above apply in relation to any other land which, under section 2 of this Act, is treated as part of a dwelling-house as they apply in relation to the dwelling-house itself.

PART III

PROVISIONS FOR DETERMINING APPLICATION OF PARAGRAPH 10 (RESIDENT LANDLORDS)

17.—(1) In determining whether the condition in paragraph 10(1)(c) above is at any time fulfilled with respect to a tenancy, there shall be disregarded—

(a) any period of not more than twenty-eight days, beginning with the date on which the interest of the landlord under the tenancy becomes vested at law and in equity in an individual who, during that period, does not occupy as his only or principal home another dwelling-house which forms part of the building or, as the case may be, flat concerned;

(b) if, within a period falling within paragraph (a) above, the individual concerned notifies the tenant in writing of his intention to occupy as his only or principal home another dwelling-house in the building or, as the case may be, flat concerned, the period beginning with the date on which the interest of the landlord under the tenancy becomes vested in that individual as mentioned in that paragraph and ending—

(i) at the expiry of the period of six months beginning on that date, or

(ii) on the date on which that interest ceases to be so vested, or

(iii) on the date on which that interest becomes again vested in such an individual as is mentioned in paragraph 10(1)(c) or the condition in that paragraph becomes deemed to be fulfilled by virtue of paragraph 18(1) or paragraph 20 below,

whichever is the earlier; and

(c) any period of not more than two years beginning with the date on which the interest of the landlord under the tenancy becomes, and during which it remains, vested—

(i) in trustees as such; or

(ii) by virtue of section 9 of the Administration of Estates Act 1925, in the Probate Judge, within the meaning of that Act. 1925 c. 23.

(2) Where the interest of the landlord under a tenancy becomes vested at law and in equity in two or more persons jointly, of whom at least one was an individual, sub-paragraph (1) above shall have effect subject to the following modifications—

(a) in paragraph (a) for the words from "an individual" to "occupy" there shall be substituted "the joint landlords if, during that period none of them occupies"; and

(b) in paragraph (b) for the words "the individual concerned" there shall be substituted "any of the joint landlords who is an individual" and for the words "that individual" there shall be substituted "the joint landlords".

18.—(1) During any period when—

(a) the interest of the landlord under the tenancy referred to in paragraph 10 above is vested in trustees as such, and

(b) that interest is or, if it is held on trust for sale, the proceeds of its sale are held on trust for any person who or for two or more persons of whom at least one occupies as his only or principal home a dwelling-house which forms part of the building or, as the case may be, flat referred to in paragraph 10(1)(a),

the condition in paragraph 10(1)(c) shall be deemed to be fulfilled and accordingly, no part of that period shall be disregarded by virtue of paragraph 17 above.

(2) If a period during which the condition in paragraph 10(1)(c) is deemed to be fulfilled by virtue of sub-paragraph (1) above comes to an end on the death of a person who was in occupation of a dwelling-house as mentioned in paragraph (b) of that sub-paragraph, then, in determining whether that condition is at any time thereafter fulfilled, there shall be disregarded any period—

(a) which begins on the date of the death;

(b) during which the interest of the landlord remains vested as mentioned in sub-paragraph (1)(a) above; and

(c) which ends at the expiry of the period of two years beginning on the date of the death or on any earlier date on which the condition in paragraph 10(1)(c) becomes again deemed to be fulfilled by virtue of sub-paragraph (1) above.

19. In any case where—

(a) immediately before a tenancy comes to an end the condition in paragraph 10(1)(c) is deemed to be fulfilled by virtue of paragraph 18(1) above, and

(b) on the coming to an end of that tenancy the trustees in whom the interest of the landlord is vested grant a new tenancy of the same or substantially the same dwelling-house to a person (alone or jointly with others) who was the tenant or one of the tenants under the previous tenancy,

the condition in paragraph 10(1)(b) above shall be deemed to be fulfilled with respect to the new tenancy.

20.—(1) The tenancy referred to in paragraph 10 above falls within this paragraph if the interest of the landlord under the tenancy becomes vested in the personal representatives of a deceased person acting in that capacity.

SCH. 1 (2) If the tenancy falls within this paragraph, the condition in paragraph 10(1)(c) shall be deemed to be fulfilled for any period, beginning with the date on which the interest becomes vested in the personal representatives and not exceeding two years, during which the interest of the landlord remains so vested.

21. Throughout any period which, by virtue of paragraph 17 or paragraph 18(2) above, falls to be disregarded for the purpose of determining whether the condition in paragraph 10(1)(c) is fulfilled with respect to a tenancy, no order shall be made for possession of the dwelling-house subject to that tenancy, other than an order which might be made if that tenancy were or, as the case may be, had been an assured tenancy.

22. For the purposes of paragraph 10 above, a building is a purpose-built block of flats if as constructed it contained, and it contains, two or more flats; and for this purpose "flat" means a dwelling-house which—

(a) forms part only of a building; and

(b) is separated horizontally from another dwelling-house which forms part of the same building.

Section 7.

SCHEDULE 2

GROUNDS FOR POSSESSION OF DWELLING-HOUSES LET ON ASSURED TENANCIES

PART I

GROUNDS ON WHICH COURT MUST ORDER POSSESSION

Ground 1

Not later than the beginning of the tenancy the landlord gave notice in writing to the tenant that possession might be recovered on this ground or the court is of the opinion that it is just and equitable to dispense with the requirement of notice and (in either case)—

(a) at some time before the beginning of the tenancy, the landlord who is seeking possession or, in the case of joint landlords seeking possession, at least one of them occupied the dwelling-house as his only or principal home; or

(b) the landlord who is seeking possession or, in the case of joint landlords seeking possession, at least one of them requires the dwelling-house as his or his spouse's only or principal home and neither the landlord (or, in the case of joint landlords, any one of them) nor any other person who, as landlord, derived title under the landlord who gave the notice mentioned above acquired the reversion on the tenancy for money or money's worth.

Ground 2

The dwelling-house is subject to a mortgage granted before the beginning of the tenancy and—

1925 c. 20. (a) the mortgagee is entitled to exercise a power of sale conferred on him by the mortgage or by section 101 of the Law of Property Act 1925; and

(b) the mortgagee requires possession of the dwelling-house for the purpose of disposing of it with vacant possession in exercise of that power; and

(c) either notice was given as mentioned in Ground 1 above or the court is satisfied that it is just and equitable to dispense with the requirement of notice;

and for the purposes of this ground "mortgage" includes a charge and "mortgagee" shall be construed accordingly.

Ground 3

The tenancy is a fixed term tenancy for a term not exceeding eight months and—

(a) not later than the beginning of the tenancy the landlord gave notice in writing to the tenant that possession might be recovered on this ground; and

(b) at some time within the period of twelve months ending with the beginning of the tenancy, the dwelling-house was occupied under a right to occupy it for a holiday.

Ground 4

The tenancy is a fixed term tenancy for a term not exceeding twelve months and—

(a) not later than the beginning of the tenancy the landlord gave notice in writing to the tenant that possession might be recovered on this ground; and

(b) at some time within the period of twelve months ending with the beginning of the tenancy, the dwelling-house was let on a tenancy falling within paragraph 8 of Schedule 1 to this Act.

Ground 5

The dwelling-house is held for the purpose of being available for occupation by a minister of religion as a residence from which to perform the duties of his office and—

(a) not later than the beginning of the tenancy the landlord gave notice in writing to the tenant that possession might be recovered on this ground; and

(b) the court is satisfied that the dwelling-house is required for occupation by a minister of religion as such a residence.

Ground 6

The landlord who is seeking possession or, if that landlord is a registered housing association or charitable housing trust, a superior landlord intends to demolish or reconstruct the whole or a substantial part of the dwelling-house or to carry out substantial works on the dwelling-house or any part thereof or any building of which it forms part and the following conditions are fulfilled—

(a) the intended work cannot reasonably be carried out without the tenant giving up possession of the dwelling-house because—

(i) the tenant is not willing to agree to such a variation of the terms of the tenancy as would give such access and other facilities as would permit the intended work to be carried out, or

(ii) the nature of the intended work is such that no such variation is practicable, or

(iii) the tenant is not willing to accept an assured tenancy of such part only of the dwelling-house (in this sub-paragraph referred to as "the reduced part") as would leave in the possession of his landlord so much of the dwelling-house as would be reasonable to enable the

SCH. 2 intended work to be carried out and, where appropriate, as would give such access and other facilities over the reduced part as would permit the intended work to be carried out, or

(iv) the nature of the intended work is such that such a tenancy is not practicable; and

(b) either the landlord seeking possession acquired his interest in the dwelling-house before the grant of the tenancy or that interest was in existence at the time of that grant and neither that landlord (or, in the case of joint landlords, any of them) nor any other person who, alone or jointly with others, has acquired that interest since that time acquired it for money or money's worth; and

(c) the assured tenancy on which the dwelling-house is let did not come into
1977 c. 42. being by virtue of any provision of Schedule 1 to the Rent Act 1977, as amended by Part I of Schedule 4 to this Act or, as the case may be,
1976 c. 80. section 4 of the Rent (Agriculture) Act 1976, as amended by Part II of that Schedule.

For the purposes of this ground, if, immediately before the grant of the tenancy, the tenant to whom it was granted or, if it was granted to joint tenants, any of them was the tenant or one of the joint tenants under an earlier assured tenancy of the dwelling-house concerned, any reference in paragraph (b) above to the grant of the tenancy is a reference to the grant of that earlier assured tenancy.

For the purposes of this ground "registered housing association" has the same
1985 c. 69. meaning as in the Housing Associations Act 1985 and "charitable housing trust" means a housing trust, within the meaning of that Act, which is a charity, within
1960 c. 58. the meaning of the Charities Act 1960.

Ground 7

The tenancy is a periodic tenancy (including a statutory periodic tenancy) which has devolved under the will or intestacy of the former tenant and the proceedings for the recovery of possession are begun not later than twelve months after the death of the former tenant or, if the court so directs, after the date on which, in the opinion of the court, the landlord or, in the case of joint landlords, any one of them became aware of the former tenant's death.

For the purposes of this ground, the acceptance by the landlord of rent from a new tenant after the death of the former tenant shall not be regarded as creating a new periodic tenancy, unless the landlord agrees in writing to a change (as compared with the tenancy before the death) in the amount of the rent, the period of the tenancy, the premises which are let or any other term of the tenancy.

Ground 8

Both at the date of the service of the notice under section 8 of this Act relating to the proceedings for possession and at the date of the hearing—

(a) if rent is payable weekly or fortnightly, at least thirteen weeks' rent is unpaid;

(b) if rent is payable monthly, at least three months' rent is unpaid;

(c) if rent is payable quarterly, at least one quarter's rent is more than three months in arrears; and

(d) if rent is payable yearly, at least three months' rent is more than three months in arrears;

and for the purpose of this ground "rent" means rent lawfully due from the tenant.

PART II

GROUNDS ON WHICH COURT MAY ORDER POSSESSION

Ground 9

Suitable alternative accommodation is available for the tenant or will be available for him when the order for possession takes effect.

Ground 10

Some rent lawfully due from the tenant—

(a) is unpaid on the date on which the proceedings for possession are begun; and

(b) except where subsection (1)(b) of section 8 of this Act applies, was in arrears at the date of the service of the notice under that section relating to those proceedings.

Ground 11

Whether or not any rent is in arrears on the date on which proceedings for possession are begun, the tenant has persistently delayed paying rent which has become lawfully due.

Ground 12

Any obligation of the tenancy (other than one related to the payment of rent) has been broken or not performed.

Ground 13

The condition of the dwelling-house or any of the common parts has deteriorated owing to acts of waste by, or the neglect or default of, the tenant or any other person residing in the dwelling-house and, in the case of an act of waste by, or the neglect or default of, a person lodging with the tenant or a sub-tenant of his, the tenant has not taken such steps as he ought reasonably to have taken for the removal of the lodger or sub-tenant.

For the purposes of this ground, "common parts" means any part of a building comprising the dwelling-house and any other premises which the tenant is entitled under the terms of the tenancy to use in common with the occupiers of other dwelling-houses in which the landlord has an estate or interest.

Ground 14

The tenant or any other person residing in the dwelling-house has been guilty of conduct which is a nuisance or annoyance to adjoining occupiers, or has been convicted of using the dwelling-house or allowing the dwelling-house to be used for immoral or illegal purposes.

Ground 15

The condition of any furniture provided for use under the tenancy has, in the opinion of the court, deteriorated owing to ill-treatment by the tenant or any other person residing in the dwelling-house and, in the case of ill-treatment by a person lodging with the tenant or by a sub-tenant of his, the tenant has not taken such steps as he ought reasonably to have taken for the removal of the lodger or sub-tenant.

SCH. 2

Ground 16

The dwelling-house was let to the tenant in consequence of his employment by the landlord seeking possession or a previous landlord under the tenancy and the tenant has ceased to be in that employment.

PART III

SUITABLE ALTERNATIVE ACCOMMODATION

1. For the purposes of Ground 9 above, a certificate of the local housing authority for the district in which the dwelling-house in question is situated, certifying that the authority will provide suitable alternative accommodation for the tenant by a date specified in the certificate, shall be conclusive evidence that suitable alternative accommodation will be available for him by that date.

2. Where no such certificate as is mentioned in paragraph 1 above is produced to the court, accommodation shall be deemed to be suitable for the purposes of Ground 9 above if it consists of either—

(a) premises which are to be let as a separate dwelling such that they will then be let on an assured tenancy, other than—

(i) a tenancy in respect of which notice is given not later than the beginning of the tenancy that possession might be recovered on any of Grounds 1 to 5 above, or

(ii) an assured shorthold tenancy, within the meaning of Chapter II of Part I of this Act, or

(b) premises to be let as a separate dwelling on terms which will, in the opinion of the court, afford to the tenant security of tenure reasonably equivalent to the security afforded by Chapter I of Part I of this Act in the case of an assured tenancy of a kind mentioned in sub-paragraph (a) above,

and, in the opinion of the court, the accommodation fulfils the relevant conditions as defined in paragraph 3 below.

3.—(1) For the purposes of paragraph 2 above, the relevant conditions are that the accommodation is reasonably suitable to the needs of the tenant and his family as regards proximity to place of work, and either—

(a) similar as regards rental and extent to the accommodation afforded by dwelling-houses provided in the neighbourhood by any local housing authority for persons whose needs as regards extent are, in the opinion of the court, similar to those of the tenant and of his family; or

(b) reasonably suitable to the means of the tenant and to the needs of the tenant and his family as regards extent and character; and

that if any furniture was provided for use under the assured tenancy in question, furniture is provided for use in the accommodation which is either similar to that so provided or is reasonably suitable to the needs of the tenant and his family.

(2) For the purposes of sub-paragraph (1)(a) above, a certificate of a local housing authority stating—

(a) the extent of the accommodation afforded by dwelling-houses provided by the authority to meet the needs of tenants with families of such number as may be specified in the certificate, and

(b) the amount of the rent charged by the authority for dwelling-houses affording accommodation of that extent,

shall be conclusive evidence of the facts so stated.

4. Accommodation shall not be deemed to be suitable to the needs of the tenant and his family if the result of their occupation of the accommodation would be that it would be an overcrowded dwelling-house for the purposes of Part X of the Housing Act 1985. SCH. 2 1985 c. 68.

5. Any document purporting to be a certificate of a local housing authority named therein issued for the purposes of this Part of this Schedule and to be signed by the proper officer of that authority shall be received in evidence and, unless the contrary is shown, shall be deemed to be such a certificate without further proof.

6. In this Part of this Schedule "local housing authority" and "district", in relation to such an authority, have the same meaning as in the Housing Act 1985.

PART IV

NOTICES RELATING TO RECOVERY OF POSSESSION

7. Any reference in Grounds 1 to 5 in Part I of this Schedule or in the following provisions of this Part to the landlord giving a notice in writing to the tenant is, in the case of joint landlords, a reference to at least one of the joint landlords giving such a notice.

8.—(1) If, not later than the beginning of a tenancy (in this paragraph referred to as "the earlier tenancy"), the landlord gives such a notice in writing to the tenant as is mentioned in any of Grounds 1 to 5 in Part I of this Schedule, then, for the purposes of the ground in question and any further application of this paragraph, that notice shall also have effect as if it had been given immediately before the beginning of any later tenancy falling within sub-paragraph (2) below.

(2) Subject to sub-paragraph (3) below, sub-paragraph (1) above applies to a later tenancy—

(a) which takes effect immediately on the coming to an end of the earlier tenancy; and

(b) which is granted (or deemed to be granted) to the person who was the tenant under the earlier tenancy immediately before it came to an end; and

(c) which is of substantially the same dwelling-house as the earlier tenancy.

(3) Sub-paragraph (1) above does not apply in relation to a later tenancy if, not later than the beginning of the tenancy, the landlord gave notice in writing to the tenant that the tenancy is not one in respect of which possession can be recovered on the ground in question.

9. Where paragraph 8(1) above has effect in relation to a notice given as mentioned in Ground 1 in Part I of this Schedule, the reference in paragraph (b) of that ground to the reversion on the tenancy is a reference to the reversion on the earlier tenancy and on any later tenancy falling within paragraph 8(2) above.

10. Where paragraph 8(1) above has effect in relation to a notice given as mentioned in Ground 3 or Ground 4 in Part I of this Schedule, any second or subsequent tenancy in relation to which the notice has effect shall be treated for the purpose of that ground as beginning at the beginning of the tenancy in respect of which the notice was actually given.

11. Any reference in Grounds 1 to 5 in Part I of this Schedule to a notice being given not later than the beginning of the tenancy is a reference to its being given not later than the day on which the tenancy is entered into and, accordingly, section 45(2) of this Act shall not apply to any such reference.

Section 24.

SCHEDULE 3

AGRICULTURAL WORKER CONDITIONS

Interpretation

1.—(1) In this Schedule—

1976 c. 80.

"the 1976 Act" means the Rent (Agriculture) Act 1976;

"agriculture" has the same meaning as in the 1976 Act; and

"relevant tenancy or licence" means a tenancy or licence of a description specified in section 24(2) of this Act.

(2) In relation to a relevant tenancy or licence—

(a) "the occupier" means the tenant or licensee; and

(b) "the dwelling-house" means the dwelling-house which is let under the tenancy or, as the case may be, is occupied under the licence.

(3) Schedule 3 to the 1976 Act applies for the purposes of this Schedule as it applies for the purposes of that Act and, accordingly, shall have effect to determine—

(a) whether a person is a qualifying worker;

(b) whether a person is incapable of whole-time work in agriculture, or work in agriculture as a permit worker, in consequence of a qualifying injury or disease; and

(c) whether a dwelling-house is in qualifying ownership.

The conditions

2. The agricultural worker condition is fulfilled with respect to a dwelling-house subject to a relevant tenancy or licence if—

(a) the dwelling-house is or has been in qualifying ownership at any time during the subsistence of the tenancy or licence (whether or not it was at that time a relevant tenancy or licence); and

(b) the occupier or, where there are joint occupiers, at least one of them—

(i) is a qualifying worker or has been a qualifying worker at any time during the subsistence of the tenancy or licence (whether or not it was at that time a relevant tenancy or licence); or

(ii) is incapable of whole-time work in agriculture or work in agriculture as a permit worker in consequence of a qualifying injury or disease.

3.—(1) The agricultural worker condition is also fulfilled with respect to a dwelling-house subject to a relevant tenancy or licence if—

(a) that condition was previously fulfilled with respect to the dwelling-house but the person who was then the occupier or, as the case may be, a person who was one of the joint occupiers (whether or not under the same relevant tenancy or licence) has died; and

(b) that condition ceased to be fulfilled on the death of the occupier referred to in paragraph (a) above (hereinafter referred to as "the previous qualifying occupier"); and

(c) the occupier is either—

(i) the qualifying widow or widower of the previous qualifying occupier; or

(ii) the qualifying member of the previous qualifying occupier's family.

(2) For the purposes of sub-paragraph (1)(c)(i) above and sub-paragraph (3) below a widow or widower of the previous qualifying occupier of the dwelling-house is a qualifying widow or widower if she or he was residing in the dwelling-house immediately before the previous qualifying occupier's death. SCH. 3

(3) Subject to sub-paragraph (4) below, for the purposes of sub-paragraph (1)(c)(ii) above, a member of the family of the previous qualifying occupier of the dwelling-house is the qualifying member of the family if—

(a) on the death of the previous qualifying occupier there was no qualifying widow or widower; and

(b) the member of the family was residing in the dwelling-house with the previous qualifying occupier at the time of, and for the period of two years before, his death.

(4) Not more than one member of the previous qualifying occupier's family may be taken into account in determining whether the agricultural worker condition is fulfilled by virtue of this paragraph and, accordingly, if there is more than one member of the family—

(a) who is the occupier in relation to the relevant tenancy or licence, and

(b) who, apart from this sub-paragraph, would be the qualifying member of the family by virtue of sub-paragraph (3) above,

only that one of those members of the family who may be decided by agreement or, in default of agreement by the county court, shall be the qualifying member.

(5) For the purposes of the preceding provisions of this paragraph a person who, immediately before the previous qualifying occupier's death, was living with the previous occupier as his or her wife or husband shall be treated as the widow or widower of the previous occupier.

(6) If, immediately before the death of the previous qualifying occupier, there is, by virtue of sub-paragraph (5) above, more than one person who falls within sub-paragraph (1)(c)(i) above, such one of them as may be decided by agreement or, in default of agreement, by the county court shall be treated as the qualifying widow or widower for the purposes of this paragraph.

4. The agricultural worker condition is also fulfilled with respect to a dwelling-house subject to a relevant tenancy or licence if—

(a) the tenancy or licence was granted to the occupier or, where there are joint occupiers, at least one of them in consideration of his giving up possession of another dwelling-house of which he was then occupier (or one of joint occupiers) under another relevant tenancy or licence; and

(b) immediately before he gave up possession of that dwelling-house, as a result of his occupation the agricultural worker condition was fulfilled with respect to it (whether by virtue of paragraph 2 or paragraph 3 above or this paragraph);

and the reference in paragraph (a) above to a tenancy or licence granted to the occupier or at least one of joint occupiers includes a reference to the case where the grant is to him together with one or more other persons.

5.—(1) This paragraph applies where—

(a) by virtue of any of paragraphs 2 to 4 above, the agricultural worker condition is fulfilled with respect to a dwelling-house subject to a relevant tenancy or licence (in this paragraph referred to as "the earlier tenancy or licence"); and

(b) another relevant tenancy or licence of the same dwelling-house (in this paragraph referred to as "the later tenancy or licence") is granted to the person who, immediately before the grant, was the occupier or one of

SCH. 3

the joint occupiers under the earlier tenancy or licence and as a result of whose occupation the agricultural worker condition was fulfilled as mentioned in paragraph (a) above;

and the reference in paragraph (b) above to the grant of the later tenancy or licence to the person mentioned in that paragraph includes a reference to the case where the grant is to that person together with one or more other persons.

(2) So long as a person as a result of whose occupation of the dwelling-house the agricultural worker condition was fulfilled with respect to the earlier tenancy or licence continues to be the occupier, or one of the joint occupiers, under the later tenancy or licence, the agricultural worker condition shall be fulfilled with respect to the dwelling-house.

(3) For the purposes of paragraphs 3 and 4 above and any further application of this paragraph, where sub-paragraph (2) above has effect, the agricultural worker condition shall be treated as fulfilled so far as concerns the later tenancy or licence by virtue of the same paragraph of this Schedule as was applicable (or, as the case may be, last applicable) in the case of the earlier tenancy or licence.

Section 39.

SCHEDULE 4

STATUTORY TENANTS: SUCCESSION

PART I

1977 c. 42.

AMENDMENTS OF SCHEDULE 1 TO RENT ACT 1977

1. In paragraph 1 the words "or, as the case may be, paragraph 3" shall be omitted.

2. At the end of paragraph 2 there shall be inserted the following sub-paragraphs—

> "(2) For the purposes of this paragraph, a person who was living with the original tenant as his or her wife or husband shall be treated as the spouse of the original tenant.
>
> (3) If, immediately after the death of the original tenant, there is, by virtue of sub-paragraph (2) above, more than one person who fulfils the conditions in sub-paragraph (1) above, such one of them as may be decided by agreement or, in default of agreement, by the county court shall be treated as the surviving spouse for the purposes of this paragraph."

3. In paragraph 3—

(a) after the words "residing with him" there shall be inserted "in the dwelling-house";

(b) for the words "period of 6 months" there shall be substituted "period of 2 years";

(c) for the words from "the statutory tenant" onwards there shall be substituted "entitled to an assured tenancy of the dwelling-house by succession"; and

(d) at the end there shall be added the following sub-paragraph—

> "(2) If the original tenant died within the period of 18 months beginning on the operative date, then, for the purposes of this paragraph, a person who was residing in the dwelling-house with the original tenant at the time of his death and for the period which began 6 months before the operative date and ended at the time of his death shall be taken to have been residing with the original tenant for the period of 2 years immediately before his death."

4. In paragraph 4 the words "or 3" shall be omitted. SCH. 4

5. In paragraph 5—

(a) for the words from "or, as the case may be" to "of this Act" there shall be substituted "below shall have effect"; and

(b) for the words "the statutory tenant" there shall be substituted "entitled to an assured tenancy of the dwelling-house by succession".

6. For paragraph 6 there shall be substituted the following paragraph—

"6.—(1) Where a person who—

(a) was a member of the original tenant's family immediately before that tenant's death, and

(b) was a member of the first successor's family immediately before the first successor's death,

was residing in the dwelling-house with the first successor at the time of, and for the period of 2 years immediately before, the first successor's death, that person or, if there is more than one such person, such one of them as may be decided by agreement or, in default of agreement, by the county court shall be entitled to an assured tenancy of the dwelling-house by succession.

(2) If the first successor died within the period of 18 months beginning on the operative date, then, for the purposes of this paragraph, a person who was residing in the dwelling-house with the first successor at the time of his death and for the period which began 6 months before the operative date and ended at the time of his death shall be taken to have been residing with the first successor for the period of 2 years immediately before his death."

7. Paragraph 7 shall be omitted.

8. In paragraph 10(1)(a) for the words "paragraphs 6 or 7" there shall be substituted "paragraph 6".

9. At the end of paragraph 11 there shall be inserted the following paragraph—

"11A. In this Part of this Schedule "the operative date" means the date on which Part I of the Housing Act 1988 came into force."

PART II

AMENDMENTS OF SECTION 4 OF RENT (AGRICULTURE) ACT 1976 1976 c. 80.

10. In subsection (2) the words "or, as the case may be, subsection (4)" shall be omitted.

11. In subsection (4)—

(a) in paragraph (b) after the words "residing with him" there shall be inserted "in the dwelling-house" and for the words "period of six months" there shall be substituted "period of 2 years"; and

(b) for the words from "the statutory tenant" onwards there shall be substituted "entitled to an assured tenancy of the dwelling-house by succession".

12. In subsection (5) for the words "subsections (1), (3) and (4)" there shall be substituted "subsections (1) and (3)" and after that subsection there shall be inserted the following subsections—

"(5A) For the purposes of subsection (3) above, a person who was living with the original occupier as his or her wife or husband shall be treated as the spouse of the original occupier and, subject to subsection

Sch. 4

(5B) below, the references in subsection (3) above to a widow and in subsection (4) above to a surviving spouse shall be construed accordingly.

(5B) If, immediately after the death of the original occupier, there is, by virtue of subsection (5A) above, more than one person who fulfils the conditions in subsection (3) above, such one of them as may be decided by agreement or, in default of agreement by the county court, shall be the statutory tenant by virtue of that subsection.

(5C) If the original occupier died within the period of 18 months beginning on the operative date, then, for the purposes of subsection (3) above, a person who was residing in the dwelling-house with the original occupier at the time of his death and for the period which began 6 months before the operative date and ended at the time of his death shall be taken to have been residing with the original occupier for the period of 2 years immediately before his death; and in this subsection "the operative date" means the date on which Part I of the Housing Act 1988 came into force."

Part III

Modifications of Section 7 and Schedule 2

13.—(1) Subject to sub-paragraph (2) below, in relation to the assured tenancy to which the successor becomes entitled by succession, section 7 of this Act shall have effect as if in subsection (3) after the word "established" there were inserted the words "or that the circumstances are as specified in any of Cases 11, 12, 16, 17, 18 and 20 in Schedule 15 to the Rent Act 1977".

(2) Sub-paragraph (1) above does not apply if, by virtue of section 39(8) of this Act, the assured tenancy to which the successor becomes entitled is an assured agricultural occupancy.

14. If by virtue of section 39(8) of this Act, the assured tenancy to which the successor becomes entitled is an assured agricultural occupancy, section 7 of this Act shall have effect in relation to that tenancy as if in subsection (3) after the word "established" there were inserted the words "or that the circumstances are as specified in Case XI or Case XII of the Rent (Agriculture) Act 1976".

15.—(1) In relation to the assured tenancy to which the successor becomes entitled by succession, any notice given to the predecessor for the purposes of
1977 c. 42. Case 13, Case 14 or Case 15 in Schedule 15 to the Rent Act 1977 shall be treated as having been given for the purposes of whichever of Grounds 3 to 5 in Schedule 2 to this Act corresponds to the Case in question.

(2) Where sub-paragraph (1) above applies, the regulated tenancy of the predecessor shall be treated, in relation to the assured tenancy of the successor, as "the earlier tenancy" for the purposes of Part IV of Schedule 2 to this Act.

Section 46.

SCHEDULE 5

Housing for Wales

Status

1.—(1) Housing for Wales is a body corporate and is in this Schedule referred to as "the Corporation".

(2) The Corporation is a public body for the purposes of the Prevention of Corruption Acts 1889 to 1916.

(3) The Corporation shall not be regarded—

(a) as the servant or agent of the Crown; or

(b) as enjoying any status, immunity or privilege of the Crown; or

(c) as exempt from any tax, duty, rate, levy or other charge whatsoever, whether general or local;

and its property shall not be regarded as property of, or held on behalf of, the Crown.

Membership

2.—(1)The members of the Corporation shall be—

(a) not less than six nor more than eight persons appointed by the Secretary of State; and

(b) the chief executive of the Corporation appointed under paragraph 7 below;

and the members appointed under paragraph (a) above are in this Schedule referred to as the "appointed members".

(2) Before appointing a person to be a member of the Corporation the Secretary of State shall satisfy himself that he will have no financial or other interest likely to affect prejudicially the exercise of his functions as a member; and the Secretary of State may require a person whom he proposes to appoint to give him such information as he considers necessary for that purpose.

3.—(1) The appointed members shall hold and vacate office in accordance with the terms of their appointment, subject to the following provisions.

(2) A member may resign his membership by notice in writing addressed to the Secretary of State.

(3) The Secretary of State may remove a member from office if he is satisfied that—

(a) he has been adjudged bankrupt or made an arrangement with his creditors;

(b) he has been absent from meetings of the Corporation for a period longer than three consecutive months without the permission of the Corporation; or

(c) he is otherwise unable or unfit to discharge the functions of a member, or is unsuitable to continue as a member.

(4) The Secretary of State shall satisfy himself from time to time with respect to every appointed member that he has no financial or other interest likely to affect prejudicially the exercise of his functions as a member; and he may require an appointed member to give him such information as he considers necessary for that purpose.

Chairman and Deputy Chairman

4.—(1) The Secretary of State shall appoint one of the appointed members to be Chairman and may appoint one to be Deputy Chairman; and the members so appointed shall hold and vacate those offices in accordance with the terms of their appointment, subject to the following provisions.

(2) The Chairman or Deputy Chairman may resign by notice in writing addressed to the Secretary of State.

(3) If the Chairman or Deputy Chairman ceases to be a member of the Corporation, he also ceases to be Chairman or Deputy Chairman.

Remuneration and allowances

5.—(1) The Secretary of State may pay the Chairman, Deputy Chairman and appointed members such remuneration as he may, with the consent of the Treasury, determine.

SCH. 5 (2) The Corporation may pay them such reasonable allowances as may be so determined in respect of expenses properly incurred by them in the performance of their duties.

Pensions

6.—(1) The Secretary of State may, with the consent of the Treasury, determine to pay in respect of a person's office as Chairman, Deputy Chairman or appointed member—

(a) such pension, allowance or gratuity to or in respect of that person on his retirement or death as may be so determined; or

(b) such contributions or other payments towards provision for such pension, allowance or gratuity as may be so determined.

(2) As soon as may be after the making of such a determination the Secretary of State shall lay before each House of Parliament a statement of the amount payable in pursuance of the determination.

1972 c. 11. (3) Sub-paragraph (1) above does not apply in the case of a member who has been admitted in pursuance of regulations under section 7 of the Superannuation Act 1972 to participate in the benefits of a superannuation fund maintained by a local authority.

(4) In such a case the Secretary of State shall make any payments required to be made to the fund in respect of the member by the employing authority and may make such deductions from his remuneration as the employing authority might make in respect of his contributions to the fund.

Staff

7.—(1) There shall be a chief executive of the Corporation.

(2) After consultation with the Chairman or person designated to be chairman of the Corporation, the Secretary of State shall make the first appointment of the chief executive on such terms and conditions as he may, with the consent of the Treasury, determine.

(3) The Corporation, with the approval of the Secretary of State, may make subsequent appointments to the office of chief executive on such terms and conditions as the Corporation may, with the approval of the Secretary of State given with the consent of the Treasury, determine.

8.—(1) The Corporation may appoint, on such terms and conditions as it may, with the approval of the Secretary of State, determine, such other employees as it thinks fit.

(2) In respect of such of its employees as it may, with the approval of the Secretary of State, determine, the Corporation shall make such arrangements for providing pensions, allowances or gratuities as it may determine; and such arrangements may include the establishment and administration, by the Corporation or otherwise, of one or more pension schemes.

(3) The reference in sub-paragraph (2) above to pensions, allowances or gratuities to or in respect of employees of the Corporation includes a reference to pensions, allowances or gratuities by way of compensation to or in respect of any of the Corporation's employees who suffer loss of office or employment or loss or diminution of emoluments.

(4) The Secretary of State with the consent of the Treasury may, by statutory instrument subject to annulment in pursuance of a resolution of either House of Parliament, make regulations providing for—

(a) the transfer to, and administration by, Housing for Wales of any superannuation fund maintained by the Housing Corporation in terms of the provisions of any scheme made under section 7 of the Superannuation Act 1972; and 1972 c. 11.

(b) the modification, for the purposes of the regulations, of that section or any scheme thereunder.

(5) If an employee of the Corporation becomes a member of the Corporation and was by reference to his employment by the Corporation a participant in a pension scheme administered by it for the benefit of its employees—

(a) the Corporation may determine that his service as a member shall be treated for the purposes of the scheme as service as an employee of the Corporation whether or not any benefits are to be payable to or in respect of him by virtue of paragraph 6 above; but

(b) if the Corporation does so determine, any discretion as to the benefits payable to or in respect of him which the scheme confers on the Corporation shall be exercised only with the approval of the Secretary of State.

(6) Any reference in the preceding provisions of this paragraph to the approval of the Secretary of State is a reference to that approval given with the consent of the Treasury.

9.—(1) Not later than such date as the Secretary of State may determine, the Corporation shall make an offer of employment by it to each person employed immediately before that date by the Housing Corporation in connection with functions in Wales; and any question as to the persons to whom an offer of employment is to be made under this paragraph shall be determined by the Secretary of State.

(2) The terms of the offer shall be such that they are, taken as a whole, not less favourable to the person to whom the offer is made than the terms on which he is employed on the date on which the offer is made.

(3) An offer made in pursuance of this paragraph shall not be revocable during the period of 3 months commencing with the date on which it is made.

10.—(1) Where a person becomes an employee of the Corporation in consequence of an offer made under paragraph 9 above, then, for the purposes of the Employment Protection (Consolidation) Act 1978, his period of employment with the Housing Corporation shall count as a period of employment by the Corporation, and the change of employment shall not break the continuity of the period of employment. 1978 c. 44.

(2) Where an offer is made in pursuance of paragraph 9 above to any person employed as mentioned in that paragraph, none of the agreed redundancy procedures applicable to such a person shall apply to him; and where that person ceases to be so employed—

(a) on becoming a member of the staff of the Corporation in consequence of that paragraph, or

(b) having unreasonably refused the offer,

Part VI of the Employment Protection (Consolidation) Act 1978 shall not apply to him and he shall not be treated for the purposes of any scheme under section 24 of the Superannuation Act 1972 or any other scheme as having been retired on redundancy.

(3) Without prejudice to sub-paragraph (2) above, where a person has unreasonably refused an offer made to him in pursuance of paragraph 9 above, the Housing Corporation shall not terminate that person's employment unless it has first had regard to the feasibility of employing him in a suitable alternative position with it.

SCH. 5

(4) Where a person continues in employment in the Housing Corporation either—

(a) not having unreasonably refused an offer made to him in pursuance of this paragraph, or

(b) not having been placed in a suitable alternative position as mentioned in sub-paragraph (3) above,

he shall be treated for all purposes as if the offer mentioned in paragraph 9 above had not been made.

11.—(1) Any dispute as to whether an offer of employment complies with sub-paragraph (2) of paragraph 9 above shall be referred to and be determined by an industrial tribunal.

(2) An industrial tribunal shall not consider a complaint referred to it under sub-paragraph (1) above unless the complaint is presented to the tribunal before the end of the period of 3 months beginning with the date of the offer of employment or, in a case where the tribunal is satisfied that it was not reasonably practicable for the complaint to be presented before the end of the period of 3 months, within such further period as the tribunal considers reasonable.

(3) Subject to sub-paragraph (4) below, there shall be no appeal from the decision of an industrial tribunal under this paragraph.

(4) An appeal to the Employment Appeal Tribunal may be made only on a question of law arising from the decision of, or in proceedings before, an industrial tribunal under this paragraph.

Proceedings

12.—(1) The quorum of the Corporation and the arrangements relating to its meetings shall, subject to any directions given by the Secretary of State, be such as the Corporation may determine.

(2) The validity of proceedings of the Corporation is not affected by any defect in the appointment of any of its members.

13.—(1) Where a member of the Corporation is in any way directly or indirectly interested in a contract made or proposed to be made by the Corporation—

(a) he shall disclose the nature of his interest at a meeting of the Corporation, and the disclosure shall be recorded in the minutes of the Corporation; and

(b) he shall not take any part in any decision of the Corporation with respect to the contract.

(2) A general notice given by a member at a meeting of the Corporation to the effect that he is a member of a specified company or firm and is to be regarded as interested in any contract which may be made with the company or firm is a sufficient disclosure of his interest for the purposes of this paragraph in relation to a contract made after the date of the notice.

(3) A member need not attend in person at a meeting of the Corporation in order to make any disclosure which he is required to make under this paragraph provided he takes reasonable steps to secure that the disclosure is brought up and read at the meeting.

14.—(1) The fixing of the Corporation's seal may be authenticated by the signature of the Chairman or of any other person authorised for the purpose.

(2) A document purporting to be duly executed under the seal of the Corporation shall be received in evidence and be deemed to be so executed unless the contrary is proved.

SCHEDULE 6

Section 59.

1985 c. 69.

Amendments of Housing Associations Act 1985

Part I

Amendments of Part I with Respect to the Housing Corporation, Housing for Wales and Scottish Homes

1. After section 2 there shall be inserted the following section—

"The Corporation. 2A.—(1) In relation to a housing association which has its registered office for the purposes of the 1965 Act in Scotland, "the Corporation" means Scottish Homes.

(2) In relation to a housing association—

(a) which is a society registered under the 1965 Act and has its registered office for the purposes of that Act in Wales, or

(b) which is a registered charity and has its address for the purposes of registration by the Charity Commissioners in Wales,

"the Corporation" means Housing for Wales.

(3) In relation to any other housing association which is a society registered under the 1965 Act or a registered charity, "the Corporation" means the Housing Corporation.

(4) Subject to subsections (1) to (3), in this Act, except where the context otherwise requires, "the Corporation" means the Housing Corporation, Scottish Homes or Housing for Wales and "the Corporations" means those three bodies."

2. Except as provided below, for the words "Housing Corporation", in each place where they occur in Part I, there shall be substituted "Corporation".

3.—(1) In section 3 (the register), in subsection (1)—

(a) for the words "the Housing Corporation" there shall be substituted "each of the Corporations"; and

(b) after the word "Corporation", in the second place where it occurs, there shall be inserted "by which it is maintained".

(2) After subsection (1) of that section there shall be inserted the following subsection—

"(1A) In this Act "register", in relation to the Corporation, means the register maintained by the Corporation under this section."

(3) In subsection (2) of that section the words "of housing associations maintained under this section" shall be omitted.

4.—(1) In section 5 (registration) for subsection (2) there shall be substituted the following subsection—

"(2) Nothing in subsection (1) shall require the Corporations to establish the same criteria; and each of them may vary any criteria established by it under that subsection."

(2) For subsection (4) of that section there shall be substituted the following subsection—

"(4) Where at any time a body is, or was, on a register maintained under section 3, then, for all purposes other than rectification of that register, the body shall be conclusively presumed to be, or to have been, at that time a housing association eligible for registration in that register."

SCH. 6

5. In section 6(4) (removal from register) for paragraphs (a) to (c) there shall be substituted the following paragraphs—

"(a) a grant under section 41 (housing association grants),

(b) a grant under section 54 (revenue deficit grants),

(c) any such payment or loan as is mentioned in paragraph 2 or paragraph 3 of Schedule 1 (grant-aided land),

(d) a grant or a loan under section 2(2) of the Housing (Scotland) Act 1988,

(e) a grant under section 50 of the Housing Act 1988 (housing association grants), or

(f) a grant under section 51 of that Act (revenue deficit grants)".

6. In section 7 (appeals against removal from the register), in subsection (1) for the words from "to the High Court" onwards there shall be substituted,—

"(a) where it is a decision of Scottish Homes, to the Court of Session; and

(b) in any other case, to the High Court".

7.—(1) In section 9 (control by Corporation of disposition of land by housing associations) for subsection (1) there shall be substituted the following subsections—

"(1) Subject to section 10 and sections 81(7), 105(6) and 133(7) of the Housing Act 1988, the consent of the Corporation is required for any disposition of land by a registered housing association.

(1A) Subject to section 10, the consent of the relevant Corporation is required for any disposition of grant-aided land (as defined in Schedule 1) by an unregistered housing association; and for this purpose "the relevant Corporation" means,—

(a) if the land is in England, the Housing Corporation;

(b) if the land is in Scotland, Scottish Homes, and

(c) if the land is in Wales, Housing for Wales."

(2) In subsection (3) of that section—

(a) for the words "the consent of the Corporation", in the first place where they occur, there shall be substituted "consent"; and

(b) for the words "the consent of the Corporation", in the second place where they occur, there shall be substituted "that consent".

(3) After subsection (5) of that section there shall be added—

"(6) References in this section to consent are references,—

(a) in the case of the Housing Corporation or Housing for Wales, to consent given by order under the seal of the Corporation; and

(b) in the case of Scottish Homes, to consent in writing."

8.—(1) In section 10 (dispositions excepted from section 9), in subsection (1) for the words from "the Charity Commissioners", in the second place where they occur, onwards there shall be substituted "before making an order in such a case the Charity Commissioners shall consult,—

(a) in the case of dispositions of land in England, the Housing Corporation;

(b) in the case of dispositions of land in Scotland, Scottish Homes; and

(c) in the case of dispositions of land in Wales, Housing for Wales."

(2) In subsection (2) of that section at the end of paragraph (b) there shall be inserted "or SCH. 6

(c) a letting of land under an assured tenancy or an assured agricultural occupancy, or

(d) a letting of land in England or Wales under what would be an assured tenancy or an assured agricultural occupancy but for any of paragraphs 4 to 8 of Schedule 1 to the Housing Act 1988, or

(e) a letting of land in Scotland under what would be an assured tenancy but for any of paragraphs 3 to 8 and 12 of Schedule 4 to the Housing (Scotland) Act 1988."

9.—(1) In section 15 (payments and benefits to committee members, etc.) at the end of subsection (2) there shall be inserted the following paragraphs—

"(f) except in the case of housing associations registered in the register maintained by Scottish Homes, payments made or benefits granted by an association in such class or classes of case as may be specified in a determination made by the Corporation with the approval of the Secretary of State;

(g) in the case of housing associations registered in the register maintained by Scottish Homes, payments made or benefits granted by such an association with the approval of Scottish Homes (which approval may be given only in relation to a class or classes of case)."

(2) After subsection (2) there shall be inserted the following subsection—

"(3) The Housing Corporation and Housing for Wales may make different determinations for the purposes of subsection (2)(f) above and, before making such a determination, the Corporation shall consult such bodies appearing to it to be representative of housing associations as it considers appropriate; and after making such a determination the Corporation shall publish the determination in such manner as it considers appropriate for bringing it to the notice of the associations concerned."

10. For section 15A (which was inserted by section 14 of the Housing (Scotland) Act 1986) there shall be substituted the following section— 1986 c. 65.

"Payments etc. in community-based housing associations in Scotland.

15A.—(1) In relation to a community-based housing association in Scotland the following are also permitted, notwithstanding section 15(1)—

(a) payments made by the association in respect of the purchase of a dwelling, or part of a dwelling, owned and occupied by a person described in subsection (2) who is not an employee of the association; but only if—

(i) such payments constitute expenditure in connection with housing projects undertaken for the purpose of improving or repairing dwellings; and

(ii) the purchase price does not exceed such value as may be placed on the dwelling, or as the case may be part, by the district valuer;

(b) the granting of the tenancy of a dwelling, or part of a dwelling, to such a person; but only if the person—

(i) lives in the dwelling or in another dwelling owned by the association; or

(ii) has at any time within the period of twelve months immediately preceding the granting of the tenancy lived in the dwelling (or such other dwelling) whether or not it belonged to the housing association when he lived there.

SCH. 6

(2) The persons mentioned in subsection (1) are—

(a) a committee member or voluntary officer of the association; or

(b) a person who at any time in the twelve months preceding the payment (or as the case may be the granting of the tenancy) has been such a member or officer; or

(c) a close relative of a person described in paragraph (a) or (b).

(3) For the purposes of subsection (1), a housing association is "community-based" if—

(a) prior to the specified date, it was designated as such by the Housing Corporation; or

(b) on or after that date, it is designated as such by Scottish Homes;

and, in this subsection, "specified date" has the same meaning as in section 3 of the Housing (Scotland) Act 1988.

(4) Scottish Homes—

(a) shall make a designation under subsection (3) only if it considers that the activities of the housing association relate wholly or mainly to the improvement of dwellings, or the management of improved dwellings, within a particular community (whether or not identified by reference to a geographical area entirely within any one administrative area); and

(b) may revoke such a designation (including a designation made by the Housing Corporation under subsection (3) above as originally enacted) if it considers, after giving the association an opportunity to make representations to it as regards such revocation, that the association's activities have ceased so to relate."

11. In section 16 (general power to remove committee member), in subsection (4) for the words from "order to the High Court" onwards there shall be substituted "order,—

(a) if it is an order of the Housing Corporation or Housing for Wales, to the High Court, and

(b) if it is an order of Scottish Homes, to the Court of Session."

12. In section 17 (power to appoint new committee members) at the end of subsection (1) there shall be added the words "and the power conferred by paragraph (c) may be exercised notwithstanding that it will cause the maximum number of committee members permissible under the association's constitution to be exceeded".

13.—(1) In section 18 (exercise of powers in relation to registered charities), in subsection (1) immediately before the entry relating to section 41 of the 1985 Act there shall be inserted the following entries—

"section 50 of the Housing Act 1988 (housing association grants),

section 51 of that Act (revenue deficit grants)".

(2) In subsection (3) of that section (appointment by Corporation of trustees of associations which are registered charities: appointments not to exceed maximum number of trustees) the words from "and the Corporation" onwards shall be omitted.

14. In section 19 (change of rules under the 1965 Act), in subsection (3) for the words "given by order under the seal of the Corporation" there shall be substituted "given,— Sch. 6

(a) in the case of the Housing Corporation or Housing for Wales, by order under the seal of the Corporation; and

(b) in the case of Scottish Homes, by notice in writing."

15. In section 21 (amalgamation and dissolution under the 1965 Act), in subsection (6) for the words from "are to an order" onwards there shall be substituted "are,—

(a) in the case of the Housing Corporation or Housing for Wales, to consent given by order under the seal of the Corporation; and

(b) in the case of Scottish Homes, to consent given in writing."

16. In section 22 (Corporation's power to petition for winding up), in subsection (1) after the word "applies" there shall be inserted "(a)" and at the end there shall be added "or

(b) on the ground that the association is unable to pay its debts within the meaning of section 518 of the Companies Act 1985.".

17.—(1) In section 24 (general requirements as to accounts and audit), in subsection (2) after the word "association" there shall be inserted "which is a registered charity".

(2) In subsection (5) of that section after the words "different areas" there shall be inserted "or for different descriptions of housing associations or housing activities".

(3) After subsection (5) of that section there shall be inserted the following subsection—

"(6) For the purposes of subsection (5)(a), descriptions may be framed by reference to any matters whatever, including in particular, in the case of housing activities, the manner in which they are financed."

18. In section 27 (responsibility for securing compliance with accounting requirements), in subsection (2) at the end of paragraph (c) there shall be added "or

(d) section 55(9) of the Housing Act 1988 is not complied with".

19.—(1) In section 28 (Corporation may appoint a person to inquire into the affairs of a registered housing association), in subsection (1) for the words "the Corporation's staff" there shall be substituted "staff of any of the Corporations" and at the end of that subsection there shall be added "and, if the appointed person considers it necessary for the purposes of the inquiry, he may also inquire into the business of any other body which, at a time which the appointed person considers material, is or was a subsidiary or associate of the association concerned".

(2) In subsection (2) of that section at the end of paragraph (b) there shall be added "or

(c) any person who is, or has been, an officer, agent or member of a subsidiary or associate of the association; or

(d) any other person whom the appointed person has reason to believe is or may be in possession of information of relevance to the inquiry";

and in the words following paragraph (b) for the words "the association's business" there shall be substituted "the business of the association or any other such body as is referred to in subsection (1)".

SCH. 6 (3) After subsection (3) of that section there shall be inserted the following subsections—

"(3A) Where, by virtue of subsection (2), any books, accounts or other documents are produced to the appointed person, he may take copies of or make extracts from them.

(3B) The appointed person may, if he thinks fit during the course of the inquiry, make one or more interim reports to the Corporation on such matters as appear to him to be appropriate."

(4) After subsection (5) of that section there shall be added the following subsections—

"(6) In this section, in relation to a housing association, "subsidiary" means a company with respect to which one of the following conditions is fulfilled,—

(a) the association is a member of the company and controls the composition of the board of directors; or

(b) the association holds more than half in nominal value of the company's equity share capital; or

(c) the company is a subsidiary, within the meaning of the Companies Act 1985 or the Friendly and Industrial and Provident Societies Act 1968, of another company which, by virtue of paragraph (a) or paragraph (b), is itself a subsidiary of the housing association;

and, in the case of a housing association which is a body of trustees, the reference in paragraph (a) or paragraph (b) to the association is a reference to the trustees acting as such and any reference in subsection (7) to the association shall be construed accordingly.

(7) For the purposes of subsection (6)(a), the composition of a company's board of directors shall be deemed to be controlled by a housing association if, but only if, the association, by the exercise of some power exercisable by the association without the consent or concurrence of any other person, can appoint or remove the holders of all or a majority of the directorships.

(8) In this section, in relation to a housing association, "associate" means—

(a) any body of which the association is a subsidiary, and

(b) any other subsidiary of such a body,

and in this subsection "subsidiary" has the same meaning as in the Companies Act 1985 or the Friendly and Industrial and Provident Societies Act 1968 or, in the case of a body which is itself a housing association, has the meaning assigned by subsection (6).

(9) In relation to a company which is an industrial and provident society,—

(a) any reference in subsection (6)(a) or subsection (7) to the board of directors is a reference to the committee of management of the society; and

(b) the reference in subsection (7) to the holders of all or a majority of the directorships is a reference to all or a majority of the members of the committee or, if the housing association is itself a member of the committee, such number as together with the association would constitute a majority."

20. In section 29(1) (extraordinary audit) after the words "section 28" there shall be inserted "into the affairs of a registered housing association".

21.—(1) In section 30 (general powers of Corporation as a result of an inquiry or audit) after subsection (1) there shall be inserted the following subsection— SCH. 6

"(1A) If at any time the appointed person makes an interim report under section 28(3B) and, as a result of that interim report, the Corporation is satisfied that there has been misconduct or mismanagement as mentioned in subsection (1),—

(a) the Corporation may at that time exercise any of the powers conferred by paragraphs (b) to (d) of that subsection; and

(b) in relation to the exercise at that time of the power conferred by subsection (1)(b), the reference therein to a period of six months shall be construed as a reference to a period beginning at that time and ending six months after the date of the report under section 28(4)."

(2) In subsection (4) of that section (appeal against certain orders) for the words from "order to the High Court" onwards there shall be substituted "order,—

(a) if it is an order of the Housing Corporation or Housing for Wales, to the High Court; and

(b) if it is an order of Scottish Homes, to the Court of Session."

22.—(1) In section 31 (exercise of powers in relation to registered charities), in subsection (1) immediately before the entry relating to section 41 of the 1985 Act there shall be inserted the following entries—

"section 50 of the Housing Act 1988 (housing association grants),

section 51 of that Act (revenue deficit grants)".

(2) At the end of subsection (2)(b) of that section there shall be added the words "and such other activities (if any) of the association as are incidental to or connected with its housing activities".

23. In section 33 (recognition of central association), in subsection (1) after "housing associations" there shall be inserted "in Great Britain or in any part of Great Britain".

24. After section 33 there shall be inserted the following section—

"Provision of services between the Corporations.

33A. Any of the Corporations may enter into an agreement with the others or either of them for the provision of services of any description by the one to the other or others on such terms, as to payment or otherwise, as the parties to the agreement consider appropriate."

25. In section 39 (minor definitions) before the definition of "mental disorder" there shall be inserted—

" "assured tenancy" has, in England and Wales, the same meaning as in Part I of the Housing Act 1988 and, in Scotland, the same meaning as in Part II of the Housing (Scotland) Act 1988;

"assured agricultural occupancy" has the same meaning as in Part I of the Housing Act 1988."

26. In section 40 (index of defined expressions in Part I)—

(a) after the entry relating to "appropriate registrar" there shall be inserted—

" "assured agricultural occupancy" ... section 39

"assured tenancy" ... ... section 39";

(b) after the entry relating to "the Companies Act" there shall be inserted—

" "the Corporation" ... ... section 2A"; and

(c) in the entry beginning "register", in the second column for "3(2)" there shall be substituted "3".

SCH. 6

PART II

AMENDMENTS OF PART II WITH RESPECT TO THE HOUSING CORPORATION AND HOUSING FOR WALES

27.—(1) In section 63 (building society advances) for the words "the Housing Corporation", in each place where they occur in subsections (1) and (2), there shall be substituted "one of the Corporations" and in subsection (1) (b) for the words "the Corporation" there shall be substituted "that one of the Corporations which is concerned".

(2) After subsection (2) of that section there shall be inserted the following subsection—

"(2A) In this section "the Corporations" means the Housing Corporation and Housing for Wales".

28.—(1) In section 69 (power to vary or terminate certain agreements) at the end of subsection (1)(a) there shall be added "(including such an agreement under which rights and obligations have been transferred to Housing for Wales)".

(2) After subsection (2) of that section there shall be inserted the following subsection—

"(2A) In the case of an agreement under which rights and obligations have been transferred to Housing for Wales, the reference to a party to the agreement includes a reference to Housing for Wales."

29. In section 69A (land subject to housing management agreement) for the words "housing association grant, revenue deficit grant or hostel deficit grant" there shall be substituted "grant under section 50 (housing association grant) or section 51 (revenue deficit grant) of the Housing Act 1988".

30.—(1) In Part I of Schedule 5 (residual subsidies)—

(a) in paragraph 5(3) the words "at such times and in such places as the Treasury may direct" and "with the approval of the Treasury" shall be omitted; and

(b) at the end of paragraph 6(2)(b) there shall be added "or Housing for Wales".

(2) In Part II of that Schedule, in paragraph 5(3) the words "at such times and in such places as the Treasury may direct" and "with the approval of the Treasury" shall be omitted.

PART III

AMENDMENTS OF PART III WITH RESPECT TO THE HOUSING CORPORATION AND HOUSING FOR WALES

31.—(1) In section 74 (constitution of Housing Corporation etc.), in subsection (1) after the words "Housing Corporation" there shall be inserted "and Housing for Wales, each of".

(2) In subsection (2) of that section for the words "the Corporation" there shall be substituted "the Housing Corporation".

(3) At the end of that section there shall be inserted the following subsections—

"(3) In this Part "registered housing association" in relation to the Corporation, means a housing association registered in the register maintained by the Corporation.

(4) In this Part,—

(a) in relation to land in Wales held by an unregistered housing association, "the Corporation" means Housing for Wales; and

(b) in relation to land outside Wales held by such an association, "the Corporation" means the Housing Corporation."

32. In section 75 (general functions), in subsection (1)(c) for the words "a register of housing associations" there shall be substituted "the register of housing associations referred to in section 3". Sch. 6

33. At the end of section 77 (advisory service) there shall be added the following subsection—

"(3) The powers conferred on the Corporation by subsections (1) and (2) may be exercised by the Housing Corporation and Housing for Wales acting jointly".

34.—(1) In section 83 (power to guarantee loans), in subsection (3) (maximum amount outstanding in respect of loans etc.) for the words "the Corporation", in each place where they occur, there shall be substituted "the Housing Corporation".

(2) After subsection (3) of that section there shall be inserted the following subsection—

"(3A) The aggregate amount outstanding in respect of—

(a) loans for which Housing for Wales has given a guarantee under this section, and

(b) payments made by Housing for Wales in meeting an obligation arising by virtue of such a guarantee and not repaid to Housing for Wales,

shall not exceed £30 million or such greater sum not exceeding £50 million as the Secretary of State may specify by order made with the approval of the Treasury".

(3) In subsection (4) of that section (procedure for orders of Secretary of State) after the words "subsection (3)" there shall be inserted "or subsection (3A)".

35.—(1) In section 93 (limit on borrowing), in subsection (2) for the words from "shall not exceed" onwards there shall be substituted "shall not exceed the limit appropriate to the Corporation under subsection (2A)".

(2) At the end of subsection (2) of that section there shall be inserted the following subsection—

"(2A) The limit referred to in subsection (2) is,—

(a) in the case of the Housing Corporation, £2,000 million or such greater sum not exceeding £3,000 million as the Secretary of State may specify by order made with the consent of the Treasury; and

(b) in the case of Housing for Wales, £250 million or such greater sum not exceeding £300 million as the Secretary of State may specify by order made with the consent of the Treasury."

(3) In subsections (3) to (5) of that section for "(2)", in each place where it occurs, there shall be substituted "(2A)".

36. In section 106(1) (minor definitions: general) for the definition of "housing activities" there shall be substituted the following—

" "housing activities", in relation to a registered housing association, means all its activities in pursuance of such of its purposes, objects or powers as are of a description mentioned in section 1(1)(a) or subsections (2) to (4) of section 4."

37. In Schedule 6, paragraph 3(3)(b) shall be omitted.

Section 62(5).

SCHEDULE 7

Housing Action Trusts: Constitution

Members

1. A housing action trust (in this Schedule referred to as a "trust") shall consist of a chairman and such number of other members (not less than five but not exceeding eleven) as the Secretary of State may from time to time appoint.

2.—(1) In appointing members of a trust the Secretary of State shall have regard to the desirability of securing the services of persons who live in or have special knowledge of the locality in which the designated area is situated and before appointing any such person as a member he shall consult every local housing authority any part of whose district is included in the designated area.

(2) Before appointing a person to be a member of a trust the Secretary of State shall satisfy himself that that person will have no financial or other interest likely to affect prejudicially the exercise of his functions as a member; and the Secretary of State may require a person whom he proposes to appoint to give him such information as he considers necessary for that purpose.

(3) For the purposes of sub-paragraph (2) above, the fact that a person is or may become a tenant of a trust shall not be regarded as giving to that person an interest likely to affect prejudicially the exercise of his functions as a member.

(4) The Secretary of State shall appoint one of the members to be chairman and, if he thinks fit, another to be deputy chairman of the trust.

3. Subject to the following provisions of this Schedule, each member of the trust as such and the chairman and deputy chairman as such shall hold and vacate office in accordance with his appointment.

4. If the chairman or deputy chairman ceases to be a member of the trust, he shall also cease to be chairman or deputy chairman, as the case may be.

5. Any member of the trust may, by notice in writing addressed to the Secretary of State, resign his membership; and the chairman or deputy chairman may, by like notice, resign his office as such.

6. If the Secretary of State is satisfied that a member of the trust (including the chairman or deputy chairman)—

(a) has become bankrupt or made an arrangement with his creditors, or

(b) has been absent from meetings of the trust for a period longer than three consecutive months without the permission of the trust, or

(c) is otherwise unable or unfit to discharge the functions of a member, or is unsuitable to continue as a member,

the Secretary of State may remove him from his office.

7. A member of the trust who ceases to be a member or ceases to be chairman or deputy chairman shall be eligible for reappointment.

Remuneration

8. The trust may pay to each member such remuneration and allowances as the Secretary of State may with the approval of the Treasury determine.

9. The trust may pay or make provision for paying, to or in respect of any member, such sums by way of pensions, allowances and gratuities as the Secretary of State may with the approval of the Treasury determine and, with that approval, the Secretary of State may undertake to meet any liabilities arising in respect of such pensions, allowances or gratuities after the dissolution of the trust.

10. Where a person ceases to be a member of a trust and it appears to the Secretary of State that there are special circumstances which make it right for him to receive compensation, the trust may make to him payment of such amount as the Secretary of State may with the approval of the Treasury determine. SCH. 7

Staff

11.—(1) There shall be a chief officer of the trust who shall be appointed by the trust with the approval of the Secretary of State.

(2) The chief officer shall be responsible to the trust for the general exercise of the trust's functions.

(3) The trust may appoint such number of other employees as may be approved by the Secretary of State.

(4) References in paragraph 12 below to employees of the trust include references to the chief officer as well as other employees.

12.—(1) Employees of the trust shall be appointed at such remuneration and on such other terms and conditions as the trust may determine.

(2) The trust may pay such pensions, allowances or gratuities as it may determine to or in respect of any of its employees, make such payments as it may determine towards the provision of pensions, allowances or gratuities to or in respect of any of its employees or provide and maintain such schemes as it may determine (whether contributory or not) for the payment of pensions, allowances or gratuities to or in respect of any of its employees; and with the approval of the Treasury the Secretary of State may undertake to meet any liabilities arising in respect of such pensions, allowances or gratuities after the dissolution of the trust.

(3) The reference in sub-paragraph (2) above to pensions, allowances or gratuities to or in respect of any of the trust's employees includes a reference to pensions, allowances or gratuities by way of compensation to or in respect of any of the trust's employees who suffer loss of office or employment or loss or diminution of emoluments.

(4) If an employee of the trust becomes a member and was by reference to his employment by the trust a participant in a pension scheme maintained by the trust for the benefit of any of its employees, the trust may determine that his service as a member shall be treated for the purposes of the scheme as service as an employee of the trust whether or not any benefits are to be payable to or in respect of him by virtue of paragraph 9 above.

(5) A determination of the trust for the purposes of this paragraph is ineffective unless made with the approval of the Secretary of State given with the consent of the Treasury.

Meetings and proceedings

13. The quorum of the trust and the arrangements relating to its meetings shall, subject to any directions given by the Secretary of State, be such as the trust may determine.

14. The validity of any proceedings of the trust shall not be affected by any vacancy among its members or by any defect in the appointment of any of its members.

Instruments, etc.

15. The fixing of the seal of the trust shall be authenticated by the signature of the chairman or of some other member authorised either generally or specially by the trust to act for that purpose.

SCH. 7 16. Any document purporting to be a document duly executed under the seal of the trust shall be received in evidence and shall, unless the contrary is proved, be deemed to be so executed.

17. A document purporting to be signed on behalf of a trust shall be received in evidence and shall, unless the contrary is proved, be deemed to be so signed.

House of Commons disqualification

1975 c. 24. 18. In Part III of Schedule 1 to the House of Commons Disqualification Act 1975 (disqualifying offices), there shall be inserted at the appropriate place the following entry—

> "Any member, in receipt of remuneration, of a housing action trust (within the meaning of Part III of the Housing Act 1988)."

Section 62(5).

SCHEDULE 8

HOUSING ACTION TRUSTS: FINANCE ETC.

PART I

PRELIMINARY

1.—(1) References in this Schedule to a trust are to a housing action trust.

(2) The financial year of a trust shall begin with 1 April and references to a financial year in relation to a trust shall be construed accordingly.

PART II

FINANCE

Financial duties

2.—(1) After consultation with a trust, the Secretary of State may, with the Treasury's approval, determine the financial duties of the trust, and different determinations may be made in relation to different trusts or for different functions and activities of the same trust.

(2) The Secretary of State shall give the trust notice of every determination, and a determination may—

(a) relate to a period beginning before the date on which it is made;

(b) contain incidental or supplementary provisions; and

(c) be varied by a subsequent determination.

Government grants

3.—(1) The Secretary of State may (out of moneys provided by Parliament and with the consent of the Treasury) pay to a trust, in respect of the exercise of its functions and in respect of its administrative expenses, such sums as he may (with the approval of the Treasury) determine.

(2) The payment may be made on such terms as the Secretary of State (with the approval of the Treasury) provides.

Borrowing

4.—(1) A trust may borrow temporarily, by way of overdraft or otherwise, such sums as it may require for meeting its obligations and discharging its functions—

(a) in sterling from the Secretary of State; or

(b) with the consent of the Secretary of State, or in accordance with any general authority given by the Secretary of State, either in sterling or in currency other than sterling from a person other than the Secretary of State.

(2) A trust may borrow otherwise than by way of temporary loan such sums as the trust may require—

(a) in sterling from the Secretary of State; or

(b) with the consent of the Secretary of State, in a currency other than sterling from a person other than the Secretary of State.

(3) The Secretary of State may lend to a trust any sums it has power to borrow from him under sub-paragraph (1) or sub-paragraph (2) above.

(4) The Treasury may issue to the Secretary of State out of the National Loans Fund any sums necessary to enable him to make loans under sub-paragraph (3) above.

(5) Loans made under sub-paragraph (3) above shall be repaid to the Secretary of State at such times and by such methods, and interest on the loans shall be paid to him at such times and at such rates, as he may determine.

(6) All sums received by the Secretary of State under sub-paragraph (5) above shall be paid into the National Loans Fund.

(7) References in this paragraph to the Secretary of State are references to him acting with the approval of the Treasury.

Guarantees

5.—(1) The Treasury may guarantee, in such manner and on such conditions as they think fit, the repayment of the principal of and the payment of interest on any sums which a trust borrows from a person or body other than the Secretary of State.

(2) Immediately after a guarantee is given under this paragraph, the Treasury shall lay a statement of the guarantee before each House of Parliament; and, where any sum is issued for fulfilling a guarantee so given, the Treasury shall lay before each House of Parliament a statement relating to that sum, as soon as possible after the end of each financial year, beginning with that in which the sum is issued and ending with that in which all liability in respect of the principal of the sum and in respect of interest on it is finally discharged.

(3) Any sums required by the Treasury for fulfilling a guarantee under this paragraph shall be charged on and issued out of the Consolidated Fund.

(4) If any sums are issued in fulfilment of a guarantee given under this paragraph, the trust shall make to the Treasury, at such times and in such manner as the Treasury may from time to time direct, payments of such amounts as the Treasury so direct in or towards repayment of the sums so issued and payments of interest, at such rates as the Treasury so direct, on what is outstanding for the time being in respect of sums so issued.

(5) Any sums received by the Treasury in pursuance of sub-paragraph (4) above shall be paid into the Consolidated Fund.

Assumed debt

6.—(1) On any acquisition to which this paragraph applies, a trust shall assume a debt to the Secretary of State of such amount as may be notified to the trust in writing by him, with the approval of the Treasury.

SCH. 8

(2) This paragraph applies to any acquisition by the trust of property held—

(a) by or on behalf of the Crown; or

(b) by a company all of whose shares are held by or on behalf of the Crown or by a wholly owned subsidiary of such a company.

(3) Subject to sub-paragraph (4) below, the amount to be notified is the aggregate of the following—

(a) the consideration given when the property was first brought into public ownership; and

(b) the costs and expenses of and incidental to its being brought into public ownership.

(4) If it appears to the Secretary of State that there has been such a change in circumstances since the property was first brought into public ownership that its true value would not be reflected by reference to the consideration mentioned in sub-paragraph (3) above, the Secretary of State, with the approval of the Treasury, shall determine the amount to be notified.

(5) The rate of interest payable on the debt assumed by a trust under this paragraph, and the date from which interest is to begin to accrue, the arrangements for paying off the principal, and the other terms of the debt shall be such as the Secretary of State, with the approval of the Treasury, may from time to time determine.

(6) Different rates and dates may be determined under sub-paragraph (5) above with respect to different portions of the debt.

(7) Any sums received by the Secretary of State under sub-paragraph (5) above shall be paid into the National Loans Fund.

Surplus funds

7.—(1) Where it appears to the Secretary of State, after consultation with the Treasury and the trust, that a trust has a surplus, whether on capital or on revenue account, after making allowance by way of transfer to reserve or otherwise for its future requirements, the trust shall, if the Secretary of State with the approval of the Treasury and after consultation with the trust so directs, pay to the Secretary of State such sum not exceeding the amount of that surplus as may be specified in the direction.

(2) Any sum received by the Secretary of State under this paragraph shall, subject to sub-paragraph (4) below, be paid into the Consolidated Fund.

(3) The whole or part of any payment made to the Secretary of State by a trust under sub-paragraph (1) above shall, if the Secretary of State with the approval of the Treasury so determines, be treated as made by way of repayment of such part of the principal of loans under paragraph 4(3) above, and as made in respect of the repayments due at such times, as may be so determined.

(4) Any sum treated under sub-paragraph (3) above as a repayment of a loan shall be paid by the Secretary of State into the National Loans Fund.

Financial limits

8.—(1) The aggregate amount of the sums mentioned in sub-paragraph (2) below shall not exceed such sum as the Secretary of State, with the consent of the Treasury, may by order made by statutory instrument specify.

(2) The sums are—

(a) sums borrowed by all trusts under paragraph 4 above minus repayments made in respect of the sums; and

(b) sums issued by the Treasury in fulfilment of guarantees under paragraph 5 above of debts of all trusts.

(3) No order shall be made under sub-paragraph (1) above unless a draft of it has been laid before, and approved by a resolution of, the House of Commons. Sch. 8

Grants and loans: accounts

9.—(1) The Secretary of State shall prepare in respect of each financial year an account—

(a) of the sums paid to trusts under paragraph 3 above;

(b) of the sums issued to him under paragraph 4(4) above and the sums received by him under paragraph 4(5) above and of the disposal by him of those sums; and

(c) of the sums paid into the Consolidated Fund or National Loans Fund under paragraph 7 above.

(2) The Secretary of State shall send the account to the Comptroller and Auditor General before the end of the month of November next following the end of that year.

(3) The Comptroller and Auditor General shall examine, certify and report on the account and lay copies of it and of his report before each House of Parliament.

(4) The form of the account and the manner of preparing it shall be such as the Treasury may direct.

Part III

General Accounts Etc.

Accounts

10.—(1) A trust shall keep proper accounts and other records in relation to them.

(2) The accounts and records shall show, in respect of the financial year to which they relate, a true and fair view of the trust's activities.

(3) A trust shall prepare in respect of each financial year a statement of accounts complying with any requirement which the Secretary of State has (with the consent of the Treasury) notified in writing to the trust relating to—

(a) the information to be contained in the statement;

(b) the manner in which the information is to be presented; and

(c) the methods and principles according to which the statement is to be prepared.

(4) Subject to any requirement notified to the trust under sub-paragraph (3) above, in preparing any statement of accounts in accordance with that sub-paragraph the trust shall follow, with respect to each of the matters specified in paragraphs (a) to (c) of that sub-paragraph, such course as may for the time being be approved by the Secretary of State with the consent of the Treasury.

(5) Section 6 of the National Audit Act 1983 (which enables the Comptroller and Auditor General to conduct examinations into the economy, efficiency and effectiveness with which certain departments, authorities and bodies have used their resources) shall apply to a trust. 1983 c. 44.

Audit

11.—(1) The trust's accounts and statements of accounts shall be audited by an auditor to be appointed annually by the Secretary of State in relation to the trust.

SCH. 8

(2) A person shall not be qualified for appointment under sub-paragraph (1) above unless he is qualified for appointment as auditor of a company under section 389 of the Companies Act 1985. 1985 c. 6.

(3) A person shall not be qualified for appointment under sub-paragraph (1) above if the person is—

(a) a member, officer or servant of the trust,

(b) a partner of, or employed by, a member, officer or servant of the trust, or

(c) a body corporate.

Transmission to Secretary of State

12. As soon as the accounts and statement of accounts of the trust for any financial year have been audited, the trust shall send to the Secretary of State a copy of the statement, together with a copy of any report made by the auditor on the statement or on the accounts.

Reports

13.—(1) As soon as possible after the end of each financial year, a trust shall make to the Secretary of State a report dealing generally with the trust's operations during the year, and shall include in the report a copy of its audited statement of accounts for that year.

(2) Without prejudice to the generality of sub-paragraph (1) above, a report shall give particulars of the name and address of every person who, in the financial year to which the report relates, has received financial assistance from the trust under section 71(1) of this Act, together with particulars of the form of the assistance, the amount involved and the purpose for which the assistance was given.

(3) The Secretary of State shall lay a copy of the report before each House of Parliament.

Information

14. Without prejudice to paragraph 13 above, a trust shall provide the Secretary of State with such information relating to its activities as he may require, and for that purpose shall permit any person authorised by the Secretary of State to inspect and make copies of the accounts, books, documents or papers of the trust and shall afford such explanation of them as that person or the Secretary of State may reasonably require.

Section 76.

SCHEDULE 9

ORDERS VESTING LAND IN HOUSING ACTION TRUSTS

PART I

PROVISIONS SUPPLEMENTING SECTION 76(1) TO (3)

1. In this Part of this Schedule "the principal section" means section 76 of this Act.

2.—(1) In the principal section and paragraph 3 below, "statutory undertakers" and "statutory undertaking" shall be construed in accordance with paragraph 4 below.

(2) In the principal section and the following provisions of this Part of this Schedule, "wholly-owned subsidiary" has the meaning given by section 736 of the Companies Act 1985.

3.—(1) In subsection (3) of the principal section the reference to the Secretary of State and the appropriate Minister— SCH. 9

(a) in relation to statutory undertakers who are also statutory undertakers for the purposes of any provision of Part XI of the Town and Country Planning Act 1971, shall be construed as if contained in that Part; and 1971 c. 78.

(b) in relation to any other statutory undertakers shall be construed in accordance with an order made by the Secretary of State.

(2) If, for the purposes of subsection (3) of the principal section, any question arises as to which Minister is the appropriate Minister in relation to any statutory undertakers, that question shall be determined by the Treasury.

4. In the principal section and, except where the context otherwise requires, in paragraph 3 above "statutory undertakers" means—

(a) persons authorised by any enactment to carry on any railway, light railway, tramway, road transport, water transport, canal, inland navigation, dock, harbour, pier or lighthouse undertaking, or any undertaking for the supply of electricity, hydraulic power or water;

(b) British Shipbuilders, the British Steel Corporation, the Civil Aviation Authority, the British Coal Corporation, the National Enterprise Board, the Post Office and any other authority, body or undertakers which, by virtue of any enactment, are to be treated as statutory undertakers for any of the purposes of the Town and Country Planning Act 1971;

(c) any other authority, body or undertakers specified in an order made by the Secretary of State; and

(d) any wholly-owned subsidiary of any person, authority, body or undertakers mentioned in sub-paragraphs (a) and (b) above or specified in an order made under sub-paragraph (c) above;

and "statutory undertaking" shall be construed accordingly.

5. An order under any provision of this Part of this Schedule shall be made by statutory instrument which shall be subject to annulment in pursuance of a resolution of either House of Parliament.

PART II

MODIFICATIONS OF ENACTMENTS

Land Compensation Act 1961

6. The Land Compensation Act 1961 shall have effect in relation to orders under section 76 of this Act subject to the modifications in paragraphs 7 to 11 below. 1961 c. 33.

7. References to the date of service of a notice to treat shall be treated as references to the date on which an order under section 76 of this Act comes into force.

8. Section 17(2) shall be treated as if for the words "the authority proposing to acquire it have served a notice to treat in respect thereof, or an agreement has been made for the sale thereof to that authority" there were substituted the words "an order under section 76 of the Housing Act 1988 vesting the land in which the interest subsists in a housing action trust has come into force, or an agreement has been made for the sale of the interest to such a trust".

9. In section 22—

(a) subsection (2) shall be treated as if at the end of paragraph (c) there were added the words "or

SCH. 9

(cc) where an order has been made under section 76 of the Housing Act 1988 vesting the land in which the interest subsists in a housing action trust"; and

(b) subsection (3) shall be treated as if, in paragraph (a), after the words "paragraph (b)" there were inserted "or paragraph (cc)".

10. Any reference to a notice to treat in section 39(2) shall be treated as a reference to an order under section 76 of this Act.

11. In Schedule 2, paragraph 1(2) shall be treated as if at the end there were added the following paragraph—

"(k) an acquisition by means of an order under section 76 of the Housing Act 1988 vesting land in a housing action trust."

Compulsory Purchase (Vesting Declarations) Act 1981

1981 c. 66.

12.—(1) In Schedule 2 to the Compulsory Purchase (Vesting Declarations) Act 1981 (vesting of land in urban development corporation), in paragraph 1 after the word "declaration)" there shall be inserted "or under section 76 of the Housing Act 1988 (subsection (5) of which contains similar provision)".

(2) At the end of sub-paragraph (a) of paragraph 3 of that Schedule there shall be added "or, as the case may be, the housing action trust".

Section 78.

SCHEDULE 10

HOUSING ACTION TRUSTS: LAND

PART I

MODIFICATIONS OF ACQUISITION OF LAND ACT 1981

1981 c. 67.

1. The Acquisition of Land Act 1981 (in this Part referred to as "the 1981 Act") shall apply in relation to the compulsory acquisition of land under section 77 of this Act with the modifications made by this Part of this Schedule.

2.—(1) Where a compulsory purchase order authorising the acquisition of any land is submitted to the Secretary of State in accordance with section 2(2) of the 1981 Act then, if the Secretary of State—

(a) is satisfied that the order ought to be confirmed so far as it relates to part of the land comprised in it, but

(b) has not for the time being determined whether it ought to be confirmed so far as it relates to any other such land,

he may confirm the order so far as it relates to the land mentioned in paragraph (a) above, and give directions postponing the consideration of the order, so far as it relates to any other land specified in the directions, until such time as may be so specified.

(2) Where the Secretary of State gives directions under sub-paragraph (1) above, the notices required by section 15 of the 1981 Act to be published and served shall include a statement of the effect of the directions.

3. The reference in section 17(3) of the 1981 Act to statutory undertakers includes a reference to a housing action trust.

PART II

LAND: SUPPLEMENTARY

Extinguishment of rights over land

4.—(1) Subject to this paragraph, on an order under section 76 of this Act coming into force or the completion by a housing action trust of a compulsory acquisition of land under Part III of this Act, all private rights of way and rights of laying down, erecting, continuing or maintaining any apparatus on, under or over the land shall be extinguished, and any such apparatus shall vest in the trust.

(2) Sub-paragraph (1) above does not apply—

(a) to any right vested in, or apparatus belonging to, statutory undertakers for the purpose of carrying on their undertaking; or

(b) to any right conferred by or in accordance with the telecommunications code on the operator of a telecommunications code system or to any telecommunications apparatus kept installed for the purposes of any such system.

(3) In respect of any right or apparatus not falling within sub-paragraph (2) above, sub-paragraph (1) above shall have effect subject—

(a) to any direction given by the Secretary of State before the coming into force of the order (or, as the case may be, by the trust before the completion of the acquisition) that sub-paragraph (1) above shall not apply to any right or apparatus specified in the direction, and

(b) to any agreement which may be made (whether before or after the coming into force of the order or completion of the acquisition) between the Secretary of State (or trust) and the person in or to whom the right or apparatus in question is vested or belongs.

(4) Any person who suffers loss by the extinguishment of a right or the vesting of any apparatus under this paragraph shall be entitled to compensation from the trust.

(5) Any compensation payable under this paragraph shall be determined in accordance with the Land Compensation Act 1961. 1961 c. 33.

Power to override easements

5.—(1) The erection, construction or carrying out, or maintenance of any building or work on land which has been vested in or acquired by a housing action trust for the purposes of Part III of this Act, whether done by the trust or by any other person, is authorised by virtue of this paragraph if it is done in accordance with planning permission, notwithstanding that it involves interference with an interest or right to which this paragraph applies, or involves a breach of a restriction as to the user of land arising by virtue of a contract.

(2) Nothing in sub-paragraph (1) above shall authorise interference with any right of way or right of laying down, erecting, continuing or maintaining apparatus on, under or over land, being a right vested in or belonging to statutory undertakers for the purpose of the carrying on of their undertaking or a right conferred by or in accordance with the telecommunications code on the operator of a telecommunications code system.

(3) This paragraph applies to the following interests and rights, that is to say, any easement, liberty, privilege, right or advantage annexed to land and adversely affecting other land, including any natural right to support.

(4) In respect of any interference or breach in pursuance of sub-paragraph (1) above, compensation shall be payable under section 7 or section 10 of the Compulsory Purchase Act 1965, to be assessed in the same manner and subject 1965 c. 56.
to the same rules as in the case of other compensation under those sections in

SCH. 10 respect of injurious affection where the compensation is to be estimated in connection with a purchase by a housing action trust or the injury arises from the execution of works on land acquired by such a trust.

(5) Where a person other than the housing action trust by or in whom the land in question was acquired or vested is liable to pay compensation by virtue of sub-paragraph (4) above and fails to discharge that liability, the liability shall (subject to sub-paragraph (6) below) be enforceable against the trust.

(6) Nothing in sub-paragraph (5) above shall be construed as affecting any agreement between the trust and any other person for indemnifying the trust against any liability under that sub-paragraph.

(7) Nothing in this paragraph shall be construed as authorising any act or omission on the part of any person which is actionable at the suit of any person on any grounds other than such an interference or breach as is mentioned in sub-paragraph (1) above.

(8) Nothing in this paragraph shall be construed as authorising any act or omission on the part of a housing action trust, or of any body corporate, in contravention of any limitation imposed by law on its capacity by virtue of the constitution of the trust or body.

Consecrated land and burial grounds

6.—(1) Any consecrated land, whether including a building or not, which has been vested in or acquired by a housing action trust for the purposes of Part III of this Act may (subject to the following provisions of this paragraph) be used by the trust, or by any other person, in any manner in accordance with planning permission, notwithstanding any obligation or restriction imposed under ecclesiastical law or otherwise in respect of consecrated land.

(2) Sub-paragraph (1) above does not apply to land which consists or forms part of a burial ground.

(3) Any use of consecrated land authorised by sub-paragraph (1) above, and the use of any land, not being consecrated land, vested or acquired as mentioned in that sub-paragraph which at the time of acquisition included a church or other building used or formerly used for religious worship or the site thereof, shall be subject to compliance with the prescribed requirements with respect to the removal and reinterment of any human remains, and the disposal of monuments and fixtures and furnishings; and, in the case of consecrated land, shall be subject to such provisions as may be prescribed for prohibiting or restricting the use of the land, either absolutely or until the prescribed consent has been obtained, so long as any church or other building used or formerly used for religious worship, or any part thereof, remains on the land.

(4) Any regulations made for the purposes of sub-paragraph (3) above—

(a) shall contain such provisions as appear to the Secretary of State to be requisite for securing that any use of land which is subject to compliance with the regulations shall, as nearly as may be, be subject to the like control as is imposed by law in the case of a similar use authorised by an enactment not contained in this Act or by a Measure, or as it would be proper to impose on a disposal of the land in question otherwise than in pursuance of an enactment or Measure;

(b) shall contain requirements relating to the disposal of any such land as is mentioned in sub-paragraph (3) above such as appear to the Secretary of State requisite for securing that the provisions of that sub-paragraph shall be complied with in relation to the use of the land; and

(c) may contain such incidental and consequential provisions (including provision as to the closing of registers) as appear to the Secretary of State to be expedient for the purposes of the regulations.

(5) Any land consisting of a burial ground or part of a burial ground which has been vested in or acquired by a housing action trust for the purposes of Part III of this Act may be used by the trust in any manner in accordance with planning permission, notwithstanding anything in any enactment relating to burial grounds or any obligation or restriction imposed under ecclesiastical law or otherwise in respect of burial grounds. SCH. 10

(6) Sub-paragraph (5) above shall not have effect in respect of any land which has been used for the burial of the dead until the prescribed requirements with respect to the removal and reinterment of human remains and the disposal of monuments in or upon the land have been complied with.

(7) Provision shall be made by any regulations made for the purposes of sub-paragraphs (3) and (6) above—

(a) for requiring the persons in whom the land is vested to publish notice of their intention to carry out the removal and reinterment of any human remains or the disposal of any monuments; and

(b) for enabling the personal representatives or relatives of any deceased person themselves to undertake the removal and reinterment of the remains of the deceased and the disposal of any monument commemorating the deceased, and for requiring the persons in whom the land is vested to defray the expenses of such removal, reinterment and disposal, not exceeding such amount as may be prescribed; and

(c) for requiring compliance with such reasonable conditions (if any) as may be imposed, in the case of consecrated land, by the bishop of the diocese, with respect to the manner of removal and the place and manner of reinterment of any human remains and the disposal of any monuments; and

(d) for requiring compliance with any directions given in any case by the Secretary of State with respect to the removal and reinterment of any human remains.

(8) Subject to the provisions of any such regulations as are referred to in sub-paragraph (7) above, no faculty shall be required for the removal and reinterment in accordance with the regulations of any human remains or for the removal or disposal of any monuments, and the provisions of section 25 of the Burial Act 1857 (which prohibits the removal of human remains without the licence of the Secretary of State except in certain cases) shall not apply to a removal carried out in accordance with the regulations. 1857 c. 81.

(9) Any power conferred by this paragraph to use land in a manner therein mentioned shall be construed as a power so to use the land, whether it involves the erection, construction or carrying out of any building or work, or the maintenance of any building or work, or not.

(10) Nothing in this paragraph shall be construed as authorising any act or omission on the part of any person which is actionable at the suit of any person on any grounds other than contravention of any such obligation, restriction or enactment as is mentioned in sub-paragraph (1) or sub-paragraph (5) above.

(11) Sub-paragraph (8) of paragraph 5 above shall apply in relation to this paragraph as it applies in relation to that.

(12) In this paragraph "burial ground" includes any churchyard, cemetery or other ground, whether consecrated or not, which has at any time been set apart for the purposes of interment, and "monument" includes a tombstone or other memorial.

(13) In this paragraph "prescribed" means prescribed by regulations made by the Secretary of State.

(14) The power to make regulations under this paragraph shall be exercisable by statutory instrument which shall be subject to annulment in pursuance of a resolution of either House of Parliament.

Sch. 10

Open spaces

7.—(1) Any land being, or forming part of, a common, open space or fuel or field garden allotment, which has been vested in or acquired by a housing action trust for the purposes of Part III of this Act may be used by the trust, or by any other person, in any manner in accordance with planning permission, notwithstanding anything in any enactment relating to land of that kind, or in any enactment by which the land is specially regulated.

(2) Nothing in this paragraph shall be construed as authorising any act or omission on the part of any person which is actionable at the suit of any person on any grounds other than contravention of any such enactment as is mentioned in sub-paragraph (1) above.

(3) Sub-paragraph (8) of paragraph 5 above shall apply in relation to this paragraph as it applies in relation to that.

Displacement of persons

8. If the Secretary of State certifies that possession of a house which has been vested in or acquired by a housing action trust for the purposes of Part III of this Act and is for the time being held by that trust for the purposes for which it was acquired, is immediately required for those purposes, nothing in the Rent (Agriculture) Act 1976 or the Rent Act 1977 or this Act shall prevent that trust from obtaining possession of the house.

1976 c. 80.
1977 c. 42.

Extinguishment of public rights of way

9.—(1) Where any land has been vested in or acquired by a housing action trust for the purposes of Part III of this Act and is for the time being held by that trust for those purposes, the Secretary of State may by order extinguish any public right of way over the land.

(2) Where the Secretary of State proposes to make an order under this paragraph, he shall publish in such manner as appears to him to be requisite a notice—

(a) stating the effect of the order, and

(b) specifying the time (not being less than 28 days from the publication of the notice) within which, and the manner in which, objections to the proposal may be made,

and shall serve a like notice—

(i) on the local planning authority in whose area the land is situated; and

(ii) on the relevant highway authority.

(3) In sub-paragraph (2) above "the relevant highway authority" means any authority which is a highway authority in relation to the right of way proposed to be extinguished by the order under this paragraph.

(4) Where an objection to a proposal to make an order under this paragraph is duly made and is not withdrawn, the provisions of paragraph 10 below shall have effect in relation to the proposal.

(5) For the purposes of this paragraph an objection to such a proposal shall not be treated as duly made unless—

(a) it is made within the time and in the manner specified in the notice required by this paragraph; and

(b) a statement in writing of the grounds of the objection is comprised in or submitted with the objection.

(6) Where it is proposed to make an order under this paragraph extinguishing a public right of way over a road on land acquired for the purposes of this Act by a housing action trust and compensation in respect of restrictions imposed under section 1 or section 2 of the Restriction of Ribbon Development Act 1935 in

1935 c. 47.

respect of that road has been paid by the highway authority (or, in the case of a trunk road, by the authority which, when the compensation was paid, was the authority for the purposes of section 4 of the Trunk Roads Act 1936), the order may provide for the payment by the housing action trust to that authority, in respect of the compensation so paid, of such sums as the Secretary of State, with the consent of the Treasury, may determine.

SCH. 10

1936 c. 5 (1 Edw. 8 & Geo. 6.)

(7) Where the Secretary of State makes an order under this paragraph on the application of a housing action trust, he shall send a copy of it to the Post Office.

10.—(1) In this paragraph any reference to making a final decision, in relation to an order, is a reference to deciding whether to make the order or what modification, if any, ought to be made.

(2) Unless the Secretary of State decides apart from the objection not to make the order, or decides to make a modification which is agreed to by the objector as meeting the objection, the Secretary of State shall, before making a final decision, consider the grounds of the objection as set out in the statement comprised in or submitted with the objection, and may, if he thinks fit, require the objector to submit within a specified period a further statement in writing as to any of the matters to which the objection relates.

(3) In so far as the Secretary of State, after considering the grounds of the objection as set out in the original statement and in any such further statement, is satisfied that the objection relates to a matter which can be dealt with in the assessment of compensation, the Secretary of State may treat the objection as irrelevant for the purpose of making a final decision.

(4) If, after considering the grounds of the objection as set out in the original statement and in any such further statement, the Secretary of State is satisfied that, for the purpose of making a final decision, he is sufficiently informed as to the matters to which the objection relates, or if, where a further statement has been required, it is not submitted within the specified period, the Secretary of State may make a final decision without further investigation as to those matters.

(5) Subject to sub-paragraphs (3) and (4) above, the Secretary of State, before making a final decision, shall afford to the objector an opportunity of appearing before, and being heard by, a person appointed for the purpose by the Secretary of State; and if the objector avails himself of that opportunity, the Secretary of State shall afford an opportunity of appearing and being heard on the same occasion to the housing action trust on whose representation the order is proposed to be made, and to any other persons to whom it appears to the Secretary of State to be expedient to afford such an opportunity.

(6) Notwithstanding anything in the preceding provisions of this paragraph, if it appears to the Secretary of State that the matters to which the objection relates are such as to require investigation by public local inquiry before he makes a final decision, he shall cause such an inquiry to be held; and where he determines to cause such an inquiry to be held, any of the requirements of those provisions to which effect has not been given at the time of that determination shall be dispensed with.

Telegraphic lines

11.—(1) Where an order under paragraph 9 above extinguishing a public right of way is made on the application of a housing action trust and at the time of the publication of the notice required by sub-paragraph (2) of that paragraph any telecommunication apparatus was kept installed for the purposes of a telecommunications code system under, in, on, over, along or across the land over which the right of way subsisted—

(a) the power of the operator of the system to remove the apparatus shall, notwithstanding the making of the order, be exercisable at any time not later than the end of the period of three months from the date on which the right of way is extinguished and shall be exercisable in respect of the

Sch. 10

whole or any part of the apparatus after the end of that period if before the end of that period the operator of the system has given notice to the trust of his intention to remove the apparatus or that part of it, as the case may be;

(b) the operator of the system may by notice given in that behalf to the trust not later than the end of the said period of three months abandon the telecommunication apparatus or any part of it;

(c) subject to paragraph (b) above, the operator of the system shall be deemed at the end of that period to have abandoned any part of the apparatus which he has then neither removed nor given notice of his intention to remove;

(d) the operator of the system shall be entitled to recover from the trust the expense of providing, in substitution for the apparatus and any other telecommunication apparatus connected with it which is rendered useless in consequence of the removal or abandonment of the first-mentioned apparatus, any telecommunication apparatus in such other place as the operator may require; and

(e) where under the preceding provisions of this sub-paragraph the operator of the system has abandoned the whole or any part of any telecommunication apparatus, that apparatus or that part of it shall vest in the trust and shall be deemed, with its abandonment, to cease to be kept installed for the purposes of a telecommunications code system.

(2) As soon as practicable after the making of an order under paragraph 9 above extinguishing a public right of way in circumstances in which sub-paragraph (1) above applies in relation to the operator of any telecommunications code system, the Secretary of State shall give notice to the operator of the making of the order.

Statutory undertakers

12.—(1) Where any land has been acquired by a housing action trust under section 77 of this Act and—

(a) there subsists over that land a right vested in or belonging to statutory undertakers for the purpose of the carrying on of their undertaking, being a right of way or a right of laying down, erecting, continuing or maintaining apparatus on, under or over that land, or

(b) there is on, under or over the land apparatus vested in or belonging to statutory undertakers for the purpose of the carrying on of their undertaking,

the trust, if satisfied that the extinguishment of the right or, as the case may be, the removal of the apparatus, is necessary for the purpose of carrying out any development, may serve on the statutory undertakers a notice stating that, at the end of the period of 28 days from the date of service of the notice or such longer period as may be specified therein, the right will be extinguished or requiring that, before the end of that period, the apparatus shall be removed.

(2) The statutory undertakers on whom a notice is served under sub-paragraph (1) above may, before the end of the period of 28 days from the service of the notice, serve a counter-notice on the trust stating that they object to all or any provisions of the notice and specifying the grounds of their objection.

(3) If no counter-notice is served under sub-paragraph (2) above—

(a) any right to which the notice relates shall be extinguished at the end of the period specified in that behalf in the notice; and

(b) if, at the end of the period so specified in relation to any apparatus, any requirement of the notice as to the removal of the apparatus has not been complied with, the trust may remove the apparatus and dispose of it in any way it may think fit.

(4) If a counter-notice is served under sub-paragraph (2) above on a trust, the trust may either withdraw the notice (without prejudice to the service of a further notice) or may apply to the Secretary of State and the appropriate Minister for an order under this paragraph embodying the provisions of the notice with or without modification. SCH. 10

(5) Where by virtue of this paragraph any right vested in or belonging to statutory undertakers is extinguished, or any requirement is imposed on statutory undertakers, those undertakers shall be entitled to compensation from the trust.

(6) Sections 238 and 240 of the Town and Country Planning Act 1971 (measure of compensation to statutory undertakers) shall apply to compensation under sub-paragraph (5) above as they apply to compensation under section 237(2) of that Act. 1971 c. 78.

(7) Except in a case in which paragraph 11 above has effect—

(a) the reference in paragraph (a) of sub-paragraph (1) above to a right vested in or belonging to statutory undertakers for the purpose of the carrying on of their undertaking shall include a reference to a right conferred by or in accordance with the telecommunications code on the operator of a telecommunications code system; and

(b) the reference in paragraph (b) of that sub-paragraph to apparatus vested in or belonging to statutory undertakers for the purpose of the carrying on of their undertaking shall include a reference to telecommunication apparatus kept installed for the purposes of any such system.

(8) Where paragraph (a) or paragraph (b) of sub-paragraph (1) above has effect as mentioned in sub-paragraph (7) above, in the rest of this paragraph and in paragraph 13 below,—

(a) any reference to statutory undertakers shall have effect as a reference to the operator of any such system as is referred to in sub-paragraph (7) above; and

(b) any reference to the appropriate Minister shall have effect as a reference to the Secretary of State for Trade and Industry.

13.—(1) Before making an order under paragraph 12(4) above the Ministers proposing to make the order—

(a) shall afford to the statutory undertakers on whom notice was served under paragraph 12(1) above an opportunity of objecting to the application for the order; and

(b) if any objection is made, shall consider the objection and afford to those statutory undertakers and to the trust on whom the counter-notice was served, an opportunity of appearing before and being heard by a person appointed by the Secretary of State and the appropriate Minister for the purpose;

and the Ministers may then, if they think fit, make the order in accordance with the application either with or without modification.

(2) Where an order is made under paragraph 12(4) above—

(a) any right to which the order relates shall be extinguished at the end of the period specified in that behalf in the order; and

(b) if, at the end of the period so specified in relation to any apparatus, any requirement of the order as to the removal of the apparatus has not been complied with, the trust may remove the apparatus and dispose of it in any way it may think fit.

14.—(1) Subject to this paragraph, where any land has been acquired by a housing action trust under section 77 of this Act and—

(a) there is on, under or over the land apparatus vested in or belonging to statutory undertakers, and

SCH. 10

(b) the undertakers claim that development to be carried out on the land is such as to require, on technical or other grounds connected with the carrying on of their undertaking, the removal or re-siting of the apparatus affected by the development,

the undertakers may serve on the trust a notice claiming the right to enter on the land and carry out such works for the removal or re-siting of the apparatus or any part of it as may be specified in the notice.

(2) Where, after the land has been acquired as mentioned in sub-paragraph (1) above, development of the land is begun to be carried out, no notice under this paragraph shall be served later than 21 days after the beginning of the development.

(3) Where a notice is served under this paragraph the trust on which it is served may, before the end of the period of 28 days from the date of service, serve on the statutory undertakers a counter-notice stating that it objects to all or any of the provisions of the notice and specifying the grounds of its objection.

(4) If no counter-notice is served under sub-paragraph (3) above, the statutory undertakers shall, after the end of the said period of 28 days, have the rights claimed in their notice.

(5) If a counter-notice is served under sub-paragraph (3) above, the statutory undertakers who served the notice under this paragraph may either withdraw it or may apply to the Secretary of State and the appropriate Minister for an order under this paragraph conferring on the undertakers the rights claimed in the notice or such modified rights as the Secretary of State and the appropriate Minister think it expedient to confer on them.

(6) Where by virtue of this paragraph or an order of Ministers made under it, statutory undertakers have the right to execute works for the removal or re-siting of apparatus, they may arrange with the trust for the works to be carried out by the trust, under the superintendence of the undertakers, instead of by the undertakers themselves.

(7) Where works are carried out for the removal or re-siting of statutory undertakers' apparatus, being works which the undertakers have the right to carry out by virtue of this paragraph or an order of Ministers made under it, the undertakers shall be entitled to compensation from the trust.

1971 c. 78. (8) Sections 238 and 240 of the Town and Country Planning Act 1971 (measure of compensation to statutory undertakers) shall apply to compensation under sub-paragraph (7) above as they apply to compensation under section 237(3) of that Act.

(9) In sub-paragraph (1)(a) above, the reference to apparatus vested in or belonging to statutory undertakers shall include a reference to telecommunication apparatus kept installed for the purposes of a telecommunications code system.

(10) Where sub-paragraph (1)(a) above has effect as mentioned in sub-paragraph (9) above, in the rest of this paragraph—

(a) any reference to statutory undertakers shall have effect as a reference to the operator of any such system as is referred to in sub-paragraph (9) above; and

(b) any reference to the appropriate Minister shall have effect as a reference to the Secretary of State for Trade and Industry.

15.—(1) The powers conferred by this paragraph shall be exercisable where, on a representation made by statutory undertakers, it appears to the Secretary of State and the appropriate Minister to be expedient that the powers and duties of those undertakers should be extended or modified, in order—

(a) to secure the provision for a designated area of services which would not otherwise be provided, or which would not otherwise be satisfactorily provided; or Sch. 10

(b) to facilitate an adjustment of the carrying on of the undertaking necessitated by any of the acts and events mentioned in sub-paragraph (2) below.

(2) The said acts and events are—

(a) the acquisition under Part III of this Act of any land in which an interest was held, or which was used, for the purpose of the carrying on of the undertaking of the statutory undertakers in question; and

(b) the extinguishment of a right or the imposition of any requirements by virtue of paragraph 12 above.

(3) The powers conferred by this paragraph shall also be exercisable where, on a representation made by a housing action trust, it appears to the Secretary of State and the appropriate Minister to be expedient that the powers and duties of statutory undertakers should be extended or modified, in order to secure the provision of new services, or the extension of existing services, for the purposes of a designated area under Part III of this Act.

(4) Where the powers conferred by this paragraph are exercisable, the Secretary of State and the appropriate Minister may, if they think fit, by order provide for such extension or modification of the powers and duties of the statutory undertakers as appears to them to be requisite in order to secure the provision of the services in question, as mentioned in sub-paragraph (1)(a) or sub-paragraph (3) above, or to secure the adjustment in question, as mentioned in sub-paragraph (1)(b) above, as the case may be.

(5) Without prejudice to the generality of sub-paragraph (4) above, an order under this paragraph may make provision—

(a) for empowering the statutory undertakers to acquire (whether compulsorily or by agreement) any land specified in the order, and to erect or construct any buildings or works so specified;

(b) for applying, in relation to the acquisition of any such land or the construction of any such works, enactments relating to the acquisition of land and the construction of works;

(c) where it has been represented that the making of the order is expedient for the purposes mentioned in sub-paragraph (1)(a) or sub-paragraph (3) above, for giving effect to such financial arrangements between the housing action trust and the statutory undertakers as they may agree, or as, in default of agreement, may be determined to be equitable in such manner and by such tribunal as may be specified in the order; and

(d) for such incidental and supplemental matters as appear to the Secretary of State and the appropriate Minister to be expedient for the purposes of the order.

16.—(1) As soon as may be after making such a representation as is mentioned in sub-paragraph (1) or sub-paragraph (3) of paragraph 15 above—

(a) the statutory undertakers, in a case falling within sub-paragraph (1), or

(b) the housing action trust, in a case falling within sub-paragraph (3),

shall publish, in such form and manner as may be directed by the Secretary of State and the appropriate Minister, a notice giving such particulars as may be so directed of the matters to which representation relates, and specifying the time within which, and the manner in which, objections to the making of an order on the representation may be made, and shall also, if it is so directed by the Secretary of State and the appropriate Minister, serve a like notice on such persons, or persons of such classes, as may be so directed.

Sch. 10 (2) Orders under paragraph 15 above shall be subject to special parliamentary procedure.

17.—(1) Where, on a representation made by statutory undertakers, the appropriate Minister is satisfied that the fulfilment of any obligations incurred by those undertakers in connection with the carrying on of their undertaking has been rendered impracticable by an act or event to which this sub-paragraph applies, the appropriate Minister may, if he thinks fit, by order direct that the statutory undertakers shall be relieved of the fulfilment of that obligation, either absolutely or to such extent as may be specified in the order.

(2) Sub-paragraph (1) above applies to the following acts and events—

(a) the compulsory acquisition under this Part of this Act of any land in which an interest was held, or which was used, for the purpose of the carrying on of the undertaking of the statutory undertakers; and

(b) the extinguishment of a right or the imposition of any requirement by virtue of paragraph 12 above.

(3) As soon as may be after making a representation to the appropriate Minister under sub-paragraph (1) above, the appropriate statutory undertakers shall, as may be directed by the appropriate Minister, either publish (in such form and manner as may be so directed) a notice giving such particulars as may be so directed of the matters to which the representation relates, and specifying the time within which, and the manner in which, objections to the making of an order on the representation may be made, or serve such a notice on such persons, or persons of such classes, as may be so directed, or both publish and serve such notices.

(4) If any objection to the making of an order under this paragraph is duly made and is not withdrawn before the order is made, the order shall be subject to special parliamentary procedure.

(5) Immediately after an order is made under this paragraph by the appropriate Minister, he shall publish a notice stating that the order has been made and naming a place where a copy of it may be seen at all reasonable hours, and shall serve a like notice—

(a) on any person who duly made an objection to the order and has sent to the appropriate Minister a request in writing to serve him with the notice required by this sub-paragraph, specifying an address for service; and

(b) on such other persons (if any) as the appropriate Minister thinks fit.

(6) Subject to the following provisions of this paragraph, an order under this paragraph shall become operative on the date on which the notice required by sub-paragraph (5) above is first published.

(7) Where in accordance with sub-paragraph (4) above the order is subject to special parliamentary procedure, sub-paragraph (6) above shall not apply.

(8) If any person aggrieved by an order under this paragraph wishes to question the validity of the order on the ground that it is not within the powers conferred by this paragraph, or that any requirement of this paragraph has not been complied with in relation to the order, he may, within six weeks from the date on which the notice required by sub-paragraph (5) above is first published, make an application to the High Court under this paragraph.

(9) On any application under sub-paragraph (8) above the High Court—

(a) may by interim order wholly or in part suspend the operation of the order, either generally or in so far as it affects any property of the applicant, until the final determination of the proceedings; and

(b) if satisfied that the order is wholly or to any extent outside the powers conferred by this paragraph, or that the interests of the applicant have been substantially prejudiced by the failure to comply with any requirement of this paragraph, may wholly or in part quash the order, either generally or in so far as it affects any property of the applicant. SCH. 10

(10) Subject to sub-paragraph (8) above, the validity of an order under this paragraph shall not be questioned in any legal proceedings whatsoever, either before or after the order has been made.

18.—(1) For the purposes of paragraphs 15 and 17 above, an objection to the making of an order thereunder shall not be treated as duly made unless—

(a) the objection is made within the time and in the manner specified in the notice required by paragraph 16 or (as the case may be) paragraph 17 above; and

(b) a statement in writing of the grounds of the objection is comprised in or submitted with the objection.

(2) Where an objection to the making of such an order is duly made in accordance with sub-paragraph (1) above and is not withdrawn, the following provisions of this paragraph shall have effect in relation thereto; but, in the application of those provisions to an order under paragraph 15 above, any reference to the appropriate Minister shall be construed as a reference to the Secretary of State and the appropriate Minister.

(3) Unless the appropriate Minister decides apart from the objection not to make the order, or decides to make a modification which is agreed to by the objector as meeting the objection, the appropriate Minister, before making a final decision, shall consider the grounds of the objection as set out in the statement, and may, if he thinks fit, require the objector to submit within a specified period a further statement in writing as to any of the matters to which the objection relates.

(4) In so far as the appropriate Minister after considering the grounds of the objection as set out in the original statement and in any such further statement, is satisfied that the objection relates to a matter which can be dealt with in the assessment of compensation, the appropriate Minister may treat the objection as irrelevant for the purpose of making a final decision.

(5) If, after considering the grounds of the objection as set out in the original statement and in any such further statement, the appropriate Minister is satisfied that, for the purpose of making a final decision, he is sufficiently informed as to the matters to which the objection relates, or if, where a further statement has been required it is not submitted within the specified period, the appropriate Minister may make a final decision without further investigation as to those matters.

(6) Subject to sub-paragraphs (4) and (5) above, the appropriate Minister, before making a final decision, shall afford to the objector an opportunity of appearing before, and being heard by, a person appointed for the purpose by the appropriate Minister; and if the objector avails himself of that opportunity, the appropriate Minister shall afford an opportunity of appearing and being heard on the same occasion to the statutory undertakers, local authority or Minister on whose representation the order is proposed to be made, and to any other persons to whom it appears to the appropriate Minister to be expedient to afford such an opportunity.

(7) Notwithstanding anything in the preceding provisions of this paragraph, if it appears to the appropriate Minister that the matters to which the objection relates are such as to require investigation by public local inquiry before he makes a final decision, he shall cause such an inquiry to be held; and where he determines to cause such an inquiry to be held, any of the requirements of those provisions to which effect has not been given at the time of that determination shall be dispensed with.

SCH. 10 (8) In this paragraph any reference to making a final decision, in relation to an order, is a reference to deciding whether to make the order or what modification (if any) ought to be made.

Interpretation

19. Any expression used in this Part of the Schedule to which a meaning is
1984 c. 12. assigned by paragraph 1 of Schedule 4 to the Telecommunications Act 1984 has that meaning in this Part.

PART III

ACQUISITION OF RIGHTS

1965 c. 56. 20.—(1) The Compulsory Purchase Act 1965 (in this Part of the Schedule referred to as "the 1965 Act") shall have effect with the modifications necessary to make it apply to the compulsory purchase of rights by virtue of section 77(5) of this Act as it applies to the compulsory purchase of land so that, in appropriate contexts, references in the 1965 Act to land are read as referring, or as including references, to the rights or to land over which the rights are or are to be exercisable, according to the requirements of the particular context.

(2) Without prejudice to the generality of sub-paragraph (1) above, in relation to the purchase of rights in pursuance of section 77(5) of this Act—

(a) Part I of the 1965 Act (which relates to compulsory purchases under the
1981 c. 58. Acquisition of Land Act 1981) shall have effect with the modifications specified in paragraphs 21 to 23 below; and

(b) the enactments relating to compensation for the compulsory purchase of land shall apply with the necessary modifications as they apply to such compensation.

21.—(1) For section 7 of the 1965 Act (which relates to compensation) there shall be substituted the following—

"7.—(1) In assesssing the compensation to be paid by the acquiring authority under this Act regard shall be had not only to the extent, if any, to which the value of the land over which the right is purchased is depreciated by the purchase but also to the damage, if any, to be sustained by the owner of the land by reason of injurious affection of other land of the owner by the exercise of the right.

(2) The modifications subject to which subsection (1) of section 44 of the Land Compensation Act 1973 is to have effect, as applied by subsection (2) of that section to compensation for injurious affection under this section, are that for the words "land is acquired or taken" there shall be substituted the words "a right over land is purchased" and for the words "acquired or taken from him" there shall be substituted the words "over which the right is exercisable"."

22. For section 8 of the 1965 Act (which relates to cases in which a vendor cannot be required to sell part only of a building or garden) there shall be substituted the following—

"8.—(1) Where in consequence of the service on a person in pursuance of section 5 of this Act of a notice to treat in respect of a right over land consisting of a house, building or manufactory or of a park or garden belonging to a house (hereafter in this subsection referred to as "the relevant land")—

(a) a question of disputed compensation in respect of the purchase of the right would apart from this section fall to be determined by the Lands Tribunal (hereafter in this section referred to as "the Tribunal"); and

(b) before the Tribunal has determined that question the person satisfies the Tribunal that he has an interest which he is able and willing to sell in the whole of the relevant land and— Sch. 10

(i) where that land consists of a house, building or manufactory, that the right cannot be purchased without material detriment to that land, or

(ii) where that land consists of such a park or garden, that the right cannot be purchased without seriously affecting the amenity or convenience of the house to which that land belongs,

the compulsory purchase order to which the notice to treat relates shall, in relation to that person, cease to authorise the purchase of the right and be deemed to authorise the purchase of that person's interest in the whole of the relevant land including, where the land consists of such a park or garden, the house to which it belongs, and the notice shall be deemed to have been served in respect of that interest on such date as the Tribunal directs.

(2) Any question as to the extent of the land in which a compulsory purchase order is deemed to authorise the purchase of an interest by virtue of the preceding subsection shall be determined by the Tribunal.

(3) Where in consequence of a determination of the Tribunal that it is satisfied as mentioned in subsection (1) of this section a compulsory purchase order is deemed by virtue of that subsection to authorise the purchase of an interest in land, the acquiring authority may, at any time within the period of six weeks beginning with the date of the determination, withdraw the notice to treat in consequence of which the determination was made; but nothing in this subsection prejudices any other power of the authority to withdraw the notice.

(4) The modifications subject to which subsection (1) of section 58 of the Land Compensation Act 1973 is to have effect, as applied by subsection (2) of that section to the duty of the Tribunal in determining whether it is satisfied as mentioned in subsection (1) of this section, are that at the beginning of paragraphs (a) and (b) there shall be inserted the words "a right over", for the word "severance" there shall be substituted the words "right on the whole of the house, building or manufactory or of the house and the park or garden" and for the words "part proposed" and "part is" there shall be substituted respectively the words "right proposed" and "right is"."

23.—(1)The following provisions of the 1965 Act (which state the effect of a deed poll executed in various circumstances where there is no conveyance by persons with interests in the land), namely—

section 9(4) (failure of owners to convey),

paragraph 10(3) of Schedule 1 (owners under incapacity),

paragraph 2(3) of Schedule 2 (absent and untraced owners), and

paragraphs 2(3) and 7(2) of Schedule 4 (common land),

shall be so modified as to secure that, as against persons with interests in the land which are expressed to be overridden by the deed, the right which is to be purchased compulsorily is vested absolutely in the acquiring authority.

(2) Section 11 of the 1965 Act (powers of entry) shall be so modified as to secure that, as from the date on which the acquiring authority has served notice to treat in respect of any right, it has power, exercisable in the like circumstances and subject to the like conditions, to enter for the purpose of exercising that right (which shall be deemed for this purpose to have been created on the date of service of the notice); and sections 12 (penalty for unauthorised entry) and 13 (entry on sheriff's warrant in the event of obstruction) of the Act shall be modified correspondingly.

SCH. 10

(3) Section 20 of the 1965 Act (compensation for short-term tenants) shall apply with the modifications necessary to secure that persons with such interests as are mentioned in that section are compensated in a manner corresponding to that in which they would be compensated on a compulsory acquisition of the interests but taking into account only the extent (if any) of such interference with such interests as is actually caused, or likely to be caused, by the exercise of the right in question.

(4) Section 22 of the 1965 Act (protection of acquiring authority's possession of land where by inadvertence an interest in the land has not been purchased) shall be so modified as to enable the acquiring authority, in circumstances corresponding to those referred to in that section, to continue to be entitled to exercise the right in question, subject to compliance with that section as respects compensation.

Section 79(13).

SCHEDULE 11

PROVISIONS APPLICABLE TO CERTAIN DISPOSALS OF HOUSES

Repayment of discount on early disposal

1.—(1) This paragraph applies where, on the disposal of a house under section 79 of this Act, a discount is given to the purchaser by the housing action trust in accordance with a consent given by the Secretary of State under subsection (1) of that section and that consent does not exclude the application of this paragraph.

(2) On the disposal, the conveyance, grant or assignment shall contain a covenant binding on the purchaser and his successors in title to pay to the housing action trust on demand, if within a period of three years there is a relevant disposal which is not an exempted disposal (but if there is more than one such disposal then only on the first of them), an amount equal to the discount, reduced by one-third for each complete year which has elapsed after the conveyance, grant or assignment and before the further disposal.

Obligation to repay a charge on the house

2.—(1) The liability that may arise under the covenant required by paragraph 1 above is a charge on the house, taking effect as if it had been created by deed expressed to be by way of legal mortgage.

(2) The charge has priority immediately after any legal charge securing an amount—

(a) left outstanding by the purchaser; or

(b) advanced to him by an approved lending institution for the purpose of enabling him to acquire the interest disposed of on the first disposal; or

(c) further advanced to him by that institution;

but the housing action trust may at any time by written notice served on an approved lending institution postpone the charge taking effect by virtue of this paragraph to a legal charge securing an amount advanced or further advanced to the purchaser by that institution.

(3) A charge taking effect by virtue of this paragraph is a land charge for the
1925 c. 21. purposes of section 59 of the Land Registration Act 1925 notwithstanding subsection (5) of that section (exclusion of mortgages), and subsection (2) of that section applies accordingly with respect to its protection and realisation.

(4) The covenant required by paragraph 1 above does not, by virtue of its binding successors in title of the purchaser, bind a person exercising rights under a charge having priority over the charge taking effect by virtue of this paragraph, or a person deriving title under him; and a provision of the conveyance, grant or

assignment, or of a collateral agreement, is void in so far as it purports to authorise a forfeiture, or to impose a penalty or disability, in the event of any such person failing to comply with the covenant. SCH. 11

(5) The approved lending institutions for the purposes of this paragraph are—

(a) a building society;

(b) a bank;

(c) an insurance company;

(d) a friendly society; and

(e) any body specified, or of a class or description specified, in an order made under section 156 of the Housing Act 1985 (which makes provision in relation to disposals in pursuance of the right to buy corresponding to that made by this paragraph). 1985 c. 68.

Relevant disposals

3.—(1) A disposal, whether of the whole or part of the house, is a relevant disposal for the purpose of this Schedule if it is—

(a) a conveyance of the freehold or an assignment of the lease; or

(b) the grant of a lease or sub-lease (other than a mortgage term) for a term of more than 21 years otherwise than at a rack rent.

(2) For the purposes of sub-paragraph (1)(b) above it shall be assumed—

(a) that any option to renew or extend a lease or sub-lease, whether or not forming part of a series of options, is exercised; and

(b) that any option to terminate a lease or sub-lease is not exercised.

Exempted disposals

4.—(1) A disposal is an exempted disposal for the purposes of this Schedule if—

(a) it is a disposal of the whole of the house and a conveyance of the freehold or an assignment of the lease and the person or each of the persons to whom it is made is a qualifying person (as defined in sub-paragraph (2) below);

(b) it is a vesting of the whole of the house in a person taking under a will or on an intestacy;

(c) it is a disposal of the whole of the house in pursuance of an order made under section 24 of the Matrimonial Causes Act 1973 (property adjustment orders in connection with matrimonial proceedings) or section 2 of the Inheritance (Provision for Family and Dependants) Act 1975 (orders as to financial provision to be made from estate); 1973 c. 18. 1975 c. 63.

(d) it is a compulsory disposal; or

(e) the property disposed of is property included with the house as being such a yard, garden, outhouse or appurtenance as is referred to in section 92(1)(b) of this Act.

(2) For the purposes of sub-paragraph (1)(a) above, a person is a qualifying person in relation to a disposal if—

(a) he is the person or one of the persons by whom the disposal is made;

(b) he is the spouse or a former spouse of that person or one of those persons; or

(c) he is a member of the family of that person or one of those persons and has resided with him throughout the period of twelve months ending with the disposal.

SCH. 11

1985 c. 68.

(3) Section 186 of the Housing Act 1985 applies to determine whether a person is a member of another person's family for the purposes of sub-paragraph (2)(c) above.

Compulsory disposal

5. In this Schedule a "compulsory disposal" means a disposal of property which is acquired compulsorily, or is acquired by a person who has made or would have made, or for whom another person has made or would have made, a compulsory purchase order authorising its compulsory purchase for the purposes for which it is acquired.

Exempted disposals ending obligation under covenants

6. Where there is a relevant disposal which is an exempted disposal by virtue of paragraph 4(1)(d) or paragraph 4(1)(e) above—

(a) the covenant required by paragraph 1 above is not binding on the person to whom the disposal is made or any successor in title of his; and

(b) that covenant and the charge taking effect by virtue of paragraph 2 above cease to apply in relation to the property disposed of.

Treatment of options

7. For the purpose of this Schedule, the grant of an option enabling a person to call for a relevant disposal which is not an exempted disposal shall be treated as such a disposal made to him.

Section 108.

SCHEDULE 12

REGISTRATION OF TITLE AND RELATED MATTERS

Interpretation

1. In this Schedule—

"transferred property" means property which is the subject of a grant under section 104(1)(a) of this Act;

"transferee", in relation to any transferred property, means the person to whom the grant is made;

"conveyance" means the instrument by which the grant is effected; and

other expressions have the same meaning as in section 104 of this Act.

Acquisitions under section 104(1)(a)

2.—(1) Where a landlord makes a grant of transferred property, it shall ensure—

(a) that the conveyance contains a statement that the grant is made under section 104(1)(a) of this Act; and

(b) that all deeds and other documents relating to land (including, in the case of registered land, the land certificate) which are in its possession or under its control and which the transferee reasonably requires on or in connection with the grant of the transferred property are made available to him for this purpose.

(2) Where the landlord's title to the whole or any part of the transferred property is not registered— Sch. 12

(a) section 123 of the Land Registration Act 1925 (compulsory registration of title) applies in relation to the conveyance whether or not the transferred property is in an area in which an Order in Council under section 120 of that Act (areas of compulsory registration) is in force; and 1925 c. 21.

(b) the landlord shall give the transferee a certificate stating that it is entitled to convey the freehold subject only to such incumbrances, rights and interests as are stated in the conveyance or summarised in the certificate.

(3) The Chief Land Registrar shall, for the purpose of the registration of title, accept such a certificate as is referred to in sub-paragraph (2)(b) above as sufficient evidence of the facts stated in it; but if as a result he has to meet a claim under the Land Registration Acts 1925 to 1986 the landlord is liable to indemnify him.

(4) On an application being made for registration of a disposition of registered land or, as the case may be, of the transferee's title under a disposition of unregistered land, the Chief Land Registrar shall, if the conveyance contains the statement required by sub-paragraph (1)(a) above, enter in the register a restriction stating the requirement under section 105 of this Act of consent to subsequent disposals.

(5) Any reference in the preceding provisions of this paragraph to a statement or a certificate is a reference to a statement or, as the case may be, certificate in a form approved by the Chief Land Registrar.

Procedures on termination of leases granted under section 104(1)(b)

3.—(1) If a lease granted under section 104(1)(b) of this Act comes to an end in such circumstances as may be prescribed, the public sector landlord which was the lessee under the lease shall, at such time as may be prescribed, furnish to the Chief Land Registrar such statement as may be prescribed.

(2) In any case where—

(a) under section 104(1)(b) of this Act the applicant has granted a lease of a flat (in this sub-paragraph referred to as "the landlord's lease"), and

(b) under Part V of the Housing Act 1985 (the right to buy) a lease of the flat (in this sub-paragraph referred to as "the right to buy lease") has been granted to a qualifying tenant, and 1985 c. 68.

(c) by virtue of requirements prescribed under section 104(2) of this Act and related to the grant of the right to buy lease, the landlord's lease comes to an end,

then, notwithstanding anything in section 64 of the Land Registration Act 1925 (production of land certificate), notice of the grant of the right to buy lease may be entered in the register without production of the applicant's land certificate, but without prejudice to the power of the Chief Land Registrar to compel production of the certificate.

SCHEDULE 13

Section 119.

Amendments of Landlord and Tenant Act 1987

1. In Part I of the Landlord and Tenant Act 1987 (tenants' rights of first refusal), in section 2 (landlords for the purposes of Part I), in subsection (1) after "(2)" there shall be inserted "and section 4(1A)". 1987 c. 31.

SCH. 13

2.—(1) In section 3 of that Act (qualifying tenants), in subsection (1) (paragraphs (a) to (c) of which exclude certain tenants) the word "or" immediately preceding paragraph (c) shall be omitted and at the end of that paragraph there shall be added "or

(d) an assured tenancy or assured agricultural occupancy within the meaning of Part I of the Housing Act 1988".

(2) In subsection (2) of that section (which excludes persons having interests going beyond a particular flat), for paragraphs (a) and (b) there shall be substituted the words "by virtue of one or more tenancies none of which falls within paragraphs (a) to (d) of subsection (1), he is the tenant not only of the flat in question but also of at least two other flats contained in those premises"; and in subsection (3) of that section for "(2)(b)" there shall be substituted "(2)".

3.—(1) In section 4 of that Act (relevant disposals) after subsection (1) there shall be inserted the following subsection—

"(1A) Where an estate or interest of the landlord has been mortgaged, the reference in subsection (1) above to the disposal of an estate or interest by the landlord includes a reference to its disposal by the mortgagee in exercise of a power of sale or leasing, whether or not the disposal is made in the name of the landlord; and, in relation to such a proposed disposal by the mortgagee, any reference in the following provisions of this Part to the landlord shall be construed as a reference to the mortgagee."

(2) In subsection (2) of that section, in paragraph (a), at the end of sub-paragraph (i) there shall be inserted "or", sub-paragraph (ii) shall be omitted and at the end of that paragraph there shall be inserted—

"(aa) a disposal consisting of the creation of an estate or interest by way of security for a loan".

4.—(1) In Part III of that Act (compulsory acquisition by tenants of their landlord's interest), in section 26 (qualifying tenants), in subsection (2) (which excludes persons having interests going beyond a particular flat) for the words following "if" there shall be substituted "by virtue of one or more long leases none of which constitutes a tenancy to which Part II of the Landlord and Tenant Act 1954 applies, he is the tenant not only of the flat in question but also of at least two other flats contained in those premises".

(2) At the end of the said section 26 there shall be added the following subsection—

"(4) For the purposes of subsection (2) any tenant of a flat contained in the premises in question who is a body corporate shall be treated as the tenant of any other flat so contained and let to an associated company, as defined in section 20(1)."

5. In Part IV of that Act (variation of leases), for subsections (6) and (7) of section 35 (which make provision about long leases) there shall be substituted the following subsection—

"(6) For the purposes of this Part a long lease shall not be regarded as a long lease of a flat if—

(a) the demised premises consist of or include three or more flats contained in the same building; or

(b) the lease constitutes a tenancy to which Part II of the Landlord and Tenant Act 1954 applies."

6. In section 40 (application for variation of insurance provisions of lease of dwelling other than a flat) for subsection (4) (which makes provision about long leases) there shall be substituted the following subsections—

"(4) For the purpose of this section, a long lease shall not be regarded as a long lease of a dwelling if— SCH. 13

(a) the demised premises consist of three or more dwellings; or

(b) the lease constitutes a tenancy to which Part II of the Landlord and Tenant Act 1954 applies.

(4A) Without prejudice to subsection (4), an application under subsection (1) may not be made by a person who is a tenant under a long lease of a dwelling if, by virtue of that lease and one or more other long leases of dwellings, he is also a tenant from the same landlord of at least two other dwellings.

(4B) For the purposes of subsection (4A), any tenant of a dwelling who is a body corporate shall be treated as a tenant of any other dwelling held from the same landlord which is let under a long lease to an associated company, as defined in section 20(1)."

7. In Part VII of that Act (general), in section 58 (exempt landlords), in subsection (1) after paragraph (c) there shall be inserted the following paragraph—

"(ca) a housing action trust established under Part III of the Housing Act 1988."

SCHEDULE 14

Section 120.

APPOINTMENT ETC. OF RENT OFFICERS

PART I

AMENDMENTS OF SECTION 63 OF RENT ACT 1977

1977 c. 42.

1. In subsection (1), paragraph (b) and the word "and" immediately preceding it shall be omitted.

2. In subsection (2)—

(a) in paragraph (a) the words "and deputy rent officers" shall be omitted;

(b) in paragraph (b) the words "or deputy rent officer" shall be omitted;

(c) in paragraph (d) the words "and deputy rent officers" and the word "and" at the end of the paragraph shall be omitted; and

(d) paragraph (e) shall be omitted.

3. After subsection (2) there shall be inserted the following subsection—

"(2A) A scheme under this section may make all or any of the following provisions—

(a) provision requiring the consent of the Secretary of State to the appointment of rent officers;

(b) provision with respect to the appointment of rent officers for fixed periods;

(c) provision for the proper officer of the local authority, in such circumstances and subject to such conditions (as to consent or otherwise) as may be specified in the scheme,—

(i) to designate a person appointed or to be appointed a rent officer as chief rent officer and to designate one or more such persons as senior rent officers;

(ii) to delegate to a person so designated as chief rent officer such functions as may be specified in the scheme; and

(iii) to revoke a designation under sub-paragraph (i) above and to revoke or vary a delegation under sub-paragraph (ii) above;

Sch. 14

(d) provision with respect to the delegation of functions by a chief rent officer to other rent officers (whether designated as senior rent officers or not);

(e) provision as to the circumstances in which and the terms on which a rent officer appointed by the scheme may undertake functions outside the area to which the scheme relates in accordance with paragraph (f) below;

(f) provision under which a rent officer appointed for an area other than that to which the scheme relates may undertake functions in the area to which the scheme relates and for such a rent officer to be treated for such purposes as may be specified in the scheme (which may include the purposes of paragraphs (c) and (d) above and paragraphs (c) and (d) of subsection (2) above) as if he were a rent officer appointed under the scheme; and

(g) provision conferring functions on the proper officer of a local authority with respect to the matters referred to in paragraphs (d) to (f) above."

4. In subsection (3) the words "and deputy rent officers" shall be omitted.

5. In subsection (7)—

(a) in paragraph (b) the words "and deputy rent officers" shall be omitted, after the words "section 7" there shall be inserted "or section 24" and for the words following "1972" there shall be substituted "or"; and

(b) at the end of paragraph (b) there shall be inserted the following paragraph—

"(c) incurred in respect of increases of pensions payable to or in respect of rent officers (so appointed) by virtue of the Pensions (Increase) Act 1971".

Part II

1977 c. 42.

Sections to be Inserted in Rent Act 1977 after Section 64

"Amalgamation schemes

64A.—(1) If the Secretary of State is of the opinion—

(a) that there is at any time insufficient work in two or more registration areas to justify the existence of a separate service of rent officers for each area, or

(b) that it would at any time be beneficial for the efficient administration of the service provided by rent officers in two or more registration areas,

he may, after consultation with the local authorities concerned, make a scheme under section 63 above designating as an amalgamated registration area the areas of those authorities and making provision accordingly for that amalgamated area.

(2) Any reference in the following provisions of this Chapter to a registration area includes a reference to an amalgamated registration area and, in relation to such an area, "the constituent authorities" means the local authorities whose areas make up the amalgamated area.

(3) A scheme under section 63 above made for an amalgamated registration area—

(a) shall confer on the proper officer of one of the constituent authorities all or any of the functions which, in accordance with section 63 above, fall to be exercisable by the proper officer of the local authority for the registration area;

(b) may provide that any rent officer previously appointed for the area of any one of the constituent authorities shall be treated for such purposes as may be specified in the scheme as a rent officer appointed for the amalgamated registration area; and

(c) shall make such provision as appears to the Secretary of State to be appropriate for the payment by one or more of the constituent authorities of the remunerations, allowances and other expenditure which under section 63 above is to be paid by the local authority for the area.

(4) A scheme under section 63 above made for an amalgamated registration area may contain such incidental, transitional and supplementary provisions as appear to the Secretary of State to be necessary or expedient.

New basis for administration of rent officer service

64B.—(1) If, with respect to registration areas generally or any particular registration area or areas, it appears to the Secretary of State that it is no longer appropriate for the appointment, remuneration and administration of rent officers to be a function of local authorities, he may by order—

(a) provide that no scheme under section 63 above shall be made for the area or areas specified in the order; and

(b) make, with respect to the area or areas so specified, such provision as appears to him to be appropriate with respect to the appointment, remuneration and administration of rent officers and the payment of pensions, allowances or gratuities to or in respect of them.

(2) An order under this section shall make provision for any expenditure attributable to the provisions of the order to be met by the Secretary of State in such manner as may be specified in the order (whether by way of grant, reimbursement or otherwise); and any expenditure incurred by the Secretary of State by virtue of this subsection shall be paid out of money provided by Parliament.

(3) An order under this section—

(a) may contain such incidental, transitional and supplementary provisions as appear to the Secretary of State to be appropriate, including provisions amending this Part of this Act; and

(b) shall be made by statutory instrument which shall be subject to annulment in pursuance of a resolution of either House of Parliament."

SCHEDULE 15

Repair Notices: Amendments of Housing Act 1985, Part VI

1.—(1) In section 189 (repair notice in respect of unfit house), in subsection (1)—

(a) at the beginning there shall be inserted the words "Subject to subsection (1A)"; and

(b) for the word "house", in each place where it occurs, there shall be substituted "dwelling-house".

(2) At the end of subsection (1) of that section there shall be inserted the following subsection—

"(1A) Where the local housing authority are satisfied that a dwelling-house which is a flat is unfit for human habitation by reason of the defective condition of a part of the building outside the flat, they shall serve a repair notice on the person having control of that part of the building, unless they are satisfied that the works which would be required to that part are such that the flat is not capable of being rendered so fit at reasonable expense."

SCH. 15

(3) In subsection (2) of that section—

(a) in paragraph (a) for the words from "within such reasonable time" onwards there shall be substituted the words "and to begin those works not later than such reasonable date, being not earlier than the seventh day after the notice becomes operative, as is specified in the notice and to complete those works within such reasonable time as is so specified, and"; and

(b) in paragraph (b) for the word "house" there shall be substituted "dwelling-house".

(4) In subsection (3) of that section for the words "the house", in each place where they occur, there shall be substituted "the dwelling-house or part of the building concerned", for the word "may" there shall be substituted "shall" and for the words "lessee or otherwise" there shall be substituted "or lessee".

(5) At the end of that section there shall be added the following subsection—

"(5) A repair notice under this section which has become operative is a local land charge."

2.—(1) In section 190 (repair notice in respect of house in state of disrepair, but not unfit), in subsection (1),—

(a) for the word "house", in each place where it occurs, there shall be substituted "dwelling-house";

(b) in paragraph (b), after the word "satisfied" there shall be inserted "whether" and after the word "tenant", in the first place where it occurs, there shall be inserted "or otherwise".

(2) At the end of subsection (1) of that section there shall be inserted the following subsection—

"(1A) Where the local housing authority—

(a) are satisfied that a building containing a flat is in such a state of disrepair that, although the flat is not unfit for human habitation, substantial repairs are necessary to a part of the building outside the flat to bring the flat up to a reasonable standard, having regard to its age, character and locality, or

(b) are satisfied, whether on a representation made by an occupying tenant or otherwise, that a building containing a flat is in such a state of disrepair that, although the flat is not unfit for human habitation, the condition of a part of the building outside the flat is such as to interfere materially with the personal comfort of the occupying tenant,

they may serve a repair notice on the person having control of the part of the building concerned."

(3) In subsection (2) of that section for the words from "within such reasonable time" onwards there shall be substituted "to execute the works specified in the notice, not being works of internal decorative repair, and—

(a) to begin those works not later than such reasonable date, being not earlier than the seventh day after the notice becomes operative, as is specified in the notice; and

(b) to complete those works within such reasonable time as is so specified."

(4) In subsection (3) of that section for the words "the house", in each place where they occur, there shall be substituted "the dwelling-house or part of the building concerned", for the word "may" there shall be substituted "shall" and for the words "lessee or otherwise" there shall be substituted "or lessee".

(5) At the end of that section there shall be added the following subsection—

"(5) A repair notice under this section which has become operative is a local land charge." SCH. 15

3.—(1) In section 191 (appeals against repair notices), after subsection (1) there shall be inserted the following subsection—

"(1A) Without prejudice to the generality of subsection (1), it shall be a ground of appeal that some person other than the appellant, being a person who is an owner in relation to the dwelling-house or part of the building concerned, ought to execute the works or pay the whole or part of the cost of executing them."

(2) In subsection (3) of that section for the words "the house" there shall be substituted "the dwelling-house".

(3) After subsection (3) of that section there shall be inserted the following subsections—

"(3A) Where the grounds on which an appeal is brought are or include that specified in subsection (1A), the appellant shall serve a copy of his notice of appeal on each other person referred to; and on the hearing of the appeal the court may—

(a) vary the repair notice so as to require the works to be executed by any such other person; or

(b) make such order as it thinks fit with respect to the payment to be made by any such other person to the appellant or, where the works are executed by the local housing authority, to the authority.

(3B) In the exercise of its powers under subsection (3A), the court shall take into account, as between the appellant and any such other person as is referred to in that subsection,—

(a) their relative interests in the dwelling-house or part of the building concerned (considering both the nature of the interests and the rights and obligations arising under or by virtue of them);

(b) their relative responsibility for the state of the dwelling-house or building which gives rise to the need for the execution of the works; and

(c) the relative degree of benefit to be derived from the execution of the works.

(3C) If, by virtue of the exercise of the court's powers under subsection (3A), a person other than the appellant is required to execute the works specified in a repair notice, then, so long as that other person continues to be an owner in relation to the premises to which the notice relates, he shall be regarded as the person having control of those premises for the purposes of the following provisions of this Part."

4.—(1) In section 192 (power to purchase houses found on appeal to be unfit etc.), in subsections (1) and (2) for the words "the house", in each place where they occur, there shall be substituted "the dwelling-house".

(2) In subsection (3) of that section for the words "the house" there shall be substituted "the dwelling-house or part of the building in question".

(3) In subsection (4) of that section for the words "the house" there shall be substituted "the dwelling-house".

5.—(1) In section 193 (power of local housing authority to execute works) for subsection (2) there shall be substituted the following subsections—

SCH. 15

"(2) For the purpose of this Part compliance with the notice means beginning and completing the works specified in the notice,—

(a) if no appeal is brought against the notice, not later than such date and within such period as is specified in the notice;

(b) if an appeal is brought against the notice and is not withdrawn, not later than such date and within such period as may be fixed by the court determining the appeal; and

(c) if an appeal brought against the notice is withdrawn, not later than the twenty-first day after the date on which the notice becomes operative and within such period (beginning on that twenty-first day) as is specified in the notice.

(2A) If, before the expiry of the period which under subsection (2) is appropriate for completion of the works specified in the notice, it appears to the local housing authority that reasonable progress is not being made towards compliance with the notice, the authority may themselves do the work required to be done by the notice."

(2) At the end of that section there shall be added the following subsection—

"(4) If, after the local housing authority have given notice under section 194 of their intention to enter and do any works, the works are in fact carried out by the person having control of the dwelling-house or part of the building in question, any administrative and other expenses incurred by the authority with a view to doing the works themselves shall be treated for the purposes of Schedule 10 as expenses incurred by them under this section in carrying out works in default of the person on whom the repair notice was served."

6.—(1) In section194 (notice of authority's intention to execute works), in subsection (1)—

(a) for the words "a house" there shall be substituted "any premises";

(b) for the word "may" there shall be substituted "shall"; and

(c) for the words "the house", in each place where they occur, there shall be substituted "the premises".

(2) In subsection (2) of that section for the words "the house", in each place where they occur, there shall be substituted "the premises".

7. In section 198 (penalty for obstruction), in subsection (2) for the words "level 2" there shall be substituted "level 3".

8. After section 198 there shall be inserted the following section—

"Penalty for failure to execute works.

198A.—(1) A person having control of premises to which a repair notice relates who intentionally fails to comply with the notice commits a summary offence and is liable on conviction to a fine not exceeding level 4 on the standard scale.

(2) The obligation to execute the works specified in the notice continues notwithstanding that the period for completion of the works has expired.

(3) Section 193(2) shall have effect to determine whether a person has failed to comply with a notice and what is the period for completion of any works.

(4) The provisions of this section are without prejudice to the exercise by the local housing authority of the powers conferred by the preceding provisions of this Part."

9. Sections 199 to 201 (recovery by lessee of proportion of works and provisions as to charging orders) shall cease to have effect.

10. In section 203 (saving for rights arising from breach of covenant, etc.), in subsection (3) for the words "a house" there shall be substituted "any premises". SCH. 15

11. In section 205 (application of provisions to parts of buildings and temporary or movable structures) paragraph (a) shall be omitted and for the word "house" there shall be substituted "dwelling-house".

12.—(1) In section 207 (definitions)—

(a) for the definition beginning "house" there shall be substituted—

""dwelling-house" and "flat" shall be construed in accordance with subsection (2) and "the building", in relation to a flat, means the building containing the flat";

(b) in the definition of "person having control" for the words "in relation to premises" there shall be substituted "subject to section 191(3A),—

(a) in relation to a dwelling-house";

(c) at the end of that definition there shall be added "and

(b) in relation to a part of a building to which relates a repair notice served under subsection (1A) of section 189 or section 190, means a person who is an owner in relation to that part of the building (or the building as a whole) and who, in the opinion of the authority by whom the notice is served, ought to execute the works specified in the notice"; and

(d) after the definition of "person having control" there shall be inserted—

""premises" includes a dwelling-house or part of a building and, in relation to any premises, any reference to a person having control shall be construed accordingly".

(2) At the end of that section there shall be inserted the following subsection—

"(2) For the purposes of this Part a "dwelling-house" includes any yard, garden, outhouses and appurtenances belonging to it or usually enjoyed with it and section 183 shall have effect to determine whether a dwelling-house is a flat."

13.—(1) In Schedule 10 (recovery of expenses incurred by local housing authority), in paragraph 2, in sub-paragraph (1) for the words following "authority" there shall be substituted—

"(a) where the works were required by a notice under section 189 or section 190 (repair notices), from the person having control of the dwelling-house or part of the building to which the notice relates; and

(b) in any other case, from the person on whom the notice was served;

and in the following provisions of this paragraph the person from whom expenses are recoverable by virtue of this sub-paragraph is referred to as "the person primarily liable"."

(2) In sub-paragraphs (2) and (3) of paragraph 2 of that Schedule for the words "on whom the notice was served", in each place where they occur, there shall be substituted "primarily liable".

(3) In paragraph 6 of that Schedule (appeals) after sub-paragraph (1) there shall be inserted the following sub-paragraph—

"(1A) Where the demand for recovery of expenses relates to works carried out by virtue of section 193(2A), it shall be a ground of appeal that, at the time the local housing authority gave notice under section 194 of their intention to enter and do the works, reasonable progress was being made towards compliance with the repair notice."

Section 135.
1987 c. 26.

SCHEDULE 16

Schedule to be Inserted in the Housing (Scotland) Act 1987

"SCHEDULE 6A

Consultation Before Disposal to Private Sector Landlord

Disposals to which this Schedule applies

1.—(1) This Schedule applies to the disposal by a local authority of an interest in land as a result of which a secure tenant of the local authority will become the tenant of a private sector landlord.

(2) For the purposes of this Schedule the grant of an option which if exercised would result in a secure tenant of a local authority becoming the tenant of a private sector landlord shall be treated as a disposal of the interest which is the subject of the option.

(3) Where a disposal of land by a local authority is in part a disposal to which this Schedule applies, the provisions of this Schedule apply to that part as to a separate disposal.

(4) In this paragraph "private sector landlord" means a person other than one of those set out in sub-paragraphs (i) to (iv) and (viii) and (ix) of paragraph (a) of subsection (2) of section 61.

Application for Secretary of State's consent

2.—(1) The Secretary of State shall not entertain an application for his consent under section 12(7) to a disposal to which this Schedule applies unless the local authority certify either—

(a) that the requirements of paragraph 3 as to consultation have been complied with, or

(b) that the requirements of that paragraph as to consultation have been complied with except in relation to tenants expected to have vacated the house in question before the disposal;

and the certificate shall be accompanied by a copy of the notices given by the local authority in accordance with that paragraph.

(2) Where the certificate is in the latter form, the Secretary of State shall not determine the application until the local authority certify as regards the tenants not originally consulted—

(a) that they have vacated the house in question, or

(b) that the requirements of paragraph 3 as to consultation have been complied with;

and a certificate under sub-paragraph (b) shall be accompanied by a copy of the notices given by the local authority in accordance with paragraph 3.

Requirements as to consultation

3.—(1) The requirements as to consultation referred to above are as follows.

(2) The local authority shall serve notice in writing on the tenant informing him of—

(a) such details of their proposal as the local authority consider appropriate, but including the identity of the person to whom the disposal is to be made,

(b) the likely consequences of the disposal for the tenant, and

(c) the effect of section 81A and the provision made under it (preservation of right to buy on disposal to private sector landlord) and of this Schedule, Sch. 16

and informing him that he may, within such reasonable period as may be specified in the notice, which must be at least 28 days after the service of the notice, make representations to the local authority.

(3) The local authority shall consider any representations made to them within that period and shall serve a further written notice on the tenant informing him—

(a) of any significant changes in their proposal, and

(b) that he may within such period as is specified (which must be at least 28 days after the service of the notice) communicate to the Secretary of State his objection to the proposal,

and informing him of the effect of paragraph 5 (consent to be withheld if majority of tenants are opposed).

Power to require further consultation

4. The Secretary of State may require the local authority to carry out such further consultation with their tenants, and to give him such information as to the results of that consultation, as he may direct.

Consent to be withheld if majority of tenants are opposed

5.—(1) The Secretary of State shall not give his consent if it appears to him that a majority of the tenants of the houses to which the application relates do not wish the disposal to proceed; but this does not affect his general discretion to refuse consent on grounds relating to whether a disposal has the support of the tenants or on any other ground.

(2) In making his decision the Secretary of State may have regard to any information available to him; and the local authority shall give him such information as to the representations made to them by tenants and others, and other relevant matters, as he may require.

Protection of purchasers

6. The Secretary of State's consent to a disposal is not invalidated by a failure on his part or that of the local authority to comply with the requirements of this Schedule."

SCHEDULE 17

Section 140.

Minor and Consequential Amendments

Part I

General Amendments

The Reserve and Auxiliary Forces (Protection of Civil Interests) Act 1951

1. In section 4 of the Reserve and Auxiliary Forces (Protection of Civil Interests) Act 1951 (recovery of possession of dwelling-houses in default of payment of rent precluded in certain cases) after subsection (2) there shall be inserted the following subsection— 1951 c. 65.

"(2A) For the purposes of the foregoing provisions of this Act, a judgment or order for the recovery of possession of a dwelling-house let on an assured tenancy within the meaning of Part I of the Housing Act 1988 shall be regarded as a judgment or order for the recovery of possession in

SCH. 17

default of payment of rent if the judgment or order was made on any of Grounds 8, 10 and 11 in Schedule 2 to that Act and not on any other ground."

2. For section 16 of that Act (protection of tenure of rented premises by extension of Rent Acts), as it applies otherwise than to Scotland, there shall be substituted the following section—

"Protection of tenure of certain rented premises by extension of Housing Act 1988.

16.—(1) Subject to subsection (2) of section 14 of this Act and subsection (3) below, if at any time during a service man's period of residence protection—

(a) a tenancy qualifying for protection which is a fixed term tenancy ends without being continued or renewed by agreement (whether on the same or different terms and conditions), and

(b) by reason only of such circumstances as are mentioned in subsection (4) below, on the ending of that tenancy no statutory periodic tenancy of the rented family residence would arise, apart from the provisions of this section,

Chapter I of Part I of the Housing Act 1988 shall, during the remainder of the period of protection, apply in relation to the rented family residence as if those circumstances did not exist and had not existed immediately before the ending of that tenancy and, accordingly, as if on the ending of that tenancy there arose a statutory periodic tenancy which is an assured tenancy during the remainder of that period.

(2) Subject to subsection (2) of section 14 of this Act and subsection (3) below, if at any time during a service man's period of residence protection—

(a) a tenancy qualifying for protection which is a periodic tenancy would come to an end, apart from the provisions of this section, and

(b) by reason only of such circumstances as are mentioned in subsection (4) below that tenancy is not an assured tenancy, and

(c) if that tenancy had been an assured tenancy, it would not have come to an end at that time,

Chapter I of Part I of the Housing Act 1988 shall, during the remainder of the period of protection, apply in relation to the rented family residence as if those circumstances did not exist and, accordingly, as if the tenancy had become an assured tenancy immediately before it would otherwise have come to an end.

(3) Neither subsection (1) nor subsection (2) above applies if, on the ending of the tenancy qualifying for protection, a statutory tenancy arises.

(4) The circumstances referred to in subsections (1) and (2) above are any one or more of the following, that is to say,—

(a) that the tenancy was entered into before, or pursuant to a contract made before, Part I of the Housing Act 1988 came into force;

(b) that the rateable value (as defined for the purposes of that Act) of the premises which are the rented family residence, or of a property of which those premises form part, exceeded the relevant limit specified in paragraph 2 of Schedule 1 to that Act;

(c) that the circumstances mentioned in paragraph 3 or paragraph 6 of that Schedule applied with respect to the tenancy qualifying for protection; and Sch. 17

(d) that the reversion immediately expectant on the tenancy qualifying for protection belongs to any of the bodies specified in paragraph 12 of that Schedule."

3. For the said section 16, as it applies to Scotland, there shall be substituted the following section—

"Protection of tenure of certain rented premises by extension of Housing (Scotland) Act 1988.

16.—(1) Subject to subsection (2) of section 14 of this Act and subsection (3) below, if at any time during a service man's period of residence protection—

(a) a tenancy qualifying for protection ends without being continued or renewed by agreement (whether on the same or different terms and conditions), and

(b) by reason only of such circumstances as are mentioned in subsection (4) below, on the ending of that tenancy no statutory tenancy of the rented family residence would arise, apart from the provisions of this section,

sections 12 to 31 of the Housing (Scotland) Act 1988 shall, during the remainder of the period of protection, apply in relation to the rented family residence as if those circumstances did not exist and had not existed immediately before the ending of that tenancy and, accordingly, as if on the ending of that tenancy there arose a statutory assured tenancy during the remainder of that period.

(2) Subject to subsection (2) of section 14 of this Act and subsection (3) below, if at any time during a service man's period of residence protection—

(a) a tenancy qualifying for protection would come to an end, apart from the provisions of this section,

(b) by reason only of such circumstances as are mentioned in subsection (4) below that tenancy is not an assured tenancy, and

(c) if that tenancy had been an assured tenancy, it would not have come to an end at that time,

sections 12 to 31 of the Housing (Scotland) Act 1988 shall, during the remainder of the period of protection, apply in relation to the rented family residence as if those circumstances did not exist and, accordingly, as if the tenancy had become an assured tenancy immediately before it would otherwise have come to an end.

(3) Neither subsection (1) nor subsection (2) above applies if, on the ending of the tenancy qualifying for protection, a statutory tenancy arises.

(4) The circumstances referred to in subsections (1) and (2) above are one or more of the following, that is to say—

(a) that the circumstances mentioned in paragraph 2 of Schedule 4 to the Housing (Scotland) Act 1988 applied with respect to the tenancy qualifying for protection;

(b) that the circumstances mentioned in paragraph 5 of that Schedule applied with respect to the tenancy qualifying for protection; and

SCH. 17

(c) that the reversion immediately expectant on the tenancy qualifying for protection belongs to any of the bodies specified in paragraph 11 of that Schedule."

4.—(1) Section 17 of that Act (provisions in case of rented premises which include accommodation shared otherwise than with landlord), as it applies otherwise than to Scotland, shall be amended in accordance with this paragraph.

(2) In subsection (1)—

(a) after the words "qualifying for protection" there shall be inserted "which is a fixed term tenancy";

(b) in paragraph (b) for the words from "subsection (2)" to "1977" there shall be substituted "section 16(4) above, subsection (1) of section 3 of the Housing Act 1988";

(c) for the words "said section 22" there shall be substituted "said section 3"; and

(d) at the end there shall be added "and, accordingly, as if on the ending of the tenancy there arose a statutory periodic tenancy which is an assured tenancy during the remainder of that period".

(3) For subsection (2) there shall be substituted the following subsections—

"(2) Where, at any time during a service man's period of residence protection—

(a) a tenancy qualifying for protection which is a periodic tenancy would come to an end, apart from the provisions of this section and section 16 above, and

(b) paragraphs (a) and (b) of subsection (1) above apply,

section 3 of the Housing Act 1988 shall, during the remainder of the period of protection, apply in relation to the separate accommodation as if the circumstances referred to in subsection (1)(b) above did not exist and, accordingly, as if the tenancy had become an assured tenancy immediately before it would otherwise have come to an end.

(3) Neither subsection (1) nor subsection (2) above applies if, on the ending of the tenancy qualifying for protection, a statutory tenancy arises."

5.—(1) The said section 17, as it applies to Scotland, shall be amended in accordance with this paragraph.

(2) In subsection (1)—

(a) in paragraph (b) for the words from "subsection (2)" to "1977" there shall be substituted the words "section 16(4) above, subsection (1) of section 14 of the Housing (Scotland) Act 1988";

(b) for the words "said section 97" there shall be substituted the words "said section 14"; and

(c) at the end there shall be added the words "and, accordingly, as if on the ending of the tenancy there arose a statutory assured tenancy during the remainder of that period".

(3) For subsection (2) there shall be substituted the following subsections—

"(2) Where, at any time during a service man's period of residence protection—

(a) a tenancy qualifying for protection would come to an end, apart from the provisions of this section and section 16 above, and

(b) paragraphs (a) and (b) of subsection (1) above apply,

section 14 of the Housing (Scotland) Act 1988 shall, during the remainder of the period of protection, apply in relation to the separate accommodation as if the circumstances in subsection (1)(b) above did not exist and, accordingly, as if the tenancy had become an assured tenancy immediately before it would otherwise come to an end.

(3) Neither subsection (1) nor subsection (2) above applies if, on the ending of the tenancy qualifying for protection, a statutory tenancy arises."

6.—(1) In section 18 of that Act (protection of tenure, in connection with employment, under a licence or rent-free letting), in subsection (1), as it applies otherwise than to Scotland,—

(a) for the words "Part VII of the Rent Act 1977" there shall be substituted "Chapter I of Part I of the Housing Act 1988"; and

(b) for the words "subject to a statutory tenancy within the meaning of the Rent Act 1977" there shall be substituted "let on a statutory periodic tenancy which is an assured tenancy".

(2) In that subsection, as it applies to Scotland,—

(a) for the words "the Rent (Scotland) Act 1971" there shall be substituted the words "sections 12 to 31 of the Housing (Scotland) Act 1988", and

(b) for the words "subject to a statutory tenancy within the meaning of the Rent (Scotland) Act 1971" there shall be substituted the words "let on a statutory assured tenancy".

(3) Subsection (2) of that section shall be omitted.

(4) In subsection (3) of that section, as it applies otherwise than to Scotland, at the end of paragraph (c) there shall be added "or

(d) is a dwelling-house which is let on or subject to an assured agricultural occupancy within the meaning of Part I of the Housing Act 1988 which is not an assured tenancy."

7. For section 19 of that Act (limitation on application of Rent Acts by virtue of sections 16 to 18), as it applies otherwise than to Scotland, there shall be substituted the following section—

"Limitation on application of Housing Act 1988 by virtue of sections 16 to 18.

19. Where by virtue of sections 16 to 18 above, the operation of Chapter I of Part I of the Housing Act 1988 in relation to any premises is extended or modified, the extension or modification shall not affect—

(a) any tenancy of those premises other than the statutory periodic tenancy which is deemed to arise or, as the case may be, the tenancy which is for any period deemed to be an assured tenancy by virtue of any of those provisions; or

(b) any rent payable in respect of a period beginning before the time when that statutory periodic tenancy was deemed to arise or, as the case may be, before that tenancy became deemed to be an assured tenancy; or

(c) anything done or omitted to be done before the time referred to in paragraph (b) above."

8. For the said section 19, as it applies to Scotland, there shall be substituted the following section—

"Limitation on application of Housing (Scotland) Act 1988 by virtue of sections 16 to 18.

19. Where by virtue of sections 16 to 18 above, the operation of sections 12 to 31 of the Housing (Scotland) Act 1988 in relation to any premises is extended or modified, the extension or modification shall not affect—

Sch. 17

(a) any tenancy of those premises other than the statutory assured tenancy which is deemed to arise or, as the case may be, the tenancy which is for any period deemed to be an assured tenancy by virtue of any of those provisions; or

(b) any rent payable in respect of a period beginning before the time when that statutory assured tenancy was deemed to arise or, as the case may be, before that tenancy became deemed to be an assured tenancy; or

(c) anything done or omitted to be done before the time referred to in paragraph (b) above."

9.—(1) Section 20 of that Act (modification of Rent Acts as respects occupation by employees), as it applies otherwise than to Scotland, shall be amended in accordance with this paragraph.

(2) In subsection (1) after the words "Case I in Schedule 15 to the Rent Act 1977" there shall be inserted "or Ground 12 in Schedule 2 to the Housing Act 1988".

(3) In subsection (2) after the words "Case 8 in the said Schedule 15" there shall be inserted "or, as the case may be, Ground 16 in the said Schedule 2" and for paragraph (b) there shall be substituted the following paragraph—

"(b) Chapter I of Part I of the Housing Act 1988 applies in relation to the premises as mentioned in section 18(1) of this Act and a dependant or dependants of the service man is or are living in the premises or in part thereof in right of the statutory periodic tenancy or assured tenancy referred to in section 19(a) of this Act".

(4) In subsection (3)—

(a) after the words "the Cases in Part I of the said Schedule 15" there shall be inserted "or, as the case may be, Grounds 10 to 16 in Part II of the said Schedule 2"; and

(b) after the words "section 98(1) of the Rent Act 1977" there shall be inserted "or, as the case may be, section 7(4) of the Housing Act 1988".

10.—(1) The said section 20, as it applies to Scotland, shall be amended in accordance with this paragraph.

(2) In subsection (1) after the words "Case 1 in Schedule 2 to the Rent (Scotland) Act 1984" there shall be inserted the words "or Ground 13 in Schedule 5 to the Housing (Scotland) Act 1988".

(3) In subsection (2) after the words "Case 7 in the said Schedule 2" there shall be inserted the words "or, as the case may be, Ground 17 in the said Schedule 5" and for paragraph (b) there shall be substituted the following paragraph—

"(b) sections 12 to 31 of the Housing (Scotland) Act 1988 apply in relation to the premises as mentioned in section 18(1) of this Act and a dependant or dependants of the service man is or are living in the premises or in part thereof in right of the statutory assured tenancy or assured tenancy referred to in paragraph (a) of section 19 of this Act".

(4) In subsection (3)—

(a) after the words "the Cases in Part I of the said Schedule 2" there shall be inserted the words "or, as the case may be, Grounds 10 to 17 in Part II of the said Schedule 5"; and

(b) after the words "section 11 of the Rent (Scotland) Act 1984" there shall be inserted the words "or, as the case may be, section 18(4) of the Housing (Scotland) Act 1988".

11. In section 22 of that Act (facilities for action on behalf of men serving abroad in proceedings as to tenancies), as it applies otherwise than to Scotland, in subsection (1)— SCH. 17

(a) after the words "Rent Act 1977" there shall be inserted "or under Part I of the Housing Act 1988";

(b) for the words "Part V of that Act" there shall be substituted "Part V of the Rent Act 1977 or Part I of the Housing Act 1988"; and

(c) in paragraph (a) after the word "tenancy" there shall be inserted "or licence".

12. In the said section 22, as it applies to Scotland, in subsection (1),—

(a) for the words "Part III of the Rent Act 1965 or under the Rent (Scotland) Act 1971" there shall be substituted the words "the Rent (Scotland) Act 1984 or under Part II of the Housing (Scotland) Act 1988";

(b) for the words "rent tribunal" there shall be substituted the words "rent assessment committee" and for the words "or tribunal" there shall be substituted the words "or committee";

(c) for the words "Part VII of that Act" there shall be substituted the words "Part VII of the said Act of 1984 or under Part II of the Housing (Scotland) Act 1988"; and

(d) in paragraph (a) after the word "tenancy" there shall be inserted the words "or licence".

13.—(1) Section 23 of that Act (interpretation of Part II), as it applies otherwise than to Scotland, shall be amended in accordance with this paragraph.

(2) In subsection (1)—

(a) after the definition of "agricultural land" there shall be inserted—

""assured tenancy" has the same meaning as in Part I of the Housing Act 1988";

(b) after the definition of "dependant" there shall be inserted—

""fixed term tenancy" means any tenancy other than a periodic tenancy";

(c) for the definition of "landlord" and "tenant" there shall be substituted—

"in relation to a statutory tenancy or to a provision of the Rent Act 1977 "landlord" and "tenant" have the same meaning as in that Act but, subject to that, those expressions have the same meaning as in Part I of the Housing Act 1988"; and

(d) after the definition of "relevant police authority" there shall be inserted—

""statutory periodic tenancy" has the same meaning as in Part I of the Housing Act 1988".

(3) At the end of subsection (1) there shall be inserted the following subsection—

"(1A) Any reference in this Part of this Act to Chapter I of Part I of the Housing Act 1988 includes a reference to the General Provisions of Chapter VI of that Part, so far as applicable to Chapter I."

(4) In subsection (3) after the words "Rent Act 1977" there shall be inserted "or Chapter I of Part I of the Housing Act 1988".

14.—(1) The said section 23, as it applies to Scotland, shall be amended in accordance with this paragraph.

SCH. 17 (2) In subsection (1)—

(a) after the definition of "agricultural land" there shall be inserted—

""assured tenancy" and "statutory assured tenancy" have the same meaning as in Part II of the Housing (Scotland) Act 1988";

(b) for the definition of "landlord" and "tenant" there shall be substituted—

"in relation to a statutory tenancy or to a provision of the Rent (Scotland) Act 1984 "landlord" and "tenant" have the same meaning as in that Act but, subject to that, those expressions have the same meaning as in Part II of the Housing (Scotland) Act 1988".

(3) At the end of subsection (1) there shall be inserted the following subsection—

"(1A) Any reference in this Part of this Act to sections 12 to 31 of the Housing (Scotland) Act 1988 includes a reference to sections 47 to 55 of that Act so far as applicable to those sections."

(4) In subsection (3) after the words "Rent (Scotland) Act 1984" there shall be inserted the words "or sections 12 to 31 of the Housing (Scotland) Act 1988".

The Leasehold Reform Act 1967

1967 c. 88. 15. In section 28 of the Leasehold Reform Act 1967 (retention or resumption of land required for public purposes) at the end of subsection (5) (bodies to whom that section applies) there shall be added "and

(g) a housing action trust established under Part III of the Housing Act 1988."

16. In section 29 of that Act (reservation of future right to develop) after subsection (6B) there shall be inserted the following subsection—

"(6C) Subsections (1) to (4) above shall have effect in relation to a housing action trust as if any reference in those subsections or in Part I of Schedule 4 to this Act to a local authority were a reference to the trust."

17.—(1) In Schedule 4A to that Act (which is set out in Schedule 4 to the
1986 c. 63. Housing and Planning Act 1986 and excludes certain shared ownership leases from Part I of the 1967 Act) at the end of paragraph 2(1) there shall be added "or to a person who acquired that interest in exercise of the right conferred by Part IV of the Housing Act 1988".

(2) In paragraph 2(2) of that Schedule, at the end of paragraph (e) there shall be added the following paragraph—

"(f) a housing action trust established under Part III of the Housing Act 1988".

The Town and Country Planning Act 1971

1971 c. 78. 18. In section 215 of the Town and Country Planning Act 1971 (procedure for making certain orders), in subsection (8) (definitions of "relevant area" and "local authority") after the words "Part IV of the Local Government Act 1985" there shall be inserted "a housing action trust established under Part III of the Housing Act 1988".

The Local Government Act 1974

1974 c. 7. 19. In section 25 of the Local Government Act 1974 (local government administration: authorities subject to investigation), in subsection (1) after paragraph (bd) there shall be inserted the following paragraph—

"(be) any housing action trust established under Part III of the Housing Act 1988".

The Consumer Credit Act 1974 SCH. 17

20. In section 16 of the Consumer Credit Act 1974 (exempt agreements), in subsection (6B), in paragraph (a) after the words "England and Wales," there shall be inserted "the Housing Corporation, Housing for Wales and". 1974 c. 39.

The Rent (Agriculture) Act 1976

21. In section 28 of the Rent (Agriculture) Act 1976 (rehousing: duty of housing authority concerned), the following subsection shall be inserted after subsection (14) of that section— 1976 c. 80.

"(14A) Notwithstanding anything in section 127(1) of the Magistrates' Courts Act 1980, an information relating to an offence under this section may be tried if it is laid at any time within two years after the commission of the offence and within six months after the date on which evidence sufficient in the opinion of the housing authority concerned to justify the proceedings comes to its knowledge."

The Rent Act 1977

22. In the Rent Act 1977, sections 68 and 69, Part II of Schedule 11 and Schedule 12 (which provide for applications by a local authority for the determination of a fair rent and make provision about certificates of fair rent) shall cease to have effect except as respects applications made before the commencement of this Act. 1977 c. 42.

23. In section 77 of that Act (which provides for the reference of restricted contracts to rent tribunals by the lessor, the lessee or the local authority) the words "or the local authority" shall be omitted.

24. Section 89 of the Rent Act 1977 (which provides for the phasing of progression to a registered rent in the case of housing association tenancies) and Schedule 8 to that Act (phasing of rent increases: general provisions) shall cease to have effect except with respect to an increase in rent up to, or towards, a registered rent in relation to which the relevant date for the purposes of the said Schedule 8 falls before this Act comes into force.

25. In section 137 of the Rent Act 1977 (effect on sub-tenancy of determination of superior tenancy), in subsection (1) the words "this Part of" shall be omitted.

The Protection from Eviction Act 1977

26. In section 7 of the Protection from Eviction Act 1977 (service of notices), in subsection (3)(c) (certain licensors treated as landlords for the purposes of the section) the words "under a restricted contract (within the meaning of the Rent Act 1977)" shall be omitted. 1977 c. 43.

The Justices of the Peace Act 1979

27. In section 64 of the Justices of the Peace Act 1979 (disqualification in certain cases of justices who are members of local authorities) at the end of subsection (6) there shall be added the words "and a housing action trust established under Part III of the Housing Act 1988". 1979 c. 55.

The Local Government, Planning and Land Act 1980

28. In Schedule 16 to the Local Government, Planning and Land Act 1980 (bodies to whom Part X applies) after paragraph 8 there shall be inserted the following paragraph— 1980 c. 65.

"8A. A housing action trust established under Part III of the Housing Act 1988."

SCH. 17 29. In Schedule 28 to the Local Government, Planning and Land Act 1980, in paragraph 10 after the words "Rent Act 1977" there shall be inserted "or the Housing Act 1988."

The Highways Act 1980

1980 c. 66. 30. In Schedule 6 to the Highways Act 1980, in Part I, in paragraph 1(3)(b)(i) after the words "Rent Act 1977" there shall be inserted "and licensees under an assured agricultural occupancy within the meaning of Part I of the Housing Act 1988".

The New Towns Act 1981

1981 c. 64. 31. In section 22 of the New Towns Act 1981 (possession of houses) after the words "Rent Act 1977" there shall be inserted "or Part I of the Housing Act 1988".

The Acquisition of Land Act 1981

1981 c. 67. 32.—(1) In section 12(2) of the Acquisition of Land Act 1981 after the words "Rent (Agriculture) Act 1976" there shall be inserted "or a licensee under an assured agricultural occupancy within the meaning of Part I of the Housing Act 1988".

(2) In Schedule 1 to that Act, in paragraph 3(2) after the words "Rent (Agriculture) Act 1976" there shall be inserted "or a licensee under an assured agricultural occupancy within the meaning of Part I of the Housing Act 1988".

The Matrimonial Homes Act 1983

1983 c. 19. 33. In section 1(6) of the Matrimonial Homes Act 1983 (occupation of one spouse by virtue of that section treated as occupation by the other for the purposes of certain enactments) after the words "Housing Act 1985" there shall be inserted "and Part I of the Housing Act 1988".

34.—(1) In Schedule 1 to that Act (transfer of certain tenancies on divorce, etc.), in paragraph 1—

(a) at the end of paragraph (c) of sub-paragraph (1) there shall be inserted "or

(d) an assured tenancy or assured agricultural occupancy, within the meaning of Part I of the Housing Act 1988"; and

(b) in sub-paragraph (2) after the words "secure tenancy" there shall be inserted "or an assured tenancy or assured agricultural occupancy".

(2) In paragraph 2 of that Schedule (orders transferring tenancies etc. from one spouse to another)—

(a) in sub-paragraph (1) after the words "Housing Act 1985" there shall be inserted "or an assured tenancy or assured agricultural occupancy within the meaning of Part I of the Housing Act 1988"; and

(b) at the end of sub-paragraph (3) there shall be inserted—

"(4) Where the spouse so entitled is for the purposes of section 17 of the Housing Act 1988 a successor in relation to the tenancy or occupancy, his or her former spouse (or, in the case of judicial separation, his or her spouse) shall be deemed to be a successor in relation to the tenancy or occupancy for the purposes of that section.

(5) If the transfer under sub-paragraph (1) above is of an assured agricultural occupancy, then, for the purposes of Chapter III of Part I of the Housing Act 1988,—

SCH. 17

(a) the agricultural worker condition shall be fulfilled with respect to the dwelling-house while the spouse to whom the assured agricultural occupancy is transferred continues to be the occupier under that occupancy; and

(b) that condition shall be treated as so fulfilled by virtue of the same paragraph of Schedule 3 to the Housing Act 1988 as was applicable before the transfer."

The County Courts Act 1984

35.—(1) In section 66 of the County Courts Act 1984 (trial by jury: exceptions), in subsection (1) at the end of paragraph (b)(iii) there shall be inserted "or 1984 c. 28.

(iv) under Part I of the Housing Act 1988".

(2) In section 77(6) of that Act (appeals: possession proceedings) after paragraph (e) there shall be inserted the following paragraph—

"(ee) section 7 of the Housing Act 1988, as it applies to the grounds in Part II of Schedule 2 to that Act; or".

The Matrimonial and Family Proceedings Act 1984

36. In section 22 of the Matrimonial and Family Proceedings Act 1984 (powers of the court in relation to certain tenancies of dwelling-houses), in paragraph (a) after the word "tenancy" there shall be inserted "or assured agricultural occupancy". 1984 c. 42.

The Local Government Act 1985

37. In section 101 of the Local Government Act 1985 (power by order to make incidental, consequential, etc. provisions) in subsection (1)(b) after second "Act" insert "or the Housing Act 1988". 1985 c. 51.

The Housing Act 1985

38. In section 32(1) of the Housing Act 1985 (power to dispose of land) after "(the right to buy)" there shall be inserted "and Part IV of the Housing Act 1988 (change of landlord: secure tenants)". 1985 c. 68.

39. In section 43(1) of that Act (consent required for certain disposals) after "(the right to buy)" there shall be inserted "or Part IV of the Housing Act 1988 (change of landlord: secure tenants)".

40. In section 115 of that Act (meaning of "long tenancy"), in subsection (2)(c) after "1980" there shall be inserted "or paragraph 4(2)(b) of Schedule 4A to the Leasehold Reform Act 1967".

41. In section 155 of that Act (repayment of discount on early disposal) after subsection (3) there shall be inserted the following subsection—

"(3A) Where a secure tenant has served on his landlord an operative notice of delay, as defined in section 153A,—

(a) the three years referred to in subsection (2) shall begin from a date which precedes the date of the conveyance of the freehold or grant of the lease by a period equal to the time (or, if there is more than one such notice, the aggregate of the times) during which, by virtue of section 153B, any payment of rent falls to be taken into account in accordance with subsection (3) of that section; and

(b) any reference in subsection (3) (other than paragraph (a) thereof) to the acquisition of the tenant's initial share shall be construed as a reference to a date which precedes that acquisition by the period referred to in paragraph (a) of this subsection."

SCH. 17

42. In section 171F of that Act (subsequent dealings after disposal of dwelling-house to private sector landlord: possession on grounds of suitable alternative accommodation) after "Rent Act 1977" there shall be inserted "or on Ground 9 in Schedule 2 to the Housing Act 1988".

43. In section 236 of that Act at the end of subsection (2) (meaning of "occupying tenant") there shall be added the words "or

(e) is a licensee under an assured agricultural occupancy."

44. In section 238 of that Act (index of defined expressions in Part VII) before the entry relating to "clearance area" there shall be inserted—

"assured agricultural occupancy ... ... section 622".

45. In section 247 of that Act (notification of certain disposals of land to the local housing authority), in subsection (5) (provision not to apply to certain disposals) after paragraph (c) there shall be inserted the following paragraph—

"(ca) the grant of an assured tenancy or assured agricultural occupancy, or of a tenancy which is not such a tenancy or occupancy by reason only of paragraph 10 of Schedule 1 to the Housing Act 1988 (resident landlords) or of that paragraph and the fact that the accommodation which is let is not let as a separate dwelling".

46. In section 263 of that Act (index of defined expressions in Part VIII) before the entry relating to "clearance area" there shall be inserted—

"assured agricultural occupancy ... ... section 622
assured tenancy ... ... section 622".

47. In Part IX of that Act (slum clearance) in the following provisions relating to the recovery of possession, namely, sections 264(5), 270(3), 276 and 286(3), after the words "Rent Acts" there shall be inserted "or Part I of the Housing Act 1988".

48. In section 309 of that Act (recovery of possession of premises for purposes of approved redevelopment), in paragraph (a) of subsection (1) after the words "the Rent Act 1977)" the following words shall be inserted "or let on or subject to an assured tenancy or assured agricultural occupancy"; and in the words following paragraph (b) of that subsection after the words "section 98(1)(a) of the Rent Act 1977" there shall be inserted "or section 7 of the Housing Act 1988".

49. In section 323 of that Act (index of defined expressions in Part IX) before the entry relating to "clearance area" there shall be inserted—

"assured agricultural occupancy ... ... section 622
assured tenancy ... ... section 622".

50. In section 368 of that Act (means of escape from fire: power to secure that part of house not used for human habitation), in subsection (6) after the words "Rent Acts" there shall be inserted "or Part I of the Housing Act 1988".

51. In section 381 of that Act (general effect of control order), in subsection (3) after the words "Rent Acts" there shall be inserted "and Part I of the Housing Act 1988".

52.—(1) In section 382 of that Act (effect of control order on persons occupying house) after subsection (3) there shall be inserted the following subsection—

"(3A) Section 1(2) of and paragraph 12 of Part I of Schedule 1 to the Housing Act 1988 (which exclude local authority lettings from Part I of that Act) do not apply to a lease or agreement under which a person to whom this section applies is occupying part of the house."

(2) In subsection (4) of that section after paragraph (b) there shall be inserted "or SCH. 17

(c) an assured tenancy or assured agricultural occupancy within the meaning of Part I of the Housing Act 1988";

and for the words "either of those Acts" there shall be substituted "any of those Acts".

53. In section 400 of that Act (index of defined expressions for Part XI) after the entry relating to "appropriate multiplier" there shall be inserted—

"assured tenancy ... ... section 622
assured agricultural occupancy ... ... section 622".

54. In section 429A of that Act (housing management: financial assistance etc.) in subsection (2), in paragraph (a) after the words "secure tenancies)" there shall be inserted "or subsection (2A)" and at the end of that subsection there shall be inserted the following subsection—

"(2A) Subsection (2)(a) applies to the following bodies—

(a) the Housing Corporation;

(b) Housing for Wales;

(c) a housing trust which is a charity;

(d) a registered housing association other than a co-operative housing association; and

(e) an unregistered housing association which is a co-operative housing association."

55. In section 434 of that Act (index of defined expressions for Part XIII) there shall be inserted, in the appropriate places in alphabetical order, the following entries—

"charity ... ... section 622"

"co-operative housing association ... ... section 5(2)"

"housing association ... ... section 5(1)"

"housing trust" ... ... section 6".

56. In section 450A of that Act (right to a loan in certain cases after exercise of right to buy) in subsection (6), in the definition of "housing authority" for the words from "housing association" onwards there shall be substituted "registered housing association other than a co-operative housing association and any unregistered housing association which is a co-operative housing association; and".

57. In section 450B of that Act (power to make loans in other cases) in subsection (4), in the definition of "housing authority" for the words from "housing association" onwards there shall be substituted "registered housing association other than a co-operative housing association and any unregistered housing association which is a co-operative housing association; and".

58. In section 459 of that Act (index of defined expressions for Part XIV) after the entry relating to "building society" there shall be inserted—

"co-operative housing association ... ... section 5(2)".

59. In section 533 of that Act (assistance for owners of defective housing: exceptions to eligibility) after the words "Rent (Agriculture) Act 1976" there shall be inserted "or who occupies the dwelling under an assured agricultural occupancy which is not an assured tenancy".

60. In section 553 of that Act (effect of repurchase of defective dwellings on certain existing tenancies) in subsection (2)—

(a) in paragraph (a) after the words "protected tenancy" there shall be inserted "or an assured tenancy";

SCH. 17

(b) at the end of paragraph (b) there shall be added the words "or in accordance with any of Grounds 1, 3, 4 and 5 in Schedule 2 to the Housing Act 1988 (notice that possession might be recovered under that ground) or under section 20(1)(c) of that Act (notice served in respect of assured shorthold tenancies); and"; and

(c) after paragraph (b) there shall be added—

"(c) the tenancy is not an assured periodic tenancy which, by virtue of section 39(7) of the Housing Act 1988 (successors under the Rent Act 1977), is an assured shorthold tenancy".

61.—(1) In section 554 of that Act (grant of tenancy of defective dwelling to former owner-occupier) at the end of subsection (2) there shall be inserted the following subsection—

"(2A) If the authority is a registered housing association, other than a housing co-operative, within the meaning of section 27B, their obligation is to grant a secure tenancy if the individual to whom a tenancy is to be granted—

(a) is a person who, immediately before he acquired his interest in the dwelling-house, was a secure tenant of it; or

(b) is the spouse or former spouse or widow or widower of a person falling within paragraph (a); or

(c) is a member of the family, within the meaning of section 186, of a person falling within paragraph (a) who has died, and was residing with that person in the dwelling-house at the time of and for the period of twelve months before his death."

(2) In subsection (3) of that section, at the end of paragraph (b) there shall be inserted "or

(c) an assured tenancy which is neither an assured shorthold tenancy, within the meaning of Part I of the Housing Act 1988, nor a tenancy under which the landlord might recover possession on any of Grounds 1 to 5 in Schedule 2 to that Act."

62. In section 577 of that Act (index of defined expressions for Part XVI) after the entry relating to "associated arrangement" there shall be inserted—

"assured agricultural occupancy ... ... section 622
assured tenancy ... ... section 622".

63. In section 612 of that Act (exclusion of Rent Act protection) after the words "the Rent Acts" there shall be inserted "or Part I of the Housing Act 1988".

64. In section 622 of that Act (definitions: general) before the definition of "bank" there shall be inserted—

""assured tenancy" has the same meaning as in Part I of the Housing Act 1988;

"assured agricultural occupancy" has the same meaning as in Part I of the Housing Act 1988".

65. In Schedule 2 to that Act, in Part IV (grounds for possession: suitability of alternative accommodation) in paragraph 1, at the end of sub-paragraph (b) there shall be added "or

(c) which are to be let as a separate dwelling under an assured tenancy which is neither an assured shorthold tenancy, within the meaning of Part I of the Housing Act 1988, nor a tenancy under which the landlord might recover possession under any of Grounds 1 to 5 in Schedule 2 to that Act".

66. In Schedule 5 to that Act, in paragraph 3, after the entry for section 58(2) of the Housing Associations Act 1985 there shall be inserted the following entries— **SCH. 17** **1985 c. 69.**

"section 50 of the Housing Act 1988 (housing association grants), or

section 51 of that Act (revenue deficit grants)."

The Landlord and Tenant Act 1985

67.—(1) In section 5 of the Landlord and Tenant Act 1985 (information to be contained in rent books), in subsection (1)(b) after the word "tenancy" there shall be inserted "or let on an assured tenancy within the meaning of Part I of the Housing Act 1988". **1985 c. 70.**

(2) In subsection (2) of that section after the word "tenancy" there shall be added "or let on an assured tenancy within the meaning of Part I of the Housing Act 1988".

68. In section 26 of that Act (tenants of certain public authorities excepted from provisions about service charges etc.) in subsection (3)(c) after the words "Housing Act 1980" there shall be inserted "or paragraph 4(2)(b) of Schedule 4A to the Leasehold Reform Act 1967".

The Agricultural Holdings Act 1986

69.—(1) In Schedule 3 to the Agricultural Holdings Act 1986 (cases where consent of Tribunal to operation of notice to quit is not required), in Part II (provisions applicable to Case A: suitable alternative accommodation), in paragraph 3 after paragraph (b) there shall be inserted "or **1986 c. 5.**

(c) premises which are to be let as a separate dwelling such that they will then be let on an assured tenancy which is not an assured shorthold tenancy (construing those terms in accordance with Part I of the Housing Act 1988), or

(d) premises to be let as a separate dwelling on terms which will afford to the tenant security of tenure reasonably equivalent to the security afforded by Chapter I of Part I of that Act in the case of an assured tenancy which is not an assured shorthold tenancy."

(2) At the end of the said paragraph 3 there shall be added the following sub-paragraph—

"(2) Any reference in sub-paragraph (1) above to an assured tenancy does not include a reference to a tenancy in respect of which possession might be recovered on any of Grounds 1 to 5 in Schedule 2 to the Housing Act 1988."

70. In Schedule 5 to that Act (notice to quit where tenant is a service man), in paragraph 2(2)(a) after the words "Rent Act 1977" there shall be inserted "or paragraph 7 of Schedule 1 to the Housing Act 1988".

The Drug Trafficking Offences Act 1986

71. In section 15 of the Drug Trafficking Offences Act 1986 (bankruptcy of defendant etc.), in subsection (2)(b) for the words "or 308" there shall be substituted "308 or 308A" and after the word "replacement" there shall be inserted "and certain tenancies". **1986 c. 32.**

72. In section 16 of that Act (sequestration in Scotland of defendant), in subsection (2)(b) for the words "under subsection (6) of that section" there shall be substituted the words "under subsection (10) of section 31 of that Act or subsection (6) of the said section 32 of that Act".

SCH. 17

The Insolvency Act 1986

1986 c. 45. 73. In section 308 of the Insolvency Act 1986 (vesting in trustee of certain items of excess value), in subsection (1), for the words "the next section" there shall be substituted "section 309".

74. In section 335 of that Act (adjustment between earlier and later bankruptcy estates), in subsection (4) after the words "replacement value)" there shall be inserted the words "or section 308A (vesting in trustee of certain tenancies)".

75. In section 351 of that Act (definitions), in paragraph (a), for the words "or 308" there shall be substituted ", section 308" and after the words "replacement value)" there shall be inserted "or section 308A (vesting in trustee of certain tenancies)".

The Social Security Act 1986

1986 c. 50. 76. In section 31 of the Social Security Act 1986 (information relating to housing benefit), in subsection (5) (information as to registered rents), after the words "housing benefit scheme" there shall be inserted "(a)", and at the end there shall be added "and

(b) where a rent is determined under section 14 or section 22 of the Housing Act 1988 or section 25 or section 34 of the Housing (Scotland) Act 1988 (determination of rents by rent assessment committee), the committee shall note in their determination the amount (if any) of the rent which, in the opinion of the committee, is fairly attributable to the provision of services, except where that amount is in their opinion negligible; and the amounts so noted may be included in the information specified in an order under section 42 of the Housing Act 1988 or, as the case may be, section 49 of the Housing (Scotland) Act 1988 (information to be publicly available)".

The Housing (Scotland) Act 1987

1987 c. 26. 77. In section 12 of the Housing (Scotland) Act 1987 (which relates, amongst other things, to the disposal by local authorities of land acquired or appropriated for housing purposes and of houses)—

(a) in subsection (1)(c), for the words "subsection (5)" there shall be substituted the words "subsections (5) and (7)";

(b) in subsection (7)—

(i) for "(1)(d)" there shall be substituted "(1)(c) or (d)";

(ii) for the words "house or any part share thereof" there shall be substituted the words "land, house or part share thereof";

(iii) for the words "it is a house" there shall be substituted the words ", in the case of a house, it is one";

(c) in subsection (8) after the word "apply" there shall be inserted the words ", in the case of a house,".

78. In section 13 of that Act (power of Secretary of State in certain cases to impose conditions on sale of local authority's houses etc.) for the words "land or dwelling" there shall be substituted the words "or land".

1987 c. 26. 79. In section 61(4)(b) of the Housing (Scotland) Act 1987 after sub-paragraph (vi) there shall be inserted the following sub-paragraphs—

"(vii) section 50 of the Housing Act 1988 (housing association grants); or

(viii) section 51 of that Act (revenue deficit grants); or".

The Access to Personal Files Act 1987 Sch. 17

80. In Schedule 1 to the Access to Personal Files Act 1987 (accessible personal information: England and Wales), in paragraph 2 at the end of sub-paragraph (2) there shall be added "and any housing action trust established under Part III of the Housing Act 1988." 1987 c. 37.

The Criminal Justice (Scotland) Act 1987

81. In section 33 of the Criminal Justice (Scotland) Act 1987 (sequestration of person holding realisable property), in subsection (2)(b) for the words "under subsection (6) of that section" there shall be substituted the words "under subsection (10) of section 31 of that Act or subsection (6) of the said section 32 of that Act". 1987 c. 41.

82. In section 34 of that Act (bankruptcy in England and Wales of person holding realisable property), in subsection (2)(b) for the words "or 308" there shall be substituted "308 or 308A" and after the word "replacement" there shall be inserted "and certain tenancies".

The Criminal Justice Act 1988

83. In section 84 of the Criminal Justice Act 1988 (bankruptcy of defendant etc.), in subsection (2)(b) for the words "or 308" there shall be substituted "308 or 308A" and after the word "replacement" there shall be inserted "and certain tenancies". 1988 c. 33.

84. In section 85 of that Act (sequestration in Scotland of defendant), in subsection 2(b) for the words "under subsection (6) of that section" there shall be substituted the words "under subsection (10) of section 31 of that Act or subsection (6) of the said section 32 of that Act".

The Housing (Scotland) Act 1988

85. In section 19 of the Housing (Scotland) Act 1988 (notice of proceedings for possession)— 1988 c. 43.

(a) in subsection (2) for the word "is" there shall be substituted the words "and particulars of it are";

(b) in subsection (3) after the word "one" where it first occurs there shall be inserted the words "in the prescribed form".

86. In section 36 of that Act (damages for unlawful eviction)—

(a) in subsection (2) for the word "calculated" there shall be substituted the word "likely";

(b) in subsection (7)(b)—

(i) after the word "of" where it first occurs there shall be inserted the words "the doing of acts or";

(ii) after the word "for" there shall be inserted the words "doing the acts or".

87. In section 38 of that Act (further offence of harassment)—

(a) for the words from "In section 22" to "after subsection (2)" there shall be substituted the words—

"(1) Subsection (2) of section 22 of the Rent (Scotland) Act 1984 (unlawful eviction and harassment of occupier) shall, as respects acts done after the commencement of this section, have effect with the substitution of the word "likely" for the word "calculated".

(2) After that subsection";

(b) after "(2A)" there shall be inserted the words "Subject to subsection (2B) below";

SCH. 17

(c) for the word "calculated" there shall be substituted the word "likely";

(d) the words "subject to subsection (2B) below" and "by reason only of conduct falling within paragraph (b) of that subsection" shall cease to have effect;

(e) after the word "for" where it second occurs there shall be inserted the words "doing the acts or".

88. In section 36 of that Act (damages for unlawful eviction)—

(a) in subsection (6), for the words "proceedings are begun to enforce the liability" there shall be substituted the words "the date on which the proceedings to enforce the liability are finally decided"; and

(b) after subsection (6) there shall be inserted the following subsections—

"(6A) For the purposes of subsection (6)(a) above, proceedings to enforce a liability are finally decided—

(a) if no appeal may be made against the decision in these proceedings;

(b) if an appeal may be made against the decision with leave and the time limit for applications for leave expires and either no application has been made or leave has been refused;

(c) if leave to appeal against the decision is granted or is not required and no appeal is made within the time limit for appeals; or

(d) if an appeal is made but is abandoned before it is determined.

(6B) If, in proceedings to enforce a liability arising by virtue of subsection (3) above, it appears to the court—

(a) that, prior to the event which gave rise to the liability, the conduct of the former residential occupier or any person living with him in the premises concerned was such that it is reasonable to mitigate the damages for which the landlord would otherwise be liable, or

(b) that, before the proceedings were begun, the landlord offered to reinstate the former residential occupier in the premises in question and either it was unreasonable of the former residential occupier to refuse that offer or, if he had obtained alternative accommodation before the offer was made, it would have been unreasonable of him to refuse that offer if he had not obtained that accommodation,

the court may reduce the amount of damages which would otherwise be payable to such amount as it thinks appropriate.".

89. In section 63 of that Act (consent for subsequent disposals) after subsection (2) there shall be inserted the following subsection—

"(2A) Before giving any consent for the purposes of subsection (1) above, Scottish Homes—

(a) shall satisfy itself that the person who is seeking the consent has taken appropriate steps to consult the tenant of the house (or, as the case may be, each house) of which the property proposed to be disposed of consists; and

(b) shall have regard to the response of such tenant to that consultation."

90. In Schedule 4 to that Act (tenancies which cannot be assured tenancies) after paragraph 11 there shall be inserted the following paragraph—

"Accommodation for homeless persons SCH. 17

11A. A tenancy granted expressly on a temporary basis in the fulfilment of a duty imposed on a local authority by Part II of the Housing (Scotland) Act 1987."

PART II

AMENDMENTS CONSEQUENTIAL ON THE ESTABLISHMENT OF HOUSING FOR WALES

The Land Commission Act 1967

91. In section 56(4) of the Land Commission Act 1967 (bodies exempted from betterment levy) after paragraph (e) there shall be inserted the following paragraph— 1967 c. 1.

"(ea) Housing for Wales".

The Parliamentary Commissioner Act 1967

92. In Schedule 2 to the Parliamentary Commissioner Act 1967 (departments etc. subject to investigation) after the entry "Housing Corporation" there shall be inserted— 1967 c. 13.

"Housing for Wales".

The Income and Corporation Taxes Act 1970

93. In section 342 of the Income and Corporation Taxes Act 1970 (disposals of land between Housing Corporation and housing societies) and in section 342A of that Act (disposals by certain housing associations) after the words "Housing Corporation" in each place where they occur there shall be inserted "or Housing for Wales". 1970 c. 10.

The Land Compensation Act 1973

94. In section 32(7B)(b) of the Land Compensation Act 1973 (supplementary provisions about home loss payments) after the words "Housing Corporation" there shall be inserted "or Housing for Wales". 1973 c. 26.

The House of Commons Disqualification Act 1975

95. In Schedule 1 to the House of Commons Disqualification Act 1975, in Part II (bodies of which all members are disqualified) there shall be inserted at the appropriate place the following entry— 1975 c. 24.

"Housing for Wales".

The Statutory Corporations (Financial Provisions) Act 1975

96. In Schedule 2 to the Statutory Corporations (Financial Provisions) Act 1975 (bodies corporate affected by section 5 of that Act as to their power to borrow in currencies other than sterling) after the entry "The Housing Corporation" there shall be inserted— 1975 c. 55.

"Housing for Wales".

The Development of Rural Wales Act 1976

97. In section 8(2) of the Development of Rural Wales Act 1976 (assistance to the Development Board for Rural Wales from public authorities and others) for the words "the Housing Corporation" there shall be substituted "Housing for Wales". 1976 c. 75.

SCH. 17

The Rent (Agriculture) Act 1976

1976 c. 80. 98. In section 5(3) of the Rent (Agriculture) Act 1976 (no statutory tenancy where landlord's interest belongs to Crown or to local authority etc.) after paragraph (d) there shall be inserted the following paragraph—

"(da) Housing for Wales".

The Rent Act 1977

1977 c. 42. 99. In section 15(2)(a) of the Rent Act 1977 (landlord's interest belonging to housing association etc.) after the words "Housing Corporation" there shall be inserted—

"(aa) Housing for Wales".

100. In each of the following provisions of that Act, that is to say, sections 86(2)(a) (tenancies to which Part VI applies), 93(1) (increase of rent without notice to quit) and Schedule 12 (certificates of fair rent), in paragraph 12 (meaning of "secure tenancy"), after the words "Housing Corporation" there shall be inserted "or Housing for Wales".

The Criminal Law Act 1977

1977 c. 45. 101. In section 7(5) of the Criminal Law Act 1977 (authorities who may authorise occupation by protected intending occupier for purposes of offence of adverse occupation of residential premises) after the words "Housing Corporation" there shall be inserted—

"(ba) Housing for Wales".

The National Health Service Act 1977

1977 c. 49. 102. In section 28A(2)(e) of the National Health Service Act 1977 (power to make payments towards expenditure on community services) at the end there shall be added the following sub-paragraph "and

(vii) Housing for Wales."

103. In section 28B(1)(b)(v) of that Act (power of Secretary of State to make payments towards expenditure on community services in Wales) for the words "the Housing Corporation" there shall be substituted "Housing for Wales".

The Local Government, Planning and Land Act 1980

1980 c. 65. 104. In Schedule 16 to the Local Government, Planning and Land Act 1980 (bodies to whom Part X of that Act applies) after paragraph 9 there shall be inserted the following paragraph—

"9a. Housing for Wales."

The Finance Act 1981

1981 c. 35. 105. In section 107(3) of the Finance Act 1981 (exemption from stamp duty in case of sale of houses at discount by local authorities etc.) after paragraph (c) there shall be inserted the following paragraph—

"(ca) Housing for Wales."

The Housing Act 1985

1985 c. 68. 106. In the Housing Act 1985 for the words "Housing Corporation" in each place where they occur there shall be substituted "Corporation".

107. In Part I of that Act (introductory provisions—authorities and bodies other than local housing authorities) after section 6 there shall be inserted the following section— SCH. 17

"6A. In this Act "the Corporation" has the meaning assigned by section 2A of the Housing Associations Act 1985."

108. In section 57 of that Act (index of defined expressions: Part II) after the entry relating to "compulsory disposal" there shall be inserted—

"the Corporation section 6A".

109. In section 117 of that Act (index of defined expressions: Part IV) after the entry relating to "co-operative housing association" there shall be inserted—

"the Corporation section 6A".

110. In section 188 of that Act (index of defined expressions: Part V) after the entry relating to "co-operative housing association" there shall be inserted—

"the Corporation section 6A".

111. In section 238 of that Act (index of defined expressions: Part VII) after the entry relating to "clearance area" there shall be inserted—

"the Corporation section 6A".

112. In section 459 of that Act (index of defined expressions: Part XIV) after the entry relating to "building society" there shall be inserted—

"the Corporation section 6A".

113. In section 577 of that Act (index of defined expressions: Part XVI) after the entry relating to "co-operative housing association" there shall be inserted—

"the Corporation section 6A".

The Landlord and Tenant Act 1987

114. In section 58(1) of the Landlord and Tenant Act 1987 (exempt landlords) after paragraph (e) there shall be inserted the following paragraph— 1987 c. 31.

"(ea) Housing for Wales".

The Income and Corporation Taxes Act 1988

115. In section 376(4) of the Income and Corporation Taxes Act 1988 (qualifying borrowers and lenders) after paragraph (k) there shall be inserted the following paragraph— 1988 c. 1.

"(ka) Housing for Wales."

116. In section 560(2)(e) of that Act (persons who are sub-contractors or contractors for the purposes of Chapter IV of Part XIII of that Act) after the words "Housing Corporation" there shall be inserted "Housing for Wales".

SCHEDULE 18

Section 140.

Enactments Repealed

Chapter	Short title	Extent of repeal
14 & 15 Geo. VI c. 65.	The Reserve and Auxiliary Forces (Protection of Civil Interests) Act 1951.	Section 18(2).
1976 c.80.	The Rent (Agriculture) Act 1976.	In section 4(2) the words "or, as the case may be, subsection (4)". In section 13(3) the words "68, 69" and "or Part II of Schedule 11 or Schedule 12 to that Act". In Schedule 4, in Part I, paragraph 2(2).
1977 c.42.	The Rent Act 1977.	Section 16A. Sections 19 to 21. In section 63, in subsection (1), paragraph (b) and the word "and" immediately preceding it; in subsection (2) in paragraph (a), the words "and deputy rent officers", in paragraph (b), the words "or deputy rent officer", in paragraph (d) the words "and deputy rent officers" and the word "and" at the end of the paragraph, and paragraph (e); in subsection (3), the words "and deputy rent officers"; and in subsection (7)(b), the words "and deputy rent officers". In section 67, in subsection (5), the words "and sections 68 and 69 of this Act" and in subsection (7), the words "Subject to section 69(4) of this Act." Sections 68 and 69. In section 74, in subsection (2), in paragraph (a) "69", in paragraph (b) the words "or II" and paragraph (c). In section 77(1) the words "or the local authority". In section 80(1) the words "or the local authority". Section 81A(1)(a).

Chapter	Short title	Extent of repeal
		In section 87, in subsection (2), in paragraph (a) "69" and in paragraph (c) the words "and 12". In section 88(2) the words "then, subject to section 89 of this Act". Section 89. In section 103(1) the words "or the local authority". In section 137 the words "this Part of". In Schedule 1, in paragraph 1 the words "or, as the case may be, paragraph 3", in paragraph 4, the words "or 3", and paragraph 7. In Schedule 2, paragraph 6(3). Schedule 8. In Schedule 11, Part II. Schedule 12. In Schedule 14, paragraph 4. In Schedule 15, in Part IV, paragraph 4(2). In Schedule 20, paragraph 2(2). In Schedule 24, paragraph 8(3).
1977 c. 43.	The Protection from Eviction Act 1977.	In section 7(3)(c) the words from "under" to "1977)".
1980 c.51.	The Housing Act 1980.	Section 52. Sections 56 to 58. Section 59(1). Section 60. Section 73(2). Section 76(2). In Schedule 9, paragraph 2. In Schedule 10, paragraph 2. In Schedule 25, paragraph 36, in paragraph 40 "68 (4)" and paragraphs 46 and 63.
1985 c. 51.	The Local Government Act 1985.	In Schedule 13, in paragraph 21, the words from "and section 19(5)(aa)" onwards.
1985 c.68.	The Housing Act 1985.	In section 80, in subsection (1) the words from "the Housing Corporation" to "charity or", the words "housing association or" and subsection (2). Sections 199 to 201.

Sch. 18

Chapter	Short title	Extent of repeal
		In Schedule 5, in paragraph 3 the word "or" immediately following the entry for section 55 of the Housing Associations Act 1985; paragraphs 6 and 8.
1985 c.69.	The Housing Associations Act 1985.	In section 3(2) the words "of housing associations maintained under this section". In section 18(3) the words from "and the Corporation" onwards. In section 40, the entries relating to housing association grant and revenue deficit grant. Sections 41 to 57. Section 62. In section 73, the entries relating to approved development programme, hostel deficit grant, housing association grant, housing project, revenue deficit grant, shared ownership agreement and shared ownership lease. Section 75(1)(d). In section 87(1) the words "registered housing associations and other". In section 107, in subsection (3) the entries relating to sections 4, 44 and 45 and 52, and in subsection (4) the words "section 4(3)(h)". In Schedule 5, in paragraph 5(3) of Part I and in paragraph 5(3) of Part II, the words "at such times and in such places as the Treasury may direct, and" and the words "with the approval of the Treasury". In Schedule 6, paragraph 3(3)(b).
1986 c.63.	The Housing and Planning Act 1986.	Section 7. Section 12. In section 13, subsections (1) to (3) and (5). Section 19. In Schedule 4, paragraphs 1(3) and 10. In Schedule 5, paragraph 8.
1986 c.65.	The Housing (Scotland) Act 1986.	Section 13(1). Sections 14 to 16.

Chapter	Short title	Extent of repeal
		In Schedule 2, in paragraph 4(8), sub-paragraph (a) and, in sub-paragraph (b), the words "section 4(3)(h)".
1987 c.26.	The Housing (Scotland) Act 1987.	In section 61(4)(b) the word "or" at the end of sub-paragraph (v) and at the end of sub-paragraph (vi).
1987 c.31.	The Landlord and Tenant Act 1987.	In section 3(1)(b) the word "or". Section 4(2)(a)(ii). Section 45. Section 60(2). In Schedule 4, paragraph 7.
1988 c.9.	The Local Government Act 1988.	Section 24(5)(b).
1988 c.43.	The Housing (Scotland) Act 1988.	Section 4(4). In section 38, the words "subject to subsection (2B) below" and "by reason only of conduct falling within paragraph (b) of that subsection". Schedule 3. In Schedule 9, paragraphs 6(b) and 7. In Schedule 10, the entry relating to the Housing Associations Act 1985.

1. The repeal of sections 19 to 21 of the Rent Act 1977 does not apply with respect to any tenancy or contract entered into before the coming into force of Part I of this Act nor to any other tenancy or contract which, having regard to section 36 of this Act, can be a restricted contract.

2. The repeal of section 52 of the Housing Act 1980 (protected shorthold tenancies) does not apply with respect to any tenancy entered into before the coming into force of Part I of this Act nor to any other tenancy which, having regard to section 34 of this Act, can be a protected shorthold tenancy.

3. The repeal of sections 56 to 58 of the Housing Act 1980 does not have effect in relation to any tenancy to which, by virtue of section 37(2) of this Act, section 1(3) of this Act does not apply.

4. The repeals in section 80 of the Housing Act 1985—

(a) have effect (subject to section 35(5) of this Act) in relation to any tenancy or licence entered into before the coming into force of Part I of this Act unless, immediately before that time, the landlord or, as the case may be, the licensor is a body which, in accordance with the repeals, would cease to be within the said section 80; and

(b) do not have effect in relation to a tenancy or licence entered into on or after the coming into force of Part I of this Act if the tenancy or licence falls within any of paragraphs (c) to (f) of subsection (4) of section 35 of this Act.

Appendix 2

Statutory Instruments

The Rent Book (Forms of Notice) (Amendment) Regulations 1988

SI 1988 No 2198

Coming into force 15th January 1989

The Secretary of State for the Environment, as respects England, and the Secretary of State for Wales, as respects Wales, in exercise of the powers conferred on them by section 5 of the Landlord and Tenant Act 1985, and of all other powers enabling them in that behalf, hereby make the following Regulations:

1. These Regulations may be cited as the Rent Book (Forms of Notice) (Amendment) Regulations 1988 and shall come into force on 15th January 1989.

2. The Rent Book (Forms of Notice) Regulations 1982 are amended as follows—

(1) at the end of regulation 2 insert—
"and
"the 1988 Act" means the Housing Act 1988";

(2) after regulation 3(1)(c) insert—

"(d) if the premises are a dwelling house let on an assured tenancy or an assured agricultural occupancy within the meaning of the 1988 Act, the form set out in Part IV of the Schedule to these regulations";

(3) in regulation 3(2) for "(a), (b) and (c)" substitute "(a) to (d)";

(4) substitute for the words in paragraph 11 of the forms in Parts I and III of the Schedule and in paragraph 13 of the form in Part II of the Schedule "You may be entitled to get help to pay your rent and rates through the housing benefit scheme. Apply to your local council for details.";

(5) for paragraphs 11 and 12 of the form in Part II of the Schedule substitute "11. If you have a protected shorthold tenancy or your tenancy was formerly a controlled one, special rules apply."; and

(6) Insert as Part IV of the Schedule the form in the Schedule to these Regulations.

SCHEDULE
(FORM FOR RENT BOOK FOR ASSURED TENANCY OR ASSURED AGRICULTURAL OCCUPANCY)

IMPORTANT—PLEASE READ THIS

If the rent for the premises you occupy as your residence is payable weekly, the landlord must provide you with a rent book or similar document. If you have an assured tenancy, including an assured *shorthold* tenancy (*see* paragraph 7 below), or an assured agricultural occupancy, the rent book or similar document must contain this notice, properly filled in.

1. Address of premises ....

***2.** Name and address of landlord ....

***3.** Name and address of agent (if any) ....

***4.** The rent payable including/excluding† rates is £ ...... per week.

5. Details of accommodation (if any) which the occupier has the right to share with other persons

....

6. The other terms and conditions of the tenancy are ....

....

7. If you have an assured tenancy or an assured agricultural occupancy you have certain rights under the Housing Act 1988. These include the right not to be evicted from your home unless your landlord gets a possession order from the courts. Unless the property is let under an assured *shorthold* tenancy, the courts can only grant an order on a limited number of grounds. Further details regarding assured tenancies are set out in the Department of the Environment and Welsh Office booklet "Assured Tenancies" no. 19 in the series of housing booklets. These booklets are available from rent officers, council offices and housing aid centres, some of which also give advice.

8. You may be entitled to get help to pay your rent and rates through the housing benefit scheme. Apply to your local council for details.

9. It is a criminal offence for your landlord to evict you without an order from the court or to harass you or interfere with your possessions or use of facilities in order to force you to leave.

10. If you are in any doubt about your legal rights or obligations, particularly if your landlord has asked you to leave, you should go to a Citizens' Advice Bureau, housing aid centre, law centre or solicitor. Help with all or part of the cost of legal advice from a solicitor may be available under the Legal Aid Scheme.

* These entries must be kept up-to-date.

† Cross out whichever does not apply.

The Assured Tenancies and Agricultural Occupancies (Rent Information) Order 1988
SI 1988 No 2199

Coming into force 15th January 1989

The Secretary of State for the Environment, as respects England, and the Secretary of State for Wales, as respects Wales, in exercise of the powers conferred upon them by section 42 of the Housing Act 1988, and of all other powers enabling them in that behalf, hereby make the following Order:

1. This Order may be cited as the Assured Tenancies and Agricultural Occupancies (Rent Information) Order 1988 and shall come into force on 15th January 1989.

2. This Order applies to cases where the rent assessment committee for an area have made a determination under section 13(4) or 22(1) of the Housing Act 1988 or are precluded from making a determination on an application under section 22(1) by reason of section 22(3) of that Act.

3. The President of the rent assessment panel for the area concerned shall, as respects those cases, make available for public inspection under section 42 of the Housing Act 1988 the information specified in the Schedule to this Order.

4. The President of each rent assessment panel shall keep the specified information available for public inspection without charge during usual office hours at the office or principal office of that panel.

5. A person requiring a copy of any specified information certified under the hand of an officer duly authorised by the President of the rent assessment panel concerned shall be entitled to obtain it on payment of a fee of £1 for the specified information relating to each determination or, where no determination is made, each application.

SCHEDULE

SPECIFIED INFORMATION

1. Address of premises.
2. Description of premises.
3. Names and addresses of landlord and tenant.
4. If granted for a term, date of commencement of the tenancy and length of term.
5. The rental period.
6. Allocation between landlord and tenant of liabilities for repairs.
7. Whether any rates are borne by the landlord or a superior landlord.
8. Details of services provided by the landlord or a superior landlord.
9. Details of furniture provided by the landlord or a superior landlord.
10. Any other terms of the tenancy or notice relating to the tenancy taken into consideration in determining the rent.
11. The rent determined, the date it was determined and the amount (if any) of the rent which, in the opinion of the committee, is fairly attributable to the provision of services, except where that amount is in their opinion negligible, or, in a case where the committee are precluded from making a

determination by section 22(3) of the Housing Act 1988, the rent currently payable under the assured shorthold tenancy.

The Rent Assessment Committees (England and Wales) (Amendment) Regulations 1988

SI 1988 No. 2200

Coming into force 15th January 1989

The Secretary of State for the Environment, as respects England, and the Secretary of State for Wales, as respects Wales, in exercise of the powers conferred on them by section 74(1) of the Rent Act 1977, and of all other powers enabling them in that behalf, and after consultation with the Council on Tribunals, hereby make the following Regulations:

1. These Regulations may be cited as the Rent Assessment Committees (England and Wales) (Amendment) Regulations 1988 and shall come into force on 15th January 1989.

2. The Rent Assessment Committees (England and Wales) Regulations 1971 are amended as follows—

(1) insert at the end of the definition of "reference" in regulation 2(2) "or which is referred or made under section 6, 13 or 22 of the Housing Act 1988";

(2) insert before "as the case may be" in regulation 2(3) "or regulation 2A(4) of these regulations";

(3) insert after regulation 2—

"*1988 Act references*

2A.—(1) This regulation applies where a reference is made under section 6, 13 or 22 of the Housing Act 1988.

(2) The committee shall serve on each party a notice specifying a period of not less than 7 days from the service of the notice during which either representations in writing or a request to make oral representations may be made by that party to the committee.

(3) A notice served under paragraph (2) above on the party who did not make the reference shall be accompanied by a copy of the reference.

(4) Where a party makes a request to make oral representations within the period specified in paragraph (2) above (or such further period as a committee may allow), the committee shall give him an opportunity to be heard in person or by a person authorised by him, whether or not that person is of counsel or a solicitor.

(5) The committee shall make such inquiry, if any, as they think fit and consider any information supplied or representation made to them in pursuance of paragraph (2) above.";

(4) insert after "the Rent Act 1977" in regulation 3(4) "or regulation 2A(2) of these regulations";

(5) insert after "dwelling-houses" in regulation 5(1)(b) "or, as the case may be, to the terms (including rent) of assured tenancies or assured agricultural occupancies of other dwelling-houses where such tenancies or occupancies have been the subject of a reference to a committee and in either case", and omit the following "and".

The Notices to Quit etc. (Prescribed Information) Regulations 1988
SI 1988 No. 2201

Coming into force 15 January 1989

The Secretary of State for the Environment, as respects England, and the Secretary of State for Wales, as respects Wales, in exercise of the powers conferred upon them by section 5 of the Protection from Eviction Act 1977, and of all other powers enabling them in that behalf, hereby make the following Regulations:

1. These Regulations may be cited as the Notices to Quit etc. (Prescribed Information) Regulations 1988 and shall come into force on 15th January 1989.

2. Where, on or after the date these Regulations come into force, a landlord gives a notice to quit any premises let as a dwelling, or a licensor gives a notice to determine a periodic licence to occupy premises as a dwelling (and the premises are not let or occupied as specified in section 5(1B) of the Protection from Eviction Act 1977), the information prescribed for the purposes of section 5 of the Protection from Eviction Act 1977 shall be that in the Schedule to these Regulations.

3. The Notices to Quit (Prescribed Information) Regulations 1980 are hereby revoked.

SCHEDULE

PRESCRIBED INFORMATION

1. If the tenant or licensee does not leave the dwelling, the landlord or licensor must get an order for possession from the court before the tenant or licensee can lawfully be evicted. The landlord or licensor cannot apply for such an order before the notice to quit or notice to determine has run out.

2. A tenant or licensee who does not know if he has any right to remain in possession after a notice to quit or a notice to determine runs out can obtain advice from a solicitor. Help with all or part of the cost of legal advice and assistance may be available under the Legal Aid Scheme. He should also be able to obtain information from a Citizens' Advice Bureau, a Housing Aid Centre or a rent officer.

The Assured Tenancies and Agricultural Occupancies (Forms) Regulations 1988
SI 1988 No. 2203

Coming into force 15 January 1989

The Secretary of State for the Environment, as respects England, and the Secretary of State for Wales, as respects Wales, in exercise of the powers conferred upon them by sections 6(2) and (3), 8(3), 13(2) and (4), 20(2), 22(1), 41(2) and 45(1) and (5) of the Housing Act 1988, and of all other powers enabling them in that behalf, hereby make the following Regulations:

1. These Regulations may be cited as the Assured Tenancies and Agricultural Occupancies (Forms) Regulations 1988 and shall come into force on 15th January 1989.

2. In these Regulations any reference to a section is to a section of the Housing Act 1988 and any reference to a numbered form is a reference to the form bearing that number in the Schedule to these Regulations, or to a form substantially to the same effect.

3. The forms prescribed for the purposes of Part I of the Housing Act 1988 shall be as follows–

(1) for a notice under section 6(2) proposing terms of a statutory periodic tenancy different from the implied terms, form no. 1;

(2) for an application under section 6(3) referring a notice under section 6(2) to a rent assessment committee, form no. 2;

(3) for a notice under section 8 informing a tenant that the landlord intends to begin proceedings for possession of a dwelling-house let on an assured tenancy which is not an assured agricultural occupancy, form no. 3;

(4) for a notice under section 8 informing a tenant that the landlord intends to begin proceedings for possession of a dwelling-house let on an assured agricultural occupancy, form no. 4;

(5) for a notice under section 13(2) proposing a new rent for an assured tenancy which is not an assured agricultural occupancy, form no. 5;

(6) for an application under section 13(4) referring to a rent assessment committee a notice under section 13(2) relating to an assured tenancy or an assured agricultural occupancy, form no. 6;

(7) for a notice under section 20 of intention to grant an assured shorthold tenancy form no. 7;

(8) for an application under section 22(1) to a rent assessment committee for a determination of rent under an assured shorthold tenancy, form no. 8; and

(9) for a notice under section 41(2) requiring a landlord or tenant to give information to a rent assessment committee, form no. 9.

SCHEDULE

FORM NO. 1

Housing Act 1988 section 6(2)

Notice Proposing Different Terms for Statutory Periodic Tenancy

- Please write clearly in black ink.
- **This notice proposes changes to the terms of the statutory periodic tenancy. If you wish to refer it to a rent assessment committee you must keep to the time limit set out in paragraph 2 below.**
- Please read this notice very carefully as it may alter the terms of the statutory periodic tenancy which arises when a fixed term assured tenancy runs out. It may also be used when a

fixed term assured agricultural occupancy ends.

- It can be used by either a landlord or a tenant.
- This notice must be served no later than the first anniversary of the day after the former fixed term tenancy or occupancy ended.
- Do not use this notice if you are a landlord only proposing an increase in rent.
- If you need help or advice about this notice, and what you should do about it, take it immediately to any of the following:
- a Citizens' Advice Bureau
- a housing aid centre,
- a law centre or a solicitor.

1. To: *Name(s) of landlord(s) or tenant(s)* *

of: *Address of premises*

2. This is to give notice that I/we* propose different terms of the statutory periodic tenancy from those in the fixed term assured tenancy which has now ended to take effect from

19

This date must be at least three months after this notice is served.

* *Cross out whichever does not apply.*

- If you agree with the new terms and rent proposed, do nothing. They will become the terms of your tenancy agreement on the date specified in paragraph 2.
- If you don't agree with the proposed terms and any adjustment of the rent (see paragraph 4), and you are unable to reach agreement with your landlord/tenant, or you do not wish to discuss it with him, you may refer the matter directly to your local rent assessment committee, **within three months of the date on which the notice was served,** using a special form.
- The committee will determine the proposed changes in the terms of the tenancy or some other different terms covering the same points, and the appropriate level of rent, if this applies.

3. Changes to the terms

(a) the provisions of the tenancy to be changed are—
Please attach relevant sections of the agreement if available.

(b) The proposed changes are—
(Continue on a separate sheet if necessary.)

4.* Changes to the rent, if applicable
The existing rent is
This includes rates* £ per
eg. week, month, year

The new rent which takes into account
the proposed changes in the terms of the tenancy
will be— £ per

eg. week, month, year

This includes rates*

- Changes to the rent are optional. A proposal to adjust the rent to take account of the proposed new terms at paragraph 3 may be made if either the landlord or the tenant considers it appropriate.

To be signed by the landlord or his agent (someone acting for him) or the tenant or his agent. If there are joint landlords or joint tenants each landlord/tenant or the agent must sign unless one signs on behalf of the rest with their agreement.

Signed:

Name(s) of landlord(s)/tenant(s):

Address of landlord(s)/tenant(s):

Tel:

If signed by agent, name and address of agent

Tel: *Date:*

**Cross out if this does not apply.*

FORM NO. 2

Housing Act 1988 section 6(3)

Application Referring a Notice Under Section 6(2) to a Rent Assessment Committee

- Please write clearly in black ink.
- Please tick boxes where appropriate.
- When you have filled in the form please send it to the appropriate rent assessment panel.
- Make sure you also send a copy of the notice served on you proposing the new terms of the statutory periodic tenancy.
- This application may be used by a landlord or a tenant who has been served with a notice under section 6(2) of the Housing Act 1988, varying the terms of a statutory periodic tenancy. It may also be used where there was an earlier assured agricultural occupancy.

1. Address of premises
2. Name(s) of tenant(s)
3. Name(s) of landlord(s)

   Address of landlord(s)
4. Details of premises.

   (a) What type of property is it, eg house, flat or room(s)?

(b) If it is a flat or room(s) say what floor(s) it is on.

(c) Give the number and type of rooms, eg living room, bathroom.

(d) Does the tenancy include any other facilities, eg garden, garage or other separate building or land? Yes ☐ No ☐

(e) If Yes, please give details.

(f) Is any of the accommodation shared?

(i) with the landlord? Yes ☐ No ☐

(ii) with another tenant or tenants? Yes ☐ No ☐

(g) If Yes, please give details.

5. What is the current rateable value of the premises? £

6. When did the statutory tenancy begin? 19

7. Services

(a) Are any services provided under the tenancy (eg cleaning, lighting, heating, hot water or gardening)? Yes ☐ No ☐

(b) If Yes, please give details.

(c) Is a separate charge made for services, maintenance, repairs, landlord's costs of management or any other item? Yes ☐ No ☐

(d) what charge is payable? £

(e) Does the charge vary according to the relevant costs? Yes ☐ No ☐

(f) If Yes, please give details.

8. (a) Is any furniture provided under the tenancy? Yes ☐ No ☐

(b) If Yes, please give details (*continue on a separate sheet if necessary*).

9. What repairs are the responsibility of

(a) the landlord?

(b) the tenant? (*continue on a separate sheet if necessary*).

10. (a) Give details of the other terms of the tenancy, eg whether the tenancy is assignable and whether a premium may be charged on an assignment (*continue on a separate sheet if necessary*).

(b) Please attach the tenancy agreement (or a copy), with a note of any variations, if you have one. It will be returned to you without delay.

11. I/We*attach a copy of the notice proposing changes to the statutory periodic tenancy and, if applicable, an adjustment of the amount of rent and apply to the rent assessment committee to consider it.

**Cross out whichever does not apply.*

To be signed by the landlord or his agent (someone acting for him), or by the tenant or his agent. If there are joint landlords or joint tenants each landlord/tenant or the agent must sign, unless one signs on behalf of the rest with their agreement.

Signed:

Name(s) of landlord(s)/tenant(s):

Address of landlord(s)/tenant(s):

Tel:

If signed by agent, name and address of agent

Tel: *Date:* *19*

FORM NO. 3

Housing Act 1988 section 8

Notice Seeking Possession of a Property Let on an Assured Tenancy

- Please write clearly in black ink.
- Do not use this form if possession is sought from an assured shorthold tenant under section 21 of the Housing Act 1988 or if the property is occupied under an assured agricultural occupancy.
- **This notice is the first step towards requiring you to give up possession of your home. You should read it very carefully.**
- If you need advice about this notice, and what you should do about it, take it as quickly as possible to any of the following–
  - a Citizens' Advice Bureau,
  - a housing aid centre,
  - a law centre,
  - or a solicitor.

  You may be able to get Legal Aid but this will depend on your personal circumstances.

1. To: *Name(s) of tenants(s)*

2. Your landlord intends to apply to the court for an order requiring you to give up possession of–

(Address of premises)

- If you have an assured tenancy under the Housing Act 1988, which is not an assured shorthold tenancy, you can only be required to leave your home if your landlord gets an order for possession from the court on one of the grounds which are set out in Schedule 2 to the Act.
- If you are willing to give up possession of your home without a court order, you should tell the person who signed this notice as soon as possible and say when you can leave.

3. The landlord intends to seek possession on ground(s) . . . . in Schedule 2 to the Housing Act 1988, which reads

Give the full text of each ground which is being relied on. (Continue on a separate sheet if necessary.)

- Whichever grounds are set out in paragraph 3 the court may allow any of the other grounds to be added at a later date. If this is done, you will be told about it so you can discuss the additional grounds at the court hearing as well as the grounds set out in paragraph 3.

4. Particulars of each ground are as follows–

Give a full explanation of why each ground is being relied. (Continue on a separate sheet if necessary.)

- If the court is satisfied that any of grounds 1 to 8 is established it must make an order (but see below in respect of fixed term tenancies).
- Before the court will grant an order on any of grounds 9 to 16, it must be satisfied that it is reasonable to require you to leave. This means that, if one of these grounds is set out in paragraph 3, you will be able to suggest to the court that it is not reasonable that you should have to leave, even if you accept that the ground applies.
- The court will not make an order under grounds 1, 3 to 7, 9 or 16, to take effect during the fixed term of the tenancy; and it will only make an order during the fixed term on grounds 2, 8 or 10 to 15 if the terms of the tenancy make provision for it to be brought to an end on any of these grounds.
- Where the court makes an order for possession solely on ground 6 or 9, your landlord must pay your reasonable removal expenses.

5. The court proceedings will not begin until after 19

Give the date after which court proceedings can be brought.

- Where the landlord is seeking possession under grounds 1, 2, 5 to 7, 9 or 16 in Schedule 2, court proceedings cannot begin earlier than 2 months from the date this notice is served on you and not before the date on which the tenancy (had it not been assured) could have been brought to an end by a notice to quit served at the same time as this notice.

- Where the landlord is seeking possession on grounds 3, 4, 8 or 10 to 15, court proceedings cannot begin until 2 weeks after the date this notice is served.
- After the date shown in paragraph 5, court proceedings may be begun at once but not later than 12 months from the date this notice is served. After this time the notice will lapse and a new notice must be served before possession can be sought.

To be signed by the landlord or his agent (someone acting for him).

Signed:

Names(s) of landlord(s):

Address of landlord(s):

Tel:

If signed by agent, name and address of agent:

Tel: *Date:* *19*

FORM NO. 4

Housing Act 1988 section 8

Notice Seeking Possession of an Assured Agricultural Occupancy

- Please write clearly in black ink.
- **This notice is the first step towards requiring you to give up possession of your home. You should read it very carefully.**
- If you need advice about this notice, and what you should do about it, take it as quickly as possible to any of the following–
- a Citizens' Advice Bureau,
- a housing aid centre,
- a law centre,
- or a solicitor.

You may be able to get Legal Aid but this will depend on your personal circumstances.

1. **To:** *Name(s) of tenant(s) or licencee(s)*
2. **Your landlord or licensor intends to apply to the court for an order requiring you to give up possession of–**

(Address of premises)

- If you have an assured agricultural occupancy under the Housing Act 1988, which is not an assured shorthold tenancy, you can only be required to leave your home if your landlord or licensor gets an order for possession from the court on one of the grounds which are set out in Schedule 2 to the Act, except ground 16.

- If you are willing to give up possession of your home without a court order, you should tell the person who signed this notice as soon as possible and say when you can leave.

3. The landlord or licensor intends to seek possession on ground(s) . . . . in Schedule 2 to the Housing Act 1988, which reads

Give the full text of each ground which is being relied on.
(Continue on a separate sheet if necessary.)

- Whichever grounds are set out in paragraph 3 the court may allow any of the other grounds to be added at a later date. If this is done, you will be told about it so you can discuss the additional grounds at the court hearing as well as the grounds set out in paragraph 3.

4. Particulars of each ground are as follows–

Give a full explanation of why each ground is being relied.
(Continue on a separate sheet if necessary.)

- If the court is satisfied that any of grounds 1 to 8 is established it must make an order (but see below in respect of fixed term tenancies or licences).
- Before the court will grant an order on any of grounds 9 to 15, it must be satisfied that it is reasonable to require you to leave. This means that, if one of these grounds is set out in paragraph 3, you will be able to suggest to the court that it is not reasonable that you should have to leave, even if you accept that the ground applies.
- The court will not make an order under grounds 1, 3 to 7 or 9, to take effect during the fixed term of the tenancy or licence; and it will only make an order during the fixed term on grounds 2, 8 or 10 to 15 if the terms of the tenancy or licence make provision for it to be brought to an end on any of these grounds.
- Where the court makes an order for possession solely on ground 6 or 9, your landlord or licensor must pay your reasonable removal expenses.

5. The court proceedings will not begin until after 19

Give the date after which court proceedings can be brought.

- Where the landlord or licensor is seeking possession under grounds 1, 2, 5 to 7 or 9 in Schedule 2, court proceedings cannot begin earlier than 2 months from the date this notice is served on you and not before the date on which the tenancy or licence (had it not been an assured agricultural occupancy) could have been brought to an end by a notice to quit or determine served at the same time as this notice.
- Where the landlord or licensor is seeking possession on grounds 3, 4, 8 or 10 to 15, court proceedings cannot begin until 2 weeks after the date this notice is served.
- After the date shown in paragraph 5, court proceedings may be begun at once but not later than 12 months from the date this notice is served. After this time the notice will lapse and a new notice must be served before possession can be sought.

To be signed by the landlord, the licensor or his agent (someone acting for him).

Signed:

Name(s) of landlord(s) or licensor(s):

Address of landlord(s) or licensor(s):

Tel:

If signed by agent, name and address of agent:

Tel: *Date:* *19*

FORM NO. 5

Housing Act 1988 section 13(2)

Landlord's Notice Proposing a New Rent Under An Assured Periodic Tenancy or Agricultural Occupancy

- Please write clearly in black ink.
- Do not use this form if there is a current rent fixing mechanism in the tenancy.
- Do not use this form to propose a rent adjustment for a statutory periodic tenancy solely because of a proposed change of terms under section 6(2) of the Housing Act 1988.
- This notice may also be used to propose a new rent or licence fee for an assured agricultural occupancy. In such a case references to "landlord"/"tenant" can be read as references to "licensor"/"licensee"etc.
- **This notice proposes a new rent. If you want to oppose this proposal you must keep to the time limit set out in paragraph 2.** Read this notice carefully. If you need help or advice take it immediately to:
  - a Citizens' Advice Bureau,
  - a housing aid centre,
  - a law centre,
  - or a solicitor.

1. To: *Name(s) of tenant(s)*
   of: *Address of premises*
2. This is to give notice that as from 19
   your landlord proposes to charge a new rent.

   The new rent must take effect at the beginning of a new period of the tenancy and not earlier than any of the following–

   (a) the minimum period after this notice was served,
   (the minimum period is–
   - in the case of a yearly tenancy, six months,
   - in the case of a tenancy where the period is less than a month, one month, and,
   - in any other case, a period equal to the period of the tenancy.)

   (b) the first anniversary of the start of the first period of the tenancy except in the case of–

- a statutory periodic tenancy, which arises when a fixed term assured tenancy ends, or
- an assured tenancy which arose on the death of a tenant under a regulated tenancy,

(c) if the rent under the tenancy has previously been increased by a notice under section 13 or a determination under section 14 of the Housing Act 1988, the first anniversary of the date on which the increased rent took effect.

3. The existing rent is £ per
eg. week, month, year

This includes/excludes* rates

4. The proposed new rent will be £ per
eg. week, month, year

This includes/excludes* rates

**Cross out whichever does not apply.*

- If you agree with the new rent proposed do nothing. If you do not agree and you are unable to reach agreement with your landlord or do not want to discuss it directly with him, you may refer the notice to your local rent assessment committee before the beginning of the new period given in paragraph 2. The committee will consider your application and will decide whether the proposed new rent is appropriate.
- You will need a special form to refer the notice to a rent assessment committee.

To be signed by the landlord or his agent (someone acting for him). If there are joint landlords each landlord or his agent must sign unless one signs on behalf of the rest with their agreement.

Signed:

Name(s) of landlord(s):

Address of landlord(s):

Tel:

If signed by agent, name and address of agent:

Tel: *Date:* *19*

FORM NO. 6

Housing Act 1988 section 13(4)

Application Referring A Notice Proposing A New Rent Under An Assured Periodic Tenancy or Agricultural Occupancy to a Rent Assessment Committee

- Please write clearly in black ink.
- Please tick boxes where appropriate.

- When you have filled the form in please send it to the appropriate rent assessment panel.
- You should use this form when your landlord has served notice on you proposing a new rent under an assured periodic tenancy.
- You will need to attach a copy of that notice to this form.
- This form may also be used to refer a notice proposing a new rent or licence fee for an assured agricultural occupancy. In such a case references to "landlord"/ "tenant" can be read as references to "licensor"/"licensee" etc.

1. Address of premises
2. Name(s) of landlord(s)
   Address of landlord(s)
3. Details of premises.
   (a) What type of property is it, eg house, flat or room(s)?
   (b) If it is a flat or room(s) say what floor(s) it is on.
   (c) Give the number and type of rooms, eg living room, bathroom.
   (d) Does the tenancy include any other facilities, eg garden, garage or other separate building or land? Yes ☐ No ☐
   (e) If Yes, please give details.
   (f) Do you share any accommodation?
      (i) with the landlord? Yes ☐ No ☐
      (ii) with another tenant or tenants? Yes ☐ No ☐
   (g) If Yes to either of the above, please give details.
4. What is the current rateable value of the premises? £
5. (a) When did the present tenancy begin? 19
   (b) When does the present tenancy end? 19
6. (a) Did you pay a premium? Yes ☐ No ☐
   (b) If Yes, please give details.
7. Services
   (a) Are any services provided under the tenancy (eg cleaning, lighting, heating, hot water or gardening)? Yes ☐ No ☐
   (b) If Yes please give details.
   (c) Is a separate charge made for services, maintenance, repairs, landlord's costs of management or any other item? Yes ☐ No ☐
   (d) What charge is payable? £
   (e) Does the charge vary according to the relevant costs? Yes ☐ No ☐
   (f) If Yes, please give details.
8. (a) Is any furniture provided under the tenancy? Yes ☐ No ☐
   (b) If Yes, please give details
   (*continue on a separate sheet if necessary*).

9. Improvements
   (a) Have you, or any former tenant(s) carried out improvements or replaced fixtures, fittings or furniture for which you or they were not responsible under the terms of the tenancy? Yes ☐ No ☐
   (b) If Yes, please give details
   (*continue on a separate sheet if necessary*).

10. What repairs are the responsibility of
   (a) the landlord?
   (b) the tenant?
   (*continue on a separate sheet if necessary*)

11. (a) Give details of the other terms of the tenancy, eg whether the tenancy is assignable and whether a premium may be charged on an assignment
   (*continue on a separate sheet if necessary*).
   (b) Please attach the tenancy agreement, or a copy (with a note of any variations), if you have one. It will be returned to you as quickly as possible.

12. Do you have an assured agricultural occupancy? Yes ☐ No ☐

13. I/We* attach a copy of the notice proposing a new rent under the assured periodic tenancy and I/we* apply for it to be considered by a rent assessment committee.

To be signed by the tenant or his agent (someone acting for him). If there are joint tenants, each tenant or his agent must sign, unless one signs on behalf of the rest with their agreement.

Signed:

Name of tenant(s):

Address of tenant(s):

Tel:

If signed by agent, name and address of agent:

Tel: *Date:* *19*

**Cross out whichever does not apply.*

FORM NO.7

Housing Act 1988 section 20

Notice of an Assured Shorthold Tenancy

- Please write clearly in black ink.
- If there is any thing you do not understand you should get advice from a solicitor or a Citizens' Advice Bureau before you agree to the tenancy.
- The landlord must give this notice to the tenant before an assured shorthold tenancy is granted. It does not commit the tenant to take the tenancy.
- **This document is important, keep it in a safe place.**

To: *Name of proposed tenant. If a joint tenancy is being offered enter the names of the joint tenants.*

1. *You are proposing to take a tenancy of the dwelling known as:*

from / /19 to / /19
day month year day month year

The tenancy must be for a term certain of at least six months.

2. This notice is to tell you that your tenancy is to be an assured shorthold tenancy. Provided you keep to the terms of the tenancy, you are entitled to remain in the dwelling for at least the first six months of the fixed period agreed at the start of the tenancy. At the end of this period, depending on the terms of the tenancy, the landlord may have the right to repossession if he wants.

3. The rent for this tenancy is the rent we have agreed. However, you have the right to apply to a rent assessment committee for a determination of the rent which the committee considers might reasonably be obtained under the tenancy. If the committee considers (i) that there is a sufficient number of similar properties in the locality let on assured tenancies and that (ii) the rent we have agreed is significantly higher than the rent which might reasonably be obtained having regard to the level of rents for other assured tenancies in the locality, it will determine a rent for the tenancy. That rent will be the legal maximum you can be required to pay from the date the committee directs.

4. This notice was served on you on 19

To be signed by the landlord or his agent (someone acting for him). If there are joint landlords each must sign, unless one signs on behalf of the rest with their agreement.

Signed

Name(s) of landlord(s):

Address of landlord(s):

Tel:

If signed by agent, name and address of agent:

Tel: *Date:* *19*

Special note for existing tenants

- Generally if you already have a protected or statutory tenancy and you give it up to take a new tenancy in the same or other accommodation owned by the same landlord, that tenancy cannot be an assured tenancy. It can still be a protected tenancy.
- But if you currently occupy a dwelling which was let to you as a protected shorthold tenant, special rules apply.
- If you have an assured tenancy which is not a shorthold under the Housing Act 1988, you cannot be offered an assured shorthold tenancy of the same or other accommodation by the same landlord.

FORM NO. 8

Housing Act 1988 section 22(1)

Application to a Rent Assessment Committee for a Determination of a Rent Under an Assured Shorthold Tenancy

- Please write clearly in black ink.
- Please tick boxes where appropriate.
- A tenant with a fixed term assured shorthold tenancy may use this form to apply to the local rent assessment committee, during the fixed term, to have the rent reduced. This form cannot be used in the cases specified at the end of this form.
- The form may also be used to apply to have the rent reduced for a fixed term assured shorthold tenancy which is an assured agricultural occupancy. In such a case, references to "landlord"/"tenant" can be read as references to "licensor"/"licensee" etc.
- When you have filled the form in please send it to the appropriate rent assessment panel.

1. Address of premises
2. Name(s) of landlord(s)
   Address of landlord(s)
3. Details of premises.
   (a) What type of property is it, eg house, flat or room(s)?
   (b) If it is a flat or room(s) say what floor(s) it is on.
   (c) Give the number and type of rooms, eg living room, bathroom etc.
   (d) Does the tenancy include any other facilities, eg garden, garage or other separate building or land? Yes ☐ No ☐
   (e) If Yes, please give details.
   (f) Do you share any accommodation?
      (i) with the landlord? Yes ☐ No ☐
      (ii) with another tenant or tenants? Yes ☐ No ☐
   (g) If Yes to either of the above, please give details.
4. What is the current rateable value of the premises? £
5. (a) When did the present tenancy begin? 19
   (b) When does the present tenancy end?
6. (a) Please confirm by ticking box that you received a notice saying that the tenancy was to be an assured shorthold tenancy before the agreement was entered into. ☐
   (b) Attach a copy of the notice if available.
   It will be returned without delay.
7. (a) Did you pay a premium? Yes ☐ No ☐
   (b) If Yes, please give details.

8. Services
   (a) Are any services provided under the tenancy (eg cleaning, lighting, heating, hot water or gardening)? Yes ☐ No ☐
   (b) If Yes, please give details.
   (c) Is a separate charge made for services, maintenance, repairs, landlord's costs of management or any other item? Yes ☐ No ☐
   (d) What charge is payable? £
   (e) Does the charge vary according to the relevant costs? Yes ☐ No ☐
   (f) If Yes, please give details.

9. (a) Is any furniture provided under the tenancy? Yes ☐ No ☐
   (b) If Yes, please give details
   (*continue on a separate sheet if necessary*).

10. What repairs are the responsibility of
   (a) the landlord?
   (b) the tenant?
   (*continue on a separate sheet if necessary*).

11. (a) Give details of the other terms of the tenancy, eg whether the tenancy is assignable, and whether a premium may be charged on an assignment
   (continue on a separate sheet if necessary).
   (b) Please attach the tenancy agreement or a copy (with a note of any variations) if you have one. It will be returned to you without delay.

12. The existing rent is £ per
eg. week, month, year

This includes/excludes rates of £ per*

13. I/We* apply to the rent assessment committee to determine a rent for the above mentioned premises.

To be signed by the tenant or his agent (someone acting for him.) If there are joint tenants each tenant or his agent must sign, unless one signs on behalf of the rest with their agreement.

Signed:

Name(s) of tenant(s):

Address of tenant(s):

Tel:

If signed by agent, name and address of agent:

Tel: *Date:* *19*

- An application cannot be made if–
   (a) the rent payable under the tenancy is a rent previously determined by a rent assessment committee; or

(b) the tenancy is an assured shorthold tenancy that came into being on the ending of a tenancy which had been an assured shorthold of the same, or substantially the same, property and the landlord and tenant under each tenancy were the same at the time.

- the rent assessment committee cannot make a determination unless it considers–
  (a) that there is a sufficient number of similar dwelling-houses in the locality let on assured tenancies (whether shorthold or not); and
  (b) that the rent payable under the shorthold tenancy in question is significantly higher than the rent which the landlord might reasonably be expected to get in comparison with other rents under the assured tenancies mentioned in (a) above.

**Cross out whichever does not apply.*

FORM NO. 9

Housing Act 1988 section 41(2)

Notice by Rent Assessment Committee Requiring Further Information

To: *Landlord(s)/tenant(s)**

of: *Address of premises*

1. An application has been made to the rent assessment committee for consideration of–

- the terms of a statutory periodic assured tenancy
- an increase in rent under an assured periodic tenancy
- the rent under an assured shorthold tenancy
- an increase in rent under an assured agricultural occupancy

of the above property. The committee needs more information from you, to consider the application.

2. The information needed is

Please send it to

no later than 19

3. If you fail to comply with this notice without reasonable cause you will be committing a criminal offence and may be liable to a fine.

Signed Date 19

for the rent assessment committee

** Cross out whichever does not apply.*

Appendix 3

The Tenants' Guarantee

Reproduced below is the Tenants' Guarantee issued by the Housing Corporation and reproduced here with their kind permission.

Guidance on the Management by Registered Housing Associations of Housing Accommodation Let on ASSURED TENANCIES Under the Housing Act 1988

Issued by the Housing Corporation under Section 36A of the Housing Associations Act 1985 (as inserted by Section 49 of the Housing Act 1988). Approved by the Secretary of State for the Environment 6 December 1988 and coming into force on 15 January 1989.

This Guidance applies to housing associations registered by the Housing Corporation under Section 5 of the Housing Associations Act 1985 which are:

a. societies registered under Industrial and Provident Societies Act 1965 having their registered office for the purposes of that Act in England, or

b. charities registered under Section 4 of the Charities Act 1960 having their address for the purposes of registration by the Charity Commissioners in England.

Separate guidance is being issued for associations registered with the Housing Corporation which are:

- fully mutual housing co-operatives;
- almshouse charities;
- providing special needs housing in shared accommodation and hostels;
- letting on long leases, including shared ownership.

Introduction

The introduction to the Guidance is provided by the Housing Corporation for explanatory purposes. It does not form part of the Guidance approved by the Secretary of State.

1. What is this Guidance?

It is issued by the Housing Corporation using its powers under Section 36A of the Housing Associations Act 1985 (as inserted by Section 49 of the Housing Act 1988). It is "The Tenants' Guarantee" which the Minister promised when the legislation was going through Parliament. Widespread consultation about its contents has taken place, and it has been approved by the Secretary of State. It cannot be changed without further consultation and approval.

It is a statement of the principles which registered housing associations should practice and the minimum standards which they should achieve, in the interests of applicants for, and tenants of, rented housing under the new statutory regime. There are also, of course, many important statutory obligations which associations are obliged to meet. Some, but not all, of these are referred to in the Guidance, which does not claim to give a full account of them. Moreover, in addition to this Guidance which is issued under statute, associations are expected to take account of the more detailed guidance on good practice issued by The Housing Corporation and the National Federation of Housing Associations, such as the 'Standards for Housing Management'. From time to time both the Corporation and the NFHA will issue further non-statutory guidance on specific subjects.

This Guidance will be a major benchmark by which the Corporation will (and the public may) assess the management of an association's affairs. Where the Corporation finds mismanagement it has powers to act as described in paragraph 5 below.

2. To whom is this Guidance addressed?

It is addressed to all English registered housing associations which let self-contained homes, which includes most sheltered schemes for the elderly. In future these lettings will, with some exceptions, be Assured Tenancies. It therefore applies to new tenants taking up tenancies with housing associations from 15th January 1989. Existing tenants will retain their existing form of tenancy, including their Fair Rents and, where they qualify for it, their Right to Buy. This is explained further under each section.

Separate guidance is being issued under Section 36A for associations letting accommodation under different tenures - i.e. fully mutual housing co-operatives, almshouses, and those providing shared housing and hostels, and long leases.

The Corporation will make it a condition of the approval of landlords under Section 94 Housing Act 1988 - to take part in the Tenants' Choice scheme - that they comply with guidance incorporating similar principles and minimum standards.

3. Why is this Guidance issued now?

It is issued now, immediately following enactment of the Housing Act 1988, because the role of housing associations is likely to grow rapidly as they take on New Town housing, make increasing use of private funding, and as council tenants choose them as new landlords. The Government and the Corporation wish to ensure that associations, while growing, continue to achieve high standards of housing management. The assured tenancy framework provides less detailed statutory rights for tenants than the secure tenancy and fair rent framework. This Guidance sets out the additional rights which the Corporation expects associations to offer as contractual rights in their tenancy agreements. A model tenancy agreement prepared by the National Federation of Housing Associations is issued to associations with this Guidance. It incorporates the provisions which the Corporation considers it essential that housing associations should include.

4. How will the Corporation monitor whether associations are following this Guidance?

Primarily this will be by monitoring visits to associations still developing schemes with public subsidy, those newly registering, those wishing to take on local authority estates, and others where reports are received of their failure to comply. In particular their tenancy agreements will be checked. In addition all associations will be required by the Guidance to lodge summaries of their lettings policies with The Housing Corporation and the local authority.

5. How can the Corporation enforce compliance with this Guidance?

In the first place we believe that associations will be anxious to maintain their reputation for good quality management and that public opinion, arising from widespread publicity, will also stimulate associations to meet the required standard.

Secondly where failings are found through monitoring associations will be advised and given a timetable to remedy them.

Thirdly, The Housing Corporation will investigate complaints from tenants of associations about their landlords when the tenant has exhausted the association's own complaints procedures.

In addition the Corporation will take into account the extent to which an association complies with this Guidance when deciding:

- *whether the association should receive Housing Association Grant,*
- *whether the association can be approved to take part in "Tenants Choice"; and*
- *whether a Higher Management Allowance is justified.*

Where The Housing Corporation has reason to believe that there is serious mismanagement of an associations affairs it can, under the Housing Associations Act 1985:

- *appoint additional people to the governing body (Section 17),*
- *institute a statutory inquiry (Section 28), and,*
- *after an inquiry which results in a finding of misconduct or mismanagement:*
- *dismiss Committees or staff (Section 30), and*
- *direct a transfer of property to another housing association (Section 32).*

Section 36A explicitly states that the extent to which an association complies with this Guidance is one of the criteria by which the Corporation may assess mismanagement.

The Guidance approved by the Secretary of State is set out in the following pages.

The Guidance

A Meeting House Demand

A1 The essential purpose of registered housing associations is to provide accommodation for those who are inadequately housed or homeless, and for whom suitable housing is not available at prices within their means, or at all, elsewhere in the local market. This section and section B is guidance for meeting that objective.

A2 To qualify for registration housing associations are required to retain their housing stock for letting (note i) and to dispose of it only in particular circumstances. Disposals require the consent of The Housing Corporation (note ii) or, where the stock has been transferred from a public housing authority, the consent of the Secretary of State. With rare exceptions it is Housing Corporation policy to refuse consent for sale of tenanted property except to the tenant or to another registered housing association.

A3 In determining their priorities for the provision of accommodation and the offer of tenancies, associations should take account of housing demand and conditions in their area. They should consult and co-operate with the local housing authority, especially about its responsibilities for homeless persons and its other statutory re-housing obligations (see note iii) and with other relevant public bodies such as social service departments and health authorities. They should also collaborate with these bodies and voluntary and community organisations to make their housing service known to the relevant members of the public.

A4 Associations are expected to respond to tenants' requirements for mobility, and to participate actively in national and local mobility and exchange schemes.

(Note i. see Section 4 (2) Housing Associations Act 1985.)

(Note ii. see Section 9 Housing Associations Act 1985.)

(Note iii. see Section 72 Housing Act 1985 which requires registered housing associations to assist with homeless persons, if requested by local authorities. Other statutory obligations are to retired agricultural workers, and persons displaced by closing orders.)

B Allocating Accommodation on Assured Tenancies

B1 Registered housing associations are expected to have publicly available policies and procedures for selecting tenants and allocating tenancies. These should be open, fair and based on housing need.

B2.1 Associations should make publicly and freely available a summary of:

a. who is eligible for their accommodation. In most cases this must exclude people on their governing bodies, or employed by them, or their close relatives (note iv). For charitable associations it may be further restricted by their rules;

b. how members of the public may apply for tenancies, including any arrangements for nominations or referrals from the local housing authority and other organisations;

c. their policies and procedures for deciding on priority as between applicants; and

d. their policies and procedures for responding to tenants wishing to move (whether or not by way of exchange of dwellings) to other dwellings let by that association or another landlord.

B2.2 Associations should send a copy of this summary to The Housing Corporation, and to the local housing authority in whose area they manage tenanted property. A copy should also be sent to local advice centres and other organisations advising the public on access to housing and be given to people who apply to the association for accommodation. Where appropriate translations should be provided.

B2.3 Larger associations will need more detailed guidelines and procedures for their staff. These should also be available to the bodies mentioned above and to any applicants or members of the public requesting to see them.

B3.1 Associations are expected to have allocation policies which are clear. They should be based upon the severity of an applicant's housing needs. Associations are expected to pay special attention to the specific housing difficulties experienced by particular groups. These will vary from time to time and from place to place. They may include - subject to the association's specific objects - elderly people, single people, families with young children, single parent families, people from ethnic minorities, young people without family support, women suffering domestic violence, disabled people, and those who care for people who would otherwise be unable to remain in their own home, but this list is not intended to be exhaustive.

B3.2 Policies and procedures must provide equality of opportunity to all sections of society, taking particular and full account of the race relations (note v) and sex discrimination (note vi) legislation. (see also section H below).

B3.3 There should be procedures which can demonstrate that policies are objective and are properly followed. For instance, among other good practices, associations are expected to keep records of applicants' own definition of their ethnic origin, and monitor them.

B3.4 Associations should prepare annual summaries of their letting activities to include a report on the number and types of lettings to different types of applicant. They should make these summaries available to inquirers.

B3.5 Associations should not deter low income applicants by requiring more than one or two weeks rent in advance, to cover the first rental period. Returnable deposits should never be required for unfurnished tenancies, and should be kept as low as possible even when furniture is provided. Associations should never charge premiums for assured tenancies covered by this Guidance.

(Note iv. see Section 15 Housing Association Act 1985.)

(Note v. see particularly Section 21 Race Relations Act 1976.)

(Note vi. see particularly Section 30 Sex Discrimination Act 1975, which, among other requirements, means that there must be a common qualifying age for men and women seeking sheltered accommodation.)

C Terms of Assured Tenancies

C1 Tenants of registered housing associations in occupation on 15 January .1989 will retain their existing status as secure tenants with registered fair rents. They will also retain that status if, after that date, they are granted a tenancy of other accommodation belonging to the same housing association; or if they exchange tenancies by mutual assignment with another secure tenant (note vii). This Guidance is about the terms of other new tenancies, which are assured tenancies.

Separate guidance is being issued for associations registered with the Housing Corporation which are:

- fully mutual housing co-operatives;
- almshouse charities;
- providing special needs housing in shared accommodation and hostels;
- letting on long leases, including shared ownership.

C2 The tenancy agreement should be in writing, and should also be explained to the tenant in clear terms. Where appropriate translations should be provided.

C3 Associations are expected to give their tenants long term security where possible. Therefore assured shorthold tenancies should be used only in exceptional circumstances, which an association may be required to justify to the Housing Corporation, where shorthold is the only practicable way of meeting the association's housing objectives. It is expected that these cases will be rare, and that most association tenancies will be periodic assured tenancies.

C4 When offering tenancies to existing tenants of another association or a local authority, associations should explain to them fully any differences in statutory or contractual rights and obligations which the new tenancy will entail, including the effects on their Right to Buy.

C5 Prospective tenants should be fully informed of the security of tenure they would have under the Housing Act 1988, and the specified grounds on which courts would be able to end the tenancy (note viii), and of the right for their spouse (or person living with the tenant as husband or wife at the time of the tenant's death) to succeed to the tenancy (note ix).

C6 Associations are expected to give their assured tenants additional contractual rights within the terms of the tenancy agreement, which should include:

a. the right to exchange tenancies with tenants of other associations, New Towns or local authorities, subject to both landlords' agreement, which the association should not unreasonably withold. (see note x).

b. the right to take in lodgers, or sub-let part of their accommodation, (provided that the sub-letting attracts no security of tenure - note xi) subject to the association's permission which should not be unreasonably witheld.

c. the right to carry out improvements, with the association's permission which should not be unreasonably witheld.

d. the right to carry out repairs and have the cost refunded in certain circumstances where the association has failed to carry out its repairing obligations. (see also Section E).

e. the right to be consulted about housing management changes, (see also Section F), and to be informed about the association's management policies (see Section G).

Associations should consider whether they wish to grant a right of succession to the tenancy to a member of the tenant's family who had been living with the tenant for the year before the tenant's death, and had been looking after the tenant, or had accepted responsibility for the tenant's dependants, or who would be made homeless if required to vacate the accommodation (note xii).

C7 In addition the tenancy agreement should:

a. state that the association is registered with the Housing Corporation and is subject to this Guidance;

b. permit assignment of the tenancy only:
- by order of the courts under the Matrimonial Causes Act, (note xiii) or,
- by way of exchange under C6.a above.

(Associations may also wish to grant a right of assignment to a person who would be entitled to succeed to the tenancy on the death of the tenant, subject to the landlord's consent which should not be unreasonably witheld.)

c. set out the initial rent payable, and, if a service charge is included, show it separately; and the procedure for altering it (see also Section D); and

d. define clearly the landlord's statutory responsibility for repairs, and the contractual responsibilities for internal decorations and repairs (and replacement of furniture and fittings where relevant) (see also Section E).

(Note vii. see Sections 35 and 38(4) Housing Act 1988 for details of tenancies which can be secure after 15 January 1989. Note also Section 1(6).)

(Note viii. see Schedule 2 Housing Act 1988.)

(Note ix. see Section 17 Housing Act 1988.)

(Note x. In deciding whether to agree to an exchange in a particular case charitable housing associations may have to take account of the objects of the association.)

(Note xi. an assured tenancy may arise where a tenant departs leaving a subtenant in possession. See Section 18 Housing Act 1988.)

(Note xii. In deciding whether to extend rights of succession charitable housing associations may have to take account of the objects of the association.)

(Note xiii. see particularly Section 24 Matrimonial Clauses Act 1973 covering property adjustment orders in connection with matrimonial proceedings.)

D Principles upon which Rent (and other Charges) for Assured Tenancies are to be Determined

D1 For tenants of registered housing associations whose tenancy commenced before 15 January 1989 rents will continue to be registered Fair Rents. That will also apply to such tenants who, after that date, are granted the tenancy of other accommodation belonging to the same housing association; or exchange tenancies by mutual assignment with another secure tenant (note xiv). This Guidance applies to other new tenancies, which are assured tenancies.

D2 Where housing association accommodation has been provided with the help of public subsidy, (including accommodation originally provided by public bodies and subsequently transferred to housing associations, for example by a local authority, a New Town or a Housing Action Trust), it is intended to be accessible to people on low incomes, whether or not they are in paid employment or in receipt of housing benefit. Associations are therefore expected to set and maintain their rents at levels which are within the reach of those in low paid employment. This will usually entail setting rents below market level. Associations should not discriminate in their rent setting between those who are eligible for housing benefit and others.

D3 In addition associations are expected to take account of the need to cover the costs (after subsidy) of loan charges, and of management and maintenance, including the requirement to make prudent provision for future repairs; and, in setting the rent for each dwelling, its size, amenities, location and condition.

D4 Associations should inform their tenants of their right to refer any proposed increases, other than those within the terms set out in the tenancy agreement, to the Rent Assessment Committee which will fix a market rent for the accommodation, above which the association should not increase the rent for 12 months, (note xv).

D5 Where associations require tenants to pay variable service charges they should provide those tenants with written information explaining their rights under the Landlord and Tenant Act 1985 (note xvi).

(Note xiv. see Sections 35 and 38(4) Housing Act 1988 for details of tenancies which can be secure and subject to the Fair Rent regime after 15 January 1989.)

(Note xv. see Section 14 Housing Act 1988.)

(Note xvi. see Section 18-30 Landlord and Tenant Act 1985, as amended by the Landlord and Tenant Act 1987.)

E Maintenance and Repair

E1 Registered housing associations must meet their statutory and contractual obligations to keep their housing property fit for human habitation. (note xvii).

E2 They should inspect their property to ensure that they meet these obligations, and can plan effectively, and make financial provision for, long term maintenance.

E3 Associations should provide their tenants with information in clear terms on:

a. who is responsible for which repairs, including the statutory position (e.g. under Section 11-14 of the Landlord and Tenant Act 1985);
b. methods for reporting the need for repairs. These should give tenants open and easy access to their landlords;
c. how long it should take for defined categories of repairs to be carried out, taking into account the importance to tenants of speed of response;
d. how emergencies should be dealt with;
e. what tenants can do if the association fails to meet its repairing obligations, including the right to be paid for carrying out the repair themselves or to contact the local authority Environmental Health Officer;
f. their policy for planned maintenance, including cyclical decorations of external and common parts; and
g. their policy for improvements, including the provision of alternative or temporary accommodation, disturbance payments, compensation, and the effect on rents.

(Note xvii. see Section 11-17 Landlord and Tenant Act 1985. also Part VI Housing Act 1985, Section 92 Public Health Act 1936 and Section 4 Defective Premises Act 1972.)

F Consultation and Tenant Involvement

F1 Registered housing associations should consult their tenants about proposed changes in management and maintenance policy or practice which may affect a substantial proportion or number of tenants, in particular,

a. where the association proposes changes in the arrangements for management or maintenance, which substantially affect tenants;
b. where physical improvements to the dwellings or environment are proposed by the association; and
c. the extent and cost of services paid for out of tenants' service charges;

and should take tenants views into account.

In addition associations are encouraged to consult tenants and/or their representative organisation(s) when an association's service is the subject of regular or serious complaint by tenants. Associations should make a reasoned response to tenants and/or their representative organisation(s) when they approach the association on a matter of concern to them or about proposals which they wish to make, including proposals for increasing tenant involvement in management.

F2 Associations should make arrangements for consultation which take into account the views of the tenants affected and the part which representative tenant organisations can play.

F3 Associations should assist representative tenant organisations to obtain reasonable facilities for meetings and for the proper conduct of their business.

F4 Associations should inform their tenants what arrangements or opportunities the association has to enable tenants to participate in the management or control of the association, or of the estate or group of dwellings of which they are tenants.

G Information to Tenants

G1 In addition to informing their tenants and other interested parties about their:

- policies and procedures for selecting tenants and dealing with transfer requests;
- terms of tenancy;
- principles and procedures for fixing rent and other charges;
- maintenance responsibilities and procedures; and
- arrangements for consultation and participation,

as described in previous sections of this Guidance, registered housing associations should have policies and procedures on the following matters and should inform their tenants of them in plain terms so that tenants and other interested parties may see how individual decisions fit in with them; namely, policy and procedures:

a. for dealing with complaints about the association's service and its treatment of tenants and applicants. This should include an appeal procedure leading to the governing body. Associations are further encouraged to set up arbitration procedures for resolving disputes between themselves and their tenants;
b. for dealing with tenants' claims for compensation for failure of services, etc;
c. for dealing with complaints about serious nuisance caused by other tenants including specific procedures for dealing with complaints of racial or other discriminatory harassment;
d. for requiring tenants to move to alternative accommodation, and the circumstances in which this might be necessary (note xviii);
e. for pursuing arrears of rent and other charges; including the circumstances in which the association may take legal action, which should be only after full investigation and consideration of the tenant's circumstances. The use of distress without a Court Order is forbidden under Section 19 of the Housing Act 1988;
f. for allowing access to personal information held by the association (see G3 below);
g. for meeting the requirements of tenants and members of their family who become disabled.

G2.1 Associations should offer tenants information advice and assistance in applying for housing benefit, so that they receive their proper entitlement.

G2.2 The information in G1 and G2 should be provided in writing in plain English, and also, where appropriate, in other languages, or in braille or on tape. It should also be explained orally at the beginning of a tenancy and/or in meetings with tenants.

G3. The Data Protection Act gives people a statutory right (subject to certain exemptions) to see and check details about themselves which are held in the form of computerised data (note xix). Associations should also allow their tenants, former tenants, and applicants for tenancies reasonable access to other personal information held about themselves or members of their family, (other than that provided in confidence by third parties).

If the tenant, former tenant or applicant considers the records inaccurate he or she should be allowed to correct, or record his/her disagreement with, the information held by the association.

(Note xviii. It is expected that these will only be fully justifiable management grounds, such as the need for vacant possession to carry out necessary works.)

(Note xix. see Data Protection Act 1984.)

H. Equal Opportunities

The Housing Corporation's commitment to equal opportunities has been strengthened by an amendment to Section 71 of the Race Relations Act 1976 (note xx) which will require the Corporation to have regard to the need to eliminate unlawful racial discrimination and to promote equality of opportunity and good relations between persons of different racial groups, in the exercise of all its functions.

Registered housing associations will be required to comply with the code of practice on race relations in the field of rented housing being prepared by the Commission for Racial Equality. (note xxi). Associations should also conform with best practice to avoid any kind of discrimination and to promote equality of opportunity both in access to accommodation and the provision of services to all members of the community who may be disadvantaged by race, sex or disability.

(note xx. As amended by Section 56 Housing Act 1988.)

(Note xxi. Under Section 47 Race Relations Act 1976, as amended by Section 137 Housing Act 1988 to cover rented housing.)

Appendix 4

Tenancy Agreement issued by the National Federation of Housing Associations

Reproduced below is the form of assured tenancy agreement issued by the National Federation of Housing Associations; it is re-printed here with the Federation's kind permission.

THIS TENANCY AGREEMENT IS BETWEEN

Name and address of Association

the .... ('the Association')

of ....

which is registered with the Housing Corporation under Section 5 of the Housing Associations Act 1985

Name of Tenant

AND .... ('the Tenant')

....

(in the case of Joint Tenants, the term 'Tenant' applies to each of them and the names of all Joint Tenants should be written above. Each Tenant individually has the full responsibilities and rights set out in this Agreement)

Address

in respect of .... ('the Premises')

Description of Premises

which comprises ....

....

....

Date of start of Tenancy

The Tenancy begins on ....
and is an assured weekly/monthly* tenancy, the terms of which are set out in this Agreement.

GENERAL TERMS

1. It is agreed as follows:–

Payments for the Premises

(1) The weekly/monthly* payments for the Premises at the date of this Agreement shall be –

	£ p
Net rent	....
Service Charge*	....
Rates	....
Water Charge*	....
Total payable	

In this Agreement the term 'Rent' refers to the sum of the net rent and service charge set out above or as varied from time to time in accordance with this Agreement.

(2) The payment of weekly/monthly* Rent, Rates and Water Charge is due in advance on the .... day of each week/month*

*delete if not applicable

Services

(3) The Association shall provide the following services in connection with the Premises for which the Tenant shall pay a Service Charge*

....

....

....

Changes in Rent

(4) The Association may increase or decrease the Rent by giving the Tenant not less than one calendar month's notice in writing of the increase or decrease. The notice shall specify the Rent and the included Service Charge proposed*. The Rent shall not be increased more than once a year and no increase shall take effect less than a year after the last increase or the date of this Agreement. The revised Rent shall be the amount specified in the notice of increase unless the Tenant exercises his/her right to refer the notice to a Rent Assessment Committee to have a market Rent determined in which case the maximum Rent payable for one year after the date specified in the notice shall be the Rent so determined.

Rates and other charges

(5) The Rates/Water Charge payable by the Tenant shall be the actual amount payable for the Premises. Any increase or decrease in the amount of Rates/Water Charge* payable by the Tenant is due immediately upon receipt of written notice served by the Association*.

Altering the Agreement

(6) With the exception of any changes in Rent, Rates or charges, this Agreement may only be altered by the agreement in writing of both the Tenant and the Association.

THE ASSOCIATION'S OBLIGATIONS

2. The Association agrees:–

Possession

(1) To give the Tenant possession of the Premises at the commencement of the Tenancy.

Tenant's right to occupy

(2) Not to interrupt or interfere with the Tenant's right peacefully to occupy the Premises except where –
- (i) access is required to inspect the condition of the Premises or to carry out repairs or other works to the Premises or adjoining property; or
- (ii) a court has given the Association possession by ending the Tenancy.

Rates and other charges

(3) To pay to the respective local authority and water authority any amounts due to them and collected from the Tenant by way of Rates and other charges*.

Repair of structure and exterior

(4) To keep in good repair, the structure and exterior of the Premises including –
- (i) drains, gutters and external pipes;
- (ii) the roof;
- (iii) outside walls, outside doors, windowsills, window catches, sash cords and window frames including necessary external painting and decorating;
- (iv) internal walls, floors and ceilings, doors and door frames, door hinges and skirting boards but not including internal painting and decoration;
- (v) chimneys, chimney stacks and flues but not including sweeping;
- (vi) pathways, steps or other means of access;
- (vii) plasterwork;
- (viii) integral garages and stores;
- (ix) boundary walls and fences.

*delete if not applicable

Repair of installations

(5) To keep in good repair and proper working order any installations provided by the Association for space heating, water heating and sanitation and for the supply of water, gas and electricity, including –

(i) basins, sinks, baths, toilets, flushing systems and waste pipes;

(ii) electric wiring including sockets and switches, gas pipes and water pipes;

(iii) water heaters, fireplaces, fitted fires and central heating installations.

Repair of common parts

(6) To take reasonable care to keep the common entrances, halls, stairways, lifts, passageways, rubbish chutes and any other common parts, including their electric lighting, in reasonable repair and fit for use by the Tenant and other occupiers and visitors to the Premises.

External decorations

(7) To keep the exterior of the Premises and any common parts in a good state of decoration and normally to decorate these areas once every .... years.

Tenants' Guarantee

(8) To provide the Tenant with information on its housing management policies as required by the guidance issued by the Housing Corporation (the Tenants' Guarantee) under the provisions of Section 36A of the Housing Associations Act 1985.

THE TENANT'S OBLIGATIONS

3. The Tenant agrees:–

Possession

(1) To take possession of the Premises at the commencement of the Tenancy and not to part with possession of the Premises or sub-let the whole of it.

Rent

(2) To pay the Rent and other charges weekly/monthly* and in advance.

Use of Premises

(3) To use the Premises for residential purposes as the Tenant's only or principal home and not to operate a business at the Premises without the written consent of the Association.

Nuisance

(4) Not to cause or allow members of his/her household or invited visitors to cause a nuisance or annoyance to neighbours or other tenants of the Association.

Racial and other harassment

(5) Not to commit or allow members of his/her household or invited visitors to commit any form of harassment on the grounds of race, colour, religion, sex, sexual orientation or disability which may interfere with the peace and comfort of, or cause offence to, any other tenant, member of his/her household, visitors or neighbours.

Noise

(6) Not to play or allow to be played any radio, television, record or tape recording or musical instrument so loudly that it causes a nuisance or annoyance to neighbours or can be heard outside the Premises between the hours of 11.00pm and 7.30am.

Pets

(7) To keep under control any animals kept at the Premises and to obtain the written consent of the Association before keeping a dog or any other animal which might cause a nuisance to neighbours.

Internal decoration

(8) To keep the interior of the Premises in good and clean condition and to decorate all internal parts of the Premises as frequently as is necessary to keep them in good decorative order.

*delete if not applicable

Damage

(9) To make good any damage to the Premises or the Association's fixtures and fittings or to the common parts caused by the Tenant or any member of the Tenant's household or any invited visitor to the Premises, fair wear and tear excepted, and to pay any costs incurred by the Association carrying out such works in default.

Reporting disrepair

(10) To report to the Association promptly any disrepair or defect for which the Association is responsible in the structure or exterior of the Premises or in any installation therein or in the common parts.

Access

(11) To allow the Association's employees or contractors acting on behalf of the Association access at all reasonable hours of the daytime to inspect the condition of the Premises or to carry out repairs or other works to the Premises or adjoining property. (The Association will normally give at least 24 hours' notice but immediate access may be required in an emergency).

Assignment

(12) Not to assign the Tenancy except in furtherance of a court order made under Section 24 of the Matrimonial Causes Act 1973 or with the written consent of the Association when exercising the right to exchange set out in 5(6) below.

Overcrowding

(13) Not to allow more than ...... persons to reside at the Premises.

Lodgers and sub-letting

(14) Before taking in any lodger or sub-letting any part of the Premises, to inform the Association of the name, age and sex of the intended lodger or sub-tenant and of the accommodation they will occupy.

Assured sub-tenancies prohibited

(15) Not to grant an assured sub-tenancy of any part of the Premises.

Ending the Tenancy

(16) To give the Association at least 4 weeks'/one calendar month's* notice in writing when the Tenant wishes to end the Tenancy.

Moving out

(17) To give the Association vacant possession and return the keys of the Premises at the end of the Tenancy and to remove all furniture, personal possessions and rubbish and leave the Premises and the Association's fixtures and fittings in good lettable condition and repair. The Association accepts no responsibility for anything left at the Premises by the Tenant at the end of the Tenancy.

THE TENANT'S RIGHTS

4. The Tenant has the following rights:–

Right to occupy

(1) The Tenant has the right to occupy the Premises without interruption or interference from the Association for the duration of this Tenancy (except for the obligation contained in this Agreement to give access to the Association's employees or contractors) so long as the Tenant complies with the terms of this Agreement and has proper respect for the rights of other tenants and neighbours.

Security of Tenure

(2) The Tenant has security of tenure as an assured tenant so long as he/she occupies the Premises as his/her only or principal home. The Association can only end the Tenancy by obtaining a court order for possession of the Premises on one of the grounds listed in Schedule 2 of the Housing Act 1988. The Association agrees that it will not give less than four weeks' notice in writing of its intention to seek a possession order. The Association will only use the following grounds to obtain an order for possession –

(i) the Tenant has not paid the Rent which is due; (Ground 10)

(ii) the Tenant has broken, or failed to perform, any of the conditions of this Tenancy; (Ground 12)

*delete if not applicable

(iii) the Tenant or anyone living in the Premises has caused damage to, or failed to look after the Premises, the building or any of the common parts; (Ground 13)

(iv) the Tenant or anyone living in the Premises has caused serious or persistent nuisance or annoyance to neighbours, or has been responsible for any act of harassment on the grounds of race, colour, sex or disability, or has been convicted of using the property for immoral or illegal purposes; (Ground 14)

(v) where the Tenancy has devolved under the will or intestacy of the Tenant subject to the provisions of Clause 4(4) (succession to a spouse) and 6 (succession to family members); (Ground 7)

(vi) suitable alternative accommodation is available to the Tenant, provided that in addition the Association can show: (Ground 9)

(a) that vacant possession is necessary to carry out work to the Premises, or

(b) that the Premises are needed for someone who requires the special amenities or services provided and the Tenant no longer does so, or

(c) that the Tenant is a Successor as defined in 6(iv) other than a spouse in whom the Tenancy has vested in accordance with 4(4) and is under-occupying the Premises.

Cessation of assured tenancy

(3) If the Tenancy ceases to be an assured tenancy the Association may end the Tenancy by giving four weeks' notice in writing to the Tenant.

Succession to a spouse

(4) On the death of the Tenant (where the Tenancy is held by one person) this Tenancy will vest in the Tenant's spouse under the provisions of the Housing Act 1988 provided that he or she occupies the Premises as his or her only or principal home at the time of the Tenant's death.

5. By way of further rights, the Association agrees:–

that the provisions of Sections 92-94, 96-99, 104-106 and Schedule 3 of the Housing Act 1985 shall be deemed to apply to this Tenancy. These rights are summarised below:

Right to take in lodgers and sub-let

(1) Subject to 3(13), 3(14) and 3(15) above, the Tenant may take in any persons as lodgers or may with the consent in writing of the Association sub-let part of the Premises provided that the Tenant may not grant an assured sub-tenancy.

Right to make improvements

(2) The Tenant may make improvements, alterations and additions to the Premises including the erection of a television aerial, external decoration and additions to, or alterations in, the Association's installations, fixtures and fittings, provided that the Tenant has first obtained the written consent of the Association and all other necessary approvals (for example, planning permission or building regulations approval). The Association will not unreasonably withhold its consent but may make it conditional upon the work being carried out to a certain standard. Failure to comply with the Association's conditions may be treated as a breach of the Tenant's obligations under this Tenancy.

Right to repair

(3) The Tenant has the right to carry out repairs which are the Association's responsibility where the Tenant has reported the need for repair in writing and where the Association has, without good reason, failed to carry out the repair within 28 days of receiving such report. This right may only be exercised in accordance with the regulations made by the Secretary of State under Section 96 of the Housing Act 1985: the Association will refund to the Tenant the agreed cost of repairs carried out in accordance with these regulations.

*delete if not applicable

Right to consultation

(4) The Association will consult the Tenant before making changes in matters of housing management or maintenance which are likely to have a substantial effect on the Tenant.

Right to information

(5) The Tenant has a right to information from the Association about the terms of this Tenancy and about the Association's repairing obligations and its policies and procedures on tenant consultation, housing allocation and transfers.

Right to exchange

(6) The Tenant has the right to exchange this Tenancy by assignment with that of another tenant of a registered housing association or a local authority or new town subject to the prior written consent of the Association, which shall only be withheld on specified grounds.

6. The Association also agrees that:–

Right of succession to a member of the family

On the death of the Tenant, provided that the Tenant was not a Successor –

(i) if the Tenancy does not vest in the Tenant's spouse under 4(4) above, subject to 6(iii) it shall be deemed to be assigned to another member of the Tenant's family who has resided with the Tenant throughout the period of twelve months ending with the Tenant's death and who occupied the premises as his or her only or principal home at the time of the Tenant's death;

(ii) if in (i) above, there is more than one member of the Tenant's family qualified to succeed to the Tenancy, they should agree between them which of them shall claim it or, if they cannot agree, each may claim in which case the Association shall decide to whom the Tenancy shall be deemed to be assigned;

(iii) all claims to succeed to the Tenancy must be made to the Association in writing within one month of the death of the Tenant. The Association shall notify all claimants of the name of the person to whom the Tenancy shall be deemed to be assigned;

(iv) for the purposes of this Agreement a Successor shall be –

(a) a spouse in whom the Tenancy was vested under the provisions of the Housing Act 1988

(b) a person to whom this Tenancy shall be deemed to be assigned under the provisions of this clause

(c) a person who was a Joint Tenant and has become a Sole Tenant.

Signed on behalf of the Association ....

Signed by the Tenant ....

....

Date ....

If the Tenant feels that the Association has broken this Agreement or not performed any obligation contained in it, he or she should first complain to the Association in writing giving details of the breach or non-performance. If the Association fails to deal with the complaint or, in the Tenant's view, continues not to comply with the Agreement the Tenant can obtain advice and information about his or her remedies at law from a local Citizens' Advice Bureau or law centre or from a solicitor.

> The Association is subject to any guidance on housing management practice issued by the Housing Corporation with the approval of the Secretary of State and this Tenancy is one to which the Tenants' Guarantee applies.

This Tenancy Agreement — NFHA assured tenancy model D — is produced for the use of members of the NFHA.

Appendix 5

The Housing Corporation's criteria for approval of a Tenants' Choice landlord

The criteria below are promulgated by the Housing Corporation and reproduced here with the Corporation's permission.

In exercise of the powers conferred by Section 94 of the Housing Act 1988, the Housing Corporation has established criteria to which the Corporation shall have regard and which must be satisfied by an applicant seeking approval to acquire property from a public sector landlord under Part IV of the Housing Act 1988. The criteria, which are effective from 15 January 1989 and may be varied by the Housing Corporation, are as follows:

1. Statutory requirements

1 Eligibility: the following bodies are not eligible for approval:

(a) a public sector landlord, ie a local housing authority within the meaning of Section 1 of the Housing Act 1985 or a new town corporation or a housing action trust or the Development Board for Rural Wales;

(b) a county council;

(c) any other body which the Corporation believes might not be independent of a public sector landlord or a county council. A body shall not be regarded as independent of a public sector landlord or a county council if the body is or appears likely to be under the control of, or subject to influence from, such a landlord or council or particular members or officers of such a landlord or council.

2 Other statutory requirements:

(a) an approval shall not be given except to a person making an application accompanied by such fee as the Corporation, with the consent of the Secretary of State, may specify;

(b) an approval may be conditional upon the person or persons concerned entering into such undertakings as may be specified by the Corporation.

2. Status

1 Any incorporated or unincorporated body or individual or group of individuals may apply for approval.

2 Unincorporated bodies which have a governing instrument and all incorporated bodies (such as a society registered under the Industrial and Provident Societies Act 1965, or a registered company) must have objects

or powers which will permit the acquisition, management, repair or improvement of housing accommodation.

3 Applicants who are unincorporated and individuals must be able to demonstrate that succession arrangements are sufficient to ensure that any tenancies acquired as a result of their Tenants' Choice landlord activity will be adequately managed in the long-term.

3. Control and accountability

1 The applicant must be, or be under the control of, a responsible person or persons with experience and skills appropriate to the anticipated scale and nature of its operations so that the activities of a Tenants' Choice landlord are likely to be conducted in a responsible and effective manner.

2 In the case of an incorporated or unincorporated body, control over its administration must be vested in a committee of management, body of trustees, board of directors or other governing body.

3 The applicant must declare any extent to which it is under the control of, or subject to influence which could prejudice its independence from another person or organisation, and be able to show that any such influence or control operates in the best interests of the applicant and does not prejudice the applicant's ability to enter into and continue to fulfil the criteria and conditions of approval.

4. Financial requirements

An applicant must be able to demonstrate that it is operating, or will operate, on a sound and proper financial basis and in particular:

1 It must keep accounting records, have adequate systems of control and produce annual accounts which have been audited by a properly qualified auditor or, if a newly formed organisation, demonstrate arrangements for meeting these requirements.

2 In order to ensure its future viability, the applicant must show that:

(a) its current and known future capital commitments are, or can be, fully financed by loans, grants or other permanent sources of capital, and

(b) its income will be sufficient for present circumstances and taking one year with another, to meet its outgoings and provisions.

3 An applicant which is a registered housing association must ensure that its overheads, eg salaries and expenses, are reasonable for its size and level of activity and are properly allocated in a consistent manner to its various functions.

5. Managerial efficiency

The Corporation will consider the applicant's skills in property acquisition, finance, housing management and maintenance. Having regard to its size, its current and intended level and nature of activity, the applicant must be able to show that it has access to professional skills and experience for the efficient acquisition, management and maintenance to a high standard, of housing either from its own staff or from other persons or organisations. These arrangements must serve the best interests of tenants and not restrict the independence of the applicant.

6. Proposed level and area of activity

The Corporation will consider the applicant's intended level and area of activity as a Tenants' Choice landlord in relation to its current size and resources, including managerial resources. The applicant's proposals for growth in levels and areas of activity should be consistent with its existing and proposed capacity without endangering, in the long term, the quality of any similar housing activities which it has already undertaken.

7. Equal opportunities

Under Section 56 of the Housing Act 1988, the Corporation has the statutory duty as set out in Section 71 of the Race Relations Act 1976 "to eliminate unlawful racial discrimination and to promote equality of opportunity, and good relations between persons of different racial groups". An applicant must be able to demonstrate that there will be equality of opportunity in its policies and procedures.

8. Other requirements

Application for approval must be made on the form provided by the Corporation. Approval will be conditional on receipt by the Corporation of a deed being executed under the seal of the applicant that will include the following undertakings:

1 not to submit any application to acquire property under Section 96 of the Housing Act 1988 if requested not to do so by the Corporation, because the property is covered by a resolution of a local housing authority that it intends to further consult its tenants under Schedule 3A paragraph 3(3) of the Housing Act 1985 about a proposed voluntary disposal, by a resolution of a Housing Action Trust under Section 79 of the Housing Act 1988 or in the case of a planned disposal by a New Town Development Corporation or the Commission for New Towns the date of the Secretary of State's instruction to initiate disposal;

2 not to submit any application to acquire property under Section 96 of the Housing Act 1988 if requested not to do so by the Corporation, because the property is covered by a resolution of a local housing authority that it intends to consult its tenants under Section 27A of the Housing Act 1985 about proposals for a management agreement with a Tenant Management Co-operative;

3 before serving any application to acquire property under Section 96 of the Housing Act 1988, to comply with the Corporation's guidance for the informal consultation of tenants to establish which of any competing applicants has the clearest support among tenants and to abide by the outcome of such informal consultation;

4 to keep tenants and the Corporation informed at all key stages of the acquisition process, and to inform tenants, the Housing Corporation and the public sector landlord should the application be withdrawn;

5 to submit to the Corporation the material to be given to tenants as part of the formal consultation under Section 102 of the Housing Act 1988 in order to allow its consistency with the approval criteria and undertakings to be assessed;

6 to obtain the Corporation's approval to the appointment and the terms of the contract with an independent teller to conduct and certify the outcome of the ballot required under Sections 102 and 103 of the Housing Act 1988 as part of the formal consultation of tenants;

7 to abide by the terms offered to tenants during the formal consultation under Sections 102 and 103 of the Housing Act 1988;

8 to treat in strict confidence any information obtained about tenants during the course of an application, and to disclose such information to third parties only where necessary for the purpose of pursuing the application;

9 to retain dwellings acquired as a Tenants' Choice landlord for letting at rents within the reach of those in low-paid employment;

10 to offer tenants rents and other charges which are consistent between properties of similar size, condition and location except where different services and amenities are to be provided;

11 to comply with the Corporation's guidance on the management by Tenants' Choice landlords of accommodation let on assured tenancies under the Housing Act 1988 or, if appropriate, the Corporation's guidance for registered housing associations letting on assured tenancies or that for fully mutual housing co-operatives, in respect of both tenancies acquired and future lettings arising from its Tenants' Choice landlord activities;

12 not to seek to have conveyed any houses specified for exclusion from the acquisition in a notice of intention to proceed served under Section 103(4)(b) of the Housing Act 1988;

13 not to seek possession under Ground 6 of Schedule 2 to the Housing Act 1988 of a dwelling acquired under Part IV of that Act;

14 to validate or substantiate within a reasonable time limit any information provided on the application form and furnish any other additional information required by the Corporation;

15 to submit within 6 months of its financial year end its audited annual accounts and an annual return relating to its activities as a Tenants' Choice landlord in such form as the Corporation may determine;

16 to provide within a reasonable time limit any additional information regarding its activities as a Tenants' Choice landlord as required by the Corporation from time to time;

17 to give the Corporation four weeks written notice of any proposed change in its objects and powers referred to at paragraph 2(2) of these criteria or, if required by Section 19 of the Housing Associations Act 1985, to obtain the Corporation's consent to such changes; and to notify the Corporation in writing within four weeks of any changes in the membership of the governing body or in the managerial and executive staff separately identified in the application form or in the registered or correspondence address of the landlord;

18 to ensure that the requirements of these criteria are observed at all times in the future.

9. Additional requirements to qualify for general approval

In addition to satisfying the criteria described in 1 to 8, to qualify for general approval an applicant must be able to demonstrate that it has:

1 not less than 2 years' experience in managing social rented housing in the manner described in the Corporation's guidance for Tenants' Choice landlords on housing management practice;

2 a high degree of financial strength and evidence of financial stability;

3 the managerial capacity to cope with the anticipated growth in the levels and areas of its Tenants' Choice landlord activity.

Index

page